Design for Wellbeing

Design for Wellbeing charts the development and application of design research to improve the personal and societal wellbeing and happiness of people. It draws together contributions from internationally leading academics and designers to demonstrate the latest thinking and research on the design of products, technologies, environments, services and experiences for wellbeing.

Part I starts by conceptualising wellbeing and takes an in-depth look at the rise of the design for wellbeing movement. Part II then goes on to demonstrate design for wellbeing in practice through a broad range of domains from products and environments to services. Among others, we see emerging trends in the design of interiors and urban spaces to support wellbeing, designing to enable and support connectedness and social interaction, and designing for behaviour change to tackle unhealthy eating behaviour in children. Significantly, the body of work on subjective wellbeing, design for happiness, is increasing, and several case studies are provided on this, demonstrating how design can contribute to support the wellbeing of people. Part III provides practical guidance for designing for wellbeing through a range of examples of tools, methods and approaches, which are highly user-centric, participatory, critical and speculative. Finally, the book concludes in Part IV with a look at future challenges for design for wellbeing.

This book provides students, researchers and practitioners with a detailed assessment of design for wellbeing, taking a distinctive global approach to design practice and theory in context. *Design for Wellbeing* concerns designers and organisations but also defines its broader contribution to society, culture and economy.

Ann Petermans is Assistant Professor at the Faculty of Architecture and Arts, Hasselt University, Belgium. She chairs the Design Research Society's Special Interest Group on Design for Wellbeing, Happiness and Health. Her research interests pertain in particular to designing for experience in designed environments and for diverse user groups, and research related to design for subjective wellbeing and how architecture and interior architecture can contribute in this respect. Ann is editorial board member of *The Design Journal* and publishes in various high-quality journals. She is also coeditor of the book *Retail Design: Theoretical Perspectives*, published by Routledge in 2017.

Rebecca Cain is Professor of Transdisciplinary Design, in the School of Design and Creative Arts, Loughborough University, UK. She also holds the position of Associate Dean for Enterprise. An industrial designer by training, her expertise is in bringing together different disciplines and working with industry and society to design and research future products, environments, services and systems that create positive outcomes for people. She works across sectors including mobility, energy and healthcare. She founded the Design Research Society's Special Interest Group for Wellbeing, Happiness and Health, which she now co-convenes.

Design for Social Responsibility
Series Editor: Rachel Cooper

Social responsibility, in various disguises, has been a recurring theme in design for many years. Since the 1960s several more or less commercial approaches have evolved. In the 1970s designers were encouraged to abandon 'design for profit' in favour of a more compassionate approach inspired by Papanek. In the 1980s and 1990s profit and ethical issues were no longer considered mutually exclusive and more market-oriented concepts emerged, such as the 'green consumer' and ethical investment. The purchase of socially responsible, 'ethical' products and services has been stimulated by the dissemination of research into sustainability issues in consumer publications. Accessibility and inclusivity have also attracted a great deal of design interest and recently designers have turned to solving social and crime-related problems. Organisations supporting and funding such projects have recently included: the NHS (research into design for patient safety); the Home Office (design against crime); and the Engineering and Physical Sciences Research Council (design decision-making for urban sustainability).

Businesses are encouraged (and increasingly forced by legislation) to set their own socially responsible agendas that depend on design to be realised. Design decisions all have environmental, social and ethical impacts, so there is a pressing need to provide guidelines for designers and design students within an overarching framework that takes a holistic approach to socially responsible design. This edited series of guides is aimed at students of design, product development, architecture and marketing, and design and management professionals working in the sectors covered by each title. Each volume includes: the background and history of the topic, its significance in social and commercial contexts and trends in the field; exemplar design case studies; and guidelines for the designer and advice on tools, techniques and resources available.

Design for Wellbeing

An Applied Approach

**Edited by Ann Petermans
and Rebecca Cain**

LONDON AND NEW YORK

First published 2020 by Routledge

2 Park Square, Milton Park, Abingdon, Oxon OX14 4RN
605 Third Avenue, New York, NY 10017

Routledge is an imprint of the Taylor & Francis Group, an informa business

First issued in paperback 2021

Publisher's Note

The publisher has gone to great lengths to ensure the quality of this reprint but points out that some imperfections in the original copies may be apparent.

British Library Cataloguing-in-Publication Data
A catalogue record for this book is available from the British Library

Library of Congress Cataloging-in-Publication Data
Names: Petermans, Ann, editor. | Cain, Rebecca, 1978- editor.
Title: Design for wellbeing: an applied approach/edited by Ann Petermans and Rebecca Cain.
Description: Abingdon, Oxon; New York, NY: Routledge, 2020. |
Series: Design for social responsibility; 12 | Includes bibliographical references and index.
Identifiers: LCCN 2019030574 (print) | LCCN 2019030575 (ebook) |
ISBN 9781138562929 (hardback) | ISBN 9781315121383 (ebook)
Subjects: LCSH: Design–Social aspects. | Well-being.
Classification: LCC NK1520 .D46535 2020 (print) | LCC NK1520 (ebook) |
DDC 745.4–dc23
LC record available at https://lccn.loc.gov/2019030574
LC ebook record available at https://lccn.loc.gov/2019030575

ISBN: 978-1-138-56292-9 (hbk)
ISBN: 978-1-03-217652-9 (pbk)
DOI: 10.4324/9781315121383

Typeset in Bembo
by Deanta Global Publishing Services, Chennai, India

Contents

Contributors

Melanie Becker is a strategic designer driven by a human-centred design approach. She is keen on translating research findings, brand values and market requirements into holistic value propositions and meaningful user experiences delivering additional value to people and businesses. She currently works as Senior Design Strategist at Noto, a product design studio in Cologne, Germany. From 2015 to 2018 she was part of the team behind the funded project 'Design for Wellbeing. Nord-Rhine-Westfalia', which resulted in a wellbeing-centred design and innovation process applicable by the creative industry. Melanie holds a Dipl.Ing. in industrial design from FH Joanneum Graz, Austria, and an MFA in advanced product design from the Umeå Institute of Design, Sweden.

Jo Broekx is architect and Professor at the Faculty of Architecture and Arts, Hasselt University, Belgium. He coordinates the first year's design studio in architecture, which focuses on the conceptual and contextual part of the design process in dwelling.

Rebecca Cain is Professor of Transdisciplinary Design, in the School of Design and Creative Arts, Loughborough University, UK. She also holds the position of Associate Dean for Enterprise. An industrial designer by training, her expertise is in bringing together different disciplines and working with industry and society to design and research future products, environments, services and systems that create positive outcomes for people. She works across sectors including mobility, energy and healthcare. She founded the Design Research Society's Special Interest Group for Wellbeing, Happiness and Health, which she now co-convenes.

Emily Corrigan-Kavanagh is currently Research Fellow in Communication Design at the University of Surrey, UK, on the 'Next Generation Paper' project. Her role involves investigating the design aspects of new augmented paper technologies, such as how associated augmented content is generated and activated, as well as planning, running and analysis of reading studies and co-design workshops with prospective users to test and reconceptualise resulting prototypes. Prior to this, she completed a PhD at Loughborough University, UK, on 'Designing for Home Happiness and Creative Design Methods'. Her research interests include designing for augmented paper, design for happiness and wellbeing, creative methods and visual research methods.

Diana Cürlis studied communication design at Folkwang University of Arts, Essen, Germany. Her work is focused on social innovation and ecological sustainability. Her current efforts aim at the improvement of the welfare of people with dementia and their caregiving relatives through participatory design. Whilst being a team member of

'Design for Wellbeing. Nord-Rhine-Westfalia' she gave birth to her second son and came in contact with new aspects of subjective wellbeing by letting go of all autonomy and working on the funded project with the least amount of sleep possible.

Liesbeth De Donder is Associate Professor in Adult Educational Sciences, Vrije Universiteit Brussel where she teaches research methodology and civil society and community development. Her research focuses on social participation and inclusion, caring communities, feelings of safety, and elder abuse, with a particular interest in participatory methodologies.

Pieter M.A. Desmet is Professor of Design for Experience at the Faculty of Industrial Design, Delft University, the Netherlands. He is founding director of the Delft Institute of Positive Design (DIOPD), a research group that focuses on emotion- and wellbeing-driven design. Pieter is partner of the research and design agency Emotion/Studio, and board member of the International Design & Emotion Society. He has published over 150 scientific (journal) papers, book chapters and books on a variety of aspects of experience-driven design, reaching an audience of both scholars and practitioners. Besides his research, he contributes to local community projects, such as a recently developed sensory wellness neighbourhood park and a cultural Rotterdam-based 'House of Happiness'.

Carolina Escobar-Tello is a progressive researcher, designer and facilitator working across industrial, service and systems design. Currently, she is Lecturer in Design at the Loughborough Design School, Loughborough University, UK. With extensive professional multicultural design and management experience in the industrial, not-for-profit and governmental arena (UK, US, Europe and South America), her work has been published in journals and international peer-reviewed conference proceedings. She is an expert in design for happiness/wellbeing, sustainable design and social innovation, and co-convenor of the Design Research Society Special Interest Group on Sustainability.

Thorsten Frackenpohl apprenticed as a merchant before starting to study design at the Köln International School of Design, Cologne, Germany. At the age of 25 he and André Poulheim founded the design studio Frackenpohl Poulheim in Cologne – which is now called Noto. Between 2007 and 2011 he was part of a newly established Chair of Industrial Design at the Technical University of Munich, Germany, and was responsible for the launch of an industrial design master program. He is fascinated by the creation of meaningful experiences that lead to business success. Many of Noto's products have received international design awards such as the Red Dot Product Design Award, the iF Product Design Award, the German Design Award and the prestigious Designpreis der Bundesrepublik Deutschland in Gold for the inflatable tent 'The Cave' for Heimplanet.

Luke Harmer, PhD (Royal College of Art, London) is Designer, Researcher and Lecturer at Loughborough University, UK. His design work has a transport focus and he has designed both public and private vehicles, as well as working on industrial, medical, electronic and packaging. His research work is concerned with embedding the user and environment into the design process.

Gitte Harzé is both architect and interior architect, and lectures at the Faculty of Architecture and Arts, Hasselt University, Belgium. She coordinates the first year's design studio in interior architecture and is a lecturer, teaching computer-aided architectural design, in the first and second bachelor in interior architecture.

Marc Hassenzahl is Professor for Ubiquitous Design/Experience and Interaction at the University of Siegen, Germany. He combines his training in psychology with a love for interaction design. With his group of designers and psychologists, he explores the theory and practice of designing pleasurable, meaningful and transforming interactive technologies. He is author of *Experience Design. Technology for All the Right Reasons* (Morgan & Claypool), co-author (with Sarah Diefenbach) of *Psychologie in der nutzerzentrierten Produktgestaltung. Mensch-Technik-Interaktion-Erlebnis (People, Technology, Interaction, Experience)* (Springer) and author of many peer-reviewed papers at the seams of psychology, design research and interaction/industrial design. More information can be found via www.marc-hassenzahl.de or https://www.facebook.com/experience.interact/.

Sander Hermsen is a Senior Researcher in Design and Behaviour Change at Utrecht University of Applied Sciences, the Netherlands. Hermsen conducts research on designing effective, evidence-driven interventions that support vulnerable people in healthy behaviour change. Another core research interest focuses on creating evidence-based and theory-driven methods and tools to enable designers and health professionals to use insights from the behavioural sciences to inform their work.

Sarah Kettley is Chair of Material and Design Innovation at Edinburgh College of Art, University of Edinburgh, UK. Her research spans disciplines in order to develop design methodologies for emerging and embedded technologies. With a background in jewellery and silversmithing, Sarah has developed craft as a methodology for the development of wearable technologies, and she leads multidisciplinary teams to engage in critical relational design research with mental health and wellbeing sectors.

Holger Klapperich studied industrial design with a focus on user experience at Folkwang University of the Arts, Essen, Germany and critical practice at Goldsmith University, London. His research interest is efficiency in the context of everyday automation. He tries to answer the question: How could an automated process/automated processes be designed to be experientially rich? Holger explores the area of tension between manual and automated activities. From 2015 to 2018 he was involved in the funded research project 'Design for Wellbeing. Nord-Rhine-Westfalia'.

Henning Köhler studied business administration with a focus on corporate development in Cologne, Germany, South Africa and India. During his studies he focused on innovation management and gained experiences with the innovation process by working for start-ups as well as corporates. His motivation for the project 'Design for Wellbeing. Nord-Rhine-Westfalia' lies in the deeper practical understanding of the sources of innovation and the business value behind subjective wellbeing. In his role as Business Designer for Noto, Henning focused within the funded project on implementing complementary lean start-up methods, testing different validation methodologies and ensuring adaptability of the developed innovation process for corporate needs.

Matthias Laschke holds a diploma in industrial design and a doctorate in philosophy, with a focus on human–computer interaction. He is Senior Research Scientist in Marc Hassenzahl's workgroup, Ubiquitous Design, at the University of Siegen, Germany. He focuses on the subject of experience design, addressing topics such as professional contexts (e.g., health care, duty roster) and mobility. Additionally, he focuses on the design and aesthetic of transformational objects (e.g., 'Pleasurable Troublemakers') and persuasive technologies, addressing diverse topics such as sustainability, procrastination, willpower, adherence or mindfulness in traffic. He is supervisor of different lectures, theses and national research projects in Germany.

Rachel Lucas is a psychotherapist currently working for the Student Counselling Service at the University of Bristol and at Affordable Talk, Bristol, UK, alongside her private practice work. Rachel took the MSc course in person-centred psychotherapy at the Sherwood Psychotherapy Training Institute in Nottingham, UK. She has provided both open-ended and short-term contracts across varied contexts including: Counselling Xtra, Nottingham, Women's Aid, Nottingham Trent University Counselling Service, NHS Employee Assistance Programmes and the Family Intervention Project. Rachel worked on an EPSRC research project at Nottingham Trent University, partnered with Mind, looking at ways to support mental health, and compiled a review of relevant UK and EU literature with Sarah Kettley.

Geke Ludden is Associate Professor and Head of Chair of Interaction Design, Department of Design, Production and Management, University of Twente, the Netherlands. She is also a research fellow of the University's Designlab. She is editor of the *Journal of Design Research* and has published in major design and (e-)health journals such as *International Journal of Design, Design Issues, Journal of Medical Internet Research* and *Journal of Personalized Medicine*. She is co-editor of the book *Design for Behaviour Change*, published by Routledge in 2018. She studies the design of products and services that support healthy behaviour and that engage people in therapy at home.

Kai Ludwigs has studied as a psychologist and economist. In 2014 he founded the Happiness Research Organisation (HRO), an independent research institute specialising in app-based research, located in Dusseldorf, Germany (www.happiness-research.org). He specialises in measuring happiness, wellbeing and quality of life with modern technologies; and is a board member of the International Society for Quality of Life Studies.

Artur Mausbach is a Senior Research Fellow and the Automotive Transitions Studio Leader at IMDC, the Intelligent Mobility Design Centre at the Royal College of Art, London. He is an architect and urban planner committed to sustainability and design research. He has worked globally as a consultant for the car industry and has had architectural designs built in the UK, Austria and Brazil. He has an MPhil on 'Environmental Urban Structures' and an 'Architecture and Urbanism' BA and MA from the University of São Paulo (USP), Brazil; and a PhD in 'Vehicle Design' from the Royal College of Art (RCA). Since 2002, he has worked in academia as lecturer, researcher, professor of design and architecture and head of Smart Cities post-graduation course, at the University of São Paulo (USP), Istituto Europeo di Design of São Paulo (IED-SP) and other institutions.

Deger Ozkaramanli is Assistant Professor in Human Centred Design at the Department of Design Production and Management and a research fellow at the DesignLab, at the University of Twente, the Netherlands. She is fascinated by the richness of the dilemmas people experience in daily life. That is why, as a designer and researcher, she pursues dilemma-driven design in her work. She has published her research in leading design journals, such as *Design Issues* and *The Design Journal*, and regularly organises workshops in dilemma-driven design to understand and increase the impact of her work on design practice. Her aim is to understand and influence the emotional, social and ethical significance of design through addressing the complex and morally loaded dilemmas evoked by products and services.

Ann Petermans is Assistant Professor at the Faculty of Architecture and Arts, Hasselt University, Belgium. She chairs the Design Research Society's Special Interest Group on Design for Wellbeing, Happiness and Health. Her research interests pertain in particular to designing for experience in designed environments and for diverse user groups, and research related to design for subjective wellbeing and how architecture and interior architecture can contribute in this respect. Ann is editorial board member of *The Design Journal* and publishes in various high-quality journals. She is also co-editor of the book *Retail Design: Theoretical Perspectives*, published by Routledge in 2017.

Anna Pohlmeyer is Assistant Professor at the Faculty of Industrial Design Engineering, Delft University of Technology, the Netherlands, Co-Director of the Delft Institute of Positive Design and board member of the Design Research Society Special Interest Group on Design for Wellbeing, Happiness and Health. Her trans-disciplinary background combines studies in psychology (Humboldt University, Berlin), a PhD in engineering (TU Berlin and University of Luxembourg) and years of teaching and doing design, which is also reflected in her research expertise on design for happiness, human-centred design methodology, and prolonging positive experiences through design.

Tiiu Poldma, PhD, FDRS, CFERDIE, is Full Professor at the School of Design, Faculty of Environmental Design/Faculté de l'Aménagement, University of Montreal, Canada. She is a regular researcher at the Center for Interdisciplinary Research in Rehabilitation of Montreal (CRIR) and Director of the FoCoLUM Lighting Lab. Her research interests include wellbeing and ageing well, how form, colour and light affect perceptions, and understanding lived experience in interior spaces from pragmatic phenomenological perspectives. Research work includes developing intersectoral projects that favour universal design integration, collaborative, co-design and participatory methodologies within Living Labs. In 2015 she was nominated Fellow of the Design Research Society for her contributions to design research.

An-Sofie Smetcoren is a postdoctoral Researcher in the Department of Adult Educational Science, Vrije Universiteit Brussel, and member of the Belgian Ageing Studies. Her main research interests concentrate on how urban environments influence the daily lives of its inhabitants (e.g., access to housing, services and care) and thus how processes of social inclusion and exclusion take place in communities. Alongside this is her particular interest in engaging with the experiences of and to give voice to socially, politically and economically marginalised groups, with a focus on older adults. Her PhD was entitled "'I'm not leaving!?" Critical perspectives on "Ageing in Place"'.

Ruth Stevens holds a PhD in Architecture and is a fellow of the research group ArcK for architecture and interior architecture at the Faculty of Architecture and Arts, Hasselt University, Belgium. Her research is focused on further developing a general frame of reference to design for human flourishing in architecture, through both theoretical work and testing a developed design tool to design for human flourishing in practice. She has presented her work at various international conferences and has published in, among others, *Interiors* and *The Design Journal*.

Marius Tippkämper studied communications design at Folkwang University of Arts, Essen, Germany, with a focus on interaction design and generative art. In 2014 he acquired his diploma, but continued to work at Folkwang University as a student assistant to Professor Claudius Lazzeroni and later as a lecturer, teaching programming. After some freelance work as an artist and as a web designer and developer he proceeded to work at ixdp. to develop hard- and software prototypes for the 'Design for Wellbeing' project. After its completion he began working as an interface designer and front-end developer at Grey Rook in Mülheim an der Ruhr, Germany.

Leandro Miletto Tonetto holds a PhD in Psychology. He is Professor of Design at Universidade do Vale do Rio dos Sinos, São Leopoldo, Brazil, and co-founder of Zooma Consumer Experience. He has coordinated research projects for organisations such as UN Women (Brazil), Dropbox and Samsung. His research focuses on design for wellbeing and emotion as a means to foster human development and health. His work has been published in *Applied Ergonomics*, *International Journal of Consumer Studies* and *Quality Management in Health Care*, among others.

Cathy Treadaway, PhD, is Professor of Creative Practice at the Cardiff School of Art and Design, Cardiff Metropolitan University, Fellow of the Royal Society of Arts, London, Fellow of the UK Higher Education Academy, York, UK, and a founder member of the CARIAD research group. She is an artist, writer and design researcher with a background in design and digital technologies. For the last six years she has been leading international interdisciplinary research investigating how to design interactive playful products for people living with advanced dementia, to help in their care and to support their wellbeing. Further information can be found at https://www.laughproject.info/.

Emmanuel Tsekleves leads design for global health at ImaginationLancaster, Lancaster University, UK. Driven by the UN's sustainable development goals, his research focuses on tackling community health challenges across the world. He is currently working on: understanding cleaning practices and driving infections from homes in Ghana; developing health and care policies for senior citizens in Malaysia; and in promoting seafood across Europe through novel packaging design. He is the convenor of the Design Research Society Special Interest Group on Global Health and editor of *Design for Health*, published by Routledge.

Jan Vanrie (PhD, Psychology) is Associate Professor of Human Sciences and Research Methodology and coordinator of research group ArcK, Faculty of Architecture and Arts, Hasselt University, Belgium. His research interests lie at the intersection of environmental psychology and perception, (interior) architecture, and design research and education. Within ArcK, he works with several colleagues in the research cluster 'Designing for More', investigating how people experience and interact with the built environment and looking for ways to support designers in design approaches such as design for subjective wellbeing, design for experience and universal design/ design for all.

Dominique Verté is Professor at the Department of Adult Educational Sciences, Vrije Universiteit Brussel. His research interests have focused on political, social and cultural participation in old age, community development, civic engagement, age-friendly communities and issues relating to health care policy. He is one of the founding directors of the Belgian Ageing Studies. This is a research project which aims to measure the living conditions and quality of life of older people in Belgian municipalities. The project promotes evidence-based policy at the local level by providing input and mobilising knowledge for planning inclusive, age-friendly policy programmes.

Preface

I am so pleased to introduce *Design for Wellbeing* as part of this series of books on design for social responsibility. Wellbeing, as Rebecca Cain and Ann Petermans state in their introductory chapter, has been a term increasingly in use over the past half-century, as an overarching paradigm with which all humans should be concerned. It is not that the dimensions of wellbeing are new, just that we have coined this term and used it increasingly to describe an attribute we should aspire to. Generally, most humans wish to be healthy and flourish through their lived experience, and many also bring into the equation happiness. This book interrogates these properties of wellbeing, whilst being concerned with the role of design in delivering human wellbeing, often alongside global wellbeing in relation to the sustainability of the earth.

Wellbeing results from both tacit and explicit engagement with a designed world that has both physical and psychological properties. This book covers ways in which we design the physical environment, ways in which we design our lives around, for instance, food and its health-giving, as well as its health-taking properties, and how we think about mental health and ageing through the course of our lives, and for a longer life. And finally, it sets these theories and practices in the context of tools developed explicitly for thinking about wellbeing by both the designers and the recipients of design.

This book is part of a series aimed at illustrating the value of design; for example, we have tackled the application of all the disciplines of design to aspects of contemporary life, such as transport and sport, services, policy-making, crime, health and sustainability, illustrating the multiplicity ways in which design is applied to serve society. Wellbeing of course sits amongst all those topics and indeed draws from them.

Designers have been attempting to be socially responsible for at least half a century if not forever, although we also know that design and designers have done some quite negative things in the name of progress. However, we have seen over the last twenty years, through this book series and others, that the design disciplines have understood their broader responsibility and have been moving into areas, or rather illustrating the work they do in relation to agendas, that will it is hoped aid the flourishing of humankind and the earth we inhabit. I am pleased to have supported Rebecca Cain and Ann Petermans in contributing this volume to the series, building a theoretical, practical and very useful reference text and baseline for future work on 'Design for Wellbeing'.

Professor Rachel Cooper
Lancaster University, UK

Part I

The rise of design for wellbeing

1 Setting the scene for design for subjective wellbeing

Ann Petermans and Rebecca Cain

Wellbeing: A hot topic

'Wellbeing' is a major, if not the ultimate goal, for every human being. Therefore, it is unsurprising that many institutions, governments and organisations worldwide are continuing to pay more attention to this important subject. There are four reasons why we are demanding more attention for 'wellbeing':

First, there is a growing societal need to focus on the wellbeing of people. There is a growing interest for people to pay the necessary time, effort and attention to the fulfilment of immaterial aspects in life, their re-appreciation of the search for and fulfilment of personal values, a good work–life balance, a healthy life, etc. However, although people increasingly have the possibilities and the willingness to work on their wellbeing, research (Easterlin, 1974; Veenhoven, 1993) shows that the average level of wellbeing remains stationary; a phenomenon known as the 'Easterlin Paradox' (De Tella & MacCulloch, 2008).

Second, from an economic point of view, paying attention to wellbeing is highly relevant, as happy people are more successful in many domains of life, and these successes are at least in part due to their happiness, according to Lyubomirsky et al. (2005a). Happy people are more social, altruistic and active, they like themselves more as well as liking others more and they have healthy bodies and immune systems as well as better conflict resolution skills. In addition, happiness seems to promote people's capacity for constructive and creative thinking (Desmet & Hassenzahl, 2012). A meta-analysis has demonstrated that being and feeling happy not only makes people feel better, more energetic and physically healthier, leading to a longer life expectancy, but happy people are also more creative and open-minded, have better relationships and are more productive in their jobs (Lyubomirsky et al., 2005b; Veenhoven, 2011). Longitudinal data indeed supports the proposition that happiness leads to success rather than vice versa (with mean effect sizes of .21 for the happiness, satisfying relationship link; .24 for the happiness, satisfying work link; and .18 for the happiness, health/longevity link) (Lyubomirsky et al., 2005b). Thus, investing in increased happiness not only leads to individuals feeling better, but also has social and public health benefits that are relevant for society as a whole (Desmet & Hassenzahl, 2012). Paying attention to wellbeing is thus highly relevant and also very much needed to enable our industries and economies to face all kinds of challenges that lie ahead of us, today and tomorrow, including, for example, ageing well, working and living well in appealing environments, and in reflecting about mobility and mental health. In this book, several of these issues and challenges will be discussed in depth.

Third, given these perspectives, it is not surprising that happiness has also become an issue on the political agenda. In 2011, the General Assembly of the United Nations accepted a resolution wherein they appealed to UN member states to undertake steps to give more attention to the pursuit of happiness of their citizens when determining how to achieve and measure social and economic development in their country (UN, 2011). In this respect, Bhutan is often a reference country: its 'Gross National Happiness Index' states that sustainable development should take a holistic view towards progress and should give equal importance to non-economic aspects of wellbeing and happiness. Similarly, in 2011 the OECD launched the OECD's 'Better Life Initiative', a pioneering project which aims to measure subjective wellbeing as an important indicator of society's progress (OECD, 2013). In line with this interest, the European Union also established an explicit aim to assess their citizens' wellbeing and design policies that help promote it in the future years (Eurobarometer, 2011).

In 2013, UN Secretary-General Ban Ki-moon pointed again to the importance of attention for people's wellbeing and happiness. In his Note to the General Assembly (2013, p. 3) he indicated that 'the creation of an enabling environment for improving people's wellbeing is a development goal in itself' and he also stated that 'the time is ripe for our measurement system [i.e., GDP] to shift emphasis from measuring economic production to measuring people's wellbeing'. Over the last five years, his call for action has been picked up by several very diverse institutions, governments and organisations all over the globe, including the UN. In 2015, UN countries adopted the 2030 Agenda for Sustainable Development and the 17 Sustainable Development Goals (SDGs) that were put forward. These goals concern a call for action to all countries to stimulate prosperity while safeguarding the protection of the planet (see Figure 1.1).

As Figure 1.1 shows, ensuring good health and promoting the wellbeing of people is 1 of these 17 SDGs, demonstrating the timeliness, relevance and importance of the topic today.

Fourth, it is clear that many designed objects and environments are silent companions in our daily lives. We are surrounded by them in almost everything we do and we interact

Figure 1.1 Sustainable Development Goals.

Source: United Nations, 2015.

with them, intentionally and unintentionally. In this respect, studying the potential of design and environments to enable people to work on their happiness holds great promise for creating a better world.

Starting from these accumulating practices and growing insights, it is not surprising that in recent years, subjective wellbeing has also emerged internationally as an important research topic. To quote Harvard psychologist Dan Gilbert (2012): 'Papers on happiness are published in Science, people who study happiness win Nobel prizes, and governments all over the world are rushing to figure out how to measure and increase the happiness of their citizens.'

This book aims to chart the development and application of design research to improve the subjective wellbeing and happiness of people. It draws together contributions from internationally leading academics and designers to demonstrate the latest thinking and research on the design of products, technologies, environments, services and experiences for wellbeing. Throughout the book, the importance of design for health is acknowledged, but it is clear that the aim of this book is to approach and explore the concept of subjective wellbeing and happiness more generally.

State-of-the-art: Researching subjective wellbeing and design

To date, researchers from diverse disciplines have tried to point to the essence of wellbeing and/or happiness. Philosophers, theorists and researchers from disciplines such as psychology, economics and neurosciences are interested in happiness. In the last few years, researchers from various design disciplines have also begun to investigate whether their discipline can contribute to the happiness of people – and, if so, what this contribution can be and/or how it can be set up or produced. However, to date, a consensus on the conceptualisation of wellbeing and happiness has not been reached, neither in design disciplines (Petermans & Pohlmeyer, 2014; Petermans & Nuyts, 2016), nor in other disciplines that focus on wellbeing and happiness (Lee et al., 2011; Desmet & Pohlmeyer, 2013).

Where researchers do agree, first, is that happiness is determined for a large part by genetics, life circumstances and intentional activities (Lyubomirsky et al., 2005a; Lyubomirsky, 2007). The fact that people can influence their happiness by focusing on the set-up of intentional activities creates tremendous opportunities for design. Throughout this book, and in particular in Part II, the contributing authors demonstrate the added value of design for wellbeing in different domains of practice. A second point of agreement among various researchers is that happiness and wellbeing have an objective and subjective component (Veenhoven et al., 2014; Petermans & Pohlmeyer, 2014).

As a consequence of these developments, researchers in academia often use the terms '(subjective) wellbeing' (SWB) and 'happiness' interchangeably (Lyubomirsky, 2007) in the popular press, daily discussions and scientific literature (Veenhoven, 2011; Desmet & Hassenzahl, 2012). In this book, we follow suit. In this respect, Chapter 2 of the book is key, as this chapter makes a detailed exploration of the rise of design for wellbeing, specifying the concepts of wellbeing, subjective wellbeing and human flourishing. In this way, a background to the growth of the area is provided.

Indeed, the way in which SWB is often connoted is close to the way in which most people interpret 'happiness' in its widest sense, that is, happiness as an overarching term for 'all that is good' (Veenhoven, 2011, p. 2). In addition, different researchers have been developing various models and strategies to increase SWB, particularly in the discipline of positive psychology (e.g., see the works of Lyubomirsky et al., 2005a; Lyubomirsky, 2007; Seligman, 2011). However, a clear consensus is still lacking.

Next, it is also recognised that 'researchers do not yet fully understand the causal role of the mediating factors that lead to improved wellbeing' (Nelson et al., 2015, p. 256). Nelson and Lyubomirsky (2014) point to the relevance and importance of future research to investigate the 'underlying mechanisms that lead positive activities to successfully improve wellbeing – that is, the "why" question' (p. 5). Such insights can facilitate creating or designing 'tools' and/or 'strategies' to enable people to develop their happiness. Part II of this book builds on this request for future research by providing examples of tools, methods and approaches that can be used by designers and researchers when designing for wellbeing.

In what follows, we elaborate further on 'objective' and 'subjective wellbeing', as these can be considered as large classification labels which provide a particular lens to look at various other approaches regarding wellbeing and happiness.

Objective wellbeing

Objective wellbeing (OWB) is the degree to which external constraints (that is, conditions that are external to an individual) for having a high quality of life are met (Constanza et al., 2007). Researchers of OWB often focus on the development and testing of lists of parameters such as social, economic, cultural and health indicators that are meaningful in this respect. Such data can be collected without subjective evaluations being made by the individuals under question (Constanza et al., 2007). OWB can be assessed by studying the objective, physical and external conditions of a designed object or environment. Regarding wellbeing, design and environment, it is also noteworthy to mention research on the concept of quality of life (with valuable work on health-related quality of life, e.g. McHorney, 1999), non-health-related quality of life, and healing environments and evidence-based design (e.g. Ulrich, 1984). In these streams of research, the focus is on how environments can be designed to contribute to the 'healing' of their respective users and, as such, can counter 'ill-being'. For instance, research in this domain reflects about the 'ideal' level of lighting, the presence of greenery, and other parameters that can be directly linked to the 'ideal objective functionality' of the concerned spaces.

Subjective wellbeing

Subjective wellbeing can be generally understood as people's self-reported evaluations of their lives as a whole (Veenhoven et al., 2014). It relates to (i) life satisfaction, (ii) emotional wellbeing, and (iii) eudaimonic or psychological wellbeing, whereby the components life satisfaction and emotional wellbeing refer to the definition of Diener (2000), who indicated that such evaluations have both cognitive and affective components. We also subscribe to the definition as proposed by Ryff (1989), whose 'psychological wellbeing' includes aspects such as personal growth and purpose in life. Finally, as an ultimate goal, SWB can lead to human flourishing if several wellbeing components, such as positive emotions, engaging activities, positive relationships and meaning are present in combination (Seligman, 2011; Huppert & So, 2013; Desmet & Pohlmeyer, 2013).

Relating objective and subjective wellbeing

In general, objective wellbeing can be considered as a determinant of subjective wellbeing (Desmet & Pohlmeyer, 2013), but, as indicated earlier, that does not cover the full spectrum of human wellbeing. There are more facets to SWB than our environmental circumstances. This becomes particularly evident when considering that different people can perceive the same circumstances differently. Moreover, lower objective standards of living do not automatically lead to lower levels of SWB. Empirical research on happiness is still fairly recent (Eid & Larsen, 2008), but Lyubomirsky et al. (2005a) have shown that inter-individual differences in SWB are more a matter of intentional activities, i.e. how we live our life, than of our circumstances. As a consequence, people have the power to actively contribute to their happiness.

When thinking about wellbeing from a design perspective, one may consider the objective measures of a design process or solution as well as people's subjective experiences with it. Typical questions in relation to objective measures are: 'Am I physically healthy in this designed environment?' or 'Is this designed product sustainable?'. The latter (i.e., people's subjective experiences of a design process or solution) then relates to questions such as: 'Can I thrive in this environment?', 'Can this object help me develop as a person?', or 'Does the space or product foster activities that are meaningful to me?'. Here, psychological and social aspects of wellbeing are at stake, whereby the person–activity fit also needs to be taken into account (Lyubomirsky & Layous, 2013). This conceptualisation brings a new, additional perspective to design sciences. Without neglecting the contribution of objective conditions of wellbeing, it is valuable to study how a design process or solution can support people to engage in or relate to activities that add meaning and pleasure to their lives. Such activities can in turn lead to sustainable increases in happiness (Lyubomirsky et al., 2005a, 2005b; Sheldon & Lyubomirsky, 2007).

Design for subjective wellbeing

Taking into account the state-of-the-art, it is intriguing to consider designed products, environments and services not only as a 'feature' of our circumstances, but also as a 'platform' where or with which people can set up intentional activities that contribute to their happiness (Petermans & Pohlmeyer, 2014). This opens up exciting opportunities for the design community.

From around 2012/2013 onwards, attention for design for wellbeing has grown in a diverse range of design disciplines, ranging from engineering design (Mackrill et al., 2014), industrial design (Desmet & Hassenzahl, 2012; Ozkaramanli & Desmet, 2012; Desmet & Pohlmeyer, 2013), interaction design (Hassenzahl et al., 2013; Karapanos et al., 2016; Diefenbach et al., 2017), ... to architecture and interior architecture (Payne et al., 2014; Vuong et al., 2012; Petermans & Pohlmeyer, 2014; Potter et al. 2018; Stevens, 2018). Particularly revealing about this interest and focus is, first, that considerations regarding what design for subjective wellbeing could be, and how designers can/could be stimulated to design for subjective wellbeing, are grounded in existing literature and insights, which are present or have come forth in studies performed in adjacent disciplines (e.g., see Jimenez et al., 2015), such as for instance psychology, philosophy, social sciences and humanities (instead of focusing on subjective wellbeing while relying [only] on a kind of gut feeling or intuition) (Stevens, 2018).

Second, new to design for subjective wellbeing as it is set up today is the call for an explicit focus on integrating design for wellbeing considerations early in the design process. It can thus be stated that research on wellbeing in design sciences can be considered pioneering work. This is supported by the fact that design conferences are only starting to set up first 'tracks' that specifically focus on 'wellbeing and happiness' (e.g., see 'Design and Emotion 2016' in The Netherlands (track Subjective Wellbeing and Happiness and

Architecture),'DRS 2016' in the UK (track Design for Health,Wellbeing and Happiness), 'DRS 2018' in Ireland (track Design Research for Wellbeing, Health and Happiness).The Design Research Society has also developed the Special Interest Group on 'Design for Wellbeing, Happiness and Health' due to a growing community of researchers in this area. These initiatives indicate that academic researchers are eager to connect and exchange knowledge and experiences on this topic. It is our hope that this book can assist in effectively organising and inspiring designers, researchers and practitioners who are active in this emerging field of knowledge.

Editing this book has enabled the involved authors to discuss various research projects that reflect on the question of how design (e.g., products, environments, services) can contribute to the wellbeing of people. Indeed, a current key question in different design disciplines is how people experience designed products, environments or services (e.g., see Petermans et al., 2013; Hassenzahl et al., 2013; Desmet & Pohlmeyer, 2013). If this question is taken one step further, aiming to link design research to research on wellbeing, one can ask: can design empower people to flourish in the environments which they occupy, and in which they live, work and/or play?

This goes beyond most current common discussions in design disciplines. Taking into account current knowledge on subjective wellbeing and happiness, it is the editors' belief that design and designers can play a very important role in this respect. In order to accommodate and answer questions on design for subjective wellbeing that are present both in design academia and design practice, this book has been set up to be of interest to different target audiences: students, teachers, researchers, but certainly also practitioners. Leading academics contributed to each of the different parts of the book, demonstrating the latest thinking and research on the design of products, environments and services for subjective wellbeing. Next to elaborating about research and theory, every contributing author has been asked explicitly to end their chapter with concrete guidelines, showcasing 'how to' translate the discussed insights into design practice.

Organisation of the book

This book brings together researchers from a diversity of disciplines who have expertise in subjective wellbeing and happiness for different user groups (e.g., older people, designers, policy-makers), but with a particular focus on products, environments and services: psychologists, social scientists, gerontologists, architects, interior architects, industrial designers, product designers, interaction designers, engineering designers and service designers. By contributing to this book, their mutual interests can converge and knowledge from a diverse range of disciplines can be exchanged.

The book is organised into four parts.

The first chapter of Part I, this chapter, sketches the background to the growth of design for subjective wellbeing. Chapter 2, a contribution from Ruth Stevens, Ann Petermans, Jan Vanrie, Anna Pohlmeyer and Rebecca Cain, then discusses the semantics of wellbeing, happiness and flourishing, and takes an in-depth look at the rise of the design for wellbeing movement.

Part II then goes on to demonstrate design for subjective wellbeing in practice, through providing a broad range of domains ranging from products to environments and services where design for subjective wellbeing has been applied.

In Chapter 3, Cathy Treadaway explores how design can be used to support the wellbeing of people living with dementia. It describes international design research that is informing the development of new products and services for dementia care and some of the particular challenges that designers face when undertaking applied design research to support the subjective wellbeing of people living with dementia. In Chapter 4, a contribution from Ann Petermans, Jan Vanrie, An-Sofie Smetcoren, Gitte Harzé and Jo Broekx, design for wellbeing in architecture and interior architecture is explored. The chapter demonstrates how research by design in a design studio exercise can help to crystallise insights and point to various possibilities that architecture and interior architecture can offer regarding the topic of 'lifelong living without care'. Next, in Chapter 5, Tiiu Poldma elaborates about social connectedness, social interaction and the design of interior environments. The chapter examines in particular how social interaction frames wellbeing from the perspective of people's experiences and how social connectedness occurs within public interior spaces. Chapter 6, developed by Luke Harmer, Rebecca Cain and Artur Mausbach, then goes on explore how social interaction within a mobility context can contribute to wellbeing. Through exploratory studies and workshops into future mobility, they explore the concept of 'joyful journeys' as moments which can be choreographed into pleasurable activities. Chapter 7 concludes Part II, with a contribution from Geke Ludden and Sander Hermsen. Their chapter elaborates about healthy eating and behaviour change, explaining why many efforts that aim to stimulate healthy eating have limited or even adverse effects on changing people's eating behaviour. They do so by adopting four views that are relevant to design. For each view, they discuss relevant literature and the role that design has played and could play when adopting that particular view. It is clear that, in the end, designing for healthy eating has great potential to contribute to people's subjective wellbeing. It is evident that the contributions that make up Part II do not present an exhaustive overview of design for subjective wellbeing in practice; on the contrary, Part II provides a 'first impression' of the broad scale of possible 'applications' of design for wellbeing in different domains. It would be wonderful to collect many more examples of design for wellbeing in practice in the near future.

Next, Part III discusses tools, methods and approaches which can be used by designers and researchers in design for wellbeing. In Chapter 8, Emmanuel Tsekleves elaborates on co-design and participatory methods and approaches for wellbeing. Following an introduction to the theory, an overview of the main areas where participatory and co-design approaches are being applied in relation to wellbeing is provided. The chapter also presents two case studies where such approaches are employed for enhancing the wellbeing of people living with dementia and Parkinson's disease. In Chapter 9, Emily Corrigan-Doyle and Carolina Escobar-Tello discuss creative methods for sustainable design for happiness and wellbeing. They elaborate about the Design for Happiness framework (DfH) and the Designing for Home Happiness framework (DfHH) as applicable, specific, creative methods to improve individuals' and ultimately society's happiness and wellbeing. They also give suggestions on how these methods might be implemented in future scenarios, and they give guidelines for their use. Chapter 10, developed by Ruth Stevens and Pieter Desmet, discusses 'Building Storey/ies': a scenario-based card game to architecturally design for human flourishing. Architectural designers can use this card game together with relevant stakeholders when they are designing for human flourishing. The chapter first discusses the development of the card game, then introduces the game components and scenario, and then reports on a workshop in which the game was tested. In Chapter 11, Holger Klapperich, Matthias Laschke, Marc Hassenzahl, Melanie Becker, Diana Cürlis, Thorsten Frackenpohl, Henning Köhler, Kai Ludwigs and Marius Tippkämper elaborate about a practice-oriented approach to begin to bridge the gap between abstract experiential design objectives and specific products and interaction. After introducing a theoretical understanding of wellbeing-driven design and showing how elements of social practice theory can inspire a set of practical design-supporting activities, a case study is discussed to highlight the challenges and opportunities of the suggested approach. Part III ends with Chapter 12, a contribution from Deger Ozkaramanli. She discusses dilemma-thinking as a means to enhance criticality in design for wellbeing. Critical design approaches require a distinct mindset and skills; in her chapter, she takes a step towards uncovering what that critical mindset can be and the role of dilemmas in supporting it.

The book concludes with Part IV with a look at future challenges facing society in terms of wellbeing, suggesting where and how design and design research can try to have a positive impact in this respect. In Chapter 13, Sarah Kettley and Rachel Lucas propose a picture of design in mental health. They outline the intersections of design research with mental health in the UK and Europe and consider challenges and future directions for designers working with the mental health service sector. A review of the literature results in their pinpointing three key challenges. Chapter 14, a contribution by An-Sofie Smetcoren, Liesbeth De Donder and Dominique Verté, discusses housing in later life. The chapter particularly focuses on housing and neighbourhood design and its relation to the (objective and subjective) wellbeing of older people. Based on a review of literature and results from a concrete research project in Brussels, Belgium, the authors set out important design principles for the future and formulate challenges relating to the home environment and wellbeing of older people. In Chapter 15, Leandro Tonetto discusses an international perspective on design for wellbeing. This contribution indicates that what seems to differentiate the scientific production within design for wellbeing from continent to continent is the underlying theoretical foundations and the social issues addressed by these studies. Part IV concludes with Chapter 16, a reflection by Pieter Desmet, wherein he discusses future agendas in design for wellbeing research and practice.

We hope that, together, these chapters will broaden the view of readers interested in design for wellbeing. With this book, we do not pretend to be able to present an exhaustive list of research projects and/or domains in design focusing on design for wellbeing. We hope that the book can be a starting point to boost research and collaboration for researchers as well as practitioners who focus on design and wellbeing, and that it can be an inspiration and foundation for further work that will help both to inspire others and to advance the body of knowledge in this field. In this way, we hope to have been able to contribute to the exchange of knowledge and experience to stimulate discussions about how design and environment can contribute to the wellbeing of people.

References

Constanza, R., Fisher, B., Ali, S., Beer, C., Bond, L., Boumans, R., Danigelis, N., Dickinson, J., Elliott, C., Farley, J., Elliott Gayer, D., MacDonald Glenn, L., Hudspeth, T., Mahoney, D., McCahill, L., McIntosh, B., Reed, B., Turab Rizvi, S., Rizzo, D., Simpatico, T., & Snapp, R. (2007). Quality of life: An approach integrating opportunities, human needs, and subjective wellbeing. *Ecological Economics, 61*(2–3), 267–276.
De Tella, R., & MacCulloch, R. (2008). Gross national happiness as an answer to the Easterlin Paradox? *Journal of Development Economics, 86*, 22–42.
Desmet, P., & Hassenzahl, M. (2012). Towards happiness: Possibility-driven design. In M. Zacarias, & J. Valente de Oliveira (Eds.), *Human-Computer Interaction: The Agency Perspective* (pp. 3–27). Berlin: Springer.

Desmet, P.M.A., & Pohlmeyer, A.E. (2013). Positive design: An introduction to design for subjective well-being. *International Journal of Design*, 7(3), 5–19.

Diefenbach, S., Hassenzahl, M., Eckoldt, K., Hartung, L., Lenz, E., & Laschke, M. (2017). Designing for well-being: A case study of keeping small secrets. *The Journal of Positive Psychology*, 12, 151–158.

Diener, E. (2000). Subjective wellbeing: the science of happiness and a proposal for a national index. *American Psychologist*, 55(1), 56–67.

Easterlin, R. (1974). Does economic growth improve the human lot? Some empirical evidence. In P. David, & M. Reder (Eds.), *Nations and Households in Economic Growth: Essays in Honour of Moses Abramovitz* (pp. 89–125). New York, NY: Academic Press.

Eid, M., & Larsen, J. (Eds.) (2008). *The Science of Subjective Wellbeing*. NY: The Guilford Press.

Eurobarometer (2011). *Well-Being in 2030*. Aggregate Report. Retrieved from http://ec.europa.eu/commfrontoffice/publicopinion/archives/quali/wellbeing_aggregate_en.pdf

Gilbert, D. (2012). The science behind the smile. *Harvard Business Review*, 90(1–2), 84–88.

Hassenzahl, M., Eckoldt, K., Diefenbach, S., Laschke, M., Lenz, E., & Kim, J. (2013). Designing moments of meaning and pleasure. Experience design and happiness. *International Journal of Design*, 7(3), 21–31.

Huppert, F., & So, T. (2013). Flourishing across Europe: Application of a new conceptual framework for defining well-being. *Social Indicator Research*, 110, 837–861.

Jimenez, S., Pohlmeyer, A.E., & Desmet, P.M.A. (2015). *Positive Design Reference* Guide. Delft: Delft University of Technology.

Karapanos, E., Gouveia, R., Hassenzahl, M., & Forlizzi, J. (2016). Wellbeing in the making: People's experiences with wearable activity trackers. *Psychology of Well-Being*, 6(4).

Lee, J., Je, H., & Byun, J. (2011). Wellbeing index of super tall residential buildings in Korea. *Building and Environment*, 46, 1184–1194.

Lyubomirsky, S. (2007). *The How of Happiness: A New Approach to Getting the Life You Want*. New York, NY: Penguin Books.

Lyubomirsky, S., King, L., & Diener, E. (2005a). The benefits of frequent positive affect: Does happiness lead to success? *Psychological Bulletin*, 131(6), 803–855.

Lyubomirsky, S., & Layous, K. (2013). How do simple positive activities increase well-being? *Current Directions in Psychological Science*, 22(1), 57–62.

Lyubomirsky, S., Sheldon, K., & Schkade, D. (2005b). Pursuing happiness: The architecture of sustainable change. *Review of General Psychology*, 9(2), 111–131.

Mackrill, J., Cain, R., & Jennings, P. (2014). Exploring positive hospital ward soundscape interventions. *Applied Ergonomics*, 45(6), 1454–1460.

McHorney C.A. (1999). Health status assessment methods for adults: Past accomplishments and future challenges. *Annual Review of Public Health*, 20, 309–335.

Nelson, S., & Lyubomirsky, S. (2014). Finding happiness: Tailoring positive activities for optimal well-being benefits. In M. Tugade, M. Shiota, & L. Kirby (Eds.), *Handbook of Positive Emotions* (pp. 275–293). New York, NY: Guilford.

Nelson, S., et al. (2015). What psychological science knows about achieving happiness. In S.J. Lynn et al. (Eds.), *Health, Happiness, and Wellbeing: Better Living Through Psychological Science* (pp. 250–271). NY: Sage.

OECD (2013). *OECD Guidelines on Measuring Subjective Well-Being*. OECD Publishing. Accessible from: https://www.oecd-ilibrary.org/economics/oecd-guidelines-on-measuring-subjective-well-being_9789264191655-en

Ozkaramanli, D., & Desmet, P. (2012). I knew I shouldn't, yet I did it again! Emotion-driven design as a means to motivate subjective well-being. *International Journal of Design*, 6(1), 27–39.

Payne, S.R., Mackrill, J., Cain, R., Streliz, J., & Gate, L. (2014). Developing interior design briefs for health-care and well-being centres through public participation. *Architectural Engineering and Design Management*, 11(4), 264–279.

Petermans, A., Janssens, W., & Van Cleempoel, K. (2013). A holistic framework for conceptualizing customer experiences in retail environments. *International Journal of Design*, 7(2), 1–18.

Petermans, A., & Pohlmeyer, A. (2014). Design for subjective wellbeing in interior architecture. *Proceedings of the 6th Symposium of Architectural Research* 2014: *Designing and Planning the Built Environment for Human Wellbeing*, pp. 206–218.

Petermans, A., & Nuyts, E. (2016). Happiness in place and space: Exploring the contribution of architecture and interior architecture to happiness. *Proceedings of the 10th Design & Emotion Conference*, Amsterdam, The Netherlands.

Potter, R., Sheehan, B., Jennings, P., & Cain, R. (2018). The impact of the physical environment on depressive symptoms of older residents living in care homes: A mixed methods study. *The Gerontologist*, *58*(3), 438–447.

Ryff, C.D. (1989). Happiness is everything, or is it? Explorations on the meaning of psychological well-being. *Journal of Personality and Social Psychology*, *57*, 1069–1081.

Seligman, M.E.P. (2011). *Flourish: A Visionary New Understanding of Happiness and Wellbeing*. New York, NY: Free Press.

Sheldon, K., & Lyubomirsky, S. (2007). Is it possible to become happier? (And if so, how?) *Social and Personality Psychology Compass*, *1*(1), 129–145.

Stevens, R. (2018). *A Launchpad for Design for Human Flourishing in Architecture. Theoretical Foundations, Practical Guidance and a Design Tool*. PhD thesis, Hasselt University, Hasselt, Belgium.

Ulrich, R. (1984). View through a window may influence recovery from surgery. *Science*, *224*, 420–421.

United Nations, General Assembly (2011). *Happiness: Towards a Holistic Approach to Development*. Retrieved from http://www.un.org/en/ga/search/view:doc.asp?symbol=A/RES/65/309

United Nations, General Assembly (2013). *Happiness: Towards a Holistic Approach to Development*. Retrieved from http://www.un.org/ga/search/view:doc.asp?symbol=A/67/697

Veenhoven, R., (1993). *Happiness in Nations: Subjective Appreciation of Life in 56 Nations, 1946–1992*. The Netherlands: Erasmus University Press.

Veenhoven, R. (2011). Greater happiness for a greater number: Is that possible? If so, how? In K.N. Sheldon, T.B. Kashdan, & M.F. Steger (Eds.), *Designing Positive Psychology* (pp. 392–409). Oxford, UK: Oxford University Press.

Veenhoven, R., Arampatzi, E., Bakker, A., Bruel, M., Burger, M., Commandeur, H., Das Gupta-Mannak, J., van Geest, P., van Haastrecht, J., Hendriks, M., Hessels, J., van Liemt, G., Oerlemans, W., Volberda, H., & van der Zwan, P. (2014). *Het rendement van geluk. Inzichten uit wetenschap en praktijk*. Den Haag: Stichting Maatschappij en Onderneming.

Vuong, K., Cain, R., Burton, E., & Jennings, P. (2012). The impact of healthcare waiting environment design on end-user perception and well-being. *International Scientific Journal Architecture and Engineering*, *2*(1), 39–44.

2 Wellbeing, happiness and flourishing

Different views on a common goal

Ruth Stevens,[1] Ann Petermans, Anna Pohlmeyer,
Rebecca Cain and Jan Vanrie

This chapter introduces design for wellbeing by looking at its evolution through its eudaimonic and hedonic roots. We explore the transition from defining wellbeing, to dimensioning its constituents, and then go on to review recent evolutions in the eudaimonic and hedonic views in domains such as philosophy, psychology, sociology, economy and design. The idea of human flourishing is then introduced, which leads us to the new movement towards positive design – inspired by positive psychology. We conclude the chapter with reflections on the work still to be done by design researchers in developing and validating tools which can be used by practising designers to design for wellbeing, happiness and flourishing.

What is wellbeing?

The roots: Eudaimonic and hedonic wellbeing

Wellbeing has been a topic of inquiry for millennia: the notion dates back to the ancient Greeks, who first mentioned the concepts of 'eudaimonia' (Aristotle) and 'hedonia' (Epicurus).

'**Eudaimonic wellbeing**' is related to *eudaimonia*, which is etymologically a combination of '*eu*', meaning 'good', and '*daimon*', meaning 'one's own spirit'. According to Greek philosopher Socrates, it was deemed the highest good for human beings, since it strived for something 'larger' and 'bigger' than just experiencing personal pleasure. Socrates' view on eudaimonia was dominated by the aspect of 'virtues', which he believed to be both necessary and sufficient for eudaimonia. Examples of these virtues are self-control, courage and wisdom, and these are, according to Socrates, deemed to guarantee eudaimonia. Later, Plato defined eudaimonia as 'the good composed of all goods; an ability which suffices for living well; perfection in respect of virtue; resources sufficient for a living creature' (Plato, 4 BCE/1854). Here, Plato argued that virtues are states of the soul, and a person who lives by virtues, has an ordered and harmonious soul, which leads to eudaimonia (Plato, 4 BCE/1854). Eudaimonia became a central topic in the work of Aristotle. His work *Nicomachean Ethics* (4 BCE/1985) furthered the conceptualisation of eudaimonia, which he believed occurs when a person *actively* expresses and exhibits his or her virtues and reasons for doing what is worth doing. Thus, consciously and actively striving for a sort of excellence is the basis of Aristotle's conception of eudaimonia. Furthermore, he believed that a person who only chases and consumes pleasure, and thereby attempts to avoid all feelings of pain, is a slavish follower of desires, which he thought was a vulgar thing (Ryan & Deci, 2001). However, there was no consensus on *how* a life should be led in order for it to count as virtuous and therefore eudaimonic. Plato's 'perfection in respect of virtue' hints at a double perspective of a person's quest for personal excellence in what one does and undertakes, and also the moral aspect of thinking in terms of what is meaningful and what is deemed good for the society one lives in. In short, Aristotle conceptualised 'eudaimonia', which he saw as a culmination of a person's idealised journey to 'actualise' their potential (Jackson, 2013).

'**Hedonic wellbeing**' on the other hand, sprouted from Greek philosophers Aristippus and Epicurus. Aristippus' viewpoint (O'Keefe, n.d. (4 BCE)) was that the goal of human life is to experience a maximum amount of pleasure, which was nuanced by Epicurus, as a life in absence of physical pain, fear and mental disturbance (Konstan, 2013). According to Epicurus, all good and bad in a person's life derives from sensations of what is pleasurable and what is painful, in which one strives for the absence of both physical and mental suffering in order to achieve a state of satiation and tranquillity of the soul, since only then does a person not need to compensate with pleasure-seeking (Folse, 2005; Konstan, 2013). Hedonism seems to only affect the personal living sphere, but it can also be seen as being broader than that, illustrated by, for instance, philosopher Jeremy Bentham (1789 (1996)) who believed that a good society is built from people who strive to maximise pleasure and self-interest. Bentham, a philosopher whose work is situated at the turn of the eighteenth- and nineteenth-century utilitarianism, in which contemporary views on hedonism are rooted, theorised that hedonic wellbeing is found in the quantity of pleasure experiences, as evidenced by his earlier statement. However, this quantitative approach to hedonism was countered by John Stuart Mill (1863 (1998)), who declared that some types of pleasure, such as friendship, knowledge or art, are *higher* and more desirable than others. In this particular evolution of hedonism, we can see traces of eudaimonic aspects as well, since friendship, for instance, concerns a rather *objectively listed value* a person would strive for in his life, that can give long-term meaning as well as short-term pleasure experiences. Objectively listed values point to values which are generally valid and acknowledged but which have different interpretations and manifestations. Still, the conclusion can be made that the hedonic view on wellbeing is founded upon affective components, focused on the personal balance between positively and negatively appraised experiences.

Eudaimonic and hedonic views on wellbeing seem to have a unique perspective on which particular components *provoke* wellbeing, which can – in short – be summed up as a set of *values* in the case of eudaimonia and *affections* in the case of hedonia.

Contemporary research in the eudaimonic and hedonic tradition

From defining wellbeing to dimensioning constituents of wellbeing

In academic literature there is currently no consensus on an actual unambiguous definition of 'wellbeing', but there is discussion on the meanings of various terms and their interrelationship. The question of how we should define wellbeing remains unanswered (Dodge et al., 2012; Huta & Waterman, 2013), not so much due to a lack of knowledge, but due to a multitude of definitions and interpretations that arose through philosophical and psychological interpretations of the eudaimonic and hedonic views. According to Pollard and Lee (2003), the construct of wellbeing is complex and multifaceted and continues to elude researchers' attempts to define and measure it, which according to Forgeard and colleagues (2011) is the reason for blurred and overly broad definitions of wellbeing in research.

Broad interpretations of wellbeing found in literature are 'the condition of life that is good for an individual creature in the broadest sense' (Tiberius, 2006, p. 494) and 'wellbeing is no less than what a group of people collectively agree makes a good life' (Ereaut & Whiting, 2008, p. 1). Both leave the question regarding the specific relation between wellbeing and hedonic and eudaimonic views unanswered but take a stance regarding the single- or multi-person profile of wellbeing. Another interesting interpretation regarding wellbeing is 'feeling good and functioning well' (Jackson, 2013, p. 22), a simple representation of wellbeing combining hedonic and eudaimonic views.[2]

A search for detailed definitions of wellbeing in contemporary literature has ended with a listing of an abundance of new terms for wellbeing, such as 'psychological wellbeing', 'happiness', 'subjective wellbeing' and many others. The very existence of all these terms is partially due to the fact that the topic was first studied in contemporary literature by philosophical researchers (e.g., Brey, 2012), but soon picked up by other disciplines such as psychology (e.g., Rogers, 1961; Bradburn, 1969). Evidently, every discipline studies wellbeing with their own lens and background, resulting in a variety of interpretations and definitions. Social sciences also became enthused to work with the topic, which quickly drew attention from economists (e.g., Layard, 2005) and policy-makers (e.g., GNH Centre Bhutan, 1970; OECD, 2013; United Nations, 2011). Even more recently, the design sciences dug into the topic of wellbeing and took some initial attempts to introduce it into actual design practice (e.g., Desmet & Pohlmeyer, 2013; Hassenzahl, 2010; Petermans & Pohlmeyer, 2014). This resulted in the existence of many interpretations of 'wellbeing', each of which entails a specific perspective that at some point overlaps with others. Meanwhile, different terms are often used interchangeably in scholarly texts. Indeed, many definitions are available, raising questions regarding the 'ingredients' of these constructs, and how they are brought together throughout different definitions (Pollard & Lee, 2003). Dodge and colleagues (2012) stated that no clear definition has risen because scholars have placed more effort in trying to pinpoint the dimensions of wellbeing: *the attention shifted from defining to rather dimensioning wellbeing, which led to a more nuanced view on the construct of 'wellbeing'.* Instead of clearly representing what wellbeing *is,* researchers started to *describe* what *constitutes* wellbeing. For instance, 'music' can be *defined* as 'vocal or instrumental sounds', but it is *dimensioned* by elements such as, principally, the pitch, the timbre and the rhythm, and by other aspects such as volume, dynamics, articulation, tempo, etc. (see Gardner, 1983). Through its constituents, a richer image of 'music' is shaped, and, additionally, this knowledge can stimulate practitioners to approach music in a more creative way by playing with its constituents. In the case of 'wellbeing', a similar process has taken place. To demonstrate this, a summary (Table 2.1) concerning the terminological diversity in wellbeing semantics was set up.

Table 2.1 compares wellbeing-related research topics regarding (i) their hedonic or eudaimonic nature and (ii) their attempt to define it or to describe it, and, in the case of descriptions, whether the components that describe wellbeing are concrete measures to be taken by a person, or rather descriptions regarding particular needs one should work on.

An overview of recent wellbeing interpretations in the light of eudaimonia versus hedonia

In the following, we review recent evolutions in the eudaimonic and hedonic views. These data were collected via a literature review in the field of wellbeing and including domains such as philosophy, psychology, sociology, economy and design.

Table 2.1 Terminological diversity of wellbeing semantics

Discipline	Authors	Year	'Wellbeing' is		'Wellbeing' defined and description	'wellbeing' constitutes
			Hedonic roots	Eudaimonic roots		
Psychology	Maslow	1954		**Self actualisation**	Achieving one's full potential, and experiencing purpose and meaning	
Psychology	Rogers	1961		**The good life**		**Fully functioning person:** Open to experiences, living in here and now, doing what is good for them, experientiall free, creative etc.
Psychology	Bradburn	1969		**Psychological wellbeing**	Preponderance of positive affect over negative affect	
Psychology	Diener	1984	**Life satisfaction**		The balance between positive and negative affect	retrospective judgement of life
Economy	Max-Neef	1991				9 basic fundamental human needs: subsistence, protection, affection, understanding, participation, leisure, creation, identity, freedom
Psychology	Cummins	1996		**Personal wellbeing**		To measure one's life satisfaction: standard of living, health, achieving in life, relationships, safety, community-connectedness, future security
Psychology	Kahneman	1999	**Happiness**			
Sociology and psychology	Keyes	2002		**Flourishing**	Diagnosis of flourishing: emotional, psychological and positive functioning	14 items: positive affect (happy and interested), purpose in life, self-acceptance, social contribution, social integration, social growth, social acceptance, social coherence, environmental mastery, personal growth, autonomy, life satisfaction
Psychology	Csikszentmihalyi	1990		**Flow**	Total engagement, being absorbed in something	mastering
Philosophy	Nussbaum	2000				10 human capabilities: life, bodily health, bodily integrity, senses and imagination and thought, emotions, practical reason, affiliation, other species, play, control over one's environment
Psychology	Ryan & Deci	2002		**Self-determination**		Answering to 3 psychological needs: autonomy, competence, relatedness

Field	Author	Year	Concept	Description	Strategies
(Positive) psychology	Seligman	2003	**Authentic happiness**	Pleasant life, engaged or good life, meaningful life	
Psychology	Eid & Diener	2004	**Subjective wellbeing**	Multidimensional evaluation of one's life, including cognitive judgements of life satisfaction as well as affective evaluations of moods and emotions	
Psychology	Peterson et al	2005	**Happiness and life satisfaction**	3 pathways to wellbeing; pleasure, engagement, meaning	
Economy	Ranis et al	2006	**Human flourishing**	8 domains: bodily wellbeing, material wellbeing, mental development, work, security, spiritual wellbeing, empowerment and political freedom, respect of other species	
Psychology	Lyubomirsky	2007	**Happiness**		12 strategies: Counting blessings, cultivating optimism, avoiding over-thinking and social comparison, practicing acts of kindness, nurturing relationships, doing more activities that truly engage you, replaying and savoring life's joys, committing to your goals, developing strategies for coping, learning to forgive, practicing religion and spirituality, taking care of your body
Psychology	Ryff & Singer	2008	**Psychological wellbeing**	Self-acceptance, purpose in life, environmental mastery, positive relationships, personal growth, autonomy	
Psychology	Cummins	2010	**Homeostasis**		
Psychology	Diener et al.	2010	**Flourishing**	Positive functioning – fulfilling a set of universal human psychological needs	Balance between threads and strengths 8 items: positive relationships, engagement, purpose and meaning, self-acceptance, competence, optimism, social contribution
(Positive) psychology	Seligman	2011	**Flourishing**	Positive emotion, engagement, relationships, meaning, accomplishment	connect, be active, take notice, keep learning, give

(*Continued*)

Table 2.1 Continued

Discipline	Authors	Year	'Wellbeing' is		'Wellbeing' defined and description	'wellbeing' constitutes
			Hedonic roots	Eudaimonic roots		
Sociology	Veenhoven	2011	**Happiness**		The degree to which an individual judges overall quality of life as a whole favourably	
Psychology	Dodge	2012	**Equilibrium theory**			Balance between psychological, physical and social resources and psychological, physical and social challenges
(Positive) design	Ruitenberg & Desmet	2012	**Meaningful activities**			enrol in activities that use and develop personal skills and talents of users, rooted in their values, that contribute to a greater good, that are rewarding and enjoyable in return
(Positive) design	Desmet & Pohlmeyer	2013	**Flourishing**			A sweet spot when pleasure, meaning and virtue occur together
Psychology	Huppert & So	2013	**Flourishing**	The combination of feeling good and functioning effectively		10 components (that are also the opposite of symptoms of depression): competence, emotional stability, engagement, meaning, optimism, positive emotion, positive relationships, resilience, self-esteem, vitality.
Psychology	Rusk & Waters	2015	**Positive functioning**			5 domains: comprehension and coping, attention and awareness, emotions, goals and habits, virtues and relationships
(Positive) psychology	Butler & Kern	2016	**Flourishing**		A dynamic optimal state of psychosocial functioning that arises from functioning across multiple psychosocial domains	

Source: Stevens, 2018.

Starting with *eudaimonia*, the work of Maslow (1954) has been considered by many researchers as a point of reference, since an essential human need that he proposes is that of *self-actualisation*, which motivates people the more it is fulfilled, in contrast to deficiency needs that tend to decrease once they are not lacking them any more (e.g., Ryff, 1989; Jackson, 2013). Also, the work of Rogers (1961) is key in this respect. He reflected on wellbeing in terms of 'the good life', and the 'fully functioning person' presented inspired other influential researchers such as Ryff and Singer (2008); he also included a more detailed view on what Aristotle's 'striving for excellence' and 'virtuous behaviour' should be. Rogers's 'good life' stands for living up to moral standards and a 'fully functioning person' was first described as a person open to experiences, living in the here-and-now, trusting and using personal values, leading an increasingly existential life, feeling in control and being creative (Rogers, 1961). Rogers attributes to such a person an active attitude towards life, continuously striving for achievement while believing in oneself. In other words, being mentally ready to fulfil one's potential, and viewing life as a process, is crucial to reach the goal of actualising oneself (Rogers, 1961). Thence, Rogers states that self-actualising complies with fulfilling a list of *objective – or objectifiable – criteria*, some of which he listed. These objective criteria entail aspects or values that are objectively preferable by everybody, such as, for instance, 'security'. This approach is in line with Parfit (1984), who views eudaimonia as an 'objective list theory', in which eudaimonic wellbeing consists of achieving certain objective values, such as perfecting one's nature or realising human capabilities. In 1998, Ryff and Singer furthered the 'objective list theory', and further detailed what self-actualising entails, by explicating their multifaceted term of 'psychological wellbeing' – which Ryff used as a synonym for eudaimonic wellbeing. *Self-actualising* is indeed the core of their concept, and it is based on one's own unique potential. Through this concept, Ryff and Singer (1998) explicitly put forward the personal responsibility and active engagement of a person to realise their full potential, implying that passively and coincidentally consuming 'life' is not enough. Moreover, besides an active attitude, a conscious understanding of what one is undertaking is part of the concept as well. This implies that people create meaning through the actions they undertake, or, as Vivenza calls it, 'action directed by thought' (2007, p. 8). In Aristotle's words of 'eudaimonia not only requires for instance a good character, but also rational activity' (*Nicomachean Ethics*, 4 BCE), clear references can be found to the active nature of eudaimonic wellbeing implying both an active attitude towards life and the need to be mindfully present in life. In this case, wellbeing is actually well-'doing'.

More accounts of eudaimonic wellbeing and its dimensions have been put forward, for example by Ryan and Deci, through their self-determination theory (1985, 2002), working on the notion that the objective list of values concern innate psychological needs that a human needs to fulfil, and by Nussbaum (2000) through the 'capabilities approach'. The latter builds from the power of a person to perform, or to obtain achievement regarding certain values they hold (Sen, 1992), and thereby stresses that a person can fulfil needs while applying their own inner strengths. Yet again, a deepening of the 'fully functioning person' is realised, in terms of describing lists of specific objective human needs and capabilities, that stimulate people to undertake action in life.

Another influential reference in eudaimonic wellbeing is the work of Martin Seligman. As one of the founders of positive psychology, he introduced the concept of 'authentic happiness' in 2003. In his view, authentic happiness implies leading a pleasant life, an engaged life and a meaningful life, all at once. Concretely, a person can attain this by, respectively, having positive feelings, pursuing involvement in all dimensions of life (e.g., work, relations, leisure) and using their signature strengths and talents to service 'bigger' things in life. In 2011, Seligman developed his theory of 'authentic happiness' further to a theory of wellbeing (2011). Hereby, he first added the dimensions of relationships and accomplishment to the already identified dimensions of positive emotions, engagement and meaning. Furthermore, rather than pursuing the goal of life satisfaction, he now proposed to strive for human flourishing (HF) by increasing positive emotions, as well as engagement, relationships, meaning and accomplishment. Seligman believes in the need for the development of personal 'character', which happens when a person cultivates and nurtures personal strengths such as kindness or originality, in order to achieve universal virtues, such as, for instance, wisdom, knowledge or love and humanity (Peterson & Seligman, 2004). In his view, it is important that people are responsible for choosing to develop their strengths over correcting weaknesses, and, in doing so, have the prospect of flourishing (Seligman, 2011). The assumption that most people can choose to work on talents and live their life in that manner has been criticised, however, because it is more difficult for people who, for instance, live under a dictatorial regime (Jackson, 2013) or in a disadvantaged context.

As for the concept of *hedonia*, Bradburn (1969) was one of the first to further expand this view. In his theory on what he calls 'psychological wellbeing' (a label which Carol Ryff later actually used as a synonym of the eudaimonic model, cf. supra), 'an individual is high in psychological wellbeing in the degree to which he has an excess of positive affect over negative affect' (1989, p. 9). Both affects (pleasure and pain) are seen as distinct aspects. Thus, wellbeing emanates when a preponderance of positive over negative affect occurs, a situation that Bradburn calls 'happiness' (1969). Happiness, here refers to a psychological state a person is in, complying with a temporary feeling of joy, a mood one is in or even a short fleeting positive emotion one goes through (see e.g., Ryff, 1989; Waterman, 1993; Tiberius, 2006). In literature, 'happiness' is often used as a synonym for the term 'wellbeing' (e.g., Seligman, 2002), however in most literature on the historic evolution of hedonic wellbeing 'happiness' is defined as a synonym of 'pleasure' (Kahneman et al., 1999; Waterman, 1993; Ryan & Deci, 2001). Researchers (e.g., Diener, 1984; Diener & Suh, 1997; Kahneman et al., 1999) have challenged the extent to which pleasure and pain are two distinct aspects or they intertwine, which leads to the argument that a cognitive component is a part of wellbeing as well, to be able to 'measure' the balance between 'pleasure' and 'pain'. Diener, under the heading of subjective wellbeing, conceptualised this cognitive component as 'satisfaction of life' (Diener, 1984), or the personal appraisal or retrospective judgement of one's life (see also Veenhoven, 2011). Thus, the hedonic interpretation is again a construct with multiple components, consisting of the *affective* 'happiness', which implies that positive affect exceeds negative affect, and the *cognitive* 'life satisfaction'.[3]

Another theory in this respect is that of Sumner, labelled 'authentic happiness theory' (1996), which, in line with Diener (1984), focuses on the evaluative question or judgement of how life is going for you. More recently, hedonism defender, Feldman (2004), seemed to shift towards a more eudaimonic interpretation, claiming 'pleasure' should not only be seen as sensory pleasure, but as part of *attitudinal pleasure*, meaning positive attitudes.

Discussion of the findings

Reviewing the summary of the evolutions in eudaimonic and hedonic viewpoints, the following aspects seem particularly relevant:

Objective versus subjective

Eudaimonic wellbeing is characterised by the fulfilment of widely shared, common or, in other words, objective values (e.g., Tiberius, 2006), such as realising one's potential, while hedonic wellbeing is characterised by subjective measures of the balance between pleasure and pain (e.g., Samman, 2007) and founded upon one's personal evaluation of life. For that reason, the hedonic view on wellbeing has also been called 'subjective wellbeing' in academic studies (e.g., Kahneman et al., 1999; Samman, 2007). The term 'subjective' is justified by Jackson (2013) stating that 'wellbeing' depends on what people personally *think* would make their lives 'better' and not on what others think would make their life better (i.e., objective values). On the contrary, the eudaimonic vision requires personal effort and drive, mindful presence and physical activity in order to fulfil certain objectified, psychological needs and values.

Active versus passive

As we have argued above, a major difference between hedonic and eudaimonic views lies in their respective connotations of passive appraisal versus actively undertaking action. Hedonist views have the connotation of relying on passively 'consuming' pleasure. Although this is combined with actively avoiding pain, the overall balance results in a rather passive attitude of evaluating. A prototypical example could be binge-watching TV. In eudaimonic views, personal effort and drive, and the choice to act upon this, are crucial, which contributes to the more active image that is attached to eudaimonia. Here, it is known that consuming pleasure in a passive way does not suffice (Pohlmeyer, 2014), and it is replaced by actively striving to function in a *positive* way as a person. In that respect, eudaimonia transcends feelings of pleasure and happiness, and strives for the feeling of leading a virtuous and full life (Ryff & Keyes, 1995; Ryff & Singer, 1998).

Timeframe: Rear-view versus forward-looking perspectives and the long term versus the short term

There seems to be a dual difference in the time-perspective between eudaimonia and hedonia. To reach eudaimonia, a person strives for future successes, and interprets their entire lifetime as the time span to achieve this goal of becoming the best person they can be, or, in other words, self-actualisation. Consequently, eudaimonia is a long-term process characterised by a forward-looking perspective. Hedonistic views, on the other hand, concern judgements in the now and evaluations in retrospect. One can say hedonists look back at what has happened in a specific period of time or what is happening in the present, and thereby take a rear-view perspective to evaluate rather shorter-term time intervals.

From wellbeing to human flourishing

A positive route/roots: Positive psychology

As stated by Huppert and So (2013, p. 838), for too long it was 'tacitly assumed that wellbeing would prevail when pathology was absent', believing that wellbeing could be reached as soon as negative aspects, such as pathology, were absent or removed. However, this line of thinking was already countered by a growing body of research explaining that 'ill' and its opposite term 'healthy' are continua that can evolve independently from one another (e.g., Keyes, 2005). So, taking away the negative does not necessarily equal more wellbeing. Instead, the positive should be added. Taking this *positive* route is key in 'positive psychology'. More concretely, positive psychology is a research field that has been developed over the last decades in an effort to counter the focus in psychology on rather negative topics, such as what causes depression or stress (Myers & Diener, 1995; Huppert & So, 2013; Tiberius, 2006; Kigen Bjering, 2014). Research into 'flourishing' grew out of positive psychology (Seligman & Csikszentmihalyi, 2000). In 1998, in his inauguration speech as president of the American Psychological Association (APA), Martin Seligman noted that psychologists should focus on studying what makes people happy instead of focusing on negative issues. He stated 'we baked the part about mental illness. … The other side's unbaked, the side of strength, the side of what we're good at' (address, Lincoln Summit, September 1999). According to Seligman, in positive psychology three things are key: (1) be as concerned with strength as with weakness; (2) be as interested in building the best things in life as in repairing the worst; and, finally, (3) be as concerned with making lives of normal people fulfilling and with nurturing their talent as with healing pathology (Seligman, 2004). Positive psychology is defined by Gable and Haidt in 2005 as 'the study of conditions and processes that contribute to the flourishing or optimal functioning of people, groups, and institutions' (2005, p. 104).

Flourishing defined or described: Is it eudaimonia or more?

Hone and colleagues defined flourishing as 'having high levels of subjective wellbeing' (2014, p. 1) and, using different semantics, as 'high levels of wellbeing', attributing a sort of comparative and superlative degree to flourishing, which is shared by other researchers (e.g., Fredrickson & Losada, 2005; Seligman, 2011). Schotanus-Dijkstra (2015, p. 2) launched a similar definition by stating that flourishing is 'having high levels of both hedonic and eudaimonic wellbeing', which she based on the interpretations of Huppert (2009), Huppert and So (2013) and Keyes (2002), stressing the multidimensional character of flourishing. Therefore, flourishing also incorporates finding the right balance in life, in line with the flow-status, as described by Csikszentmihalyi (1990), in which the right balance between challenges and resources is achieved. An understanding of Keyes (2002), Huppert and So (2013) and Seligman (2011) also acknowledges the hedonic aspects in flourishing. Hence, although flourishing seems to refer to a superlative, it cannot simply be called the *summum* of eudaimonia, since hedonics are mentioned too.

Huppert and So (2013, p. 838) stated that flourishing is 'the experience of life going well … feeling good and functioning effectively'. Here, a shift is noticed from viewing flourishing as a 'state of mind' towards stressing its dynamic nature, and viewing it as actively chased. This also illustrates that flourishing seems to be approached as a more active concept compared to its neighbouring concepts of 'happiness' or 'wellbeing'.

Next to descriptions of flourishing, contemporary research (e.g., Keyes, 2002) has made progress in reflecting on the constituents of flourishing, or the properties and particularities of what can be labelled as 'flourishing people'. Keyes (2002) also acknowledged the presence of hedonic symptoms in a person to be part of flourishing and went on to define 14 items representing the 3 types (emotional, psychological and social) of wellbeing (see Keyes, 2005).

While slight variations occur in the listing of constituents of flourishing, many notions on HF encompass personal development in combination with virtuous living in the broader context of society. Indeed, as different scholars have concluded to date (e.g., Hone et al., 2014; Schotanus-Dijkstra, 2015), knowledge about HF is still in its infancy. However, from the previous sections of text, we learn that HF is a concept that takes a positive outlook, that is described as a multidimensional construct with a comparative degree, incorporating hedonic pleasure with a multitude of eudaimonic aspects, characterised by a dynamic nature, and that it is built from constituents on a personal and more social scale, such as personal development and virtuous behaviour.

From positive psychology to positive design

Following the elaboration on the semantics of wellbeing, it is valuable to specify how wellbeing as a general topic has started to be integrated and translated in different design disciplines. Although wellbeing has often been marked as an important topic in the field of design research (e.g., Brey, 2015), one would expect a great deal of research and literature to be available on the topic of *design* for wellbeing. However, only in the first decades of the twenty-first century, did design for wellbeing start to make an impression on design science. The introduction of positive design (Desmet & Pohlmeyer, 2013) was key in this respect, being rooted in positive psychology and specifically applied in industrial and interaction design.

A positive design framework

The positive design framework (Desmet & Pohlmeyer, 2013) is one of the pioneering works that explicitly introduce the notion of designing for human flourishing to the field of design (Figure 2.1).

Desmet and Pohlmeyer (2013) developed this framework based on theories as well as empirical evidence in positive psychology and philosophy. Central to the framework is a multi-angle perspective of three prominent wellbeing components: pleasure, personal significance and virtues. Designers are invited to address all three components in order to stimulate pleasurable as well as meaningful experiences for people (Pohlmeyer & Desmet, 2017). Thus, eudaimonic aspects of meaning and objective lists of virtues reside next to hedonic views of pleasure.

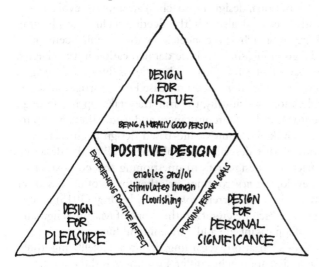

Figure 2.1 Positive design framework.

The framework can be read in detail in Desmet and Pohlmeyer (2013) and Pohlmeyer and Desmet (2017), so it is useful here to illustrate its application with some examples. One of the first deliberate and explicate 'positive design' projects, is *Tiny Tasks* by Ruitenberg and Desmet (2012), a tool to sensitise and help people on their path to flourishing by inciting them to perform and commit to meaningful activities that are pleasurable as well as virtuous, to different extents, but nevertheless always connected with human values. In the *Tiny Task* project, participants receive small key chains that communicate a specific task to the participant in a thoughtful way. Examples of these tasks are 'take a different route home' or 'guerrilla planting'. These small and seemingly trivial tasks help people to engage in meaningful activities that help them to develop skills, contribute to the greater good and that feel rewarding in and of themselves. Via this approach, Ruitenberg and Desmet (2012) emphasise a strategy to think in terms of actions a person can undertake linked to specific human values, that a person is or is not directly aware of. In the case of *Tiny Tasks*, a person's daily routine is broken, and new, surprising and wellbeing-enhancing routines are proposed, thereby demonstrating that good design merely needs to trigger people, and thereby support and motivate them to positively change their behaviour.

Other authors have also produced models and/or frameworks in order to study if and how design (home-based in various design disciplines) can contribute to emotion, experience, happiness and wellbeing (e.g., Hassenzahl, 2010; Ozkaramanli & Desmet, 2012; Pohlmeyer, 2012; Hassenzahl et al., 2013; Escobar-Tello, 2016; Petermans & Pohlmeyer, 2014; Petermans & Nuyts, 2016; Escobar-Tello, 2016; Stevens, 2018).

Broadening the scope for implementing positive design

Searching for directions to implement positive psychology into positive design, or for approaches to design for wellbeing, philosopher of technology Philip Brey, in 2015, saw four directions that design for wellbeing encompasses: 'emotional design approaches', 'capability approaches', 'life-based design' and 'positive psychology approaches'.

Brey's first two approaches – 'emotional design approaches' and 'capability approaches' – seem to be best described as operationalisations of, respectively, hedonic and eudaimonic wellbeing. The former (emotional design approaches) attempts to evoke emotional experiences, and consequently merely deals with 'the fleeting feelings of pleasure' (Brey, 2015, p. 9). The latter (capability approaches) is concerned with the enhancement of basic capabilities, necessary to lead a good life, such as those defined earlier in the chapter by Nussbaum (2000). A third approach that Brey (2015) identifies is 'life-based design'. This approach aims to improve people's wellbeing by designs based on information about people's 'whole life' – their lifestyle, more specifically, the role they take up in life (e.g., 'being a soccer fan', 'being an inventor'), and the circumstances and values they live up to. So, whereas the previous approaches lacked a context, life-based design is characterised by a clearly defined and broad context that describes the 'playing field' of the designer. However, at the same time, it restricts the designer from questioning this context, challenging the existing routines and developing *new* routines, or other forms of life based on the knowledge of a person's wellbeing in their current role. Fourthly, Brey (2015) recognised 'positive psychology approaches', which he credits to the work of Martin Seligman's (2002) wellbeing model consisting of a pleasant life and a meaningful life.

Throughout the discussion of Brey's variations regarding design for wellbeing, three aspects were found on which these design approaches differ. First, there is the presence or absence of a clear context to design in. Second, there is a narrow to a broader focus, illustrated by aiming to raise product experience (narrow) up to changing a complete lifestyle (broad). And, third, there is the difference regarding improving the existing practice, or adding new and positive practices. Differences should be used in a way that they exhibit compatibility with the specifics of the particular 'market' in which design operates. For instance, the design field of architecture is a very contextualised one, since architecture is about designing a spatial context for actions to happen in. These actions can range from daily routines that are limited in time, such as 'cooking', 'sleeping', 'working', up to entire lifestyles that are carried out in, for instance, a monastery building or a prison building. Thus, the specifics of the design field one wants to use to positively influence a person's wellbeing, are crucial elements in the choice for a particular approach.

Indeed, more work is required on methodological developments to translate positive design theories into positive design results. Initial inspiring works are present (e.g., see Ruitenberg & Desmet, 2012; Jacobse et al., 2016; Stevens, 2018) but the challenge is to open up the scope and find more applications in other design fields as well. Considering the specifics of the concerned design disciplines seems key in this respect.

Conclusion

It is clear that positive design is a design field still in development (see, for example, Ozkaramanli et al., 2016; Yoon et al., 2016; Stevens, 2018). The idea that it is worthwhile to research how design can positively influence wellbeing is commonly shared, as is the hypothesis that 'positively designed' *products* could enhance our wellbeing. To date, for positive design, industrial and interaction design is the main design field in which positive design or other wellbeing-related approaches have been applied and researched so far, but it is clear that applications in other design fields are highly encouraged. For instance, next to 'positively designed' *products,* it can also be assumed that the designed *built environment* can have an influence on our wellbeing (see also Petermans & Pohlmeyer, 2014). Indeed, as Paul Hekkert mentioned in his Foreword to the *Positive Design Reference Guide* (Jimenez et al., 2015), positive design is about the overarching question of the relationship people have with the designed world. Nonetheless, it is necessary to explore characteristic 'features' in possible application fields of positive design. In Part II of this book, five chapters present and demonstrate a diversity of approaches regarding the translation of positive design in various design disciplines, illustrating how reflecting about positive design brings with it various considerations that need to be taken into account, such as ethical issues, issues regarding 'ownership' of design, life expectancy and permanence, and the flexibility and adaptability of a design.

The journey from positive psychology research towards design applications has been progressive. From a theoretical point of view, a number of directions for design to become 'positive' are present, and some *frameworks and models* have been developed regarding positive design. But there are still very few concrete applicable *tools*[4] for designers to design for wellbeing (see also Fokkinga et al., 2014; Yoon et al., 2016). Among other aspects, this specific gap in knowledge has particularly inspired us in composing this book. Therefore, Part III of this book elaborates about tools, methods and approaches that can be used by designers and researchers to design for wellbeing. Further research in this respect will be highly valuable to further develop, validate and establish these. It is our hope that this book stimulates designers and researchers all over the world to take up this challenge.

Notes

1   The PhD thesis of the first author has been key in composing this chapter.
2   Nevertheless, the choice of words hints at the nature of these two views on wellbeing; since 'good' is an adjective and 'well' is an adverb. 'Good' modifies a noun, in this particular case modifying 'the feeling', which is what Jackson (2013) meant by using the abbreviated pronunciation of 'feeling good' for 'feeling *the good feeling*'. 'Well' modifies a verb, here 'functioning'. Thus, 'good' and 'well' are hinting at the passive and active nature, respectively, of hedonic and eudaimonic wellbeing, respectively, with regard to the person. In the eudaimonic view, a more active attitude is required.
3   In the context of the evolution of hedonism, the cognitive component of 'life satisfaction' is in fact based on subjective evaluations of people with regard to their personal situation, raising questions regarding the influence of both people's frame of reference and the expectations they hold for themselves in that matter. In that respect, Brickmann and Campbell (1971) speak in terms of the hedonic treadmill, explaining that people can get used to a specific situation in a way that much of the subjectively evaluated impact of an objective gain, such as a lottery win are negated. In this case, it has been shown that these persons are not necessarily happier than they had been before. Thus, 'elements' in life that provide pleasure by evoking positive emotions and a happy mood can eventually lose their *happy power* since people get used to them and therefore there will no longer have the same reactions to them. Evidently, adaptation and habituation play an important role in this respect, since people will adapt to a situation and will need to seek pleasure elsewhere. Also, in negative affect adaptation can occur; people can come to terms with their at first negatively appraised situation in a sense that it will no longer provide much negative affect due to habituation, as in the example of the paraplegic returning to his previous level of happiness (Brickmann et al., 1978), or to his hedonic neutrality (Diener et al., 2006). On a final note, the argument and mentioning of the hedonic treadmill does not directly inform about what hedonic wellbeing is, however it is relevant to mention in this context, since it had Diener adjust his definition of wellbeing to the following: 'an umbrella term for the different valuations people make regarding their lives, the events happening to them, their bodies and minds, and the circumstances in which they live' (Diener, 2006, pp. 399–400).
4   A tool here refers to a concrete application, mostly based on a theoretical framework or model, that is directed at the designer and can be used while designing.

References

Aristotle (4 BCE/1985). *The Nicomachean Ethics* (Irwin, Terence, Trans.). Indianapolis, IN: Hackett Pub. Co. (Original work written in 350 B.C.).

Bentham, J. (1996 [1789]). *An Introduction to the Principles of Morals and Legislation.* J. Burns and H.L.A. Hart (Eds.), Oxford: Clarendon Press.

Bradburn, N. (1969). *The Structure of Psychological Well-being.* Chicago, IL: Aldine.

Brey, P. (2012). Well-being in philosophy, psychology and economics. In P. Brey, A. Briggle, & E. Spence (Eds.), *The Good Life in a Technological Age* (pp. 15–34). New York, NY: Routledge.

Brey, P. (2015). Design for the value of human well-being. In J. van den Hoven, P. Vermaas, & I. van de Poel (Eds.), *Handbook of Ethics, Values, and Technological Design. Sources, Theory, Values and Application Domains* (pp. 365–382). Dordrecht: Springer.

Brickman, P., & Campbell, D.T. (1971). Hedonic relativism and planning the food society. In M.H. Appley (Ed.), *Adaptation-Level Theory* (pp. 287–305). New York: Academic Press.

Brickmann, P., & Coates, D., & Janoff-Bulman, R. (1978). Lottery winners and accident victims: Is happiness relative? *Journal of Personality and Social Psychology, 36,* 917–927.

Butler, J., & Kern, M.L. (2016). The PERMA-profiler: A brief multidimensional measure of flourishing. *International Journal of Wellbeing, 6*(3), 1–48.

Csikszentmihalyi, M. (1990). *Flow: The Psychology of Optimal Experience.* New York, NY: Harper & Row.

Csikszentmihalyi, M. (2000). *Beyond Boredom and Anxiety: Experiencing Flow in Work and Play.* San Francisco, CA: Jossey-Bass.

Cummins, R.A. (1996). The domains of life satisfaction: An attempt to order chaos. *Social Indicators Research, 38,* 303–332.

Cummins, R.A. (2010). Subjective well-being, homeostatically protected mood and depression: A synthesis. *Journal of Happiness Studies, 11*, 1–17.

Desmet, P.M.A., & Pohlmeyer, A.E. (2013). Positive design: An introduction to design for subjective well-being. *International Journal of Design, 7*(3), 5–19.

Diener, E. (1984). Subjective well-being. *Psychological Bulletin, 95*, 542–575.

Diener, E., Lucas, R.E., & Scollon, C.N. (2006). Beyond the hedonic treadmill: Revising the adaptation theory of well-being. *American Psychologist, 61*(4), 305–314.

Diener, E., & Suh, E. (1997). Measuring quality of life: Economic, social, and subjective indicators. *Social Indicators Research, 40*, 189–216.

Diener, E., Wirtz, D., Tov, W., Kim-Prieto, C., Choi, D., Oishi, S., & Biswas-Diener, R. (2010). New well-being measures: Short scales to assess flourishing and positive and negative feelings. *Social Indicators Research, 97*(2), 143–156.

Dodge, R., Daly, A., Huyton, J., & Sanders, L. (2012). The challenge of defining wellbeing. *International Journal of Wellbeing, 2*(3), 222–235.

Eid, M. & Diener, E. (2004). Global judgments of subjective wellbeing: Situational variability and long-term stability. *Social Indicators Research, 65*(3), 245–277.

Ereaut, G., & Whiting, R. (2008). *What Do We Mean by 'Wellbeing'? And Why Might It Matter?* Linguistic Landscapes, Research Report. UK: Department for Children, Schools and Families.

Escobar-Tello, C. (2016). A design framework to build sustainable societies: Using happiness as leverage. *The Design Journal, 19*(1), 93–115.

Feldman, F. (2004). *Pleasure and the Good Life: Concerning the Nature, Varieties, and Plausibility of Hedonism.* Oxford: Oxford UP.

Fokkinga, S.F., & Desmet, P.M.A. (2014). Run for your life! Using emotion theory in designing for concrete product interactions. Paper Presented *at the* 9th *International Conference on Design and Emotion*, 8–10 October 2014, Bogota, Colombia.

Folse, Henry (2005). *How Epicurean Metaphysics Leads to Epicurean Ethics.* New Orleans, LA: Department of Philosophy, Loyola University.

Forgeard, M.J.C., Jayawickreme, E., Kern, M., & Seligman, M.E.P. (2011). Doing the right thing: Measuring wellbeing for public policy. *International Journal of Wellbeing, 1*(1), 79–106.

Fredrickson, B.L., & Losada, M.F. (2005). Positive affect and the complex dynamics of human flourishing. *American Psychologist, 60*, 678–686.

Gable, S.L., & Haidt, J. (2005). What (and why) is positive psychology? *Review of General Psychology, 9*, 103–110.

Gardner, H. (1983). *Frames of Mind: The Theory of Multiple Intelligences.* London, UK: Heinemann.

GNH Centre Bhutan (1970). *The Story of GNH.* Accessed from: http://www.gnhcentrebhutan.org/what-is-gnh/the-story-of-gnh/

Hassenzahl, M. (2010). *Experience Design: Technology for All the Right Reasons.* San Rafael, CA: Morgan & Claypool.

Hassenzahl, M., Eckoldt, K., Diefenbach, S., Laschke, M., Lenz, E., & Kim, J. (2013). Designing moments of meaning and pleasure. Experience design and happiness. *International Journal of Design, 7*(3), 21–31.

Hone, L.C., Jarden, A., Schofield, G.M., & Duncan, S. (2014). Measuring flourishing: The impact of operational definitions on the prevalence of high levels of wellbeing. *International Journal of Wellbeing, 4*(1), 62–90.

Huppert, F.A. (2009). Psychological well-being: Evidence regarding its causes and consequences. *Applied Psychology: Health and Well-being, 1*(2), 137–164.

Huppert, F., & So, T. (2013). Flourishing across Europe: Application of a new conceptual framework for defining well-being. *Social Indicator Research, 110*, 837–861.

Huta, V., & Waterman, A.S. (2013). Eudaimonia and its distinction from Hedonia: Developing a classification and terminology for understanding conceptual and operational definitions. *Journal of Happiness Studies, 15*, 1425–1456.

Jackson, N.J. (2013). Exploring subjective wellbeing and relationships to lifewide education, learning and personal development. In N.J. Jackson, & G.B. Cooper (Eds.), *Lifewide Learning, Education & Personal Development e-Book*. Accessible from: http://www.learninglives.co.uk/e-book.htm

Jacobse, C., Pohlmeyer, A., & Boess, S. (2016). Still in its infancy: Design for co-wellbeing among different user groups. In P. Desmet, S. Fokkinga, G. Ludden, N. Cila, & H. Van Zuthem (Eds.), *Proceedings of the Tenth International Conference on Design and Emotion: Celebration and Contemplation* (pp. 211–221). 27–30 September 2016. Amsterdam, The Netherlands: The Design and Emotion Society.

Jimenez, S., Pohlmeyer, A., & Desmet, P. (2015). *Positive Design Reference Guide*. Delft, The Netherlands: Delft University of Technology.

Kahneman, D., Diener, E., & Schwarz, N. (Eds.) (1999). *Well-being: Foundations of Hedonic Psychology* (pp. 3–25). New York, NY: Russell Sage Foundation Press.

Keyes, C. (2002). The mental health continuum: From languishing to flourishing in life. *Journal of Health and Behavior Research, 43,* 207–222.

Keyes, C. (2005). Mental illness and/or mental health? Investigating axioms of the complete state model of health. *Journal of Consulting and Clinical Psychology, 73*(3), 539–548.

Kigen Bjering, A. (2014). *Designing for Happiness. How Design Can Contribute to People's Subjective Well-being*. Accessible from: https://www.ntnu.no/documents/10401/1264435841/Artikkel+Anne+Berit+Kigen+Bjering.pdf/dbefba38-2687-4778-8907-b17aafc22053

Konstan, D. (2013). *Epicurus, The Stanford Encyclopedia of Philosophy* (Fall 2013 Edition). Accessible from: https://plato.stanford.edu/entries/epicurus/

Layard, Richard. (2005). *Happiness: Lessons from a New Science*. London: Penguin.

Lyubomirsky, S. (2007). *The How of Happiness: A New Approach to Getting the Life You Want*. New York: Penguin Books.

Maslow, A. (1954). *Motivation and Personality*. New York, NY: Harper.

Max-Neef, M. (1991). *Human-Scale Development*. New York and London: Apex Press.

Mill, J.S. (1863/1998). *Utilitarianism*. London: Parker, Son & Bourn.

Myers, D.G., & Diener, E. (1995). Who is happy? *Psychological Science, 6,* 10–19.

Nussbaum, M. (2000) *Women and Human Development: The Capabilities Approach*. Cambridge: Cambridge University Press.

OECD (2013). *OECD Guidelines on Measuring Subjective Well-being*. OECD Publishing. Accessible from: https://www.oecd-ilibrary.org/economics/oecd-guidelines-on-measuring-subjective-well-being_9789264191655-en

O'Keefe, T. (n.d.). Aristippus (c. 435–356 B.C.E.). *Internet Encyclopedia of Philosophy*. A Pear reviewed academic resource. Accessible from: http://www.iep.utm.edu/aristip/#H2

Ozkaramanli, D., & Desmet, P. (2012). I knew I shouldn't, yet I did it again! Emotion-driven design as a means to motivate subjective well-being. *International Journal of Design, 6*(1), 27–39.

Ozkaramanli, D., Desmet, P.M.A., & Özcan, E. (2016). Beyond resolving dilemmas: Three design directions for addressing intrapersonal concern conflicts. *Design Issues, 32*(3), 78–91.

Parfit, D. (1984). *Reasons and Persons*. Oxford: Oxford UP.

Petermans, A., & Nuyts, E. (2016). Happiness in place and space: Exploring the contribution of architecture and interior architecture to happiness. *Proceedings of the 10th Design & Emotion Conference*, Amsterdam, The Netherlands.

Peterson, C., Park, N., & Seligman, M. (2005). Orientations to happiness and life satisfaction: The full life versus the empty life. *Journal of Happiness Studies, 6*(1), 25–41.

Petermans, A., & Pohlmeyer, A. (2014). Design for subjective wellbeing in interior architecture. *Proceedings of the 6th Symposium of Architectural Research 2014: Designing and Planning the Built Environment for Human Wellbeing*, pp. 206–218.

Peterson, C., & Seligman, M.E. (2004). *Character Strengths and Virtues: A Handbook and Classification* (Vol. 1). Oxford: Oxford University Press.

Plato (1854). *Works of Plato: A New and Literal Version, Chiefly From the Text of Stallbaum* (Vol. 6). London: Emerson's Library.

Pohlmeyer, A. (2012). Design for happiness. *Interfaces, 92,* 8–11.

Pohlmeyer, A. (2014). *A Design Approach to Human Flourishing.* Accessible from: http://adaptivepath.org/ideas/a-design-approach-to-human-flourishing/

Pohlmeyer, A., & Desmet, P. (2017). From good to the greater good. In J. Chapman (Ed.), *The Routledge Handbook of Sustainable Product Design* (pp. 469–486). London: Routledge.

Pollard, E., & Lee, P. (2003). Child well-being: A systematic review of the literature. *Social Indicators Research, 61*(1), 9–78.

Ranis, G., Stewart, F., & Samman, E. (2006). Human development: Beyond the human development index. *Journal of Human Development, 7*(3), 323–358.

Rogers, C.R. (1961). *On Becoming A Person.* New York, NY: Houghton Mifflin Harcourt.

Ruitenberg, H., & Desmet, P. (2012). Design thinking in positive psychology: The development of a product-service combination that stimulates happiness-enhancing activities. In J. Brassett, P. Hekkert, G. Ludden, M. Malpass, & J. McDonnell (Eds.), *Out of Control; Proceedings of the 8th International Conference on Design and Emotion* (pp. 1–10). London, UK: Central Saint Martins College of Art & Design.

Rusk, R., & Waters, L. (2015). A psycho-social system approach to wellbeing: Empirically deriving the five domains of positive functioning. *The Journal of Positive Psychology, 10*(2), 141–152.

Ryan, R.M., & Deci, E.L. (1985). *Intrinsic Motivation and Self-determination in Human Behaviour.* New York, NY: Plenum Press.

Ryan, R.M., & Deci, E.L. (2001). On happiness and human potentials. A review of research on hedonic and eudaimonic well-being. *Annual Revue of Psychology, 52,* 141–166.

Ryan, R.M., & Deci, E.L. (2002). Overview of self-determination theory: An organismic dialectical perspective. In R.M. Ryan, & E.L. Deci (Eds.), *Handbook of Self-determination Research* (pp. 3–33). Rochester, NY: The University of Rochester Press.

Ryff, C.D. (1989). Happiness is everything, or is it? Explorations on the meaning of psychological well-being. *Journal of Personality and Social Psychology, 57,* 1069–1081.

Ryff, C.D., & Keyes, C.L.M. (1995). The structure of psychological well-being revisited. *Journal of Personality and Social Psychology, 69*(4), 719–727.

Ryff, C.D., & Singer, B.H. (1998). The contours of positive human health. *Psychological Inquiry, 9*(1), 1–28. Retrieved from http://www.tandfonline.com/doi/abs/10.1207/s15327965pli0901_1

Ryff, C.D., & Singer, B.H. (2008). Know thyself and become what you are: A eudaimonic approach to psychological well-being. *Journal of Happiness Studies, 9*(1), 13–39.

Samman, E. (2007). *Psychological and Subjective Wellbeing: A Proposal for Internationally Comparable Indicators.* Oxford: Oxford Development Studies.

Schotanus-Dijkstra, M., Pieterse, M.E., Drossaerts, C.H.C., Westerhof, G.J., de Graaf, R., ten Have, M., Walburg, J.A., & Bohlmeijer, E.T. (2016). What factor are associated with flourishing? Results from a large representative national sample. *Journal of Happiness Studies, 17,* 1351–1370.

Seligman, M.E.P. (2002). *Authentic Happiness: Using the New Positive Psychology to Realize your Potential for Lasting Fulfillment.* New York, NY: Free Press.

Seligman, M.E.P. (2003). *Authentic Happiness: Using the New Positive Psychology to Realize your Potential for Lasting Fulfillment.* New York: Free Press.

Seligman, M.E.P. (2004). Can happiness be taught? *Daedalus, 133*(2), 80–87.

Seligman, M.E.P. (2011). *Flourish: A Visionary New Understanding of Happiness and Wellbeing.* New York, NY: Free Press.

Seligman, M., & Csikszentmihalyi, M. (2000). Positive psychology: An introduction. *American Psychologist, 55*(1), 5–14.

Sen, A. (1992). *Inequality Re-examined.* New York, NY and Cambridge, MA: Russell Sage Foundation, Harvard University Press.

Stevens, R. (2018). *A Launchpad for Design for Human Flourishing in Architecture. Theoretical Foundations, Practical Guidance and a Design Tool.* PhD thesis, Hasselt University, Hasselt, Belgium.

Tiberius, V. (2006). Well-being: Psychological research for philosophers. *Philosophy Compass, 1,* 493–505.

United Nations, General Assembly (2011). *Happiness: Towards a Holistic Approach to Development.* Retrieved from http://www.un.org/en/ga/search/view:doc.asp?symbol=A/RES/65/309

Veenhoven, R. (2011). Greater happiness for a greater number: Is that possible? If so, how? In K.N. Sheldon, T.B. Kashdan, & M.F. Steger (Eds.), *Designing Positive Psychology* (pp. 392–409). Oxford, UK: Oxford University Press.

Vivenza, G. (2007). Happiness, wealth and utility in ancient thought. In L. Bruni, & L. Porta (Eds.), *Handbook on the Economics of Happiness* (pp. 3–23). Northampton, MA: Edward Elgar.

Waterman, A.S. (1993). Two conceptions of happiness: Contrasts of personal expressiveness (Eudaimonia) and hedonic enjoyment. *Journal of Personality and Social Psychology, 64*, 678–691.

Yoon, J., Desmet, P., & Pohlmeyer, A. (2016). Developing usage guidelines for a card-based design tool: A case of the positive emotional granularity cards. *Archives of Design Research, 29*(4), 5–19.

Part II

Domains in design for wellbeing

3 Designing for people living with dementia

Cathy Treadaway

Introduction

This chapter explores how design can be used to support the wellbeing of people living with dementia. According to the World Health Organisation (WHO),[1] the numbers of people with a diagnosis of dementia are increasing globally and there are few signs of an imminent cure for the disease. A compassionate society, in which all human life is valued and celebrated, should be concerned with the wellbeing of people living with dementia; they should be enabled to continue to experience pleasure, joy and laughter through the illness until the end of life[2] (Hughes, 2014; Brooker, 2007). Designers have an important role to play in ensuring this is possible. This chapter discusses ways in which dementia impacts on wellbeing and its implication for design. It describes international design research that is informing the development of new products and services for dementia care and some of the particular challenges that designers face when undertaking applied design research to support wellbeing. The final section of the chapter describes research in which Compassionate Design has been used to guide the development of playful objects to support the wellbeing of people living with advanced dementia.

Wellbeing in the context of dementia

Contemporary definitions of wellbeing including physical, psychological, spiritual and emotional aspects of lived experience and *living well* (flourishing), *subjective wellbeing* (happiness) and *physical health* are considered interconnected.[3] In the UK, finding ways to improve wellbeing and increase happiness in society has been a government imperative. In 2008, the New Economics Foundation was commissioned to develop a set of evidence-based actions to improve personal wellbeing (Aked et al., 2008). The result was an influential government report that recommended the following five activities:

1. connect
2. be active
3. take notice
4. keep learning
5. give

For people living with dementia,[4] particularly in the more advanced stages, these wellbeing guidelines are increasingly difficult to incorporate into daily life. As the disease progresses, people become increasingly disconnected from others and withdraw from the world around them, largely due to the impact of dementia on memory, perception and

communication. Cognitive aspects of learning become a challenge and mobility and physical activity are increasingly curtailed. People living with the disease often become socially
withdrawn and feel they have little to give. Encouraging them to keep taking notice of
the world around them, to connect with others and to feel valued and loved are essential
ingredients in quality dementia care that supports wellbeing.

The design challenge

There is currently no cure for dementia and, despite recent scientific advances in understanding the disease, an imminent medical solution seems unlikely (Livingston et al., 2017).
With the rapid increase in numbers of people being diagnosed globally, finding ways to
help people to have a good quality of life for as long as possible and to live well with the
disease is now an imperative (Ógáin and Mountain, 2015). However, the complexity and
individualised impact of the disease presents a huge challenge to designers (Hendricks et
al., 2017). Understanding how someone living with the disease is personally affected, the
context in which they live and the communities and systems that support them is essential.
To support wellbeing, designs need to be appropriate, meaningful and comforting; they
need to help maintain a person's sense of *self* even when they may no longer remember
for themselves who they are. Loneliness and social isolation have a huge negative impact
on wellbeing and so keeping people connected to their carers and the world around them
is also vitally important (Rahman, 2017).

User-centred, inclusive, participatory and co-design methods fit very well with current *person-centred* approaches to care (Brooker, 2007; Kitwood, 1997). The humanistic
approach of person-centred care advocates seeing the person living with dementia in
context, adapting communication with them to the sense of reality they perceive – 'to see
the person and not the disease'. Person-centred care acknowledges an individual's need to
sustain their psychological and emotional wellbeing throughout the disease. Recent theories of relational care build on this, suggesting that the context of care, and especially the
relationships with caregivers, impact on a person's wellbeing and should also be considered
(Rahman, 2017; Nolan et al., 2004).

Design research for dementia

Traditional desk-based top-down design processes are ill-equipped to address the challenge
of designing for a disease that affects people in such profoundly different and personal
ways. Approaches that enable designers to become immersed in the care environment,
develop empathic relationships and have direct contact with people living with dementia have been shown to provide deep insights and inspiring outcomes (Hendricks et al.,
2017; Brankaert et al., 2015). Qualitative research methodologies that acquire data through
observations and communication about real-life activities, such as grounded practical theory, ethnography and the use of case studies, have been widely used by design researchers in the field (Craig and Tracy, 2014; Krippendorff, 2006; Kenning, 2017). These social,
reflexive and responsive research methods provide rich information about the context and
relationships between all those involved in a study.

Participatory and co-design methods

Participatory and co-design approaches have been found particularly valuable in yield-
ing perceptive insights, especially when involving a range of participants from a variety

of disciplines or backgrounds (Jakob et al., 2017; Treadaway et al., 2016c; Kenning, 2017; Lindsay, 2012). Co-design methods that involve a mix of participants in creative activities have been used successfully in a number of studies (Hendricks et al., 2017; Kenning, 2017; Treadaway et al., 2016a; Rijn et al., 2010; Windle et al., 2014). The inclusion of key experts in relation to dementia and dementia care ensures that the design process is socially aware, inclusive and human-centred. People living with dementia at an early stage and carers with personal experience of the disease, can share rich knowledge about how dementia impacts on daily life. Traditional participatory methods can also have their limitations, however, and may not always be appropriate depending on the design problem to be addressed. Participatory design activities that require cognition, abstracted thinking and decision-making can be particularly challenging for people living with dementia (Hendriks et al., 2014). Many people living with the disease have altered perceptions and can make *over-* or *under*estimations of their capabilities or 'confabulate' their experiences. In addition, participation can be stressful for someone living with dementia when it confronts his or her insecurities and highlights abilities once possessed but no longer accessible because of impaired memory or physical disability. This can lead to a participant's frustration, inertia or withdrawal.

Involving people

Despite these concerns, the inclusion of people living with dementia in participatory and co-design activities can provide mutual benefit to all involved (Kenning, 2017).[5] *Experts by experience* (people living with the disease) can provide researchers with unique insights into the design problem. Rodgers used a *disruptive design* approach with activities that were fun, safe and failure free in research to co-design a signature tartan fabric with people living with dementia for Alzheimer's Scotland (Rodgers, 2015). The MinD project is involving people living with dementia to design a mindfulness framework 'to enable individuals to manage their condition, to develop perceptions of self-empowerment, and to gain confidence with engaging socially'.[6] This large international multidisciplinary research project is including the voice of people living with dementia in the early to mid-stages, through self-reflection and creative activities. MinD research methods include the use of visual cards to prompt conversations and visual diaries or activity books to glean deeper insights into the personal life context of people living with dementia.[7]

Design probes, including visual cards, have been developed in a number of design for dementia projects to prompt conversations and open up spaces for discussion about personal experiences of living with the disease. Design researchers from Imagination at Lancaster University have created a set of Ageing Playfully[8] cards with practical recommendations to help in creative workshop facilitation with people living with dementia. A similar approach has been taken by researchers from the FIT project in the Netherlands, who have developed a *decision aid* to match the needs of people living with dementia and their carers with products and services to assist in their wellbeing (Cila et al., 2017). These tools start with exploring the users' needs and goals in contrast to more common design strategies that are product- or problem-oriented. This bottom-up research empowers the user and helps them to consider how best to improve their own wellbeing and quality of life at home.

Assistive technology

A wide range of assistive technologies that exploit digital technologies is being developed to support people living with dementia in their everyday challenges. These include, for example, navigation tools, memory aids for administrating medication and apps for prompting conversations when visiting relatives with dementia (Maiden et al., 2013; Bennett et al., 2017). Bennett et al. (2017) contend that the positive attributes of assistive technologies include the potential to delay entry into institutional care, reduce the burden on caregivers and improve the quality of life for people living with dementia. However, they also caution designers to consider ethical and human rights issues that may be associated with devices that track, store or share personal data of some of the most vulnerable people in society. There is also concern that assistive technologies may be designed to reduce or replace human contact to the detriment of people living with dementia (Livingston et al., 2017). Ethical concerns involved in designing for people living with dementia are complex and cannot be ignored.

Ethical issues in designing for dementia

Gaining informed consent from research participants is essential; however, this also requires the consenting individual to have decisional capacity. The complexity of this issue in relation to a disease that is progressive, impacts on memory and fragments a person's sense of self cannot be underestimated (Hughes, 2014). Designers with experience of working in the field advocate approaches that are *situated* and co-designed with all those involved. This requires an ongoing process of informed consent that is clearly communicated at each point of contact (Hendricks et al., 2017). The independence and autonomy of the person living with dementia needs to be considered paramount and their right to withdraw at any stage is an imperative. Withdrawal may be expressed in non-verbal behaviour and require the design researcher to be empathic, observant and attentive to the person's body language. Nevertheless, the ongoing process of gaining ethical consent also helps to reaffirm an individual's personhood, validating their importance as a member of society and dignity as a human being.

One of the most contentious ethical aspects of dementia care concerns how to deal with distress resulting from altered perception and memory loss; for instance, if a person can no longer remember that their partner has died and keeps asking for them; or that they no longer live in their own home and constantly ask to return there. Facing this reality can be very upsetting for a person living with dementia and also for a carer who needs to align the present circumstance with the alternative perceived reality of that person living with dementia. Some argue that affirming this reality may destroy trust, can be considered to be deceitful, and so undermine their personhood (Kitwood, 1997; Mitchell, 2016). However, others contend that recognition that each person's experience of reality has its own psychological validity can overcome the ethical dilemma of how to navigate such situations (Brooker, 2007; Killick, 2013; Hughes, 2014).

Carers and family members play a crucial role in informing design specifications. Including them early in the design process as active participants ensures that ethical considerations remain central to the design process.

Dementia and memory

Although memory loss is considered a major symptom of dementia, each person is affected differently and not all types of memory are compromised (Sabat, 2006). *Explicit* or declarative memories of lived experience are most frequently affected, whereas memories that are *implicit,* such as those that are emotional or procedural, can be retained into the advanced stages of the disease. For this reason, a person living with dementia may have strong preferences about how they feel about something or someone, but they may not remember why. Changes in memory impact profoundly on how a person will be able to experience the present, resulting in confusion and stress. Early memories of facts or life experiences may be retained clearly, yet recent events or familiar situations can be forgotten. As the disease progresses it is the implicit memories that are more likely to remain. These may include embodied skills accrued over a lifetime through practical experience that have become automatic. Activities such as knitting, folding clothes or even playing a musical instrument may continue to bring pleasure to a person living with advanced dementia, although following a knitting pattern or reading music might no longer be possible. In the same way, emotional memories can be experienced outside of conscious awareness, which is why feelings are often difficult to verbalise (LeDoux, 1998). Understanding how a person living with dementia experiences memories can be of great use to the designer interested in supporting wellbeing. Appreciating personal preferences, interests and capabilities makes it much easier to develop concepts that may stimulate positive emotion by rekindling feelings of pleasure, security, comfort and attachment.

Shared experiences that are 'in the moment', playful and imaginative bring immense relief and joy to people who can no longer experience the world as they did (Killick, 2013; Treadaway et al., 2016c). Humour, fun, playfulness and music are key ingredients that have been found to build spaces where shared meaning can be experienced, and mutuality occurs. These 'magic spaces' provide common ground, are affirming, comforting and pleasurable. Objects can help stimulate an imaginative playful experience that enables transition into a shared reality that maintains and builds caring relationships (Kenning and Treadaway, 2017).

Objects can also provide *meaningful activity*, which is known to be particularly beneficial for the wellbeing of people living with dementia (Livingston et al., 2017; Cohen-Mansfield et al., 2012; Chenoweth et al., 2014). As the disease progresses there are diminishing opportunities to engage in hobbies or daily activities that have been important or have given structure to a person's life. People living with dementia in residential care can become bored, frustrated and agitated, or increasingly passive and reluctant to engage socially (Brooker, 2008). Research has found that the active inclusion of people living with dementia in arts and creative activities can be particularly beneficial to wellbeing (Windle et al., 2014). Opportunities for creativity, such as by using the hands and manipulating physical materials, have been shown in a number of studies to provide a sense of competency and self-esteem thereby affirming personhood (Kenning, 2017; Algar-Skaife et al., 2017). Visits to art galleries and participating in musical activities have also been shown to enhance wellbeing (Kenning, 2016; Shibazaki & Nigel, 2017; Zeisel, 2011).

Design for advanced dementia

One-to-one *individualised* design research approaches may be more insightful when working with people who live with impaired cognition, communication, memory or perceptual challenges in the later stages of the disease (Hendricks et al., 2017). Including people with profound dementia in research demands great sensitivity, empathy, creativity and flexibility in attitude and approach, as well as a deep appreciation of the complex ethical issues involved. Consequently, until quite recently, there has been little published design research addressing how to design specifically to support the wellbeing of people living with advanced dementia (Rijn et al., 2010). Recent work has explored the design of sensory textiles (Treadaway & Kenning, 2016; Branco et al., 2017), multisensory enriched environments (Jakob et al., 2017), tangible technologies (Bennett et al., 2016) and playful objects (Treadaway et al., 2016b).

The final section of this chapter will describe in more detail design research that has been designing playful objects to support the wellbeing of people living with advanced dementia.

The LAUGH Project

LAUGH, a three-year international design research project,[9] has investigated ways of supporting the wellbeing of people living with advanced dementia through the development of playful hand-held objects. The acronym LAUGH (Ludic Artefacts Using Gesture and Haptics) reflects the research aim to understand hand-use and touch, in order to develop playful objects for people with profound dementia. People living with the disease were included in the study along with carers, health professionals, technologists and designers. The project partner, Pobl Gwalia Care, provided access to residents living with advanced dementia in three of its residential care facilities in South West Wales and contributed staff time and expertise throughout the project. (See Figure 3.1.)

A qualitative interpretivist methodology was used in the LAUGH research.[10] This included action research and grounded theory approaches, in which both verbal and non-verbal social interaction and engagement in activities were observed in detail (Craig & Tracy, 2014). Participatory workshops, visits and interviews in the care homes, a series of Live Lab evaluations and team reflections were used to gather data. The tools and methods of data collection included audio and video recording, collaborative creative worksheets capturing ideas and commentary, participant feedback sheets, still photography and research journals. The initial phase of the research involved a period of knowledge gathering. This was followed by a period of reflection leading to an iterative cycle of making and

Figure 3.1 LAUGH participatory workshop.

testing, followed by Live Lab evaluations (Brankaert et al., 2015), with people living with advanced dementia in residential care.

The first year of the LAUGH research sought to understand what constitutes wellbeing in the context of dementia, informed by those who have knowledge of the disease and intimate experience of care provision. This initial stage included a case study comprising a series of six semi-structured interviews with carers. Professional and informal carers were selected following advice from an advisory group comprising health professionals, representatives from dementia charities, and carers. This was followed by six participatory workshops with 20 participants: a core team of 10 participants who attended at least three workshops and 70 others who contributed to one or more events, plus six researchers from the LAUGH team. The workshops used creative and playful approaches to help participants reflect on playfulness, hand-use, positive emotion and memory in the context of wellbeing for people living with advanced dementia. The workshops were documented using video, photography and participants' responses collated from feedback sheets, interviews and sketches.

Compassionate Design

Compassionate Design[11] underpins the LAUGH design process (Treadaway et al., 2018a; Treadaway & Fennell, 2017). This approach builds on positive design methodology (Desmet & Pohlmeyer, 2013) and is specifically concerned with designing for wellbeing in advanced dementia. It focuses on three vital components that are key when designing for people who are cognitively impaired: design that stimulates the senses, that is highly personalised and that helps to foster connections between people. Compassionate Design places loving kindness at the heart of the design process, ensuring that design validates and maintains the dignity of the individual and provides them with sensory stimulation that connects them to others and the physical world around them (even when it is perceived differently by them and they may not be able to remember who they are) (Treadaway et al., 2018b). (See Figure 3.2)

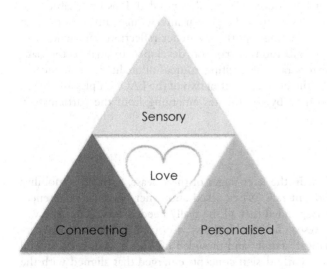

Figure 3.2 Compassionate Design.

Theories of wellbeing in dementia identify five core human needs: attachment, comfort, identity, inclusion and occupation, with love being the central constituent (Kitwood, 1997; Mitchell, 2016). The three key themes in Compassionate Design embrace these psychological needs, directing the designer's attention to ways in which designs might be developed to meet them. The focus on *personalisation* reinforces a person's psychological need for identity; the *connection* theme addresses the need for inclusion and attachment and *sensory stimulation* provides ways of delivering occupation and comfort. By emphasising the need to design for moments of meaningful connection that validate personhood and stimulate lived experience, it may be possible to encourage moments of love described by Fredrickson (2014) as *positivity resonance*. These connections between people have been found to contribute to both psychological and physical wellbeing (Fredrickson, 2014) and align with Kitwood's theories concerning the psychological needs of people living with dementia (Kitwood, 1997, Brooker, 2007).

LAUGH research, guided by Compassionate Design, has developed a collection of playful objects for people living with advanced dementia. Each concept is informed by findings from participatory workshops. Key themes arising from these workshops were identified as being vitally important to support the wellbeing of people living with the later stages of the disease and were represented in six thematic words used to guide design development: Nurturing, Security, Movement, Purposeful, Replay and Attention.

In order to ensure that the design concepts were highly personalised, six participants with advanced dementia were recruited for the study from the partner organisation.[12] Detailed 'portraits' (comprising information about personal preferences and life history) were developed for each of them in collaboration with family members, carers and the person living with dementia.[13] Design concepts were explored in two co-design workshops with an interdisciplinary group of key dementia experts, technologists and designers. These were later developed and prototyped by the LAUGH team. The final workshop event provided an opportunity for key experts to critique the prototype designs and identify any health and safety concerns before they were taken to the people they were designed for.

Each object was introduced to the person living with dementia by the team and left with them. The LAUGH team returned after one week, one month and three months, to gather detailed information about how the resident had responded. This Live Lab evaluation process included detailed observation of the person interacting with the object in situ, carer and family interviews, wellbeing reports, researcher reflections and video and photographic documentation. An evaluation matrix was developed to analyse the data, identify recurrent themes and corroborate the multiple sources of qualitative evidence.

The following sections describe the development of two of the LAUGH playful objects and explain how they were informed by the themes emerging from the participatory workshops.

Hug

'Hug' was developed for a resident in the later stages of the disease, with little mobility, limited speech and who had frequent falls. When asked about her personal preferences and immediate needs, her carers responded that all she really needed was a hug. She was unable to communicate with the researchers and had few visitors, so her professional carers asked to be considered a surrogate family and provided life history information and identified her personal preferences. Early design concepts emerged that aligned with the theme 'Nurturing'. This recognises a fundamental instinctive human desire to nurture others (and things) and includes activities such as cuddling, cradling and grooming. Design concepts were explored that focused on soft tactile materials and methods of simulating a hugging sensation. A soft textile solution was proposed, with a beating heart and extended arms to wrap around the body. A soft cushion, doll-like wearable was developed in an iterative process of prototype development. Electronics were added to provide a simulated beating heart and a sound module with speakers, enabling songs from a 'favourites' playlist to be played when the object was being hugged.

The positive response of the participant to the prototype was immediate; she snuggled into it, rested her head and closed her eyes to enjoy the sensation of the heartbeat and music. (See Figure 3.3.)

A few moments later she spoke a few words for the first time in many weeks to the amazement of the care staff. During subsequent visits the research team observed a rapid and progressive improvement in her general health and wellbeing. Her professional carers corroborated this, confirming that her appetite had improved, she was socialising with other residents, talking, smiling and, perhaps most significantly, had not fallen since she had been given the Hug object. The care home manager stated that she was convinced nothing had changed for the resident other than being given the Hug and believed it had definitely contributed to her improved wellbeing.

Steering wheel

LAUGH case study interviews with men who had been recently diagnosed with dementia, found that not being able to drive a car is particularly detrimental to self-esteem and has a negative impact on wellbeing. A person living with advanced dementia who had worked as a mechanic for a roadside rescue organisation and had enjoyed driving all his life was subsequently recruited as a participant. He was in the advanced stages of the disease and in very poor physical health, was bed-bound, anxious and depressed. A LAUGH co-design workshop, involving dementia experts, technologists and designers, explored

Figure 3.3 LAUGH Hug prototype.

Figure 3.4 LAUGH steering wheel prototype.

ideas for a personalised hand-held device that might be able to simulate the haptic experience of driving for him.

Early design concepts were influenced by detailed *portrait* information about the man's preferences and life history. These ideas were later developed by the LAUGH team into a prototype hand-held steering wheel object that could provide haptic and sensory feedback, including vibration to simulate the running engine, flashing indicator lights and an old-fashioned tune-in radio, preprogrammed with a playlist of favourite music. (See Figure 3.4.)

During the Live Lab evaluation in the residential care home, the research team observed and documented the resident's positive body language, engagement, increased communication and delight (observed in his facial expression) in response to the steering wheel. He sat in his wheelchair alongside two carers who acted out an imaginary road trip to the seaside. This involved him in role-playing the physical activity of manoeuvring the vehicle, parking and going to buy ice cream. The care home manager reported that the steering wheel had resulted in the most positive interaction they had ever experienced with this particular resident. The object had helped to engineer a shared playful experience that was clearly enjoyed by all involved.

Discussion

Research described in this chapter has shown that by placing compassion for the person living with dementia at the heart of the design process, it is possible to design appropriate and meaningful objects that help sustain wellbeing and bring moment-by-moment opportunities for happiness and hope.

The two highly personalised LAUGH objects described in the previous section were developed in response to preferences and life history information of two specific people living with advanced dementia. The guiding principles of Compassionate Design have ensured that the objects created were *personalised*, meeting individual needs and preferences; *sensory* and with low cognitive demand; and *connecting* the person living with dementia to objects and people in the world around them. Although highly personalised, each design also corresponds to one of six key themes that resonate with universal human needs. These include the desire to nurture and be nurtured (1, Nurturing); to feel safe and secure (2, Security); to have agency and a sense of purpose (3, Purposeful); to move and interact with others (4, Movement); to be creative and playful (5, Replay); and to attend to the moment (6, Attention). These themes emerged from the LAUGH partici-patory research and have been found to be critical in designing to support the wellbeing of people living with dementia. The predicted increase in the numbers of people living with the disease means that finding ways to scale up highly personalised solutions, to assist in care and support wellbeing, are urgently needed. Findings from the LAUGH research indicate that it may be possible to develop highly bespoke yet generic designs suitable for manufacture, by responding to the universal themes and incorporating interactive and programmable digital technology to provide personalisation.

Although there may be no sign of an imminent cure for dementia, there remains hope that people's life satisfaction can be improved and their happiness increased by designs that enable them to keep connected to the world around them, maintain their identity and focus on 'in the moment' pleasure. Compassionate Design has been found to be a useful approach to guide the design process, ensuring that loving kindness for the person living with dementia remains at its heart.

Acknowledgements

LAUGH design research was funded under AHRC Standard Grant Ref. AH/M005607/1.

Notes

1 WHO (2012). Dementia: A Public Health Priority. UK, World Health Organisation Alzheimer's Disease International.
2 Article 10 of the United Nations Resolution A/RES/61/106. Convention on the Rights of Persons with Disabilities. In: Sixty-first United Nations General Assembly, New York, 13 December 2006. New York: United Nations; 2006. Available from: http://www.un-documents.net/a61r106.htm (acc. 17/12/17).
3 The WHO defines 'health' as: *'a state of complete physical, mental and social wellbeing and not merely the absence of disease or infirmity'. Constitution of the World Health Organization, New York, July 1946.*
4 Dementia describes a collection of progressive neurodegenerative diseases that impact on memory, behaviour, cognition and perception.
5 Kenning calls this 'reciprocal design', which can *'contribute to quality of life, promote social engagement, provide physical interaction with objects and bring in the moment pleasure'* Kenning (2017 p.18).
6 http://minddesingingforpeop.apps-1and1.net (acc. 20/12/17).
7 https://designingfordementia.eu/resources/mind-tools/visual-diaries (acc. 20/12/17).
8 http://imagination.lancs.ac.uk/activities/Ageing_Playfully (acc. 20/12/17).
9 LAUGH research based at CARIAD, Cardiff Metropolitan University, Wales and funded by the AHRC Grant: AH/M005607/1.
10 https://research-methodology.net/research-philosophy/interpretivism/ (acc. 20/12/17).
11 www.compassionatedesign.org (acc. 20/12/17).
12 Pobl Gwalia Care.
13 Ethical consent was seen as an on-going process throughout the project and aligned with university and Alzheimer's International guidelines.

References

Aked, J., Marks, N., Cordon, C., & Thompson, S. (2008). *5 Ways to Wellbeing: A Report Presented to the Foresight Project on Communicating the Evidence Base for Improving People's Well-being.* London: The New Economics Foundation.

Algar-Skaife, K., Caulfield, M., & Woods, B. (2017). cARTefu: Creating artists in residence. Evaluation Report 2015–2017. Bangor, UK: DSDC Wales Report.

Bennett, B., Mcdonald, F., Beattie, E., Carney, T., Freckelton, I., White, B., & Willmott, L. (2017). Assistive technologies for people with dementia: Ethical considerations. *Bulletin of the World Health Organization Policy and Practice, 95*(11), 749–755.

Bennett, P., Hinder, H., & Cater, K. (2016). Rekindling imagination in dementia care with the resonant interface rocking chair. *CHI EA '16 Proceedings of the 2016 CHI Conference Extended Abstracts on Human Factors in Computing Systems, San Jose, CA, USA.* New York, NY: ACM, pp. 2020–2026.

Branco, R.M., Quental, J., & Ribeiro, Ó. (2017). Personalised participation: An approach to involve people with dementia and their families in a participatory design project. *CoDesign, 13*, 127–143.

Brankaert, R., Den Ouden, E., & Brombacher, A. (2015). Innovate dementia: The development of a living lab protocol to evaluate interventions in context. *Info, 17*, 40–52.

Brooker, D. (2007). *Person-centred Dementia Care: Making Services Better.* London and Philadelphia, PA: Jessica Kingsley Publishers.

Brooker, D. (2008). What makes life worth living. *Aging & Mental Health, 12*, 525–527.

Chenoweth, L., Forbes, I., Fleming, R., King, M.T., Stein-Parbury, J., Luscombe, G., Kenny, P., Jeon, Y.-H., Haas, M., & Brodaty, H. (2014). PerCEN: A cluster randomized controlled trial of person-centered residential care and environment for people with dementia. *International Psychogeriatrics, 26*, 1147–1160.

Cila, N., Zuthem, H.V., Thomése, F., Otten, W., Meiland, F., & Kröse, B. (2017). FIT decision aid: Matching the needs of people with dementia and caregivers with products and services. In Dr. Regina Bernhaupt, G. Dalvi, A. Joshi, D.K. Balkrishan, J. O'Neill, & M. Winckler (Eds.), *16th IFIP TC 13 International Conference on Human-Computer Interaction, INTERACT 2017*, Mumbai, India: Springer International Publishing.

Cohen-Mansfield, J., Marx, M.S., Freedman, L.S., Murad, H., Thein, K., & Dakheel-Ali, M. (2012). What affects pleasure in persons with advanced stage dementia? *Journal of Psychiatric Research, 46*, 402–406.

Craig, R.T., & Tracy, K. (2014). Building grounded practical theory in applied communication research: Introduction to the special issue. *Journal of Applied Communication Research, 42*, 229–243.

Desmet, P.M.A., & Pohlmeyer, A.E. (2013). Positive design: An introduction to design for subjective well-being. *International Journal of Design, 7*, 5–19.

Fredrickson, B.L. (2014). *Love 2.0: Creating Happiness and Health in Moments of Connection.* New York, NY: Penguin Group.

Hendriks, N., Huybrechts, L., Wilkinson, A., & Slegers, K. (2014). Challenges in doing participatory design with people with dementia. *Proceedings of the 13th Participatory Design Conference* (Vol. 2). Windhoek, Namibia: ACM.

Hendricks, N., Wilkinson, A., & Dirk, S. (Eds.) (2017). *Dementia Lab: The Role of Design.* Belgium: Dementia Lab.

Hughes, J.C. (2014). *How We Think About Dementia: Personhood, Rights, Ethics, the Arts and What They Mean for Care.* London: Jessica Kingsley.

Jakob, A., Manchester, H., & Treadaway, C. (2017). Design for dementia care: Making a difference. *Nordes 2017, 7th Nordic Design Research Conference*, Oslo, Norway.

Kenning, G. (2016). Art engagement for people with dementia. *Independent Evaluation of the Art Access Program Art Gallery of New South Wales, Sydney.* Sydney, Australia: Art Gallery New South Wales.

Kenning, G. (2017). *Making It Together: Reciprocal Design to Promote Positive Wellbeing for People Living with Dementia.* Sydney, Australia: University of Technology Sydney.

Kenning, G., & Treadaway, C. (2017). Designing for Dementia: Iterative grief and transitional objects. *Design Issues, 34*, 42–53.

Killick, J. (2013). *Playfulness and Dementia: A Practice Guide.* London: Jessica Kingsley Publishers.

Kitwood, T.M. (1997). *Dementia Reconsidered: The Person Comes First.* Buckingham: Open University Press.

Krippendorff, K. (2006). *The Semantic Turn: A New Foundation for Design.* Boca Raton, FL: CRC/Taylor & Francis.

Ledoux, J.E. (1998). *The Emotional Brain: The Mysterious Underpinnings of Emotional Life*. London: Weidenfeld & Nicolson.

Lindsay, S. (2012). Designing to support wellbeing in dementia. *DIS 2012 Designing Wellbeing*, Newcastle, UK.

Livingston, G., Sommerlad, A., Orgeta, V., Costafreda, S.G., Huntley, J., Ames, D., Ballard, C., Banerjee, S., Burns, A., Cohen-Mansfield, J., Cooper, C., Fox, N., Gitlin, L.N., Howard, R., Kales, H.C., Larson, E.B., Ritchie, K., Rockwood, K., Sampson, E.L., Samus, Q., Schneider, L.S., Selbæk, G., Teri, L., & Mukadam, N. (2017). Dementia prevention, intervention, and care. *The Lancet*, *390*(10113), 2673–2734.

Maiden, N., D'Souza, S., Jones, S., Müller, L., Pannese, L. Pitts, K. Prilla, M., Pudney, K. Rose, M., Turner, I., & Zachos, K. (2013). Computing technologies for reflective, creative care of people with dementia. *Communications of the ACM*, *56*, 60–67.

Mitchell, G. (2016). *Doll Therapy in Dementia Care*. London: Jessica Kingsley.

Nolan, M.R., Davies, S., Brown, J., Keady, J., & Nolan, J. (2004). Beyond 'person-centred' care: A new vision for gerontological nursing. *Journal of Clinical Nursing*, *13*, 45–53.

Ógáin, E.N., & Mountain, K. (2015). *Remember Me: Improving Quality of Life for People with Dementia and Their Carers Through Impact Investment*. London: NESTA.

Rahman, S. (2017). *Enhancing Health and Wellbeing in Dementia*. London: Jessica Kingsley.

Rijn, H.V., Hoof, J.V., & Stappers, P.J. (2010). Designing leisure products for people with dementia: Developing 'the Chitchatters' game. *American Journal of Alzheimer's Disease and Other Dementias*, *25*, 74–89.

Rodgers, P. (2015). Designing with people living with dementia. *Design4Health*, 13th–16th July 2015, Sheffield, UK.

Sabat, S.R. (2006). Implicit memory and people with Alzheimer's disease: Implication for caregiving. *American Journal of Alzheimer's Disease & Other Dementias*, *21*, 11–14.

Shibazaki, K.M., & Nigel, A. (2017). Exploring the impact of music concerts in promoting well-being in dementia care. *Aging & Mental Health*, *21*, 468–476.

Treadaway, C., & Fennell, J. (2017). How do we create attractive personalised and customised care? In P. Rodgers (Ed.), *Does Design Care*, September 2017. Lancaster University, Lancaster, UK.

Treadaway, C., Fennell, J., Kenning, G., Prytherch, D., & Walters, A. (2016a). Designing for wellbeing in late stage dementia. *Well-Being 2016: Co-Creating Pathways to Well-Being*, 5th–6th September 2016. Birmingham: Birmingham City University.

Treadaway, C., Fennell, J., Prytherch, D., Kenning, G., Prior, A., & Walters, A. (2018a). *Compassionate Design: How to Design for Advanced Dementia*. Cardiff: Cardiff Metropolitan University.

Treadaway, C., & Kenning, G. (2016). Sensor e-textiles: Person centered co-design for people with late stage dementia. *Working With Older People*, *20*, 76–85.

Treadaway, C., Kenning, G., Prytherch D., & Fennell, J. (2016b). LAUGH: Designing to enhance positive emotion of people living with dementia. *10th Design and Emotion Conference*, 27–30 September 2016, Amsterdam.

Treadaway, C., Prytherch, D., Kenning, G., & Fennell, J. (2016c). In the moment: Designing for late stage dementia. In P. Lloyd, & E. Bohemia (Eds.), *DRS2016* (pp. 1442–1457), 27–30th June 2016. Brighton, UK: De1sign Research Society.

Treadaway, C., Taylor, A., & Fennell, J. (2018b). Compassionate creativity: Co-design for advanced dementia. *The Fifth International Conference on Design Creativity (ICDC2018)*, Bath, UK.

Windle, G., Gregory, S., Newman, A., Goulding, A., O'Brien, D., & Parkinson, C. (2014). Understanding the impact of visual arts interventions for people living with dementia: A realist review protocol. *Systematic Reviews*, *3*, 91.

Zeisel, J. (2011). *I'm Still Here: Creating a Better Life for a Loved One Living with Alzheimer's*. London: Piatkus.

4 Design for wellbeing in architecture and interior architecture

Educating future designers on ageing well in place

Ann Petermans, Jan Vanrie, An-Sofie Smetcoren, Gitte Harzé and Jo Broekx

Introduction

'Wellbeing' is a major, if not *the* ultimate goal, for every human being. Setting up initiatives to work on people's wellbeing is very relevant and also timely. Indeed, there seems to be a societal need to focus on the wellbeing of people and there is a growing interest in people to pay the necessary time, effort and attention to the fulfilment of some of these immaterial aspects of life. Moreover, from an economic point of view, paying attention to wellbeing is also highly relevant as 'happy' people are more successful in many domains of life, and these successes are, at least in part, due to their happiness (Lyubomirsky et al., 2005). Given these perspectives, it is not surprising that happiness has become an issue on the political agenda. Already in 2011 and 2013, UN Secretary-General Ban Ki-moon pointed to the importance of attention to people's wellbeing and happiness. In his Note to the General Assembly (2013b, p. 3) he indicated that 'the creation of an enabling environment for improving people's wellbeing is a development goal in itself'. Many designed environments and objects are indeed the silent companions in our daily lives that surround us in almost everything we do, and we interact with them, intentionally or not. In that respect, studying their potential to enable people to work on their happiness holds great promise for creating a better world.

Also in Flanders, Belgium, the Flemish government seems to value people's wellbeing more and more. The most recent policy plan of the Flemish government (2014–2019), for instance, demonstrates the thought that the government gives to these issues, including in relation to people's housing. Issues such as attention for all age groups, working on age-friendly neighbourhoods and the promotion of ageing in place and living at home for as long as possible, are key topics to be considered in this respect.

The government's focus for these topics doesn't come out of the blue. Research has demonstrated that a lot of people, young and old, prefer to be able to live for as long as possible in a place where they feel good and feel connected with the people around them, the street, and the neighbourhood (Smetcoren, 2016). A dwelling that enables people to live in a home where they can reside for life, without (much) care, and which can answer their changing dwelling needs and wishes, seems indispensable in this respect (Wahl et al., 2012). A house has also to be a 'home' for its inhabitants, a dynamic environment where people can undertake activities that can make them happy and give them meaning and 'sense' in life. Looking at a 'house' in this way implies that architects and interior architects bear an important responsibility when designing places where people can spend their lives without (much) care.

After discussing insights arising from a review of the literature on the contribution of architecture and interior architecture to older adults' subjective wellbeing, this chapter demonstrates how research by design can help to crystallise insights and point to various possibilities that architecture and interior architecture can offer in this respect. A selection of four projects from a design studio exercise on the topic of 'lifelong living without care' demonstrates various views and explorations of future designers.

Housing for older adults in Belgium

An ageing population

Population ageing, which refers to the increasingly large proportion of older people within the total population, is according to United Nations (2017a) one of the most significant and important challenges of our twenty-first century and without parallel in the history of humanity. At present, Europe has the highest percentage of its population aged 60 and over, namely 24 per cent, and this proportion is expected to reach 34 per cent in 2050 (United Nations, 2017b). As in Europe, Belgium is challenged by a growing number of people reaching retirement age. In 2017, 24.6 per cent of the Belgian population was 60 years and older, and demographic projections predict that by 2050 this will shift to 32.4 per cent (United Nations, 2017b). Even more, the older population is itself ageing. In Belgium the share of persons aged 80 years and over (also referred to as 'the oldest old') was 5.5 per cent in 2015 and it is projected that 10.6 per cent of Belgians will be 80 years or older by 2050.

These demographic projections are having implications for social protection systems such as pensions and health care (United Nations, 2013a; European Union, 2015) but also clearly underline the need to ensure adequate and qualitative home environments for older people (Pittini & Laino, 2011), all the more because, in Belgium, a large number of older people are living independently in the community. For the community-dwelling older people, data from the Belgian Ageing Studies (BAS) pointed out that 95.2 per cent of older people live independently (alone or with a partner) in a single-family house, an apartment or a studio. Only a minority live together with their children (2.5 per cent) or in alternative housing (2.3 per cent), such as sheltered housing, kangaroo housing[1] or collective housing (De Witte et al., 2012).

Inadequate housing for older adults in Belgium

To date, the Belgian housing stock can be described as 'rather old, with many older people households concentrated in badly equipped and badly isolated houses, which are often too large for their needs' (De Decker & Dewilde, 2010, p. 258). Vanneste et al. (2007) indicate that in Belgium, 15 per cent of dwellings were built before 1919, and 17 per cent between 1919 and 1945. A large number of the oldest houses are being occupied by older people. Because Belgium is recognised to have a low level of household mobility (van der Heijden et al., 2011), and relocation rate decreases with age, it is argued that dwellings tend to age together with their inhabitants. Results from the Belgian Ageing Studies have indicated that 40.1 per cent of people aged 60 and over in Flanders live in dwellings that are highly inadequate for old age. Recent analyses also indicate that 82.9 per cent of people aged 60 and over are homeowners (De Witte et al., 2012), which helps clarify why older people are not likely to leave their proper house and home environment. Having a home of one's own is considered to be an important step in our housing career and older people hold on strongly to this conviction (Meeus & De Decker, 2015). Moreover, despite the presence of this unadjusted housing stock for older people, not many of them are likely to adjust their dwellings. In fact, the older people get, the less likely they are to do so (De Witte et al., 2012). As a result, a considerable number of older people continue to live in their proper, but problematic, dwellings.

Because of different events in the areas of health and housing, living requirements and preferences about the most suitable housing among future generations of older people can change (Smetcoren, 2016). Therefore it is necessary to have a wide variety of housing to choose from. Unfortunately, at present, this is rather limited in Belgium, as the following brief overview of housing possibilities available for older people demonstrates:

(i)   A 1st option regarding housing possibilities for older people concerns moving into a residential care facility, referring to the larger-scale traditional nursing homes where there is a strong medical approach. However, previous research has emphasised that the majority postpone a move to an institutional care setting, and for most older people this is only considered as a last resort, when other options are no longer possible (Löfqvist et al., 2013; Smetcoren, 2016). Reasons why older people do not want to move into nursing homes often entail negative stereotypes, such as the fear of losing autonomy, lack of privacy and poor quality of care (Löfqvist et al., 2013), but also high costs are mentioned as hindrances (Walloon Government, 2014). Looking at the Belgian residential housing landscape, it is predicted that there will be a shortage of 22,000 places in retirement homes in the years to come (Belga, 2016), which will bring about a shortage of places for dependent older people for whom care by friends and family can no longer be provided.

(ii) A 2nd option would be for older people to live together with their children. Although this was once a more common living arrangement, at present co-residence with children occurs less and less in Belgium (De Witte et al., 2012). In 1990, there were 20,000 Flemish people aged 80 and up who lived together with one of their children; in 2007 this number was half as large (Lodewijckx, 2008).

(iii) A 3rd option refers to alternative supportive housing types, such as assisted living facilities (service flats) and collective housing or living-in-groups, or whatever forms that cannot be placed within the previously mentioned types. These are typically small-scaled living environments where the focus is more on the ability of the resident to live independently and to a lesser extent on the availability of medically oriented care. Furthermore, they are usually custom-built for older people who cannot find a solution for their needs within the traditional groups of residences. Examples for collective or intergenerational housing are still rare in Belgium. However, they entail several benefits: for example, according to older residents, the presence of mutual support that goes beyond helping each other in times of need (Glass, 2013; Gerards, 2016). Although such alternative supportive housing types are still rare in Belgium, it seems highly valuable and worthwhile to explore this aspect further. To date, there have been studies on this matter (e.g., see Vlaams Bouwmeester, 2014; Abbeyfield projects, Abbeyfield, 2014). In Belgium, Abbeyfield is already present in Brussels (e.g., Etterbeek) and Wallonia (e.g., Lixhe) and there are future projects being planned in both Flanders and Wallonia. Regarding these initiatives, we think that there is also added value not only in presenting additional *new* perspectives, but also in reflecting about how *existing* initiatives (such as existing dwellings) could be improved in terms of older people's wellbeing.

(iv) This brings us to a 4th option, which seems to be highly valued by older people (De Witte et al., 2012; Smetcoren, 2016): if possible, to try to continue to live in one's proper dwelling, at home, and try to 'age in place'. A recent study, which questioned 2,000 Belgians aged from 60 to 85, shows that more than 80 per cent of older people wish to continue living at home as long as possible (Fondation Roi Baudouin, 2017). Home is a source of attachment for inhabitants. The meaning one can attach to a home confirms that the dwelling is much more than solely a 'physical' place. Often, the time lived in a particular home helps to develop a feeling of belonging to the place and the neighbourhood. In Belgium, this attachment is referred to by 84 per cent of older people (Fondation Roi Baudouin, 2017).

If necessary, there are several services available which can support older people in their proper dwelling and enable them to age in place. There is a huge challenge to further explore how the existing housing stock where older people age can be improved in terms of older people's SWB. Later in this chapter, the output of the 'research by design' demonstrates various views and explorations in this respect.

Ageing in place: The importance of the home environment in later life

During the last decade, there has been a growing attention for the concept of 'ageing in place', which can be defined as 'the ability to live in one's own home and community safely, independently and comfortably, regardless of age, income or ability level' (Centers for Disease Control and Prevention, 2013, n.p.). Extensive academic literature on the preferences of older people themselves has shown their desire to age in place (Means, 2007). As the definition of 'ageing in place' demonstrates, it is not limited to the presence of a particular 'bricks and mortar' environment; it also relates to the surroundings of a person's neighbourhood. Recently, also, Flemish and Walloon policy has started to acknowledge the importance of the immediate surroundings in the neighbourhood of people's residences and of a qualitative and liveable living environment (Flemish Government, 2014; Walloon Government, 2014). Indeed, it is clear that, in line with the older people themselves, both policy-makers as well as the general public have responded to people's desire for ageing in place (Cutchin, 2003). It is explicitly recognised that people's subjective wellbeing is key in this aspect.

Although policy objectives regarding 'ageing in place' are being set up, they are ambitious and the road to success brings with it many queries and challenges that will need to be tackled. Indeed, notwithstanding the popularity of the concept of 'ageing in place' among policy-makers and older people, recent studies stress the need for a broader approach (Golant, 2011; Hillcoat-Nallétamby & Ogg, 2014), in the course of which 'ageing in place' is seen as a *possible* option rather than 'a "one-stop" solution to later-life aspirations and needs' (Hillcoat-Nallétamby & Ogg, 2014, p. 1790). Furthermore, ageing in place might not signify that all older people should stay put or want to stay put (Means, 2007; Smetcoren, 2016).

Ageing in place and the subjective wellbeing of older people

As discussed earlier in this book (see Chapter 2), to date, no universally accepted definition of 'wellbeing' can be given, but most researchers agree that the concept has affective, cognitive and contextual components (Desmet & Pohlmeyer, 2013). Considering 'wellbeing' from an architectural perspective, we tend to differentiate between 'objective' and 'subjective' wellbeing. 'Objective wellbeing' (OWB) concerns the realisation of objective parameters regarding wellbeing, that is, conditions that are external to an individual. Such data can be collected without subjective evaluations being made by individual people. 'Subjective wellbeing' relates to more subjective parameters regarding wellbeing, where psychological parameters are at stake, which can at least in part be considered as possible 'consequences' of the environment wherein one resides.

In general, OWB can be considered as a determinant of SWB (Desmet & Pohlmeyer, 2013). Empirical research on happiness is still fairly recent (Eid & Larsen, 2008), but Lyubomirsky et al. (2005) have shown that inter-individual differences in SWB are more a matter of intentional activities, that is, how we live our lives, than of our circumstances. So, people have the power to actively contribute to their happiness. It is therefore intriguing to consider architecture and interior architecture not only as a feature of our circumstances, but also as a platform for intentional activities that can be stimulated through design. This opens up exciting opportunities for the design community in general, and architecture and interior architecture in particular (Petermans & Nuyts, 2016).

Research by design in architecture and interior architecture

The preparation, set-up and aim of design studio assignment

Architectural practice has its own kind of knowledge production, relying on the capacity of designing. As a consequence, in the last few years, 'research by design' has become a buzzword, used in the contexts of professional, educational and research environments (van de Weijer et al., 2014). According to Loeckx (2009, p. 25),

> we take Research by Design to mean: an exploration of the spatial possibilities and limitations of the site; 'mapping' the spatial sensibilities, interests, agendas, and skills of various urban stakeholders; [and] exploring the spatial convergences that could suggest new forms of collaboration and open up new trajectories of development.

Looking at the application of research by design for our research purposes, it is clear that this can bring valuable insights in the understanding of wellbeing of older people and the contribution of architecture and interior architecture in this respect.

The aim of the design studio was to develop spatial scenarios on 'lifelong living without care' and ageing well in place for a selected semi-detached house close to the central train station of Hasselt, Belgium. No particular specificities were provided to the students as to the (future) inhabitants of the project; they were asked to be creative and come up with valuable and insightful proposals and scenarios.

Figure 4.1 shows the selected 'case' for the design exercise, which can be considered to be a typical example of a Belgian architectural project.

Contents of the studio exercise

In their studio assignment, students were asked to explore different possibilities intended to stimulate lifelong and 'care-less' ageing in place in this particular setting, and reflect and design 'broadly', without taking too many practical considerations into account.

Figure 4.1 Semi-detached house, location of design studio exercise.

For this particular exercise, the first bachelor design studios of both the architectural and interior architectural training program collaborated. In total, 132 students participated, divided into 44 mixed design teams (mostly two architecture students and 1 interior architecture student). The design exercise was organised in March 2017, at the start of the second semester, and it took four weeks from start to finish.

At the start of the design studio, every group received the plans of the location, as well as a short theoretical introduction on design for wellbeing and challenges regarding housing for older people in the Belgian housing landscape. The concrete assignment entailed three key challenges for each design team, which were intended to foster diversity in design output:

1. Reorganise the ground floor of the semi-detached house to a compact and appealing living environment.
2. Prepare the house for lifelong living by adding polyvalent living spaces (e.g., a communal space and/or a multifunctional room).
3. Optimise the relation between the inside and outside spaces and organise the outer space as a fully-fledged living space.

Under the supervision of experienced architects and interior architects and the involved researcher, the 44 groups of students developed new spatial scenarios for the selected setting.

At the end of the exercise, each design team presented their output to a jury, consisting of presentation drawings (scale 1/50), a presentation model of their design as a whole (scale 1/50), a detailed model (scale 1/20) highlighting an important aspect of the design and including key aspects of the furniture, and a visual project summary, bringing key aspects together.

Discussion of results

In order to show how research by design can help to demonstrate valuable explorations of future architectural and interior architectural designers as to the proposed key challenges, in collaboration with the design studio teachers, four projects were selected from the total sample of 44 projects presented. The key criterion for selecting these was the score obtained from the jury, which can be interpreted as a reflection of the quality of the project. In what follows, every selected project is presented in brief. In analysing these projects, the three key challenges that were discussed earlier (i.e., attention for lifelong living, use/role of communal space and relation between inside and outside spaces) will act as key lenses.

Project 1

This design team proposed a compact solution regarding the polyvalent space between the new bedroom and the existing home (see Figures 4.2a and 4.2b).

Regarding the aspect of attention for lifelong living, the team introduced new functions on the house's ground floor (i.e., bedroom and multifunctional space), which were connected to the rest of the dwelling while still guaranteeing privacy. As to the newly introduced communal space, Figure 4.2a demonstrates students' efforts to open up the existing dwelling to the garden, so that more light and brightness could be introduced to lighten the residence. Evidently, at the same time, the new extension brings about extra space and shows how the spatial experience of the whole has been a key topic for this design team. Concerning the relation of inside and outside, Figures 4.2a and 4.2b show how the new extension, containing a lot of glass, has almost no threshold between inside and outside, which fortifies the interior atmosphere and living quality in both the new extension and in the existing spaces of the dwelling. The roof of the new extension is also placed in a playful way in relation to the original house.

Project 2

As Figure 4.3a demonstrates, this team came up with a clear plan in which the kitchen and a new bedroom were housed in two separate extensions, which were connected to the existing dwelling by means of a communal garden room/corridor. The whole is organised around a courtyard that is accessible from the common parts (Figure 4.3b).

Concerning attention for lifelong living, this design team organised the main functions at the ground floor of the existing dwelling. In the newly added extensions, a kitchen and a bedroom were placed for new inhabitants. As to the role of the communal space, Figures 4.3a and 4.3b demonstrate how the courtyard has a key role in this project, being the space that connects the original dwelling and the new extensions. Regarding the relation of the inside and outside, the courtyard helps to create intimacy in the city, but also brings openness and brightness in the new kitchen and bedroom. In addition, this courtyard can truly interconnect the existing dwelling and new extensions via its functioning as a corridor. The glass enclosing both new extensions guarantee a wonderful connection between the inside and outside, which heightens the living quality of these new interior spaces.

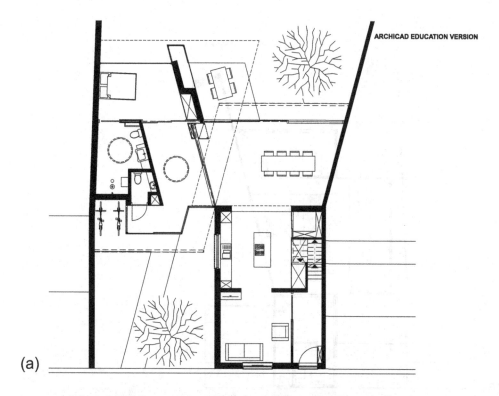

Figure 4.2 a. Design project HSN, floor plan. b. Design project HSN, model.

Source: Heeman, Slijpen, Naveed, 2017.

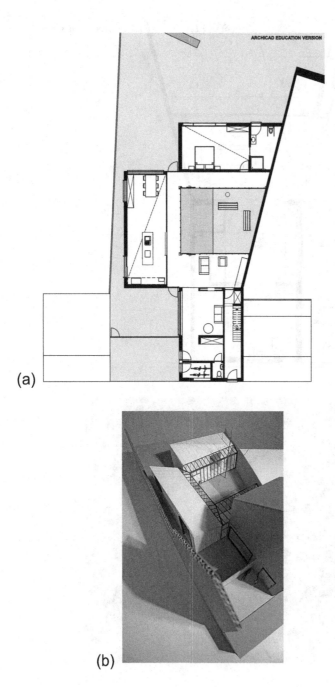

Figure 4.3 a. Design project JUV, floor plan. b. Design project JUV, model.

Source: Jamar, Ulrichts & Verheyden, 2017.

Project 3

This design team came up with a clear floor plan which had good proportions. In addition, the context was taken into account well, while providing, for instance, easy access to the garden from the street. As Figure 4.4a demonstrates, over the whole length of the terrain, getting to the garden was made possible by a path that ran from the street to deep into the garden.

Regarding attention for lifelong living, the open plan ensures a flexible layout, which can be highly valuable when striving for lifelong living. As to the communal space, the kitchen added in one of the new extensions connects a family (foreseen to live in the existing dwelling in this project) and an elderly couple (foreseen to live in the newly added extensions). Next to the kitchen, a seating area and a bedroom are placed in the new extensions. Concerning the relation of the inside and outside, the awning (extension of the roof) connects inside and outside. As Figures 4.4a and 4.4b show, by providing a front garden and an enclosed garden behind the house, two different outdoor areas are created, each with their own character and function. Consequently, the division of the house is relatively easy to realise.

Project 4

As Figures 4.5a and 4.5b demonstrate, in this project the enfilade[2] of spaces (properly dimensioned) ensures a flexible interpretation and use of space. This pattern was also extended outside. In this way, the transition between inside and outside is very gradual. The outdoor space is an extension of the interior space. The context of the dwelling was taken into account nicely. An outdoor space that is located back from the street offers access to the new extension. In this way, both the existing home and the extension can function separately.

Regarding attention for lifelong living, this design team opted for a flexible interpretation of the rooms. Figures 4.5a and 4.5b demonstrate the way the design team integrated various functions in the different spaces. In this project, 'communal spaces' (now a kitchen, living space and dining space) were interpreted in a flexible way so that, over time, the functions as they are currently foreseen, can alter. In the current design set-up, both simultaneous and non-simultaneous use of these spaces is possible. Concerning the relation inside to outside, the design team decided to persevere in the use of the enfilade pattern, safeguarding a logical connection between inside and outside.

Analysis of results

As the projects discussed demonstrate, although every design team worked on the same location, there is a great variety in the architectural and interior translation and formulation of proposals as to the three key challenges on lifelong living, the communal space in between and the relation between the inside and outside. Overall, most design teams proposed a project wherein 'grandparents' would be introduced as new inhabitants in the dwelling, which their children inhabited together with their loved ones, and whose dwelling would be adapted in order to guarantee (or, at least, facilitate) 'lifelong living without (much) care'. Regarding the aspect of lifelong living, each of the selected teams proposed different scenarios and 'solutions', depending on the key issues that each of them wanted to put forward. This is also clear in the various architectural and interior translations as to the use of the communal space that needed to be incorporated in between, or the relation between the interior spaces and the garden. The projects share each team's careful

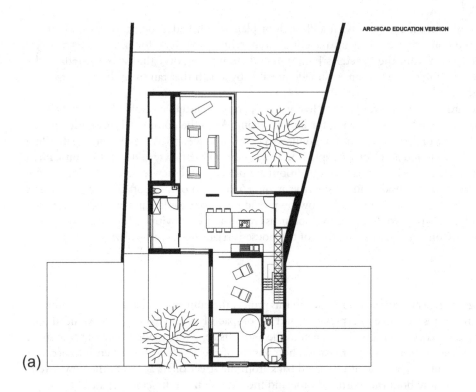

(a)

(b)

Figure 4.4 a. Design project VCLJ, floor plan. b. Design project VCLJ, model.

Source: van Cornoedus, Lenaerts & Jaspers, 2017.

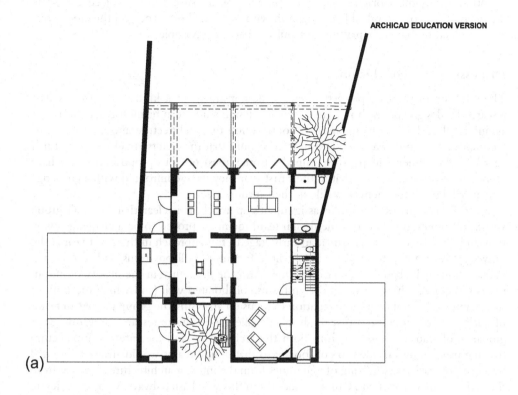

(a)

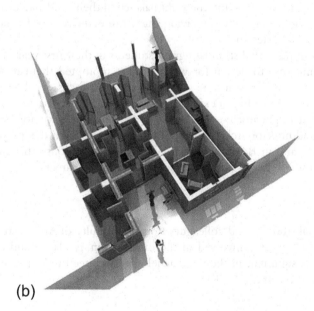

(b)

Figure 4.5 a. Design project VDB, floor plan. b. Design project VDB, model.

Source: Vangronsveld, Dekkers & Boon, 2017.

attention for lightness, brightness and the integration of nature. Most projects also share the safeguarding of the valuable connection with the neighbourhood and the city, so that easy connections between 'private' and 'public' spaces are possible.

Discussion and conclusion

The selection of the four projects discussed demonstrates what kind of diverse results a research by design approach in a first bachelor design studio can bring forth, focusing on ageing in place, lifelong living and the contribution that architecture and interior architecture can have in this respect. Taking into account that the results entail projects of first year bachelor students helps to explain the (sometimes) obvious propositions they have come up with, but it is good that in their first year they were confronted with a challenge which will be key for them to tackle in their future careers.

As to limitations of our studio assignment's approach, it is clear that, as in all group work, collaboration between some design team members proved to be a challenge every now and then. By exposing them at an early stage to this approach in their first year at the university, we wanted to prepare them a little for future collaborations with fellow students, who may be based in other disciplines. Also, the difference in the quality of output presented quickly showed which design teams collaborated well (and which did not). In this chapter, it has not been our intention to focus on analysing the group process in terms of quality of collaboration – that might be a challenge for future research. Regarding the guidance of students, teachers from both the architecture and the interior architecture training programmes needed to collaborate so that design teams would always be guided by a team of teachers consisting of colleagues from the interior architecture as well as from the architecture department. Guiding students in this way hasn't always been self-evident, as the teachers themselves had to try to find the right balance in their guidance team (i.e., 'steering' students in the 'right' direction, or giving them more 'degrees of freedom' to translate their insights into their design projects).

As to future research, we hope that stimulating our students in their first year of architecture and interior architecture to design for wellbeing has prompted them to further explore this topic, and delve deeper in it. The same goes for their focus on older people and housing, and renovation/adaptation of existing houses in this respect. In a sense, working on such an assignment might not be considered as appealing or 'sexy' for first year students in architecture and interior architecture, but taking into account the 'greying' of the population worldwide, and in Belgium in particular, there is no doubt that students will be confronted with these kinds of housing issues in their future careers.

Acknowledgements

We would like to thank all students and colleagues from the Faculty of Architecture and Arts of Hasselt University, Belgium, involved in the organisation, guidance and evaluation of this design studio assignment in the first bachelor in Architecture and in Interior Architecture in the academic year 2016–2017.

Notes

1 In this dwelling typology, two families live on one piece of land. In this concept, an original home can be converted into two independent accommodation units. In this way, two families can live separately and retain their privacy while still requesting each other's help. It is often parents and children

who create such a win-win situation. But there doesn't necessarily have to be a family bond between the two families. Kangaroo housing is a creative solution for the often high land and construction prices.

2 An 'enfilade' concerns a series of connecting rooms along with the door openings lying in line with each other on a continuous axis, so that a view 'throughout' the rooms is possible. This avoids narrow corridors that connect spaces with each other.

References

Abbeyfield (2014). *Een vernieuwend woonconcept.* Retrieved 2 February 2017 from http://abbeyfieldvlaanderen.be/nl

Belga (2016, 23 November). *Ouderenzorg kan vergrijzing niet volgen. Tekort van 22000 rusthuisbedden in Vlaanderen.* Retrieved 13 February 2017 from http://www.standaard.be/cnt/dmf20161123_02586883

Centers for Disease Control and Prevention (2013). *Health Places Terminology.* Retrieved January 2016 from http://www.cdc.gov/healthyplaces/terminology.htm

Cutchin, M. (2003). The process of mediated aging-in-place: A theoretically and empirically based model. *Social Science & Medicine, 57,* 1077–1090.

De Decker, P., & Dewilde, C. (2010). Home-ownership and asset-based welfare: The case of Belgium. *Journal of Housing and the Built Environment, 25*(2), 243–262.

De Witte, N., Smetcoren, A.-S., De Donder, L., Dury, S., Buffel, T., Kardol, T. & Verté, D. (2012). *Een huis? Een thuis! Over ouderen en wonen.* Brugge: Uitgeverij Vanden Broele.

Desmet, P., & Pohlmeyer, A. (2013). Positive design: An introduction to design for subjective wellbeing. *International Journal of Design, 7*(3), 5–19.

Eid, M., & Larsen, J. (Eds.) (2008). *The Science of Subjective Wellbeing.* New York, NY: The Guilford Press.

European Union (2015). *Social Protection Systems in the EU: Financing Arrangements and the Effectiveness and Efficiency of Resource Allocation.* Report jointly prepared by the Social Protection Committee and the European Commission Services. Retrieved January 2016 from http://ec.europa.eu/social/main.jsp?catId=738&langId=en&pubId=7743&type=2&furtherPubs=yes

Flemish Government (2014). *Regeerakkoord Vlaamse Regering 2014–2019. Vertrouwen, verbinden, vooruitgaan.* Retrieved from https://www.vlaanderen.be/publicaties/het-regeerakkoord-van-de-vlaamse-regering-2014-2019

Fondation Roi Baudouin (2017). *Choix de Vie Durant Les Vieux Jours : Enquête Auprès de plus de 2000 Personnes de 60 Ans et +.* Bruxelles: Fondation Roi Baudouin.

Gerards, S. (2016). *One Home, Three Generations: A Habitological Study on Multigenerational Dwelling as a Renewed Dwelling Concept for Flanders.* PhD thesis, Hasselt University, Hasselt, Belgium.

Glass, A. (2013). Lessons learned from a new elder cohousing community. *Journal of Housing for the Elderly, 27*(4), 348–368.

Golant, S.M. (2011). The quest for residential normalcy by older adults: Relocation but one pathway. *Journal of Aging Studies, 25*(3), 193–205.

Walloon Government (2014). *Oser, innover, rassembler.* 2014–2019. Retrieved from http://mobilite.wallonie.be/files/eDocsMobilite/politiques%20de%20mobilit%C3%A9/dpr_2014-2019.pdf

Hillcoat-Nallétamby, S., & Ogg, J. (2014). Moving beyond 'ageing in place': Older people's dislikes about their home and neighbourhood environments as a motive for wishing to move. *Ageing & Society, 34*(10), 1771–1796.

Lodewijckx, E. (2008). *Veranderende leefvormen in het Vlaamse Gewest 1990–2007 (en 2021). Een analyse van gegevens uit het rijksregister.* Studiedienst van de Vlaamse Regering. Retrieved December 2015 from http://www4.vlaanderen.be/dar/svr/afbeeldingennieuwtjes/demografie/bijlagen/2008-11-20-svr-rapport-2008-3.pdf

Loeckx, A. (2009). Project and design, amending the project mode. In A. Loeckx (Ed.), *Framing Urban Renewal in Flanders* (p. 25). Amsterdam: SUN Architecture Publishers.

Löfqvist, C., Granbom, M., Himmelsbach, I., Iwarsson, S., Oswald, F., & Haak, M. (2013). Voices on relocation and aging in place in very old age – A complex and ambivalent matter. *The Gerontologist, 53*(6), 919–927.

Lyubomirsky, S., Sheldon, K., & Schkade, D. (2005). Pursuing happiness: The architecture of sustainable change. *Review of General Psychology, 9*(2), 111–131.

Means, R. (2007). Safe as houses? Ageing in place and vulnerable older people in the UK. *Social Policy & Administration, 41*(1), 65–85.

Meeus, B., & Decker, P.D. (2015). Staying put! A housing pathway analysis of residential stability in Belgium. *Housing Studies, 30*(7), 1116–1134.

Petermans, A., & Nuyts, E. (2016). Happiness in place and space: Exploring the contribution of architecture and interior architecture to happiness. In P. Desmet, S. Fokkinga, G. Ludden, N. Cila, & H.Van Zuthem (Eds.), *Proceedings of the Tenth International Conference on Design and Emotion: Celebration and Contemplation* (pp. 114–122). 27–30 September 2016. Amsterdam, The Netherlands: The Design and Emotion Society.

Pittini, A., & Laino, E. (2011). *Housing Europe Review 2012. The Nuts and Bolts of European Social Housing Systems.* Published by CECODHAS Housing Europe's Observatory. Retrieved from http://www. housingeurope.eu/resource%105/the%housing% europe%review%2012/

Smetcoren, A. (2016). I'm not leaving!? *Critical Perspectives on 'Ageing in Place'.* Unpublished doctoral dissertation, Vrije Universiteit Brussel, Brussels.

United Nations (2013a). *World Population Ageing 2013.* Published by the Department of Economic and Social Affairs Population Division. Retrieved January 2016 from http://www.un.org/en/development/desa/population/publications/pdf/ageing/WorldPopulationAgeing2013.pdf

United Nations, General Assembly (2013b). *Happiness: Towards a Holistic Approach to Development.* Retrieved from http://www.un.org/ga/search/view:doc.asp?symbol=A/67/69

United Nations, Department of Economic and Social Affairs, Population Division (2017a). *World Population Prospects: The 2017 Revision.* Retrieved 22 August 2018 from https://esa.un.org/unpd/wpp/DataQuery/

United Nations, Department of Economic and Social Affairs, Population Division (2017b). *World Population Prospects 2017: The 2017 Revision.* Retrieved 22 August 2018 from https://esa.un.org/unpd/wpp/DataQuery/

van de Weijer, M.,Van Cleempoel, K., & Heynen, H. (2014). Positioning research and design in academia and practice: A contribution to a continuing debate. *Design Issues, 30*(2), 17–29.

van der Heijden, H., Dol, K., & Oxley, M. (2011). Western European housing systems and the impact of the international financial crisis. *Journal of Housing and the Built Environment, 26*(3), 295–313.

Vanneste, D., Thomas, I., & Goossens, L. (2007). *Woning en woonomgeving in België.* Brussel :Federaal Wetenschapsbeleid.

Vlaams Bouwmeester (2014). *Pilootprojecten onzichtbare zorg – innoverende zorgarchitectuur. Ten laatste geraadpleegd.* 29 January 2017 from http://www.vlaamsbouwmeester.be/nl/publicaties/pilootprojecten-onzichtbare-zorg

Wahl, H.-W., Iwarsson, S., & Oswald, F. (2012). Aging well and the environment: Toward an integrative model and research agenda for the future. *The Gerontologist, 52*(3), 306–316.

5 Social connectedness, social interaction and the design of interior environments

Tiiu Poldma

Introduction

In this chapter we will examine how social interaction frames wellbeing from the perspective of people's experiences and how social connectedness occurs within public interior spaces. How spaces are designed impacts on the conditions that favour (or hamper) social interactions, social inclusion and connectedness for people from all walks of life. When social connectedness is only available to some and not to others, such as people with disabilities, too often this is due in part to the design of the interior environment. Whether it is getting together for a coffee with a friend or going shopping together, all people want to have social connections, and yet they cannot engage in social connectivity when the spaces designed for them are not accessible. We will examine what constitutes social connectedness and wellbeing as lived experience, what various constructs govern human social relations and how these are manifested in the design of public places for people from all walks of life. Through the lens of a Living Lab[1], lived experiences are understood from a universal perspective and explored as the catalyst to implementing design changes to a public space within a commercial mall interior environment. Researchers and stakeholders from diverse backgrounds investigated the issues faced by all people at all stages of life and, in particular, for people with disabilities. Design researchers explored what issues hamper or support access for people with disabilities, and how interior spaces are supported by socially inclusive practices such as the implementation of universal design principles. In the past 20 years there has been an escalation in understanding the role of social connectedness and interaction within architecture and the built environment from more holistic perspectives. Issues include how the design of products and environments affect and support wellbeing, and how the interior environment specifically might better promote social interaction and connectedness through its very design.

We will explore major factors that may contribute to social connectivity, what issues lead to less than optimal social spaces, and how a universally designed environment contributes to social connectivity in specific ways. Social issues in the environment, space and place as salient aspects of social connectivity and the personal and social experiences we have, are the factors affecting social connectivity that we will explore in this chapter. The personal and social ways that we experience environments play a vital role in contributing to our wellbeing and capacity for social connectivity, and the built environment can either hinder or facilitate access and social engagement. What are the lived experiences of people who use public spaces, and, in particular, persons with disabilities?

How does the built interior environment contribute to positive experiences, and, conversely, how do social constructions and biases affect the relative ability of people to feel well and be socially active? What do people need to live well in interior environments, and what constitutes the social wellbeing of the individual? The environment, when designed appropriately, can contribute to the social connectedness of people, by providing 'added value' in how the spaces are designed to support the wellbeing of people via their 'connectedness' and/or possibilities for social interaction within the interior environment.

A secondary perspective in this chapter is understanding wellbeing from the perspective of universally designed places as social spaces, and how the interior environment is a democratic place that frames a person's personal and social experiences. From a universal design perspective, we are interested in understanding how people from all ages and stages of life perceive and navigate spaces, and what constitutes a universal approach to designed space. Social connectedness depends on a universal approach, in that design accounts for broader concerns of including people from all walks of life in all interior environments. While in the past, as well as currently, spaces and places are too often designed for some at the exclusion of others. An inclusive approach that includes social integration and places for people of all ages and stages of life to participate together in meaningful experiences means adapting physical interior environments accordingly.

These ideas will be examined in the context of how interior public spaces are a vital source for social connectedness in an urban rehabilitation Living Lab in Montreal, Canada, known as the RehabMALL . Through the lens of this research/design project, we will explore what factors contribute to creating environments that are responsive to people's lived experiences within the context of both interior social activities. The RehabMALL Living Lab is an intersectoral and multidisciplinary Living Lab with over 45 researchers who explored social inclusion and social participation in the live setting of the public spaces of a commercial mall/office complex. The researchers investigated the issues faced by people with disabilities and what obstacles and facilitators affect social participation (Poldma et al., 2014; Swaine et al., 2014). Ultimately part of the goal was to change the existing environment by using design elements as a means to support and promote social connectivity in the social relations of people, using design as a catalyst for change.

Wellbeing in the design of the interior built environment: Human connectedness in the design process and in strategic decision-making

Wellbeing for everyone, however, remains an elusive concept when wellbeing is defined with a broader view towards connectedness and social interaction. In the world of architecture and interiors, the wellbeing of occupants is not always central to the building and its design (Malnar & Vodvarka, 1992). Places have not always been designed with the user as an integrated person relating to their environment. The way that places and buildings are designed can induce isolation and stigma. For example, a food service retail counter at a height for able-bodied people is an instant barrier for people in wheelchairs, as it is too high for them to reach and be served. Much work is still needed to be done in the development of the design of interior spaces using universal principles, designing for all people with all types of abilities and cognitive/physical capacities and with inclusive wellbeing practices in both institutional and public spaces.

Sensory issues in the built environment

Our visual world is often designed with a primacy to the visual within a particular aesthetic and at the expense of all five senses working together. This ocular primacy in our society at large then plays itself out in the social relations we have with one another and as we navigate the built environment. The architect Juhani Pallasmaa has criticised the importance of the visual in architecture at the expense of other senses (1990), as 'a critique of the ocular bias of our culture at large and of architecture in particular' (Pallasmaa, 1990, p. 9). For individuals, all senses are involved when identifying with a well-designed environment. In institutional settings, while attention is paid to providing a suitable environment for the institutional purpose, the environment is often hostile rather than welcoming for persons with specific sensory issues. The design of the spatial environment becomes a salient issue in terms of the capacity of the environment to adequately support people with varying degrees of sensory responses and capacities.

The complexity of designing environments with the input of users and stakeholders

The creation of suitable environments for wellbeing when in the public domain considers places such as large public environments, for example institutions or commercial retail environments, where large segments of society congregate for leisure, work and play. In this type of designed environment, products, services and environments, and all aspects of the design are considered. Both users and stakeholders are necessary for the initial understanding of what is required and the subsequent creation of these environments. This type of design touches on what Richard Buchanan refers to as an emergent area of design

> of complex systems or environments for living, working, playing and learning … This area is more and more concerned with exploring design as sustaining, developing and integrating human beings in broader ecological and cultural environments, shaping these environments when possible or adapting to them when necessary.
>
> (Buchanan, 1995, pp. 7–8)

In essence, in the past 25 years, this move towards design disciplines that allow an understanding of the role of complex systems reflects the emergence of the necessity of including users and stakeholders with designers in designing places that hold design solutions for multiple needs. The voices of all stakeholders then inform the decisions needed to change the environment to respond to them.

In terms of research, these types of considerations necessitate a strategic and innovative approach that is grounded in the collaborations and on-the-ground knowledge of the lived experiences of users. Living Labs, as a research mechanism, offer a research environment that favours the conditions that Buchanan and Van Patter speak to: a place for exploring design as a sustaining place for solutions to human problems (Buchanan, 1995) from the perspective of collaborating and sense-making within the framework of a complex range of stakeholders (Van Patter, 2013). These concepts are foundational to understanding how to create suitable social environments for the people who will be using these environments, which might be commercial buildings or public spaces, for example.

We will now consider how people actually respond within the physical environment and what factors play a role in supporting wellbeing both from personal and social perspectives of people living within the built environment.

Social connectedness

In terms of social connectedness, Van Bel, IJsselteijn and de Kort (2008) define this as

> The momentary affective experience of belonging to a social relationship or network. Social connectedness can be the outcome of subtle events in one's peripheral area of attention, or it may be caused by explicit acts, such as by making a phone call or visiting a friend.

This momentary experience can happen spontaneously, or it can be supported by the interior environment within which these types of activities happen. For example, in the RehabMALL Living Lab we explore in this chapter later on, researchers examine the ways that people used the interior of a commercial mall in terms of the level of social connectedness. How can people in their everyday lives go to the mall to meet a friend or have a coffee together to add meaning to their lives, and what factors hamper or create opportunities for these types of activities that also promote social inclusion and social participation (Poldma et al., 2014).

Social interactions and the social constructions of space and place as intersubjective experience

Meanings of life are held within the context of the interrelationships with others as well as perspective of self. Berger & Luckmann (1966) propose that we construct our social reality based on the intersubjective realities we share in the world with others. As they state:

> The reality of everyday life presents itself to me as an intersubjective world, a world that I share with others ... there is an ongoing correspondence between *my* meanings and *their* meanings in this world.
>
> (Berger & Luckman, 1966, p. 34)

The personal and social perceptions we have form the framework of the world we share with others, an 'intersubjective' world when we are in the world in social situations, with others.

Furthermore, Berger & Luckmann suggest that 'The world of everyday life is structured both spatially and temporally' (p. 26). And while the temporal is what they go on to talk about, the spatial parameters are what are of interest here, as the social constructions of space as place often determine social relations and whether these are positive or negative (Vaikla-Poldma, 2013). Historically, interior environments as spaces have been built to promote certain relations and often, to prevent other social relations. Examples include the gender segregation of environments such as the home environments of various cultures and, in particular, in Western society, or the interior spaces of the Victorian era (Ardener, 1981; Spain, 1992).

Changing perceptions of spaces and intersubjective experiences

The development of the breakdown of these finite roles in gender relations took place in the 1990s, with seminal authors discussing the relationship of architecture and spaces in terms of cultural, historic and social concerns, and how various other types of spaces were increasingly determined as shaping life experiences. Early discussions of the shaping of social spaces and social relations were pioneered by authors such as Shirley Ardener (1981) and other authors have considered these issues more recently. Within the reality that people increasingly live in urban areas and that the United Nations (2010) and World Health Organisation (WHO) predict that more people will live in urban areas than ever before, we can surmise that social spaces, and the use of interior spaces as social places, will become even more important. Interior spaces can reflect authority, bias and privilege on the one hand, and, on the other hand, inclusively designed spaces can be democratic, welcoming and positive for as many people as possible who want to come and socialize for various reasons. These arguments reveal some of the issues hampering the ability of architectural environments to freely engage social interaction and connectedness as essential elements of people's wellbeing.

Towards connectedness and social interaction in the design of spaces

Social interaction thus manifests itself in the ways that spaces are appropriated as places. Spatial appropriation requires all of the senses to be engaged – for all types of people in all types of situations. For spaces to actually serve the interests of those occupying the space, the complex human senses and ways of being in temporal spaces need to be taken into account. To this we add the universal nature of design and the possibilities of place-making as a means to social interaction and connectedness. Three concepts will be explored here: place-making, 'third place' and 'third space' as social environment and connectedness.

First, in terms of place-making, Lefebvre considers in the context of space as a place and the construction of meanings of that place over time. Wilwerding discusses Lefebvre's idea of 'space to be the product of a system of individuals and objects that occupy it' (Wilwerding, 2013, p. 74). He explores the meaning of space thus

> the meaning of space does not emerge from the working out of social relations, but is rather constructed in an intentional and calculated manner ... space is not a real thing that has any actual permanence but rather is constructed, destroyed and reconstructed as a set of meaningful relations.
>
> (p. 74)

Second, the idea of 'third place', developed by Ray Oldenburg (1989), proposes alternative spaces as places. In considering this idea, we consider the first place as home, the second place as work and third place as a place of spontaneous congregation where social relations can occur (Oldenburg, 1989).

Third, the evolution of the idea of 'third space' emerged as a salient element within the RehabMALL Living Lab quite by accident. The spaces that were conceived within the RehabMALL Living Lab were developed out of both commercial need and evidence-based metrics that showed a lack of adequate access into the mall. Once easier access was provided, a higher concentration of older people entered the mall, wanting to congregate together for social purposes, independent of the mall's use as a primarily commercial place (yet one that provided places for social congregation). This emergent third space thus became a meeting place and also became a place for social interaction and connectedness. In urban centres these occasions are in public places such as cafes and restaurants and places to congregate in the malls and urban places we frequent. And yet, these spaces can be blocked from access due to the ways that such buildings are designed, and, when they are, people who are not afforded access are indeed kept away. A universal design approach is thus needed to provide the conditions for everyone to have equal and easy access without social discrimination influenced by the physical design of the interior environment.

In summary, considerations for wellbeing include the social constructions of spaces and places to capture the meaningful experiences of people as they congregate for social experiences (Poldma et al., 2014) The integration of meaningful social activities inside supportive interiors within everyday life has emerged recently as primordial for social interaction and connectedness in society as a whole.

Understanding, navigating and controlling one's personal relationship with the physical environment

Related to social connectedness are the ways that we navigate our world when we want to socialise and what universal design elements are present or absent. Interior spatial cues act on us physiologically and physically and either enhance and stabilise, or destabilise, our reactions to that same environment. Factors in this spatial perception include design factors such materials and lighting choices, our reactions to all sensory cues including light, noise and smell, and access issues such as stairs, elevators and escalators, as well as our own personal life experiences that influence how we evaluate various cues as we receive them and then how we experience social relations with others. These factors are all affected by our personal physical and psychological state, our cultural background, our age and relative capacity to navigate an environment and many other contextual factors. These factors may hamper social connectedness in sometimes subtle ways.

Considerations about spatial cues and the ageing person as elements of social connectedness

As we age, in particular, we tend to shift our perceptions of the environment. Our way that we attribute meanings to places and things, and personal cues, are increasingly affected by our physiological and psychological ability to navigate environments, to remain autonomous and have social relations with others in comfort and security. The physiological changes that occur to our vision and other senses change our relationship with the world around us. Studies have shown, for example, that the wellbeing of a person is affected specifically by the size of the environment (Zakus & Lysak, 1998; Poldma et al, 2017; Poldma et al., 2014). Depending on our mental and physical state, we may ascribe meanings to things in a smaller and more intimate setting more positively. These factors then affect the possibility of maintaining social connectedness, as we may choose to stay home rather than venture into social situations that could be uncomfortable. Lawton's study (1974) of patients in mental hospitals 'found large size associated with less patient movement … and more "institutional" staff attitudes' (Lawton et al., 1974, p. 601). The resultant lack of movement was a contributor to declining social relations and subsequent lack of social connectedness.

While this can be more often subconscious, environments provide both sensory and visual stability when people can 'read' the visual environment with their eyes, in terms of their overall view (peripheral vision) and also in terms of the detailed vision needed to stabilise themselves in the environment. In the interior environment this becomes heightened, especially when poor contrast or poor lighting prevent stability within the environment (Poldma, 2006). In one study on older people in long-term care institutions, simple changes in colour, materials and light, combined with the strategic placement of certain activities, accounted for a dramatic increase in social connectedness through better orientation and the feeling that spaces were welcoming for patients, as well as for family and friends, for social purposes such as conversation while being visited by friends and relatives (Poldma, 2006). The combination of size and contrast of materials, when appropriate for age and stage of life, provides ease of movement and personal control.

Disruptive factors within the environment

Another issue is how the environment plays a significant role in how 'disruptive factors' can affect a person. Studies have shown how the environment can include disruptive factors specifically in residential care facilities (Nelson, 1995).

Everyday activities where institutions employ control are the antithesis of providing wellbeing in the environment, even when social activities are promoted. Activities such as coming together in a dayroom at a long-term care centre, while positive for some, are very stressful for others for a host of reasons. In the Nelson study, disruptive factors were identified in behaviour rather than in the influence of the setting. However multiple studies show that the setting and the environment also play a role in creating disruptive reactions, where 'environment' is defined as

> all physical and interpersonal variables that surround an individual and interact with an individual in a given situation
>
> (Nelson, 1995)

Personal and social factors as environmental factors

Community participation in interior environments has been shown to have a positive impact on health (Zakus & Lysak, 1998; Ahmed et al., 2017). When people are socially engaged and when they can access social activities easily within a community setting, then they are shown to be healthier and generally happier (Carbonneau et al., 2017; Poldma et al, 2017). In one study the factors that emerged and were tested among social housing tenants included friendship, housing satisfaction, morale, mobility and activity participation (Lawton et al., 1974). These factors are intrinsically tied to a person's personal self-motivation and social motivation. While done some time ago, the study is significant as it suggests that personal control of the environment and the social activities is essential to one's capacity to partake socially in the surrounding environment and provides the basis for social participation. When personal variables such as the environment were controllable by the person, then friendship and activity participation increased substantially (Lawton et al., p. 604). These earlier studies paved the ground for understanding the value of place as a physical space with intrinsic properties that promote wellbeing or conversely present psychological and physical obstacles to social motivation.

Social experiences in places

In terms of space and place, the social nature of public places as places of congregation and active leisure can be affected by the relative design and the willingness of people to engage in social activities provided. Places can facilitate social interaction and connectedness when they are structured to provide universally designed places for all people to congregate. Places provide anchors for individuals in different ways and are a means to providing meaningful social boundaries for social and cultural groups. Terence Mann (2013) considers these questions and describes how places become spaces of personal meaning in various ways. Mann then says 'Many of us choose not to consider the role that place plays in our individual and collective identity. Yet at the same time almost all people seem to have specific places that in some way anchor them' (Mann, 2013, p. 117). The local cafe or mall becomes a meeting place, or the local church becomes a community space for a particular culture, when the conditions favour access and social interaction.

Issues arise when 'cultural place-making' is at the expense of others. In terms of gender identity, for example, the creation of home for certain cultures also defines social relations in terms of space appropriation and division (Spain, 1992). Additionally, people can create spaces that specifically target certain groups. Often, in our public places, even if they are considered accessible by all, certain places and spaces, by virtue of how they are designed, ignore the broader universal principles allowing access for everyone.

Personal and social meanings of things as lived experience

Finally, a person's state of wellbeing is also tied to the meanings that they ascribe to things and to how they experience their environment in the phenomenological sense. For social connectedness to occur, people need to find meaning in the things that matter to them, and in the real-time experiences that they have. We will look at these two concepts next.

The significance of things within contemporary urban life and the meaning of lived experiences as social experiences

Each person's 'voice', context, meaning and experience all construct meaning in interior spaces and contribute to the conditions for both personal wellness and social connectivity. Csikszentmihalyi and Rochberg-Halton (1981) suggest that each person ascribes meanings to the self, to their surroundings and to their identity and that these personal and social experiences frame how we navigate our world as a 'life-world' (Habermas, 1981); and then they engage in social interaction that provides their 'social construction of reality' (Berger & Luckann, 1966). In terms of how we ascribe meaning to things, Csikszentmihalyi and Rochberg-Halton limit their definition to things

> that are the object of human intentionality. Man-made things are twice as dependent on intention for their existence. Like any other object, they can be interpreted through the psychic activity of the interpreter.
>
> (Csikszentmihalyi and Rochberg-Halton, 1981, p. 14)

And yet, each person ascribes their own meanings to the objects that surround them (Vaikla-Poldma, 2013). Meanings are constructed based on the person's own intention and sense of lived experience, with each lived experience contributing to the making of meanings over time. Meanings of home, for example, are constructed through a person's lived experience and collections of perceptions and are often tied to the objects of home, perhaps a chair, a kitchen or a favourite toy (Vaikla-Poldma, 2013, pp. 102–103). For example, in a study done on long-term care patients, their sense of wellbeing was in the things they recalled in their past, despite being in a new environment (Poldma, 2006). Meanings of wellbeing are often constructed from the position of the person in their subjective lived experience, in the phenomenological sense, and these experiences can be both positive and negative.

Phenomenological experience as subjective social experience

Related to the meaning of things is our perception of our life-world from the perspective of phenomenological experience (Vaikla-Poldma, 2003). In essence, a phenomenological understanding of self in our life-world includes how we navigate the social world, how this is intertwined with the moving around in the environments and then, when we arrive at a place, how we experience that environment both personally and socially. As we move around in our world, we are in a temporal state of movement; space and time collapse as we experience everyday life (Poldma & Wesolkowska, 2005; Vaikla-Poldma, 2003). Thus meanings are ascribed within the context of what we see, what we experience and our perception of it in real time.

The connection between intersubjective experiences, social relations and spaces as places

Perceptions of space and the surrounding interior environment are intrinsically tied to human perception and action, as each person has their personal meanings and social interactions within environments. Aesthetic choices are thus grounded in the voices of the various people who are part of the construction of spaces (Vaikla-Poldma, 2013, p. 105). This is amplified when a person ages, as their world diminishes in size and scope. These issues become complex when other people contribute to this world, an increasingly institutional world for people who are elderly, for example. The constructions of these interior environments are many and include users, stakeholders, designers, architects and participants. For those who design spaces 'understanding intersubjective experiences requires understanding how spaces act on our perceptions and perpetuate social relations' (Vaikla-Poldma, 2013, p. 105). This means accounting for the meanings people hold in the things that they find pleasurable and how activities provide opportunities for social connectedness and generate feelings of comfort, contentment and wellbeing; and then considering how best to communicate these needs with all stakeholders concerned when designing public places and institutions in particular.

Putting these ideas into practice: The Rehabilitation Living Lab

The Rehabilitation Living Lab is a research project that took place within the context of a 'Living Lab', a place for collaboration, social action and constructing new ways to understand lived space within the context of wellbeing, social connectedness and accessibility. In this multi-sectorial project, over 45 researchers from diverse backgrounds, got together to examine these issues, to experiment and to propose technological aids and various solutions for people in the context of accessing and using the public spaces of a commercial mall complex. This research project occurred in the context of both virtual and physical environments, and research projects were carried out both before and after changes were made to the interior environment of the mall's public spaces with the support of the mall's developer/owner. Goals included determining social and environmental factors, obstacles and facilitators to social inclusion, and social participation for persons with disabilities through the lens of accessible and universal design approaches (Lidwell et al, 2003).

The RehabMALL Living Lab methodological approach

The physical interior environment was documented before and after changes to the interior environment were made. Collaborative and constructive research processes were also employed to assess with collaborators and participants how the interior environment itself might facilitate changes in the social connections people make in their everyday experiences. Core issues included understanding the nature of the public space and that

> 'Although public environments provide opportunities for participation and social inclusion, they are not always designed to accommodate the diversity of its patrons'
> (Ahmed et al., 2017, p. 2).

The Living Lab uses cooperative and constructivist forms of inquiry (Guba & Lincoln, 1994; Heron & Reason, 2001) as a means to frame the various issues and perspectives encountered. In this project, real-life settings interject with applied, basic and clinical research problems (Friedman 2003), all aimed at using technological innovation, and investigating issues to support the development of emergent practices.

Several research studies were undertaken to glean a complete picture of the obstacles and barriers hampering both social and physical accessibility to the environment (Ahmed et al., 2017; Poldma et al., 2014; Swaine et al., 2014). Metrics were collected both from a physical environmental perspective and statistics about people's movements. Accessibility factors in the mall were evaluated and the lighting and spatial characteristics were documented prior to any renovations. In a study counting people, extensive counts were carried out in order to understand people's movements, who was coming into the mall and how they were arriving and navigating within the spaces (Ahmed et al., 2017; Poldma et al., 2017) Issues that were salient were the existing conditions of the physical and social environment that were barriers to supporting social connectivity. Removing the social and physical barriers meant understanding first what these barriers might be, from the perspective of the intersubjective experiences of the people who used the space.

One of the foundational studies was conducted with people making a series of walkabouts in two stages – both before and after the changes were made to the mall, and each time with the social goal of going to meet at the mall to have a coffee together. These walkabouts were conducted at the outset of the project, before the mall was renovated, and again after the changes had been made to the mall. The studies had an overarching visual and verbal approach in two stages as follows: (1) An adapted version of visual content analysis (Rose, 2001) was employed to study the existing conditions within the mall; and (2) walkabouts were conducted using a participatory approach to glean the experiences of people as they navigated the interior spaces of the mall environment (Poldma et al., 2014). Researchers wanted to understand what experiences they had and how they interacted socially with other people. A real-time phenomenological approach was used, in that lived experiences were documented in situ, each time ending in a discussion in one of the food court areas of the mall. Observations of the spaces and a visual content analysis study were done to determine the existing issues from the perspective of designers and architects were also conducted (Poldma et al., 2014; Poldma et al., 2017). We see in Figure 5.1 a view of the mall levels before changes were made.

The author's research team organised walkabouts with people to glean their experiences in real time (Poldma et al., 2014). In an initial walkabout study, a walk was organised with two teams taking different paths from the local college to a rendezvous point at the

Figure 5.1 Mall view before changes are made, the experimental walking tour.

mall. Stigmatisation was evident when the participants tried to order a coffee or a sand-wich. Access issues added to the stigmatisation, when the two teams took different routes to arrive at the rendezvous point. In the walkabout experience, one team (able-bodied with vision issues) took eight minutes to arrive at the organised rendezvous point, while the second team, accompanying persons with motorised wheelchairs, took 43 minutes to get to the same point. When the second team arrived at the entrance door (needing wheelchair access), the people in wheelchairs had to wait for someone else to push the handicap button to open the door, as the button was too far away, thus obligating those in wheelchairs to ask for help as people walked by. Then, when the teams went to order coffee and snacks at the coffee shop, everyone would stand back when the person with a wheelchair approached the counter, making them feel uncomfortable. A specific person behind the counter was called to serve the person in the wheelchair, despite our accompaniment, and these issues became evidence of stigma and social obstacles present.

These experiences provided the team with the understanding of how the physical barriers accelerated and supported discrimination and stigma. As Ahmed et al. (2017) state:

> Removing environmental barriers can accelerate the rehabilitation process by enhancing function and in turn increase the individuals' participation and quality of life ...

Social obstacles include others' attitudes towards people with disabilities, or subtle forms of discrimination and bias, which negatively impacts interactions.

(9, 20, 22)

Thus spatial realities collided with the lived experience of the wheelchair user, and the disparity led to lack of comfort and lack of social connectivity. Several issues emerged that were then presented to the design team, who made changes to the design. In Figure 5.2 we see the changes implemented in the mall.

Some of the changes literally changed the lives of some users. Similar walkabouts took place after the mall changes had been made, with some of the same original user participants invited to do the same walkabout once again. Clearly the changes made had simplified access, and the ease of finding and using public washrooms, finding the information desk and generally navigating the wider and clearly defined spaces were positive outcomes. Some issues remained in terms of stigmas that were still evident in the use of the space by persons with disabilities, a lack of engagement with the tenants of the mall (Ahmed et al., 2017) and some design elements still needing adjustment as not all universal design principles (Lidwell et al, 2003) were implemented. And yet, for one person interviewed, the addition of an access ramp from the college allowed him access to an environment he had never frequented in the 20 years he had been teaching, due to its inaccessibility previously. As he said: 'You changed my life.'

Figure 5.2 Mall view after changes were made.

Discussion

When barriers to social participation can be identified and design features integrated within the spaces to be assistive, and when these features can also serve the larger societal needs (such as branding for commercial use), then a universal approach is enacted and social connectedness becomes possible. This was the case in the RehabMALL Living Lab. The RehabMALL research revealed issues of social participation and connectedness. First, physical changes that allowed for independent access were essential changes that were needed and that were made, while the subtle spatial changes to the environment changed the relationship of the person to both the environment and the resultant social engagement they could now have. Second, while significant changes were made, the after-walkabouts revealed social issues that were solved, as well as those that were not.

The changes made to the mall were carried out considering the spatial and temporal complexities and how these become salient issues to solve in the interior space. Barry Dainton (2001) cites Talmy's philosophical concepts of how literacy combines spatial and temporal. Talmy speaks about the frame of reference used: 'The meaning of spatial and temporal expressions is dependent upon a. scale; b. frame of reference ... all of these complexities ... deal with cognitive interpretations of subjective spatial and temporal relationships' (pp. 19–20). And he goes on to link these ideas with 'designed environments or designed services that frame concepts of meaning' (p. 20). In other words, the spatial design (circulation, pathways, location of elevators and escalators, spatial features) and a person's ability to find their way through references are important components of how they are able to find their way independently, and hence how they can socialise with others in the environment and find enjoyment and meaning. These were essential issues to solve, and the informing of stakeholders of specific issues within the mall contributed to solving positively many issues in the renovation that were implemented for the benefit of users of the mall, while providing access to those who were previously shut out.

Conclusion

If we return to the issue of wellbeing and social connectedness, we are confronted with the more philosophical question of what makes a person happy. Within the context of social connectedness, how might their activities and experiences be supported by actions of the environment that favour happiness and wellbeing? It is within these contexts that the RehabMALL Living Lab investigated how people's actual, lived experiences were affected by stigmas both inherent in the physical environment and in the capacity of people to engage in the social environment of the mall. Through renovation, the changes made provided them with an easier means to cope with issues of access, and to become aware of physical environmental factors. Furthermore, when designed universally and with these issues in mind, the design of the environment provided a backdrop to facilitate better social connectedness and enjoyment of temporal experiences such as shopping or doing a leisure activity. While not all the social stigmas and issues were resolved, the changes implemented did facilitate the social connectedness, by providing easier access for persons with disabilities to meet together with friends, and to navigate the mall, moving from place to place with more ease. In this sense social connectedness depends on the interior and a social environment that promotes wellbeing and meaningful relationships to those who use them.

Acknowledgements

I would like to acknowledge the following research team that contributed to the creation of the Living Lab. This innovative research project was conducted from 2011 to 2016. It was entitled 'A Rehabilitation Living Lab: Creating Enabling Physical and Social Environments to Optimize Social Inclusion and Social Participation of Persons with Physical Disabilities', and was funded by FRQ_S funds in Quebec, Canada. The RehabMALL, Rehabilitation Living Lab research team includes co-principal investigators Eva Kehayia and Bonne Swaine, with co-investigators (in alphabetical order) Philippe Archambault, Joyce Fung, Dahlia Kairy, Anouk Lamontagne, Guylaine Le Dorze, Helene Lefebvre, Olga Overbury and Tiiu Poldma.

Note

1   See Brankaert et al., 2015.

References

Ahmed, S., Swaine, B., Milot, M., Gaudet, C., Poldma, T., Bartlett, G., Mazer, B., Le Dorze, G., Barbic, S., Rodriguez, A.M., Lefebvre, H., Archambault, P., Kairy, D., Fung, J., Labbé, D., Lamontagne, A., & Kehayia, E. (2017). Creating an inclusive mall environment with the Precede-Proceed model: A living lab case study. *Disability and Rehabilitation, 39*(21), 2198–2206.

Ardener, S. (1981). *Women and Space: Ground Rules and Social Maps*. New York, NY: St. Martin's Press.

Berger, P.L., & Luckmann, T. (1966). *The Social Construction of Reality*. New York, NY: Anchor Books.

Buchanan, R. (1995). Wicked problems in design thinking. In V. Margolin, & R. Buchanan (Eds.), *The Idea of Design* (pp. 3–20). Cambridge, MA: The MIT Press.

Carbonneau, H., Poldma, T., Miaux, S., Mazer, B., LeDorze, G., Gilbert, A., Hammouni, Z., & El-Khatib, A. (2017). The Urban Park Living Lab: Interdisciplinary research exploring universal design to create an accessible park for persons with disabilities. World Design Summit Congress 2017, Montreal, Canada.

Csikszentmihalyi, M. & Rochberg-Halton, E. (1981). *The Meaning of Things: Domestic Symbols and the Self*. Cambridge, UK: Cambridge University Press.

Dainton, B. (2001). *Time and Space*. McGill: Queen's University Press.

Friedman, K. (2003). Theory construction in design research: Criteria, approaches and methods. *Design Studies, 24*, 507–522.

Habermas, J. (1981). *The Theory of Communicative Action* (Vol. 2, translated by Thomas McCarthy). Boston, MA: Beacon Press.

Heron, J., & Reason, P. (2001). The practice of co-operative inquiry: Research 'with' rather than 'on' people. In P. Reason, & H. Bradbury (Eds.), *Handbook of Action Research: Participatory Inquiry and Practice*. London and Thousand Oaks, CA: Sage.

Lawton, M.P., Nahomow, L., & Teaff, J. (1974). Housing characteristics and the well-being of elderly tenants in federally assisted housing. *Journal of Gerontology, 30*(5), 601–607.

Lidwell, W., Holder, K., & Butler, J. (2003). *Universal Principles of Design*. Gloucester, MA: Rockwell Publishers.

Malnar, J.M., & Vodvarka, F. (1992). *The Interior Dimension: A Theoretical Approach to Enclosed Space*. New York, NY: Van Nostrand Reinhold, Inc.

Mann, T. (2013). Digging in: Attempting to Affix Place in Place. . In T. Vaikla-Poldma (Ed.), *Meanings of Designed Spaces*. New York, NY: Fairchild Publications.

Nelson, J. (1995, May). The influence of environmental factors in incidents of disruptive behaviour. *Journal of Gerontology Nursing, 21*(5), 19–24.

Oldenburg, R. (1989). *The Great Good Place*. New York, NY: Paragon Books.

Pallasmaa, J. (1990). *The Eyes of the Skin: Architecture and the Senses*. London: Academy Editions.

Poldma, T., Carbonneau, H., Miaux, S., Mazer, B., Le Dorze, G., Gilbert, A., Hammouni, Z., & El-Khatib, A. (2017, July). Chapter 26: Lived experiences and technology in the design of urban nature parks for accessibility. In M. Antona, & C. Stephanidis (Eds.), *Universal Access in Human-Computer Interaction: Design and Development Approaches and Methods. Human and Technological Environments. UAHCI 2017 11th International Conference, UAHCI 2017 Vancouver, BC Canada Proceedings, Part III, LNCS 10279* (pp. 308–319). Cham, Switzerland: Springer International Publishing AG 2017.

Poldma, T., Labbé, D., Bertin, S., De Grosbois, È., Mazurik, K., Desjardins, M., Barile, M., Herbane, H., & Artis, G. (2014). Understanding people's needs in a community public space: About accessibility and lived experience. *ALTER. European Journal of Disability Research, Journal européen de recherche sur le handicap, 8*(3), 206–216.

Poldma, T., & Wesolkowska, M. (2005). Globalization and Changing Conceptions of Time-Space: A Paradigm Shift for Interior Design? In-Form 5, University of Nebraska, Lincoln, Nebraska, USA, Volume 5: A Global View of Interior Design, pp. 54–61.

Poldma, T. (2006). Adapting the interior environment. *Interior and Sources.* July–August 2006, pp. 58–59.

Rose, G. (2001). *Visual methodologies.* London: Sage.

Spain, D. (1992). *Gendered Spaces.* Chapel Hill, NC and London: The University of North Caroline Press.

Swaine, B., Kehayia, E., Poldma, T., Longo, C., Ahmed, S., Archambault, P., Kairy, D., Fung. J., Lamontagne, A., Le Dorze, G., Lefebvre, H., & Overbury, O. (2014). Creating a rehabilitation living lab to optimize social participation and inclusion for persons with physical disabilities, *ALTER. European Journal of Disability Research, Journal européen de recherche sur le handicap, 8*(3), 151–157.

Swaine, B., Poldma, T., Labbé, D., Barile, M., Fichten, C., Havel, A., Kehayia, E., Mazer, B., McKinley, P., & Rochette, A. (2014). Exploring the facilitators and barriers to shopping mall use by persons with disabilities and strategies for improvements: Perspectives from persons with disabilities, rehabilitation professionals and shopkeepers. *ALTER. European Journal of Disability Research, Journal européen de recherche sur le handicap, 8*(3), 217–229.

UN-Habitat (2010). *State of the World's Cities 2010/2011 – Cities for All: Bridging the Urban Divide.* Available from: http://www.unhabitat.org

Vaikla-Poldma, T. (2003). *An Investigation of Learning and Teaching Processes in an Interior Design Class: An Interpretive and Contextual inquiry.* Unpublished doctoral thesis. Montreal: Author, p. 246.

Vaikla-Poldma, T. (2013). *Meanings of Designed Spaces.* New York, NY: Fairchild Publications.

Van Bel, D.T., IJesselsteijn, W.A., & de Kort, Y. (2008). Interpersonal connectedness: Conceptualization and direction for a measurement instrument. *Extended Abstracts Proceedings of the 2008 Conference on Human Factors in Computing Systems, CHI 2008,* Florence, Italy, 5–10 April 2008. Retrieved from research gate.net 27 May 2018.

Van Patter, G.K. & Jones, P. (2013). NextDesign geographies: Understanding 1,2,3,4: The rise of visual sensemaking. In T. Vaikla-Poldma (Ed.), *Meanings of Designed Spaces* (pp. 331–341). New York, NY: Fairchild Books, A Bloomsbury Imprint.

Wilwerding, J. (2013). A history of aesthetics and structuring of space. In T. Vaikla-Poldma (Ed.), *Meanings of Designed Spaces* (pp. 66–87). New York, NY: Fairchild Books, A Bloomsbury Imprint.

Zakus, J.D.L., & Lysack, C.L. (1998). Revisiting community participation. *Healthy Policy Plan, 13,* 1–12.

6 'Joyful journeys'

Putting wellbeing at the centre of future travel

Luke Harmer, Rebecca Cain and Artur Mausbach

Journeys are changing – how can future journeys be joyful?

Mobility has become essential for our modern way of life. It provides people with access to services, opportunities, entertainment and health. Mobility is traditionally associated with progress, contributing to, and a consequence of, economic development in industrialised countries (Andrews et al., 2006). Nevertheless, the environmental impacts of current mobility have been questioned and the industry is facing the challenge to shift its paradigms towards new and more sustainable mobility (Gott, 2009).

Ettema et al. (2013) demonstrate the connection between wellbeing and good access to mobility. However, the Office for National Statistics (2014) discovered that those who commute report lower levels of happiness and satisfaction, higher anxiety and a reduced feeling that their activities are meaningful than those who don't commute. The motivations behind mobility appear critical to wellbeing; people enjoy travelling it appears, but on their terms. Whilst mobility may foster economic prosperity and for some bring wellbeing (De Vos et al., 2015) efficient mobility provision is an increasing issue for the UK's future (Chartered Institution of Highways & Transportation, 2016).

Shifting work and leisure patterns, congestion, sustainability and autonomous vehicles pose significant challenges, changes and opportunities in transport. These future challenges and changes also present opportunities for the development of more inclusive vehicle designs (Alessandrini et al., 2015) thereby extending the impact of mobility wellbeing to a greater number of people. Advances in autonomous technologies could provide solutions for mobility for those with limited access to transport as shown by concepts demonstrated in the Gateway project (Greenwich Automated Transport Environment, 2018) shifting interaction from 'human to human' to 'human to machine'. However, the Connections project at the Royal College of Art (RCA) with rural communities in Ireland (Kunur & Gheerawo, 2007) found that access to transport is not the only mobility aspiration respondents have for their transport, and that fears of social isolation and loss of privacy are also present as mobility changes occur. Fagnant and Kockelman (2015) discuss these social concerns in relation to autonomous vehicles and the additional risk of technology encouraging urban sprawl. Meyer et al. (2017) and Guerra (2016) suggest autonomy will reduce the viability of public transport for all but the most highly trafficked areas and Currie (2018) argues future predictions of autonomy are already being used as a rationale for limiting public transport spending.

A new mobility paradigm is therefore needed, one that builds with greater empathy and understanding of design for wellbeing, to ensure that the technological opportunity of mobility is met with solutions that are increasingly human–centred, inclusive and 'joyful'.

The 'joyful journey', is defined in this chapter as not only a journey that is enjoyable, bringing pleasure or happiness, but one that is imbued with meaning and that might be described as such in spite of difficulty or hardship faced in completing a journey.

Advances in computing, navigation and autonomy are creating a technology push (Di Stefano et al., 2012) with the social benefits of future transport solutions redolent to those mooted for the online social network revolution. As with autonomy, social media promised increased social connectivity. However, we are beginning to understand some of the unintended consequences that social media is having, for example social exclusion and challenges to mental wellbeing (Baccarella et al., 2018). The potential unintended consequences of autonomous mobility in this context are therefore worthy of exploration. For example, in rural areas where the connections between the social and transport are complex and interwoven, autonomy could improve transport accessibility but degrade wellbeing by fostering social exclusion.

Designing for positive experiences requires user involvement (Desmet & Pohlmeyer, 2013). In the joyful journeys research we have begun by identifying and understanding the positive attributes of current rural journeys so that the most appropriate features can be built into new journeys. For current journeys, both those that are public and private, the research aim is to understand what makes a journey joyful and subsequently identify the tools required to design meaningful future mobility experiences.

In this chapter we discuss historical perspectives of enjoyable journeys and the exploratory studies undertaken with travellers to understand where joyful journeys occur now and how they might be undertaken in the future. Finally, we offer reflections on how these studies might be incorporated into future solutions and designs that put subjective wellbeing (SWB) at the centre of travel.

Joyful journeys in leisure and commuting

Mobility is freedom. Travel freedom is characterised by the ease of unrestricted, affordable movement as we wish. Mobility is a key indicator of contemporary notions of subjective wellbeing and along with the resultant mobility, the physicality of travelling is part of objective and subjective notions of wellbeing. However, mobility wellbeing doesn't have to be characterised by predictable, uneventful and benign physical transport. Whether comfortable or uncomfortable, the physicality of travel is rooted in historical notions of movement. A journey can be either a painfully necessary return home, such as in Homer's *Odyssey* (Knox & Fagles, 1990); rewarding, as in the German *Wanderjahre* apprenticeships (Ericson, 1984); or ill-fated, as in the individualistic quest in *Don Quixote* (Watt, 1997). The travel stories told often incorporate some of these elements (Moscardo, 2010), stressing the purpose to which the mobility itself created such adventure and misadventure.

Mobility wellbeing is a much richer concept than simply efficient transportation. In describing designing for experiences that promote wellbeing, six factors can be applied to SWB and mobility: Autonomy (personal independence), Stimulation, Competence, Relatedness, Popularity and Security. From these definitions offered by Hassenzahl et al. (2013), these last four factors have a direct social component. Transport and mobility (especially public) are rich sources of social interactions; wanted or unwanted, planned or unplanned.

The grand tour, once a wealthy rite of passage, has transformed into a universal 'right' of tourism (Towner, 1985). The experience of the journey, however, has remained an integral part of a holiday throughout the expansion of tourism. These expectations, initially popularised by Thomas Cook (Brendon, 1991) of an enjoyable, managed experience of travel, as important as the destination, are still prevalent today. The distinction between leisure and commuting travel was explored by Stradling et al. (2007), who discovered that commuting respondents were concerned with the functional convenience rather than the emotional aspects of their journeys. For leisure journeys, however, equal emphasis was placed on the functional and emotive.

The distinction of joyful journeys as ones undertaken for leisure set against the drudgery of commuting necessity is not one shared universally. Certeau (1984) describes walking in the city in voyeuristic terms and travel in a railway carriage as an 'incarceration vacation' creating a 'melancholy pleasure' that comes from the forced separation of the window between the external and the internal. A space in which thoughts, memories and dreams might flourish as your gaze looks out through 'glass and iron'. These interstitial experiences appear increasingly at risk as we become gadget-enthralled, connected and constantly entertained (Gardner, 2018).

The commute is not without emotion. Commuting can be a means of 'catharsis from the pressures and frustrations of everyday life' (Freedman, 2002) and a buffer between work and home. There are those who enjoy their commute: as preparation, relaxation, time available to work, or explicitly not to work, an opportunity for exercise and for sociability (Lorenz, 2018). Guell et al. (2012) reported that SWB in commuting is linked to modal choice. They reported that enjoyable commuting journeys aren't typically to be had whilst driving but by those who reported being more aware of their surroundings because they cycled or walked. Those respondents that used the park-and-ride also found some 'welcome time out'. Amongst all those that enjoyed their commute, they took note of the natural world and experienced these sensual joys because their transport choice enabled them to do so. Commuting is not just about functionally travelling between home and work, it can enrich the experiences of the spaces we inhabit, becoming psychogeography (Richardson, 2015) or the commuter as *flâneur* (Tester, 2014).

Guell et al. (2012) also discovered that switching from car driving to active travel improved a commuter's wellbeing and that whilst wellbeing increased with travel time for walkers, it decreased for drivers. Commuting can quickly become frustrating if control is lost, typified as the driver experiencing congestion, where the scenery remains unchanged or it is not possible to enjoy or make use of the time travelling.

SWB in mobility concerns more than just promoting a change in transport modes. Logistical and environmental factors often play a significant part in creating real or perceived poor-quality mobility experiences, but how travellers behave in relation to these experiences is complex (Dickinson & Dickinson, 2006). Barriers to creating joyful journeys, such as Infrastructure, punctuality, congestion, low quality, unsavoury social interactions, fear and time pressures, deter many from public transport and direct them to the perceived independence and security of the personal vehicle.

Choreography of mobility

'Joyful journeys' is a stage of the Choreography of mobility research project being carried out by the RCA and Loughborough University School of Design and Creative Arts. The Choreography of mobility project is an attempt to rethink how we design our journeys. It explores the concept of mobility wellbeing in the transition from materiality to immateriality, the transition from physical products to services of future mobility designs. The project explores the importance of social empathy to wellbeing and proposes to design mobility as a collective subject, observing the dynamics and interactions between people, vehicles, internalities and externalities, as part of a choreography.

Exploring methods to investigate joyful journeys

Experiencing joyful journeys and mobility wellbeing has a direct link to established research in SWB. Until recent developments in mobile technology the majority of SWB travel studies were captured through surveys and interviews undertaken after completing a journey. Friman et al. (2018) highlight the gaps in SWB transport research, and the Joyful journeys project seeks to explore these gaps, particularly the contributions of the physical vehicle and the functional nature of mobility, which are layered with meaning, and contribute to wellbeing. Through investigating the extremes and contrasting joyful and joyless travel, urban and rural, old and young, commuting and leisure, it seeks to expose the differing perceptions about key mobility aspects between age groups, countryside and city.

Our research employed a mix of contextual methods (Johnson & Onwuegbuzie, 2004) as a means of discovering the components that make up current joyful journeys in the context of SWB. An exploratory user-centred approach to understanding the whole journey experience was used, undertaking the following stages to explore qualitatively how those travelling express wellbeing about their journeys:

1. **Journey shadowing and interviews**. Four semi-structured interviews with older people exploring how interviewees express their experiences during their journeys.
2. **Current and future journey mapping and rating**. Thirty-seven respondents at the London Design Festival and a workshop with eight participants at Loughborough University School of Design and Creative Arts.

Journey shadowing and interviews

The research began by seeking out joyful journeys that were part of everyday mobility but outside the requirements of commuting. At this first stage the research began by engaging with those in a position to be able to choose or 'choreograph' the journeys they make, creating journeys that are intended to be pleasurable (Figure 6.1). Retired or semi-retired older age groups in a rural context were selected to investigate how the most joyful journeys might be choreographed. These investigations were with people in a position to choose how they travelled in an environment that was pleasant and aspirational, all outside the purposes of commuting: the drive, the lift, the bus journey and the cycle ride.

Four journey shadows and interviews took place in rural North Norfolk, making use of researcher familiarity with the area. Journey shadowing and semi-structured interviews were selected to provide deep qualitative data, particularly useful when investigating the intangible elements of services (Penin, 2018). These methods allowed for the gathering of insights on general behaviour, actions and social interactions, rather than collecting specific information from individuals.

The use of video and semi-structured interviews (Kallio et al., 2016) was chosen as a means of engaging respondents in their environment during the activity, allowing participants to add context and inspiration to their responses.

Key questions and responses are shown in Table 6.1, covering observations from the journey, current experiences and thoughts about the future, capturing people's perceptions, emotions and aspirations.

Figure 6.1 Giving a lift – Journey shadowing and interview 1.

Identified themes from journey shadowing and interviews

All the interviewees were drivers and owners of cars but their relationship to their car in each instance was subtly different. It became apparent that with all the interviewees that owning a car in a rural environment created the confidence to choose other transport modes. The two driving interviews conducted illustrated how the car met social and logistical needs – car ownership compensating for the sometimes-sporadic nature of public transport in rural areas.

> I love driving and it's lovely to take people. One of the things I like to be is useful, it's one of the better parts of my life. I'm getting old. I can't do much, but one of the things I can do is get in a car and drive.
>
> (Interviewee 1)

The responses in Table 6.1 have been selected from the main themes of the semi-structured interviews.

Discussion of journey shadowing and interviews

For all the interviewees, as their need to commute has diminished, the psychosocial in mobility wellbeing came to the fore. Interview 1 (where the purpose of driving was to provide a lift) perhaps gives the best indication of how SWB can be promoted in mobility. Comparing the actions of the lift provider onto the six factors presented by Hassenzahl et al. (2013) suggests that providing lifts can create not only the social benefits necessary for SWB but the competence and stimulation as a car driver. Musselwhite (2018) reports that for older people the car can be a critical part of maintaining wellbeing satisfying utility, psychosocial and aesthetic needs and that 'transport provision beyond the

Table 6.1 Comparison of responses to journey shadowing pilot

Transport mode	1. Lift	2. Car	3. Bus	4. Cycle
Approximate distance	2 miles	9 miles	42 miles	11 miles
Journey rationale	Giving a less physically able person a lift to church	Hair appointment	Leisure trip to city to visit Castle Museum	Trip to pub
What do you most enjoy about your journeys?	'I love driving and it's lovely to take people.'	'The independence … I can listen to music and can do errands on the way.'	'… for a day out, time is irrelevant to us and also its enjoyment to sit back and relax and not think about the traffic.'	'I cycle weekly for the exercise but most enjoy pub crawl cycle trips with friends.'
What was the most memorable, joyful journey of this type?	'I used to do was to drive to Scotland … It's just the most wonderful place to go and awe-inspiring in so many ways. Scenery and good companionship.'	'We went to Blakeney and Cley … and that was really lovely … we were with friends so we were chattering away as we went.'	'Being stuck on a bus that could only do 35 mph …'	'Cycling with friends in north west Norfolk earlier in the year – when there was no traffic …'
What would you do if you could no longer travel this way?	'I'd take the bus.'	'I might take taxis but I'd also try to get lifts with friends, I'd hate it having to ask … I'm so used to being independent …'	'If I'd still able to drive I'd take the car.'	'… I don't know, it would take away something from my life …'
What music would you choose to describe your journey?	Beethoven No. 6 *Pastoral Symphony*	A Mozart symphony – calm and peaceful.	Vaughan Williams: *The Lark Ascending*	Vaughan Williams: *The Lark Ascending*
How will your journey be done in 50 years' time?	'I always think of having an aeroplane attachment …'	'… we've always said people will be flying to work in helicopters, but I don't know, it's hard to imagine.'	'Would hope there is still public transport … in 50 years' time … it might be all electric.'	'… maybe we will have autonomous bikes … but human beings will still want to do their own thing.'

car neglects psychosocial needs of mobility and sporadically meets practical and aesthetic needs depending upon the wider social context' (p. 235).

After the introduction of bus passes in England for older people in 2008, bus travel, particularly in rural communities, has taken on a richer purpose and meaning according to Andrews et al. (2012). Outside the requirements of the commute and without the pressure of time the bus is a social entity for many older users. These attributes suit the nature of the rural bus; its progress is often considerably slower than the car and its use requires planning and preparedness only marginally different in practice than the earliest omnibus.

Rural cycling too now exists increasingly as a leisure and social activity than a functional one, suiting the lifestyles of those able to choreograph their journeys.

All the interviewees reported a social aspect to their joyful journeys, but this social element did not come to the fore when they described how they imagined future transport.

Current and future journey mapping and rating

Journey shadow video as provocation

Design provocations are used to start a discussion and engage people's imagination to produce their own responses. To explore what future SWB might be like a provocation piece for the London Design Festival used the video of the first journey shadow and interview. Through editing and augmentation with illustrations, festival attendees were encouraged to explore their current journeys and how they would like to choreograph their future journeys (see Figures 6.2 and 6.3). This video explores a journey in the countryside, where people independently organise lifts to the local church. The interview shows surprising social aspects of mobility and the significance of experiences of driving and sharing. At the same time, it presents a view about the comfort provided by technology and innovation, from handle-start to flying cars. The attention to these issues is enhanced by the addition of drawn animated cartoon inserts to the video. The casual drawings style adopted aims to connect to the audience and invite them to also make drawings in response to the video.

Responses to provocation

The process was trialled as part of the Design Festival and validated as part of the workshop at Loughborough Design School as described later in this chapter. Attendees at the festival were asked to draw a cognitive map (Golledge, 1999) of how they see their current

Figure 6.2 Still from video provocation.

Drawing by Luka Kille-Speckter.

Figure 6.3 Video provocation installation at the 2018 London Design Festival.

and future joyful journeys by writing and drawing on three different cards, which presented the following questions:

- Your current journey card: (1) How do you normally travel? How far? (2) Please draw a map of one of your typical journey's (include landmarks). (3) if your journey was a piece of music, what would it be?
- Your joyful journey card: (1) What was your most joyful journey? (2) Please, can you draw what this joyful journey looks like? (3) If this joyful journey was a piece of music, what would it be?
- Your future journey card: (1) What has changed the most in your journeys in the past years? (2) Can you draw and/or write how people will undertake your joyful journey in 50 years' time?

During the four days of the exhibition, 37 response cards were completed. The responses showed that the provocation was an effective method to engage the public to draw, write and also talk about their mobility experiences. The outcomes were also used to identify which aspects of a Choreography of mobility were mentioned and remembered by the attendees.

It was observed that the current journey maps created by the respondents were inform-ative, including landmarks, but less emotional. The responses to joyful journeys were more complex, with drawing including references to landscape, weather, wind, trees, other vehi-cles and animals. The social interaction with family and friends were also found in joyful journeys. On the future journey cards, respondents referenced flying vehicles, but had greater difficulty imagining future journeys.

The responses indicated that meaningful experiences are more complex than the func-tional view of mobility: elements of companionship, music and environment are essential to the joyful journey experience. The responses suggest that attempts to 'choreograph' journeys could be more effective in promoting wellbeing than those based on improving the efficiency of mobility.

Workshop at Loughborough Design School

To further validate the methodology the exercise was repeated with eight younger people, PhD students, as part of a formal workshop at Loughborough University. The responses were intended to facilitate the beginnings of journey choreography. The participants were asked to watch the video provocation and then asked (without conferring) to create visual descriptions of their current, joyful and future journeys. They were then asked to rate these using a radar diagram with the key factors attributed to SWB as identified by Hassenzahl et al. (2013). The definitions of these factors were made available and the visual responses were used to promote group discussions. (See Figure 6.4.)

Discussion of observations from research, SWB, modal choice and future journeys

The participants of the workshop reported the most pleasurable current journeys were walking or cycling, and they featured a connectedness to the environment as a positive fac-tor. By contrast their joyful journeys were often imbued with meaning – the expectation of meeting with a loved one rather than just the pleasure of the journey itself. The radar ratings revealed overall that regular journeys undertaken by cycle or foot scored almost as highly as those described as joyful journeys. Future journeys, however, were generally seen

Figure 6.4 Example of participants' response in the video provocation workshop.

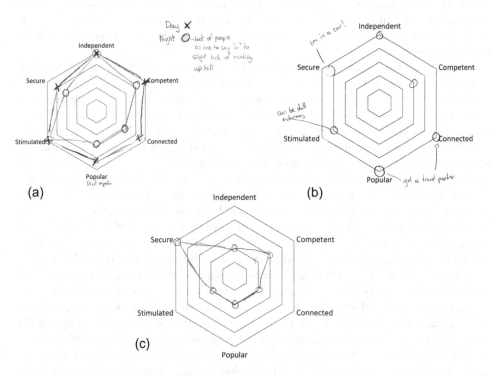

Figure 6.5 A workshop respondent's radar maps of wellbeing factors for current cycling journey (a), joyful car journey (b) and future autonomous vehicle journey (c).

as more negative than their contemporary counterparts. Future journey maps included travel by autonomous vehicles and respondents reported lower perceived levels of connectedness and popularity but increased security. Youthful predictions of future travel were overall focused on autonomous vehicles and appeared less adventurous than those from older people in the journey shadow interviews.

Whilst pop and rock music were selected as soundtracks for current journeys, future journeys were described mostly through jazz music. (See Figure 6.5.)

Investigating future joyful journeys

As vehicles become more refined, they can become increasingly like other transport and stationary environments we experience. The budget bus, train and aeroplane ride are arguably similar to the waiting lounges that often precede them. In these similar environments, passengers rely increasingly on the electronic, virtual and augmented for security, information and entertainment. For example, online journey planning is now considered a normal part of the mobility of many. Both in the public and private transport domain, connected devices now form part of the information and entertainment landscape of journeys – for example, the high level of use in the UK of Smartphones for navigation (Statista, 2017).

Aesthetic properties in transport have been traditionally associated with the vehicle itself, the physicality of the object creating emotive resonance (Bayley, 2012). The potential transition to intelligent and autonomous vehicles and the muted 'mobility as a service'

(Smith et al., 2018) could extend the scope of potential emotive resonance to digital components and graphic representations of movement. This scope extends from simple interfaces of navigation systems, which might include avatars, to interaction with complex artificial intelligence.

Modal choice for regular journeys is based to a large degree on practical and financial constraints; *mobility as function*. This focus, with an emphasis on controlling the natural environment and the utilitarian corresponds to Maslow's first two levels of the hierarchy of human needs: physiological and safety needs. Transport has expanded to include social needs, belongingness, love needs, cognitive needs and aesthetic needs. As the remit of mobility has expanded through history the objects that transport us have become imbued with more complex, subjective meaning: *mobility as beauty*.

However, the physicality of transport is being eroded by the virtual experience. Nevertheless, it is possible to design with these new mobility components and add in values that promote SWB, to create more joyful and beautiful mobility experiences that, in turn, could encourage wellbeing. Design has the capacity to facilitate the complete joyful journey, including, but venturing beyond, the transporting object, in order to avoid the potential monotony, exclusion and resulting loss of SWB that automation could bring.

The promises of future autonomous vehicles, reduced cost, increased efficiency and ease of use, makes it probable that increased amounts of time will be spent travelling. The technology that will enable our future travel may make our vehicles more sterile and foster the melancholy that Certeau describes occurring in the isolation and confines of the railway carriage. In this future transport of the amalgamated personal and public, travel frustration may increase, as on occasion the vehicles inevitably slow or stop. It is possible these situations may become more frustrating than current congestion if perceived personal control is no longer possible.

More time spent travelling, virtually connected but physically alone, could mean a lonely autonomous future. Humans are of course social, emotive physical beings. As commuters become increasingly disconnected from those around them, they may not easily be able to share their frustrations. A challenge for nurturing mobility wellbeing in future journeys is to allow and encourage social interactions and experiences of the natural world and its sensual joys; safe and secure regular travel that can be less cossetted and allow for the stimulation and relatedness of pleasant sights, sounds and smells. These factors question the form and function of the autonomous vehicle and how these desirable experiences might translate into future designs that will promote wellbeing.

Conclusions and implications for designers

The social import of 'Joyful journeys' has become apparent through this explorative research. For both young and old, many of the joyful journeys involved engaging with others and with the environment. They were 'choreographed' in the sense that mode travel time, vehicle, musical accompaniment, distractions and company were chosen. The selected soundtrack of these journeys reflected both the landscape and the attitude of their aspirational journeys. These individual journeys are a reminder of individual actions and a contrast to how we might see urban travel where logistics and congestion can dictate possibilities.

The provocation video shows how the act of driving can be treasured, as well as creating empowerment for both the driver and the driven. When designing future mobility, in particular SWB in mobility, a cognisant effort is required to design for all of Hassenzahl's

(2013) six factors linked to wellbeing. Future vehicle autonomy, whilst making possible transport for those who are currently excluded, also risks creating new types of social exclusion. For example, a future of driverless pods may make a local bus service and the lift-giving car driver redundant – removing an important social aspect of a rural community. A joyful journey is facilitated by the vehicle and its design, not as might be the case for the autonomous vehicle, dictated by it. However, autonomy also creates a potential to increase social inclusion as well as creating opportunities for others to assist those who are less able to undertake these journeys. Autonomy creates opportunities to control our journeys more, and to choreograph the elements that make up the experience. Current travel creates limits to distractions, which may result in uncommunicated but wanted time away from usual day to day pressures. Whilst driving we may be limited (legally) to audio distraction, the potential for other distractions with autonomy however, becomes an almost limitless continuation of our other activities, risking further social 'siloing' or exclusion.

This 'Joyful journeys' project suggests some key areas that can assist designers and planners in considering future mobility. Transport is only one component of mobility. The social component of unintended or intended interactions occurring both inside and outside social or family groups appears to be a key component of joyful journeys. Using journey shadowing and semi-structured interviews to determine the 'joyful' is a first step in choreographing and allowing space for these elements in new modes and design solutions. Music, cognitive maps and rating wellbeing elements of journeys could also provide insight into SWB factors. Through considering not just the functional, but the joyful journey, new types of differential, social and meaningful journey experiences can be choreographed and, in so doing, some of the potential potholes of vehicle autonomy can be avoided.

References

Alessandrini, A., Campagna, A., Delle Site, P., Filippi, F., & Persia, L. (2015). Automated vehicles and the rethinking of mobility and cities. *Transportation Research Procedia, 5*, 145–160.

Andrews, D., Nieuwenhuis, P., & Ewing, P.D. (2007). Living systems, 'total design' and the evolution of the automobile: The significance and application of holistic design methods in automotive design, manufacture and operation. *Design and Information in Biology from Molecules to Systems*. WIT Press, 13, 381–446.

Andrews, G., Parkhurst, G., Susilo, Y.O., & Shaw, J. (2012). The grey escape: Investigating older people's use of the free bus pass. *Transportation Planning and Technology, 35*, 3–15.

Baccarella, C.V., Wagner, T.F., Kietzmann, J.H., & McCarthy, I.P. (2018). Social media? It's serious! Understanding the dark side of social media. *European Management Journal, 36*, 431–438.

Bayley, S. (2012). *Cars: Freedom, Style, Sex, Power, Motion, Colour, Everything.* UK: Hachette.

Brendon, P. (1991). Thomas Cook: *150 Years of Popular Tourism.* London: Secker (Martin) & Warburg Ltd.

de Certeau, M. (1984). *The Practice of Everyday Life.* Berkeley, CA: University of California Press.

Chartered Institution of Highways & Transportation (2016). *A Transport Journey to a Healthier Life: A Discussion Paper on How Transport Policy and Procedure Can Contribute to the Health and Wellbeing Agenda.* London: Chartered Institution of Highways & Transportation.

Currie, G. (2018). Lies, damned lies, AVs, shared mobility, and urban transit futures. *Journal of Public Transportation, 21*, 3.

De Vos, J., Schwanen, T., Van Acker, V., & Witlox, F. (2015). How satisfying is the scale for travel satisfaction? *Transportation Research Part F: Traffic Psychology and Behaviour, 29*, 121–130.

Desmet, P.M.A., & Pohlmeyer, A.E. (2013). Positive design: An introduction to design for subjective wellbeing. *International Journal of Design, 7*(3), 5–19.

Di Stefano, G., Gambardella, A., & Verona, G. (2012). Technology push and demand pull perspectives in innovation studies: Current findings and future research directions. *Research Policy, 41,* 1283–1295.

Dickinson, J.E., & Dickinson, J.A. (2006). Local transport and social representations: Challenging the assumptions for sustainable tourism. *Journal of Sustainable Tourism, 14,* 192–208.

Ericson, K. (1984). The Wanderjahre: New lessons from an old way of learning. *Change: The Magazine of Higher Learning, 16,* 42–46.

Ettema, D., Gärling, T., Olsson, L.E., Friman, M., & Moerdijk, S. (2013). The road to happiness: Measuring Dutch car drivers' satisfaction with travel. *Transport Policy, 27,* 171–178.

Fagnant, D.J., & Kockelman, K. (2015). Preparing a nation for autonomous vehicles: Opportunities, barriers and policy recommendations. *Transportation Research Part A: Policy and Practice, 77,* 167–181.

Freedman, A. (2002). Commuting gazes: Schoolgirls, salarymen, and electric trains in Tokyo. *The Journal of Transport History, 23,* 23–36.

Friman, M., Ettema, D., & Olsson, L.E. (2018). Travel and wellbeing: future prospects. In *Quality of Life and Daily Travel* (pp. 255–265). Cham, Switzerland: Springer.

Gardner, C. (2018). iPhone. In L. Schofield (Ed.), *The Future Starts Here* (pp. 28–34). London: V&A Publishing.

Golledge, R.G. (1999). *Wayfinding Behavior: Cognitive Mapping and Other Spatial Processes.* Baltimore, MD: Johns Hopkins University Press.

Gott, P. (2009). *Is Mobility As We Know It Sustainable?* SAE Technical Paper. SAE International.

Greenwich Automated Transport Environment (2018). *This is Just the Beginning: Positioning the UK at the Forefront of Automated Mobility.* Greenwich: Greenwich Automated Transport Environment Project.

Guell, C., Panter, J., Jones, N.R., & Ogilvie, D. (2012). Towards a differentiated understanding of active travel behaviour: Using social theory to explore everyday commuting. *Social Science & Medicine, 75,* 233–239.

Guerra, E. (2016). Planning for cars that drive themselves: Metropolitan Planning Organizations, regional transportation plans, and autonomous vehicles. *Journal of Planning Education and Research, 36,* 210–224.

Hassenzahl, M., Eckoldt, K., Diefenbach, S., Laschke, M., Len, E., & Kim, J. (2013). Designing moments of meaning and pleasure. Experience design and happiness. *International Journal of Design, 7,* 21–31.

Johnson, R.B., & Onwuegbuzie, A.J. (2004). Mixed methods research: A research paradigm whose time has come. *Educational Researcher, 33,* 14–26.

Kallio, H., Pietilä, A., Johnson, M., & Kangasniemi, M. (2016). Systematic methodological review: Developing a framework for a qualitative semi-structured interview guide. *Journal of Advanced Nursing, 72,* 2954–2965.

Knox, B., & Fagles, R. (1990). Homer, The Iliad (Trans. Robert Fagles). New York, NY: Penguin.

Kunur, M., & Gheerawo, R. (2007). *Connections-Mobility, Ageing and Independent Living.* London: The Helen Hamlyn Research Centre.

Lorenz, O. (2018). Does commuting matter to subjective well-being? *Journal of Transport Geography, 66,* 180–199.

Meyer, J., Becker, H., Bösch, P.M., & Axhausen, K.W. (2017). Autonomous vehicles: The next jump in accessibilities? *Research in Transportation Economics, 62,* 80–91.

Moscardo, G. (2010). The shaping of tourist experience: the importance of stories and themes. In Morgan, M., Lugosi, P. & Ritchie, J. (Eds.), *The Tourism and Leisure Experience: Consumer and Managerial Perspectives.* Aspects of Tourism, pp. 43–58. Buffalo, NY: Channel View Publications.

Musselwhite, C. (2018). Mobility in Later Life and Wellbeing. In *Quality of Life and Daily Travel* (pp. 235–251). Cham, Switzerland: Springer.

Office for National Statistics, . (2014). Measuring National Well-being, Commuting and Personal Well-being. https://webarchive.nationalarchives.gov.uk/20160105232639/; http://www.ons.gov.uk/ons/rel/wellbeing/measuring-national-well-being/commuting-and-personal-well-being--2014/index.html.

Penin, L. (2018). *An Introduction to Service Design: Designing the Invisible.* New York, NY: Bloomsbury Publishing.

Richardson, T. (2015). *Walking Inside Out: Contemporary British Psychogeography.* Washington, DC: Rowman & Littlefield International.

Smith, G., Sochor, J., & Karlsson, I.C.M. (2018). Mobility as a service: Development scenarios and implications for public transport. *Research in Transportation Economics, 69,* 592–599.

Statista. (2017). Share of navigation application use on smartphones in the United Kingdom (UK) in 2017 [Graph]. In *Statista.* Retrieved March 09, 2019, from https://www.statista.com/statistics/717382/use-of-smartphone-navigation-applications-in-the-uk/

Stradling, S.G., Anable, J., & Carreno, M. (2007). Performance, importance and user disgruntlement: A six-step method for measuring satisfaction with travel modes. *Transportation Research Part A: Policy and Practice, 41,* 98–106.

Tester, K. (2014). *The Flaneur (RLE Social Theory).* London: Routledge.

Towner, J. (1985). The grand tour: A key phase in the history of tourism. *Annals of Tourism Research, 12,* 297–333.

Watt, I. (1997). *Myths of Modern Individualism: Faust, Don Quixote, Don Juan, Robinson Crusoe.* Cambridge: Cambridge University Press.

7 Healthy eating and behaviour change

Geke Ludden and Sander Hermsen

Introduction

Every day, we encounter a broad range of information about what food to eat ('eat this butter for improved heart functioning', 'eat five portions of fruit and vegetables every day') and about what not to eat ('drink less sugary drinks'). These messages are supported by a growing body of knowledge about nutrients and their effect on our health. However, despite the increase in available knowledge about our food and how it may influence our health, there is an ongoing rise in lifestyle-related diseases directly associated with our food intake.

Worldwide obesity has nearly tripled since 1975 (WHO, 2017) and the number of people affected by type II diabetes and cardiovascular diseases is rising steadily (Lee et al., 2012). Statistics from countries such as the UK and the US (Bates et al., 2014; Stark Casagrande et al., 2007) tell us that only a small proportion of people meet general dietary recommendations (consuming little saturated fat, added sugars and salt and eating enough fruit and vegetables). Eventually, these unhealthy nutrition patterns will negatively affect the wellbeing of many people and lead to an ever-increasing demand for health care, with an associated increase in cost. Healthy nutrition, therefore, is key to people's health and vitality. This chapter makes a contribution to *Design for Wellbeing* that focuses on how to support people in changing their eating behaviour in order to improve their wellbeing.

In recent years, efforts to raise people's awareness of the importance of living a healthier life as well as to support healthier food intake have widened from traditional information campaigns to monitoring and coaching systems, changes to the public environment and the design of other artefacts for healthy eating (Ludden, 2017; see also Ludden & Hekkert [2014] for a more thorough categorisation). In this chapter, we will explain why many efforts that aim to stimulate healthy eating have limited or even adverse effects on changing people's eating behaviour. We do so by adopting four views that are relevant to design. For each view, we will discuss relevant literature and the role that design has played and could play when adopting that particular view. Finally, we discuss what bringing the different views together might mean for the future of how to design for healthy eating.

Current efforts to design for healthy eating behaviour

Similar to what Clark (2010) has described as the 'agency divide', all efforts to design products and services that support people to adopt healthier eating behaviour can be placed on a continuum with purely informative, non-directive designs targeted at individuals on the one end, and interventions in the public environment that remove all freedom of choice on the other end. We will use this continuum to provide an overview of current design for healthy eating behaviour. A similar categorisation was made for design for behaviour change approaches by Niedderer, Clune & Ludden (2017).

One end of the continuum consists mostly of designs that communicate a norm or try to increase our knowledge. We are probably all familiar with traditional campaigns raising awareness of the importance of eating fruit and vegetables on television, in schools or in the public domain – these include '2 Fruit 'n' 5 Veg Every Day' in Australia, see Dixon et al. (1998), and '5 a day for Better Health' in the US, see Kramish Campbell et al. (1999). Valuable initiatives to support people who have decided they want to change their eating behaviour – or at least who want to have better insight in what they are eating on a daily basis – are web-based eating diaries and mobile applications such as the Healthy Weight Assistant and Lifesum (see Figures 7.1a and 7.1b).

The Healthy Weight Assistant (Kelders et al., 2011) is an online tool aimed at adults with a healthy weight or who are slightly overweight. It provides users with healthy recipes, provides the opportunity to keep a nutrition diary and supports planning healthy eating goals. An evaluation of this tool (ibid.) shows users were mainly female and highly educated, which is a recurring pattern in eating behaviour interventions: they typically tend to reach only high-socioeconomic status audiences, whereas the problems are more serious among low status groups, at least in industrialised countries (Wang & Lim, 2012). Moreover, adherence to this intervention was as low as 3 per cent; low adherence is another recurring phenomenon in eating behaviour interventions.

The other end of the continuum consists of efforts to influence eating behaviour in the public environment, ranging from healthier (school and business) canteens to attempts at regulating the number of fast-food outlets in inner city areas. Like mass media campaigns, such interventions can potentially reach large groups of people, simply because they can be placed in environments where many people encounter them, but unlike these campaigns, these interventions generally limit the freedom of choice people have.

(a)

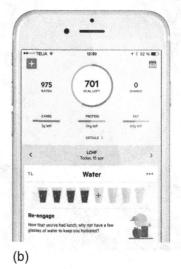

(b)

Figure 7.1 (a) Healthy Weight Assistant (left); and (b) Lifesum (right).

Their potential efficacy is large because, in general, environments influence our behaviour more than our intentions or attitudes (Marteau, 2018). Changing the availability and pricing to promote fruit and salad purchases in cafeterias may be seen as an example of a true environmental intervention. One such intervention (Jefferey et al., 1994) consisted of doubling the number of fruit choices, increasing salad ingredient selection by three and reducing the price of salad and fruit by 50 per cent, with very positive results; both fruit and salad purchases increased markedly. When the interventions were removed, fruit and salad purchases dropped again to remain slightly above baseline. Hanks and colleagues (2012) came up with another example of an environmental intervention, following the strategy of making healthy choices more convenient relative to less healthy choices by arranging one of two lunch lines in a cafeteria as a convenience line that only displayed healthier food and beverage options. They found that as a result of their intervention sales of healthier foods increased and that of unhealthier options decreased.

There have as yet been only a few 'true' environmental interventions for healthy eating. Most interventions involve some form of self-management. The ETE-plate by Annet Bruil, for instance, uses coloured lines to provide eaters with guidance of preferred portion sizes for balanced meals. The plate has sections for proteins, vegetables and starch-based food, and is designed to accommodate both European and South-East Asian cuisines. A recent study among hospital staff in Singapore showed that, even after six months, users of the plate ate more vegetables and fewer carbohydrates than a control group who did not use the plate (De Korne et al., 2017). The design of the MindFull plate and bowl (Andereae, 2017, see Figure 7.2) follows a different approach following from the idea that how full we feel depends more on how much we think we have eaten than on the actual

Figure 7.2 The MindFull soup bowl seems bigger than it actually is. This illusion is meant to trick people into feeling fuller than they actually are.

amount of food consumed. Mindful exploits errors in sensory perception to influence people into feeling full.

Although diverse and plentiful, many interventions for healthier eating tend to lack effect; a fact that is partly hidden by publication bias: unsuccessful interventions more often than not end up in the proverbial filing drawer (but see, e.g., Dassen et al., 2017, on an ineffective gamified training for overweight individuals, or Lloyd et al., 2018, on a failed lifestyle programme to prevent obesity in UK primary school children). This shows that changing eating behaviour is complex and difficult. In many cases, merely suggesting that we should change our eating behaviour (think of, for example, a school council that suggests to parents that they should prepare healthier food for their children), can cause quite some resistance. One reason for this resistance is the strength of cultural and emotional connotations of eating. Food is connected to social contexts, cultural values and identities that we are reluctant to let go of or change in any way.

The next sections will introduce four views on why the effects of current designed interventions to changing people's eating behaviour are limited: (1) the knowledge view, (2) the automaticity view, (3) the social/cultural view and (4) the engagement view. From our analysis of how these different views can explain the limited effects of current interventions, we will distil design directions for more effective designs.

(1) The knowledge view: Too much focus on knowledge of healthy eating

The majority of designed artefacts aimed at healthier nutrition consist of designs that inform us about what, when and how much we eat or should eat. This approach seems logical, considering the lack of knowledge some people seem to have about these subjects and the increasing knowledge that is available about how our nutrition affects our health.

Many designers and health professionals therefore consider knowledge to be the key issue for healthy eating and see teaching nutritional facts as the preferred strategy for behavioural change designs. This is most apparent when we look at designs aimed at children, such as the Alien Health Game (Johnson-Glenberg & Hekler, 2013), in which children make food choices. The (correct) healthier choices improve the alertness and health state of an alien avatar. Although the game evidently led to a greater knowledge about healthy nutrition in the participants, this approach has some problematic aspects that illustrate why, generally, an approach aimed at increased knowledge has only limited success.

First, while it seems obvious to start teaching about nutrition at a young age, we should not overestimate how much influence children have over their diets. Parents and – in many cultures – schools and daycare centres determine children's diets. Adults, too, often have only limited control over their diets. We will address the importance of integrating social systems and environments in interventions for healthy nutrition later in this chapter.

Second, when you attempt to sow knowledge, you are likely to harvest a reaction. Many adolescents, for example, eat unhealthily. At first glance, this seems to be a knowledge problem: adolescents have a low risk perception of (the consequences of) their unhealthy diet (Hermans et al., 2017). But attempting to increase their knowledge will only lead to their rejection of your persuasive attempt. Adolescents feel that others may be in danger, but they certainly are not. Moreover, they are seeking food choice autonomy, and will reject any limitation of that autonomy (ibid.).

This process of attitudinal bolstering does not limit itself to adolescents. Adults are also likely to resist persuasion. Reactance to the persuasion attempt is often accompanied by scepticism about the reliability of the source. When the Netherlands Health Council

(2015) published new guidelines for healthy nutrition, they encountered some prime examples of both reactance ('they are always trying to deny me nice things') and scepticism ('this is the food industry talking').

Third, more often than not, there is no lack of knowledge, even though it seems that way. Often, we do know what is right for us, but we fail to act in an appropriate manner: the famous intention-behaviour gap (Sheeran, 2002). This gap between what we know and how we would want to act on the one hand, and our actual behaviour on the other hand, can be seen in many parts of our eating behaviour. Research shows a gap between knowledge and proliferation of hygiene standards in the kitchen (McCarthy et al., 2007), of knowledge of and adherence to healthy diets at work (Mhurchu, Aston & Jebb, 2010) and of parental intentions when it comes to children's snacking and their actual behaviour (Larsen et al., 2018).

Even though knowledge is often not the problem, and even though knowledge often leads to reactance, food and eating education can still be successful in some cases. A good example is the Child Feeding Guide, developed by researchers from Loughborough University in the UK (Haycraft, Witcomb & Farrow, 2016). This app and the website provide parents with tips and tools to deal with picky eaters. During evaluation, caregivers commented that using the Child Feeding Guide had made them aware of how their feeding behaviour can inadvertently affect their child. For instance, when introducing new food to a picky child's diet, most parents will give up after less than ten attempts. However, research suggests that it can take 15 to 20 exposures before children are willing to put new foods in their mouths. In this case, factual knowledge makes it easier for parents to remain patient when dealing with their child's choosiness. When knowledge is evidently lacking, there is a reasonable chance that more knowledge will lead to different behaviour, and the chances of reactance are limited because your design directly supports people to achieve their goals.

(2) The automaticity view: Eating behaviour is largely automatic, but we design for reflective processing

One reason for the relatively small effect of knowledge on eating behaviour lies in the fact that a very large part of our daily eating behaviour is automatic. Eating-related behaviour often occurs (at least partially) outside conscious awareness, are executed regardless of intent and are hard to control or stop through conscious scrutiny. We describe two different kinds of largely automatic eating behaviour: habits and impulses. Both have their unique impact on healthy eating. To change these different forms of automatic eating behaviour requires different kinds of design solutions.

Habits, defined here as 'behaviour prompted automatically by situational cues, as a result of learned cue–behaviour associations' (Wood & Neal, 2009, p. 580), determine the major part of our eating behaviour. Habit strength predicts our consumption of fruit and vegetables, soft drinks, meat, fish, snacks and crisps (see Van 't Riet et al., 2011, for an overview). Our habits help us to come to terms with the enormous complexity of everyday life, by taking away the burden of conscious deliberation from many uncritical decisions. Unfortunately, many of our habits have detrimental effects on our health (Hermsen et al., 2016). These undesired habits are hard to change because the rigid cue – response chain of a strong habit overrides contradictory behavioural intentions.

Eating rate, the speed at which we take in our food, is an example of a habit that is so deeply engrained, that it is nearly impossible to change by will power alone. A high eating rate is strongly associated with stomach disorders and being overweight (Robinson et al., 2014), which in itself causes a range of debilitating health issues, such as diabetes type 2 and some forms of cancer (Berenson, 2011). Conscious scrutiny is unable to change this kind of habitual behaviour, but a design that disrupts the habitual behaviour may enable us to slow down our eating rate. The 10sFork (SlowControl, Paris) gives gentle vibrations when we eat too fast (i.e., taking more than one bite per 10 seconds). New evidence (Hermsen et al., 2018) suggests that even a relatively short, one-month training period with the fork may be enough to slow down a person's eating rate, with training effects still visible after two months without eating with the fork.

Changing existing habits is difficult; easier gains can be made with the introduction of new, beneficial feeding habits. For instance, many Australian schools take part in a program called Crunch & Sip, a set time during the school day to eat vegetables and fruit and drink water in the classroom. Children bring their own vegetables and fruit to school each day for the Crunch & Sip break. Each child also has a small clear bottle of water in the classroom to drink throughout the day to prevent dehydration. This is a simple, but powerful way to routinely establish an increased habitual consumption of fruit and vegetables. Similar interventions in scientific research have shown that even a short training period involving parents and children is able to instil healthier feeding habits that may very well last a lifetime (McGowan et al., 2013).

Habitual behaviours are automatically executed regardless of context. Other automatic eating behaviours, on the contrary, are more impulsive and completely set off by environmental cues. A powerful example of such impulsive behaviours can be found in supermarkets, where music, store design, product placement, advertisements, etc. influence food purchasing behaviour in ways that people cannot recognise or resist (Cohen & Babey, 2012). Key factors in our environment associated with overconsumption are the availability and easy accessibility of tempting, often high-calorie foods, the presence of overly large food portion sizes and price and marketing strategies that persuade purchasers to buy even more high-calorie or low-nutrient-dense products: 'if you buy this, we will add a large soft drink for only €1' (Poelman et al., 2014).

All these cues towards overconsumption are the result of designed interventions, be it in the form of marketing, urban planning or product and service design. If design can be used to drive us towards unhealthy eating, then designs that nudge us towards a healthier diet, or increase our awareness of our eating patterns, could also have great potential benefits. An example is the placement of products at the checkout counter. When unhealthy food at the checkout counter is replaced by healthy alternatives, two things happen. The strongest effect comes from removing the unhealthy cues and creating a new 'default' situation that does not invite you to do unhealthy impulse purchases. A smaller beneficial effect lies in an increase in sales of the healthy alternatives. Evidence for whether this latter strategy actually works is mixed, with some studies (e.g., Van Gestel, Kroese & De Ridder, 2017) finding support, and some studies (e.g., Chapman & Ogden, 2012) finding contrary results.

All in all, we can expect good designs that influence impulsive eating behaviour to be effective, but we cannot expect miracles. This is largely because our designed interventions have to compete with a myriad of other impulses. Moreover, it is useful to make a distinction between 'upstream' and 'downstream' interventions for healthy behaviour (Verplanken & Wood, 2006). Downstream interventions enable the easier performance of desired behaviour, such as improved designs for crossroads that speed up the circulation of traffic. Unfortunately, most interventions for healthy eating are 'upstream', i.e., aimed at avoiding or disrupting undesired behaviour. Poelman et al. (2014) list 32 different strategies to improve our food consumption, but all of them depend on a certain amount of willpower to succeed. To empower individuals to cope with the impulses generated by our food environment, we need to provide people with designs that improve their ability to self-regulate the amount of food they select and consume. How we achieve this remains a challenge.

(3) The social/cultural view: Too little focus on the (social) role of eating and its cultural connotations

Adding to the challenge sketched above is that food is about far more than just regulating our impulses and habits to optimalise the nutritional values that we consume. There is more than just an instrumental relationship between food and health, where food is seen as the instrument that can help us to acquire or sustain good health. The role that food plays in our daily lives is much more significant; food is connected to social contexts, cultural values and identities (Nordström et al., 2013).

Writing this just after the festive December month, it is very apparent how many socially and culturally defined food moments we encounter on a daily basis. The more traditional food moments during the end-of-year festivities are especially notable. In the Netherlands, for example, we eat 'oliebollen' (literally: '*oil spheres*') at New Year's – these are made by dropping a spoon full of dough into a deep fryer with hot oil. Certainly not the healthiest of traditions but we all indulge, later strengthening our New year's resolutions to make up for our unhealthy behaviour. It's the many smaller social and cultural food traditions that we encounter throughout the year that make it hard to stick to these resolutions. People are essentially social beings and from a very early age, we learn how to behave socially, including how, what, when and with whom we eat.

Starting at a very early age, cultural connotations and social interactions (with parents, siblings, friends) influence what children eat. Behaviour at the dinner table, parents' own ideas about what constitutes a healthy meal, as well as their ideas of what constitutes a palatable meal, all influence what and how children eat. The Loughborough Child Feeding Guide mentioned earlier therefore not only provides knowledge about what is healthy, but also about how social interactions influence eating. As an example, Walton et al. (2017) describe that parents of children who will not eat vegetables, eat fewer vegetables themselves as well.

Later in life, our peers more often than not influence our food choices. People are very sensitive to social norms, and are always, consciously and unconsciously, on the lookout for potential norm violations. Social modelling in eating behaviour is a robust and often-replicated phenomenon (Robinson et al., 2014). We automatically adapt our portion size, and even our menu choices, to those around us, regardless of whether we know or like those who influence us (Christie & Chen, 2018).

This implies that, even if we have made the decision to adapt to a healthier lifestyle, it is extremely difficult to balance this with the cultural and social norms we are confronted with. The mere desire to live a healthier life introduces food dilemmas on a daily basis. This can cause people to stay in a phase of contemplation, thinking about a desire to change while not being able to actually make any sustained changes (Ludden et al., 2017). A 'process of change' that people reported to have used to progress through the contemplation stage is self-reevaluation (Prochaska et al., 1992) which involves cognitive reappraisal of how behaviour change is part of one's identity. This process has, for example, been found to be important for women's decisions to eat more fruit (Chung et al., 2006). Lifestyle interventions might be more successful if this concept is integrated in their design in a way that it connects to people's direct social environment.

While the social and cultural ties to our decisions to consume food are complex and strong, understanding them offers new prospects for designed interventions. For example, we might incorporate social modelling in our designs. There is no better way to get toddlers to accept new foods than repeatedly seeing parents eat them, and there is no stronger influence on adolescents' and adults' behaviour than seeing peers or idols perform the desired behaviour. When Dutch researchers (Zeinstra, Kooijman & Cremer, 2017) exposed children to movie clips of famous, well-liked TV stars eating carrots, this increased the number of carrots the children ate, even after nine months. However, as with all designs aimed at unconscious processing, the effects of such designs may be limited by competing impulses. Evidence tells us that we adapt the amount we eat to those we eat with (Hermans et al., 2008), but this effect is mitigated by a range of factors such as the weight, gender and familiarity of the co-eater, the quality of the social interaction between co-eaters and the initial hunger rate (see Houldcroft, Haycraft & Farrow, 2014, for an overview of sources).

Difficulties notwithstanding, any design that does not take cultural and social aspects into account will never be successfully, let alone sustainably, adopted. Social and cultural food traditions such as those described in this section are of course defined by and often limited to a specific group of people (living in a cultural tradition, family, etc.). This means that any designed intervention should take into account the specific traditions of the group it is designed for. All efforts aimed at designing one healthy behaviour guide for everyone are bound to fail.

(4) The engagement view: Designed interventions aimed at healthy eating are often unengaging and frustrating

The automaticity of much behaviour related to eating and the strong cultural and social connotations associated with eating, make it hard to change undesired nutritional behaviour for the better. This problem calls for engaging designs, that optimally support people in their behaviour changes. Unfortunately, most designs for healthy eating have engagement issues that can be explained by looking at the key components of engagement: involvement and enjoyment (Crutzen, Van 't Riet & Short, 2016; Perski et al., 2017). Involvement relates to the actual use of the intervention (behavioural component) and enjoyment relates to positive affect and feelings of control (experiential component).

Looking at these components, it is not difficult to find examples of how current design interventions aimed at healthier eating are not engaging. The 10sFork may be an effective tool in decelerating eating rate, but it has trouble engaging its target group. Self-perceived fast eaters with eating rate-related complaints such as overweight and stomach problems, often will not consider using the fork: they tend to see using the fork as just too much hassle. Besides, eating rate, however detrimental, is not seen as a priority by this group (Hermsen et al., 2016).

As another example, consider the SmartBite-system, a device that is placed in the mouth only when eating. It reduces the volume within the mouth while supporting more mindful eating. The device showed promising effects: people using the SmartBite-system lost weight (Ryan et al., 2017). However, the system faced serious adherence problems despite the good results that were obtained. Apparently, people were not willing to use the device for longer periods of time, possibly because it diminished their joy and comfort while eating.

Other designed interventions, which are less invasive, also face serious adherence problems that can be related back to a lack of engagement. Generally, 80 per cent of health apps are abandoned in the first week (Chen, 2015). Using designs for healthy eating is often hard, boring work and not at all enjoyable. For example, tracking food intake still requires manual input of every bite we take. So far, we haven't been able to develop sensors that do this task for us although serious efforts to solve this problem have been made recently (Tseng et al., 2018). The amount of effort that is required to use the currently available interventions combined with the lack of joy and the feeling of not being in control stands in the way of the sustained use of such interventions. Arguably, there have been efforts to increase enjoyment while using health behaviour change interventions, but these have mostly focused on introducing (elements of) gaming in interventions and as such do not really make the change itself more enjoyable (Hopkins & Roberts, 2015).

Current efforts also lack an important further dimension that comes into play when longer-term use of interventions is warranted: dynamics. O'Brien and Toms (2008) critically deconstructed the term engagement in design and describe four different phases within a process of engagement: the point of engagement, the period of engagement, disengagement and re-engagement. These phases are supported by different attributes, which means that what makes a person engage for the first time (point of engagement) might differ from what keeps a person engaged. From a design perspective, this makes perfect sense: we need to design for the way people actually behave, and not for the way designers or policy-makers and health professionals want them to behave (Norman, 2007). This may seem contradictory, since the aim of these interventions *is* to change people (or at least their behaviour). However, if we see people's behaviour as dynamic rather than static, and design interventions that can adapt to such changes, we might be able to come to sustained engagement.

Conclusion and discussion

The previous sections have made clear that lifestyle behaviour change (specifically, adopting healthier nutrition behaviour) is difficult to accomplish. Together, the four views that we have discussed lay out the challenges that people face in trying to follow healthy nutrition patterns. Unhealthy nutrition behaviour is not only a matter of (lack of) knowledge or of the attitudes of an individual. The social/cultural view described above has shown that it is also affected by social (eating and being physically active are often social activities), cultural and societal (e.g., (un)healthy food availability, built environment) conditions.

The four views adopted thus show how our complete food system works against adopting healthy nutrition patterns. Parkinson and colleagues (2017) have introduced the food system compass that introduces different levels in the system of food consumption. Next to a way of mapping how our food system can work against adopting healthy food patterns, we can also use it as a starting point for thinking about how to connect the different levels through design in order to support healthier eating behaviour. The most successful endeavours to change people's behaviour have combined interventions in multiple environments (at home, at school, at the sports club) and have focused on groups rather than on individuals (Arden-Close & McGrath, 2017; Steenkamer et al., 2017). If we see behaviour as a consequence of both environment and the individual acting in that environment it makes sense to design interventions that include both of these rather than focusing on one or the other. Design and technology, as contextual factors, can take a mediating role in human interaction with the environment. Promising opportunities to create change lie in designing for both ends of the agency divide as well as in the interaction between the two. Monitoring and coaching technology has developed towards personalised solutions but have so far not always included environmental and social context. Arguing from the other end of the continuum, larger numbers of people can be reached by designing (interventions in) the environment as a trigger and connecting to personal interventions once the trigger has worked, using a sequential design.

In the next sections, we will discuss a series of promising avenues for design to initiate change at different levels of the food system in a more creative and more holistic way.

Food design aimed at healthy eating behaviour

The design of food itself offers a largely untapped potential to influence the way we perceive food. Whereas the food industry has for decades focused on innovating food so that people would find it most desirable (sweet, fat), they are now to some extent taking responsibility by trying to find solutions to decrease percentages of sugar and salt while preserving taste. Schifferstein (2016) has elaborately discussed what design can bring to the food industry. Indeed, independent designers and researchers are using health as well as sustainability challenges as starting points to design alternative food products. Think for example of the different view on food and health that Naomi Jansen presents with her 'chocobombes' (www.chocobombes.nl), a series of boxes with chocolates designed to provide pregnant women with much needed moments of comfort whilst pointing out the benefits of healthy nutrition during pregnancy. Or, consider the variety of ways in which food designer Marije Vogelzang creates new perspectives on food by design, for example by designing new vegan eating experiences (e.g., Plantbones, www.marijevogelzang.nl). Alternative strategies for food (and food packaging) designers lie in the application of insights from research on multisensory perception. Research on cross-modal interactions have indicated that these can influence our perception of food (Harrar & Spence, 2013; Spence, 2017; Becker et al., 2011). There is much to be gained in designing improved experiences of taste, texture and smell of healthy nutritional alternatives to readily available snacks, for example. Such designs do not overly rely on knowledge, can contribute to encourage healthier impulsive eating, are not affected by social and cultural functions of eating and increase engagement.

Designing a healthy food environment

A second promising possibility for design to initiate change towards healthy nutrition lies in designing the environment, both in retail and in public space. Our current obesogenic environment does not encourage healthy eating at all. This situation has direct consequences, especially for those with limited health literacy (Ball, 2015). Groups with lower socioeconomic status often face financial barriers to purchasing healthy food. Furthermore, particularly in the US, they may have limited access to healthy food, have experienced limited exposure to healthy foods in early life, which has negatively shaped taste preferences and habits, and experience a lack of social support and negative social norms related to healthy eating. In many countries, low-status occupations also pose additional challenges, with long, inflexible hours, challenging conditions and low benefits (ibid.). Finally, poverty limits people's cognitive resources, which decreases their ability to self-regulate behaviour (Mullainathan & Shafir, 2013). Health disparities, therefore, need addressing at an environmental level, by reducing the availability and attractiveness of unhealthy choices, increasing the availability and attractiveness of healthy alternatives, and placing our designs in environments that are within the reach of less fortunate groups. Such changes cannot be achieved by designers alone. For healthy food environments, policy changes are necessary. The potential for (local) governments to positively affect citizens' health is large. An example is the effect of the introduction of a sugar tax, which decreased peoples' intake of sodas in Mexico and some communities in the United States (Roach & Gostin, 2017). All in all, a healthy food environment makes healthy automatic eating behaviour possible and makes it easier to engage with healthy eating without the need for infinite amounts of willpower.

Designing for social systems

Most of our designed interventions for healthier eating are aimed at the individual. However, there is a growing body of evidence that shows that for groups with lower health literacy, only interventions that contain a social element are effective (Cleland et al., 2012). Community-based programmes, or interventions that involve some sort of support group, can be a successful way not only to increase engagement in socioeconomically disadvantaged groups, but also to support them in achieving lasting behaviour change. A vital ingredient is the embedding of interventions in existing settings, such as the workplace (with ample support from colleagues and management) or the local supermarket.

A social system that has a profound influence on eating behaviour, and is currently largely overlooked in (design) research, is the family. Families shape our nutritional habits and preferences, and the family setting is the backdrop for most of our eating behaviour. The effect of our 'individual' designs on a family setting is an under-researched, but potentially beneficial topic. Does the 10sFork (that reduces eating rate) affect other eaters in a family? Does the MindFull soup bowl 'work' in a family setting, or does its trickery get called out? Future research will tell us. In the meantime, designs aimed at the social system will increase engagement, and encourage healthy interpretation of the social and cultural functions of eating.

Healthy eating, greater wellbeing

All in all, designing for healthy eating has great potential to contribute to our wellbeing. Well-designed interventions for healthy eating help us achieve a greater quality of life for a longer period. Furthermore, they can do so without us having to give up enjoyment. Future healthy food designs will hopefully allow us to consume healthy foods and drinks we enjoy without concessions to the self-indulgent, social and cultural functions of eating. To do so, we must carefully orchestrate our designs so that they contain components aimed at knowledge and attitudes towards healthy eating, components affecting the social context of our eating behaviour, and components aimed at a healthier food environment.

References

Andereae, H. (2017). MindFull: Tableware to manipulate sensory perception and reduce portion sizes. In Dr. Elif Ozcan (Ed.), *Proceedings of the Conference on Design and Semantics of Form and Movement – Sense and Sensitivity, DeSForM 2017.* InTech.

Arden-Close, E., & McGrath, N. (2017). Health behaviour change interventions for couples: A systematic review. *British Journal of Health Psychology, 22*(2), 215–237.

Ball, K. (2015). Traversing myths and mountains: Addressing socioeconomic inequities in the promotion of nutrition and physical activity behaviours. *International Journal of Behavioral Nutrition and Physical Activity, 12*(1).

Bates, B., Lennox, A., Prentice, A., et al. (2014). *National Diet and Nutrition Survey: Results from Years 1, 2, 3 and 4 Combined of the Rolling Program (2008/9 – 2011/12)*. England: Public Health.

Becker, L., Van Rompay, T.J.L., Schifferstein, H.N.J., & Galetzka, M. (2011). Tough package, strong taste: The influence of packaging design on taste impressions and product evaluations. *Food Quality and Preference,* (22), 17–23.

Berenson, G.S. (2011). Health consequences of obesity. *Pediatric Blood & Cancer, 58*(1), 117–121.

Chapman, K., & Ogden, J. (2012). Nudging customers towards healthier choices: An intervention in the university canteen. *Journal of Food Research, 1*(2).

Chen, A. (2015). *New Data Shows Losing 80% of Mobile Users is Normal, and Why the Best Apps Do Better.* Retrieved 17 May 2016. Available from: http://andrewchen.co/new-data-shows-why-losing-80-of-your-mobile-users-is-normal-and-that-the-best-apps-do-much-better/(archived by Webcite at http://www.webcitation.org/6hjwoLkyM).

Christie, C.D., & Chen, F.S. (2018). Vegetarian or meat? Food choice modeling of main dishes occurs outside of awareness. *Appetite, 121,* 50–54.

Chung, S.J., Hoerr, S., Levine, R., & Coleman, G. (2006). Processes underlying young women's decisions to eat fruits and vegetables. *Journal of Human Nutrition and Dietetics, 19,* 297–298.

Clark, G.L. (2010). Human nature, the environment, and behaviour: Explaining the scope and geographical scale of financial decision-making. *Geografiska Annaler: Series B, Human Geography, 92*(2), 159–173. doi:10.1111/j.1468-0467.2010.00340.x.

Cleland, V., Granados, A., Crawford, D., Winzenberg, T., & Ball, K. (2012). Effectiveness of interventions to promote physical activity among socioeconomically disadvantaged women: A systematic review and meta-analysis. *Obesity Reviews, 14*(3), 197–212.

Cohen, D.A., & Babey, S.H. (2012). Contextual influences on eating behaviours: Heuristic processing and dietary choices. *Obesity Reviews, 13*(9), 766–779.

Crutzen, R., van't Riet, J., & Short, C.E. (2016). Enjoyment: A conceptual exploration and overview of experimental evidence in the context of games for health. *Games for Health Journal, 5*(1), 15–20.

Dassen, F.C.M., Houben, K., Van Breukelen, G.J.P., & Jansen, A. (2017). Gamified working memory training in overweight individuals reduces food intake but not body weight. *Appetite.*

De Korne, D.F., Malhotra, R., Lim, W.Y., Ong, C., Sharma, A., Tan, T.K., ... and Østbye, T. (2017). Effects of a portion design plate on food group guideline adherence among hospital staff. *Journal of Nutritional Science, 6.*

Dixon, H., Borland, R., DSegan, C., Stafford, H., & Sindall, C. (1998). Public reaction to Victoria's '2 Fruit "n" 5 Veg Every Day' campaign and reported consumption of fruit and vegetables. *Preventive Medicine, 27,* 572–582.

Hanks, A.S., Just, D.R., Smith, L.E., & Wansink, B. (2012). Healthy convenience: Nudging students toward healthier choices in the lunchroom. *Journal of Public Health, 34*(3), 370–376.

Harrar, V., & Spence, C. (2013). The taste of cutlery: How the taste of food is affected by the weight, size, shape, and colour of the cutlery used to eat it. *Flavour, 2*(1), 21.

Haycraft, E., Witcomb, G., & Farrow, C. (2016). Development and preliminary evaluation of the Child Feeding Guide website and app: A tool to support caregivers with promoting healthy eating in children. *Frontiers in Public Health, 4.*

Hermans, R.C.J., Larsen, J.K., Herman, C.P., & Engels, R.C.M.E. (2008). Modeling of palatable food intake in female young adults: Effects of perceived body size. *Appetite, 51,* 512–518.

Hermans, R.C., de Bruin, H., Larsen, J.K., Mensink, F., & Hoek, A.C. (2017). adolescents' responses to a school-Based Prevention Program Promoting healthy eating at school. *Frontiers in Public Health, 5*(309), 1–11.

Hermsen, S., Frost, J., Renes, R.J., & Kerkhof, P. (2016). Using feedback through digital technology to disrupt and change habitual behaviour: A critical review of current literature. *Computers in Human Behaviour, 57,* 61–74.

Hermsen, S., Frost, J.H., Robinson, E., Higgs, S., Mars, M., & Hermans, R.C.J. (2016). Evaluation of a smart fork to decelerate eating rate. *Journal of the Academy of Nutrition and Dietetics, 116*(7), 1066–1068.

Hermsen, S., Mars, M., Higgs, S., Frost, J., & Hermans, R. (2018, December 12). Effects of eating with an augmented fork with vibrotactile feedback on eating rate and body weight: A randomized controlled trial. Preprint ahead of publication, https://doi.org/10.31234/osf.io/n328p

Hopkins, I., & Roberts, D. (2015). 'Chocolate-covered Broccoli'? Games and the teaching of literature. *Changing English, 22*(2), 222–236.

Houldcroft, L., Haycraft, E., & Farrow, C. (2014). Peer and friend influences on children's eating. *Social Development, 23*(1), 19–40.

Jefferey, R.W., French, S., Raether, C., & Baxter, J.E. (1994). An environmental intervention to increase fruit and salad purchases in a cafeteria. *Preventive Medicine, 23*, 788–792.

Johnson-Glenberg, M.C., & Hekler, E.B. (2013). 'Alien Health Game': An embodied exergame to instruct in nutrition and MyPlate. *Games for Health Journal, 2*(6), 354–361.

Kramish Campbell, M., Reynolds, K.D., Havas, S., Curry, S., Bishop, D., Nicklas, T., … and Heimendinger, J. (1999). Stages of change for increasing fruit and vegetable consumption among adults and young adults participating in the national 5-a-day for better health community studies. *Health Education Behavior, 26*(4), 513–534.

Kelders, S.M., Van Gemert-Pijnen, J.E.W.C., Werkman, A., Nijland, N., & Seydel E. (2011). Effectiveness of a Web-based intervention aimed at healthy dietary and physical activity behaviour: A randomized controlled trial about users and usage. *Journal of Medical Internet Research, 13*(2), e32.

Larsen, J.K., Hermans, R.C.J., Sleddens, E.F.C., Vink, J.M., Kremers, S.P.J., Ruiter, E.L.M., & Fisher, J.O. (2018). How to bridge the intention-behaviour gap in food parenting: Automatic constructs and underlying techniques. *Appetite, 123*, 191–200.

Lee, I.M., Shiroma, E.J., Lobelo, F., Puska, P., Blair, S.N., & Katzmarzyk, P.T. (2012). Effect of physical inactivity on major non-communicable diseases worldwide: An analysis of burden of disease and life expectancy. *The Lancet, 380*(9838), 219–229.

Lloyd, J., Creanor, S., Logan, S., Green, C., Dean, S.G., Hillsdon, M., … and Wyatt, K. (2018). Effectiveness of the Healthy Lifestyles Programme (HeLP) to prevent obesity in UK primary-school children: A cluster randomised controlled trial. *The Lancet Child & Adolescent Health, 2*(1), 35–45.

Ludden, G.D.S. (2017). Design for healthy behaviour. In K. Niedderer, S. Clune, & G. Ludden (Eds.), *Design for Behaviour Change – Theories and Practices of Designing for Change*. London: Routledge.

Ludden, G. Ozkaramanli, D., & Karahanoğlu, A. (2017). Can you have your cake and eat it too? A dilemma-driven approach to design for the early stages of health behaviour change. *Proceedings of Design4Health*, 4–7 December, Melbourne, Australia.

Ludden, G.D.S., & Hekkert, P. (2014). Design for healthy behavior. design interventions and stages of change. Paper Presented at The Ninth International Conference on Design and Emotion, Bogota, Colombia, October 6–9.

Marteau, T.M. (2018). Changing minds about changing behaviour. *The Lancet, 391*(10116), 116–117.

McCarthy, M., Brennan, M., Kelly, A.L., Ritson, C., De Boer, M., & Thompson, N. (2007). Who is at risk and what do they know? Segmenting a population on their food safety knowledge. *Food Quality and Preference, 18*(2), 205–217.

McGowan, L., Cooke, L.J., Gardner, B., Beeken, R.J., Croker, H., & Wardle, J. (2013). Healthy feeding habits: Efficacy results from a cluster-randomized, controlled exploratory trial of a novel, habit-based intervention with parents. *American Journal of Clinical Nutrition, 98*(3), 769–777.

Mhurchu, C.N., Aston, L.M., & Jebb, S.A. (2010). Effects of worksite health promotion interventions on employee diets: A systematic review. *BMC Public Health, 10*(1), 62.

Mullainathan, S., & Shafir, E. (2013). *Scarcity: Why Having Too Little Means So Much*. New York, NY: Time Books, Henry Holt & Company LLC.

Netherlands Health Council (2015). *Richtlijnen goede voeding 2015*. The Hague, Netherlands: Gezondheidsraad; Publication No. 2015/24. Retrieved from: https://www.gezondheidsraad.nl/sites/default/files/201524_richtlijnen_goede_voeding_2015.pdf. Accessed 08 January 2018. (Archived by WebCite® at http://www.webcitation.org/6wJgIG9BR).

Niedderer, K. Clune, S., & Ludden, G. (2017). Summary of design for behavioural change approaches. In K. Niedderer, S. Clune, & G. Ludden (Eds.), *Design for Behaviour Change – Theories and Practices of Designing for Change*. London: Routledge.

Nordström, K., Coff, C., Jönsson, H., Nordenfelt, L., & Görman, U. (2013). Food and health: Individual, cultural, or scientific matters? *Genes & Nutrition, 8*(4), 357–363.

Norman, D.A. (2007). *The Design of Future Things*. New York, NY: Basic Books.

O'Brien, H.L., & Toms, E.G. (2008), What is user engagement? A conceptual framework for defining user engagement with technology. *Journal of the Association for Information Science and Technology, 59*, 938–955.

Parkinson, J., Dubelaar, C., Carins, J., Holden, S., Newton, F., & Pescud, M. (2017). Approaching the wicked problem of obesity: An introduction to the food system compass. *Journal of Social Marketing, 7*(4), 387–404.

Perski, O., Blandford, A., West, R., et al. (2017). *Behavioral Medicine: Practice*, Policy, Research, 7(2), 254–267.

Poelman, M.P., de Vet, E., Velema, E., Seidell, J.C., & Steenhuis, I.H.M. (2014). Behavioural strategies to control the amount of food selected and consumed. *Appetite, 72*, 156–165.

Prochaska, J.O., DiClemente, C.C., & Norcross, J.C. (1992). In search of the structure of change. In Y. Klar, J.D. Fisher, J.M. Chinsky, & A. Nadler (Eds.), *Self Change - Social Psychological and Clinical Perspectives* (pp. 87–114). New York: Springer -Verlag.

van't Riet, J., Sijtsema, S.J., Dagevos, H., & De Bruijn, G.-J. (2011). The importance of habits in eating behaviour. An overview and recommendations for future research. *Appetite, 57*(3), 585–596.

Roache, S.A., & Gostin, L.O. (2017). The untapped power of soda taxes: Incentivizing consumers, generating revenue, and altering corporate behavior. *International Journal of Health Policy and Management, 6*(9), 489–493.

Robinson, E., Almiron-Roig, E., Rutters, F., de Graaf, C., Forde, C.G., Tudur Smith, C., … and Jebb, S.A. (2014). A systematic review and meta-analysis examining the effect of eating rate on energy intake and hunger. *American Journal of Clinical Nutrition, 100*(1), 123–151.

Robinson, E., Thomas, J., Aveyard, P., & Higgs, S. (2014). What everyone else is eating: A systematic review and meta-analysis of the effect of informational eating norms on eating behaviour. *Journal of the Academy of Nutrition and Dietetics, 114*(3), 414–429.

Ryan, D.H., Parkin, C.G., Longley, W., Dixon, J., Apovian, C., & Bode, B. (2017). Efficacy and safety of an oral device to reduce food intake and promote weight loss. *Obesity Science & Practice*.

Schifferstein, H.N.J. (2016). Food design: Connecting disciplines. *International Journal of Food Design, 1*(2), 79–81.

Sheeran, P. (2002). Intention – behaviour relations: A conceptual and empirical review. *European Review of Social Psychology, 12*(1), 1–36.

Spence, C. (2017). *Gastro-physics. The New Science of Eating*. London, UK: Viking. ISBN:9780241270097.

Stark Casagrande, S., Wang, Y., Anderson, C., & Gary, T.L. (2007). Have Americans increased their fruit and vegetable intake? The trends between 1988 and 2002. *American Journal of Preventive Medicine, 32*(4), 257–263.

Steenkamer et al. (2017). *Outcome monitor aanpak gezond gewicht 2017*. Gemeente Amsterdam, Amsterdam.

Tseng, P., Napier, B., Carbarini, L., Kaplan, D.L., & Omenetto, F.G. (2018). Functional, RF-trilayer sensors for tooth mounted, wireless monitoring of the oral cavity and food consumption. *Advanced Materials, 30*(18).

Van Gestel, L.C., Kroese, F.M., & De Ridder, D.T.D. (2017). Nudging at the checkout counter – A longitudinal study of the effect of a food repositioning nudge on healthy food choice. *Psychology & Health*, 1–10.

Verplanken, B., & Wood, W. (2006). Interventions to break and create consumer habits. *Journal of Public Policy & Marketing, 25*(1), 90–103.

Walton, K., Kuczynski, L., Haycraft, E., Breen, A., & Haines, J. (2017). Time to re-think picky eating?: A relational approach to understanding picky eating. *International Journal of Behavioural Nutrition and Physical Activity, 14*(1).

Wang, Y., & Lim, H. (2012). The global childhood obesity epidemic and the association between socio-economic status and childhood obesity. *International Review of Psychiatry, 24*(3), 176.

WHO (2019). Factsheet Obesity and overweight. https://www.who.int/news-room/fact-sheets/detail/obesity-and-overweight. Accessed September 5 2019.

Wood, W., & Neal, D.T. (2009). The habitual consumer. *Journal of Consumer Psychology, 19*, 579e592.

Zeinstra, G.G., Kooijman, V., & Kremer, S. (2017). My idol eats carrots, so do I? The delayed effect of a classroom-based intervention on 4–6-year-old children's intake of a familiar vegetable. *Food Quality and Preference, 62*, 352–359.

Part III

Tools, methods and approaches for design for wellbeing

8 Co-design and participatory methods for wellbeing

Emmanuel Tsekleves

Introduction

Design does not only result in form and function, it also results in feelings, affecting our state of wellbeing (Gaudion et al., 2014). The evolution of health care services could actually be described, following the same paradigm changes, from centralised and sequential models of value creation to more distributed and open paradigms, where citizens are looked at as co-creators of their own wellbeing (Freire and Sangiorgi, 2010). Especially, in the case of participatory design, participation shares an obvious similarity with the concept of wellbeing, as they are both highly contested, internally diverse umbrella terms (White & Pettit, 2007).

Wellbeing is a complex notion with many different dimensions whose definition is disputed (Mattelmäki & Lehtonen, 2006; White & Pettit, 2007). It is a broad concept that represents an individual's overall quality of life. Studies of wellbeing can be categorised into two separate but interrelated traditions: objective wellbeing and subjective wellbeing research (Desmet & Pohlmeyer, 2013). Objective wellbeing is the degree to which external requirements for having a high quality of life are met (Keinonen et al., 2013). Subjective wellbeing can mean different things to different people (Dolan & Metcalfe, 2012; Diener et al., 2002). Thus its meaning is determined by a number of factors, including people's culture, values, preferences and relationship with the world in which they live (Gaudion et al., 2014). Within the context of this chapter wellbeing refers to a positive state of being that includes the interconnected dimensions of external and internal as well as physical, mental and social wellbeing.

The opposite of wellbeing is ill-being. This is defined as the negative affect and refers to physiological complaints and a state of worry that develop from a perceived sense of low personal competence, a lack of control and planning over life, socioeconomic deprivation and a poor family situation (Heady et al., 1984 in Boyko, 2017: 261).

Designers have a social responsibility to design products and services for the common good. Design should therefore also promote healthy behaviour and enhance wellbeing. However it is not always clear at the time of design, to know what constitutes wellbeing for the intended users, and how this product, service or environment may affect that wellbeing. This knowledge may be difficult to gather because design typically concerns products or services that do not yet exist (Van de Poel, 2012). This is where co-design can have a real impact, by designing 'with' as opposed to designing 'for' people.

Co-design and participatory research methods

In this chapter, co-design is defined as collective creativity as it is applied across the whole span of a design process. Its practices are understood to be situated within the broad range of participatory design (Sanders & Stappers, 2008; Simonsen & Robertson, 2012). Participatory design has its roots in Europe where labour unions raised the public awareness of the interrelation between technology in the workplace and its social effects (Muller & Kuhn, 1993; Simonsen & Robertson, 2012). It originated in Scandinavia in the late 1960s as workers pushed for input into the design of technology being introduced into their workplaces (Schuler & Namioka, 1993). It involves the interaction of stakeholders at all stages of the design process.

According to Sanders and Stappers, co-design 'refers to the creativity of designers and people not trained in design working together in the design development process' (2008, p. 7). Co-design presents a fundamental shift in the traditional designer–user relationship. The co-design approach enables a wide range of people to make a creative contribution to the solution but, critically, also to the formulation of a problem, a task that was previously predominantly led by designers. This approach goes beyond consultation by building and deepening equal collaboration between users and designers at resolving a particular challenge. A key element of co-design is that users, as 'domain experts' of their own needs and experiences (Visser et al., 2005), become central to the design process. In this process the designer's role shifts from that of a translator (of user experiences/needs) to that of a facilitator (Sanders and Stappers, 2008), providing ways for people to engage with each other as well as providing ways to communicate, be creative, share insights and test out new ideas. Building and deepening equal collaboration between users and designers is a critical aspect of the co-design philosophy (White & Pettit, 2007). Engaging with each other, communicating and sharing insights is an important part of co-design, as it helps to develop an empathetic relationship between researchers and research participants. This contributes to an improved understanding of the research domain and the issues that research participants, as experts in their own domain, encounter.

The co-design process begins with the 'pre-design research phase that focuses on the larger context of experience' (Sanders & Stappers, 2014, p. 8) and often makes extensive use of probes. This is followed by the generative research phase, where generative tools are mainly employed (Stappers, 2006). The generative research design phase is followed by a more 'traditional design process where the resulting ideas for product, service, interface, etc., are developed first into concepts, and then into prototypes that are refined on the basis of the feedback of future users' (Sanders & Stappers, 2008, p. 5). Finally, 'post-design research looks at how people actually experience the product, service or space' (Sanders & Stappers, 2014, p. 8).

Co-design and participatory design for wellbeing

Given the close association between participation and wellbeing (as presented in the Introduction), there have been numerous research projects employing co-design research methods that enhance the wellbeing of their target audience (Mattelmäki & Lehtonen, 2006; White & Pettit, 2007; Crivello et al., 2009; Wallace et al., 2013; Giorgi et al., 2013; Tsianakas et al., 2015; Treadaway et al., 2016; Myerson & Ramsen, 2017).

This includes projects aimed specifically at enhancing or improving the subjective well-being of individuals, typically living with a chronic health condition. For example, projects aimed at people living with dementia, where co-design methodologies are used to design tools that facilitate reminiscing to enhance a sense of personhood (Wallace et al., 2013; Giorgi et al., 2013). Other projects such as the work of Treadaway et al. (2016) have focused on supporting people living in the moment and generating positive moods.

There are also co-design research projects, which focus beyond people living with chronic disease, to their caregivers. For instance, Tsianakas et al. (2015) have developed a complex intervention for caregivers that was co-designed by staff and caregivers of patients starting chemotherapy looking at their emotional wellbeing. They conducted a fully powered randomised control trial to evaluate its efficacy and it was found that that caregivers felt reassured and supported emotionally by the intervention. This is in contrast to previous reports of caregivers feeling isolated by, and distressed with, their carer role and the emotional 'burden' it generates (Tsianakas et al., 2015). Thus the intervention developed had a positive contribution to carer's emotional wellbeing.

Other projects have explored the use of participatory methods in international development research and ask what contribution these can make to the definition and measurement of wellbeing (White & Pettit, 2007). The Young Lives project, for instance, following the lives of 12,000 children in Ethiopia, India, Peru and Vietnam, developed a methodology based on child-focused qualitative and participatory approaches to capture what children, caregivers and other community members understand by child wellbeing and how these understandings change over time (Crivello et al., 2009).

Other research projects have focused more on the use of co-design as a process for generating wellbeing as opposed to a tool for developing wellbeing-related interventions. The EU-funded Active@work project explored how one could enable and support individual workers' sustainable wellbeing and increase the motivation to work longer. They found that giving ageing workers the possibility to actively participate in the design of the workplace environment helps in enhancing physical, social and cognitive wellbeing (Mattelmäki & Lehtonen, 2006). Moreover, the RCA–Gensler Workplace and Wellbeing study provides evidence that participation in the design of the workplace can have some beneficial effect on wellbeing at work. They explored giving employees a greater sense of control over their work environment through participation in the design of their workspace. They co-designed a 'Life and Light' intervention with the research team. This comprised the introduction of plants in the space, a range of salad crops, and herbs and chillies to eat that the team would cultivate. Additionally, blinds were fully retracted to increase light. At the end of the study it was observed that teams of workers who were engaged in the participatory design project at any level (whether high or low participation) registered higher levels of mental wellbeing than the team not invited to participate (Myerson & Ramsen, 2017).

Case studies

The following two case studies present projects that employed co-design research methods aimed (i) at the wellbeing of people living with Parkinson's, and (ii) people living with dementia.

Living Playfully

Living Playfully was a research initiative aimed at scoping potential research in the area of playfulness and Parkinson's. The main goal was to facilitate and empower people affected by Parkinson's and their caregivers to co-design research from the bottom up. The focus was to have the research questions set by people living with Parkinson's, recognising their tacit knowledge and experience on what works best for them. This was done by offering people the opportunity to voice their needs, views and aspirations and to drive the formation of a research project, rather than simply participate in the research.

The scoping exercise engaged four local Parkinson's UK groups in the north-west of the UK (a total of 75 people, of whom 44 were female and 31 male; age mean 72 years; MDS-UPDRS Scale[1] slight to moderate), exploring any potential value for playfulness in order to increase motivation, perceived control and subjective wellbeing.

People affected by Parkinson's disease can experience significant impairments in their quality of life. A number of contributing factors exist, but one construct increasingly seen as important in positively affecting quality and life, is 'perceived control' (Rotter, 1990). Perceived control in relation to an illness such as Parkinson's disease can be defined as an individual's belief in their ability to control the progress of the disease generally and symptoms more specifically (Eccles et al., 2011; Delaney et al., 2012). Evidence also suggests that control can be manipulated therapeutically, with concomitant effects on psychological wellbeing (Weiss et al., 2016). Play and playfulness can add joy to life, relieve stress, supercharge learning, stimulate the mind, boost creativity and connect us to others and the world around us (Gordon, 2014). Play has the potential to foster greater motivation by satisfying three fundamental human needs: the needs for competence, autonomy and relatedness (Tieben et al., 2014). Growing evidence from research reveals that playfulness could serve to promote physical and emotional health, subjective wellbeing as well as greater levels of physical activity in later life (Staempfli, 2007; Fozard et al., 2009; Proyer, 2014; VanVleet & Feeney, 2015).

Two co-design workshops were run with each of the four groups (between May 2016 to March 2017). These workshops employed very creative, visual and playful tools to empower people living with Parkinson's and their caregivers to express their lived experiences, set research priorities, develop new ideas and concepts and provide feedback. An important aspect of the workshops was inclusiveness and playfulness, so that all group members were involved and most importantly had a great time in doing so. Each of the workshops with each Parkinson's UK group produced: (a) a list of priorities for people living with Parkinson's and their caregivers, where research should be focusing (see Figure 8.1); and (b) a number of concepts and ideas for the design and development of interactive playful interventions for improving motivation, movement and perceived control in the home environment. Table 8.1 illustrates the top priorities for people living with Parkinson's. This includes several of the priorities already identified by Parkinson's UK[2] as well as ones specific to the four groups engaged with the co-design activities.

A total of 24 unique ideas for interactive playful activities/interventions for improving people's motivation and subjective wellbeing were developed. One of these ideas was

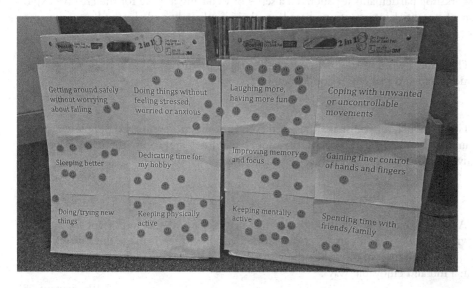

Figure 8.1 Priorities as selected by people with Parkinson's for improving their everyday life.

Table 8.1 The most important priorities for improving everyday life for people living with Parkinson's

Ranking	Priority
1	Laughing more, having more fun
2	Keeping physically active
3	Doing things without feeling stressed, worried or anxious
4	Getting around safely without worrying about falling
5	Sleeping better
6	Improving memory and focus
7	Keeping mentally active
8	Spending time with friends/family
9	Dedicating time for my hobby
9	Doing/trying new things
10	Gaining finer control of hands and fingers
11	Coping with unwanted or uncontrollable movements

taken forward and developed into a proof-of-concept prototype, which was pilot tested with one of the existing Parkinson's UK groups (22 people).

Beyond the impact this case study had in the formation of a new research proposal, it created additional value to researchers and workshop participants alike. The research scoping initiative opened a door for the research team to develop research interests in new forms of care and support how they matter in the context of involving playfulness to mediate experiences of chronic disease, as the following research quotes demonstrate.

For workshop participants it generated a sense of value and a space for the creative exploration of potential interventions based on their implicit knowledge and experience of their condition.

> These ideas would really help people like these [with Parkinson's] to be more active, motivated and feel better about themselves.
>
> [Participant 58]

> The more playful you make these interventions the more engaged people will be … and the more engaged they are, the more likely [they are] to use them and have positive outcomes.
>
> [Participant 46]

> 'Anything that makes you laugh and feel better, every day, is important for a person with Parkinson's as it can affect their mood and how they manage their health.
> You need interventions like these that have a positive spin and make you do things in a fun and enjoyable way'.
>
> [Participant 23]

Furthermore, all the connections, exploratory conversations, theoretical research and work have reshaped not just our research, but have also transformed the research team and our vision of our future practice. We felt that in the context of the workshops we were both (researchers and participants) sharing, learning, taking more control and having an enjoyable time that spanned beyond talking about research but life too. As such, we found there was an increasing interest in continuing to work together as co-researchers with people affected by Parkinson's. This case study demonstrated several points. First that the act of involving people in co-designing interventions aimed at increasing subjective wellbeing through playful means generated positive moods, such as a greater sense of value. Second, it showed that the implicit knowledge and experience of people living with chronic conditions, such as people living with Parkinson's, are well suited in co-designing interventions for subjective wellbeing, leading to research agenda setting and innovative concepts for researchers to take further.

Ageing Playfully

Social isolation is increasingly acknowledged as a major problem for people with dementia and their carers in the UK (Alzheimer's Research UK, 2018). As Alzheimer's Research UK (2013) found, 35 per cent of people with dementia (PWD) go out once a week and 28 per cent have stopped going out of the house; 23 per cent have had to give up doing their own shopping and 9 per cent say they have given up doing everything. Of those respondents, 35 per cent wanted more support and 14 per cent wanted to access activities, but they explained that lack of confidence was one of the biggest barriers to accessing activities. People with dementia were found to be afraid of becoming confused in public and getting lost, or of being a burden to their family or carers. These feelings can leave them isolated and depressed.

The research project 'Ageing Playfully', was developed in order to explore co-design with a small group of people with dementia and their carers, within a series of participatory arts workshops (for a detailed description of the research design see Escalante et al., 2017). Several workshops were set up, which included an introductory session followed by three workshops run at weekly intervals. Twelve people with dementia were recruited via an Age UK, Lancashire 'circle of support' group. The aim of the workshops was to offer a playful space where participants, their carers, two support workers and the research team could engage in an enjoyable and imaginative process of co-design using a range of arts and tactile materials.

At the outset, the project aimed at following a conventional co-design approach as defined by Sanders and Stappers (2008) with three distinct design stages, namely the pre-design, design, post-design research phase (Sanders & Stappers, 2014). During the pre-design phase the research team established trust by joining, participating and observing the activities of the targeted research participant group at their weekly local meetings for a period of two months. This provided an invaluable insight into the ways different people expressed their experience of dementia and the problems and challenges the research team would face in co-designing with such a unique group in terms of capabilities and needs. The first lesson that the team learned in this pre-design phase, was to focus on 'people' as people rather than on dementia and to concentrate on 'wellbeing' instead of 'ill-being'.

Twelve participants with dementia provided consent to take part in Ageing Playfully and were supported at the workshop sessions by two carers. The team of researchers facilitated a series of playful workshops inserted in the programme of the weekly local meetings. Co-design processes meant that researchers facilitated and encouraged the distribution of control over the process. In this spirit, the activities, themes, objectives and expected outcomes would arise from a collaborative iterative process that accounts for people living with dementia, caregivers, researchers and knowledge that emerged from the activities. The project included four workshops, each of these informing the next one. The first one was more exploratory whilst the last one focused on refining ideas that emerged in the process. As such, the co-design activity theme selection allowed for a degree of equity in research hierarchies, whether participant or researcher, but also encouraged flexibility in the methodology.

A multi-method qualitative approach was used, which included observations, audio recordings, photography and video recordings of each workshop. Carers and support workers participated in a post-workshop focus group to reflect on the workshop findings. Participant observation made it possible to include people with dementia of differing levels of verbal skill, where verbal interviewing would be difficult (Hubbard et al., 2003). The recorded observations were analysed thematically (following Graham, 2007) with the various data triangulated across recorded field notes, visual and audio data from the workshops and focus group audio recordings. Themes were identified through the process of coding, indexing and categorisation. Four key themes were identified; engagement, imagination, social interaction and the reclaiming of a sense of self.

The research team experimented with different activities during the workshops. By modelling in groups, participants could open up imaginative narratives through different materials. This was demonstrably a very engaging method of connecting with people and their ideas, allowing them to go beyond conversation into the visual image and tactile

3D model. Providing the range of modelling materials encouraged the groups to agree that one or another object would represent different things, and that it would be perfectly acceptable to change an object's meaning in combination with other materials. Changes in scale and colour led, at times, to humorous situations and so the stories would develop and transform, inspiring participants to immerse into some intricate representations with fully developed storylines. (See Figure 8.2.)

Participants started to recognise the space that was being created through the activities. By the final workshops, the team experienced much more relaxed participation. Spontaneous storytelling, which was triggered by the activities, was combined with personal tales. Importantly carers noticed how participants were looking forward to the workshops and family members reported positive moods in the participants after the 'Ageing Playfully' activities, as illustrated by the following quotes.

> I've never seen them [the people with dementia in the workshops] engaged so much before.
>
> (Age UK caregiver)

> They are really looking forward to coming to the workshops. They've been asking what we are making today.
>
> (Family caregiver)

> Some have been talking about them [workshops] with their families. They [their families] report that when they come home after the workshops, they seem happier and they keep these positive feelings.
>
> (Age UK caregiver)

Figure 8.2 Modelling activities encouraging people with dementia to socialise and develop rich narratives.

The original aim of the project was to co-design one or more models to inspire digital–physical technologies that foster wellbeing and motility for people living with dementia. However, the surprising aspect of the research was the realisation that, more than an artefact, the subjective wellbeing and mood of people with early signs of dementia did benefit significantly (as reported by the carers, support workers and family members of the people with dementia participating in the study) from the collaborative creative space, the 'magic circle', that the workshops created. The human contact, the social activity, creativity, the opportunity to be relevant and at the centre of an activity, proved to be more important for the wellbeing of the participants.

In the light of this, the project's main outcome was a set of practical recommendations for researchers, informal carers and professional carers. Being loyal to the playful nature of the research, these recommendations are presented as a set of 'playful' cards that offer guidance and ideas on how to run workshops using playful activities that mediate active social interaction, stimulate engagement and contribute to knowledge. The Ageing Playfully card game provides themes and offers practical questions to consider when working in similar activities with people living with dementia, for phases of before, during and after the workshops. The card game opens up a space in which to rehearse possible scenarios, and, at the same time, by playing, the cards offer an invitation into that co-creative space is better played – experienced – than explained. The cards are thought of as a co-design kit to facilitate activities with people who are planning to engage in participatory design projects. (See Figure 8.3.)

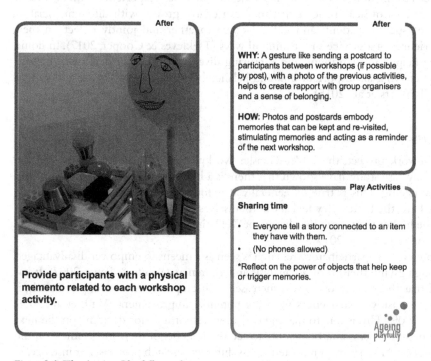

Figure 8.3 The Ageing Playfully cards.

Benefits and challenges of co-designing and participatory approaches for wellbeing

In this section we examine the value and benefits of co-design in wellbeing. We will then discuss the challenges related to employing co-design and participatory research activities for design for wellbeing.

Benefits

The inclusiveness of participatory design approaches, based on our experiences with self-organising creative and design activities, can affect the subjective wellbeing of the engaging participants in many different ways (De Couvreur et al., 2013). Some of the benefits that can be attributed to co-design with regards to wellbeing include: social and cultural value, control and empowerment, knowledge generation and empathy, and responsibility and acceptance.

Social and cultural value

One of the most obvious contributions of participatory design research to the understanding of wellbeing lies in its capacity to draw out culture, location and social group-specific understandings of the dimensions of wellbeing (White & Pettit, 2007). This is true as co-design employs very social and interactive activities to engage research participants, which often then lead to the development of shared views and values. Experience with co-design projects in the area of health shows that they can enable groups with different social or cultural values, such as patients and staff, to come together and jointly reflect on their shared experiences of a service in meaningful ways (Tsekleves & Cooper, 2017). In doing so they have helped in identifying and capturing diverse cultural perspectives, which in turn assist in creating an important link and balance between staff wellbeing and patient experience (Roberts et al., 2015)

Control and empowerment

The Active@work project, the RCA–Gensler Workplace and Wellbeing study and the Living Playfully case study, have shown that there is a link between perceived control and subjective wellbeing. This is true, as generally it is found that the more control people believe they have, the better they feel about themselves (Eccles et al., 2011; Simpson et al., 2016) and the higher they score in subsequent Wellbeing Scales (Mattelmäki & Lehtonen, 2006; Myerson & Ramsen, 2017).

Apart from control, participatory research is seen as a means to empower disadvantaged people through giving them tools of analysis and awareness (White & Pettit, 2007). It has been noted that the chance of success increases with empowerment and, particularly, if end-users have positive experiences with the potential improvement (Vink et al., 2006; Francis et al., 2009). This is due to making end-users responsible for deciding on the next steps in the design process and being able to see the benefits of their involvement in the co-design process. This has been reported across different research projects. For instance, in their study, Tsianakas et al. (2015) found that the co-design process prepared, empowered and reassured caregivers, and increased their confidence.

Knowledge generation and empathy

Empathy forms one of the key benefits of co-design. By interacting with and observing a person in conjunction with his or her physical environment, the designer can unravel clues and insights to develop empathy and a better understanding of a person's everyday experiences, which can thereby inform empathetic designs that enhance and sustain a state of wellbeing (Gaudion et al., 2014). Studies, such as that of Vaajakallio et al. (2013), have found empathy to be a helpful vehicle for project stakeholders in understanding individuals' wellbeing as personal experiences. Moreover, Tsianakas et al. (2015) found that, on top of empathy, co-design enhanced knowledge of symptoms and side effects of health conditions, prepared, empowered and reassured caregivers, and increased confidence (Tsianakas et al., 2015). Furthermore, the Living Playfully case study demonstrated that sharing of knowledge and generation of new learning was created among the co-designers. As they shared their experiences of living with Parkinson's they generated implicit knowledge on how to individually and collectively employ playful interventions and strategies to tackle some of the challenges of living with Parkinson's. As such, these case studies demonstrate that knowledge generation forms a key component of co-design and participatory research approaches.

Responsibility and acceptance

A participatory design approach helps us to develop interventions that are engaging to people and therefore are more likely to be used, increasing the overall reach and impact of the intervention (Hagen et al., 2012). Crucial to this is the ongoing involvement of co-designers throughout the design process, as it increases the feasibility and acceptability of the proposed concepts and ideas and ensures that recommendations generated by them, and then interpreted by researchers or designers into design briefs, products or services, still effectively reflect their input. The act of participation is valuable in itself, apart from any value it may have in helping to achieve other good things (Szebeko & Tan, 2010). It provides people with an opportunity to become more active. Especially in health and wellbeing research projects where co-design is employed, it encourages research participants to take greater responsibility for their own health and wellbeing. Enhancing co-designing by collective prototyping and making together provides a powerful method. The physical and social experiences within the process of making together are found to facilitate pleasure, leading engaging agents to new sources of happiness (De Couvreur et al., 2013).

Challenges

Despite the numerous benefits of participatory research methods for wellbeing, there are several challenges, which design researchers embarking in this area should be aware of.

One of the main issues in participatory research is not so much the techniques used as the way in which the research is conducted, and the relationships established between researchers and research participants (White & Pettit, 2007). Although participatory and co-design research is inherently ethical, due to its democratic relationships within the research process, there are ethical challenges too. For instance, there can be problems arising from limited resources, covert or overt agenda-setting, the unmet or mistaken expectations of the many different parties involved, failures of inclusion, and contestation over the criteria by which outcomes should be judged and evaluated.

Additional ethical challenges can arise (White & Pettit, 2007) when one engages in participatory research with people living with dementia or with people with cognitive disorders, such as autism or Asperger's syndrome (Francis et al., 2009). This is because such groups face many barriers when being involved in the co-design of products, tools or services.

More precisely, Hendriks et al. (2014) note that to collaboratively design with people with dementia in a co-design process is very challenging. Having looked at several case studies that employed a co-design approach whilst working with people living with dementia, they developed 33 guidelines. These were intended as a starting point for researchers and designers who were setting up participatory projects with people living with dementia (Hendriks et al., 2013). A couple of years later, their work along with workshops held with other researchers active in the field, led them to advocate a highly individual approach towards adjusting co-design techniques (Hendriks et al., 2015). Similarly, a set of guidelines for co-design techniques to enable people with autism spectrum disorders to participate in ICT design have been developed by Francis et al. (2009).

Furthermore, often challenges arise from the social and inclusive nature of co-design. When we design for wellbeing, we need to account somehow for the fact that people have different goals (Van de Poel, 2012). Typically co-design aims at developing shared views based on similar values. This however does not always account for diverse groups of individuals who may have different aspirations and needs. One way of approaching this is to enable and encourage different voices and views to be expressed in the co-design process, which may lead to the development of diverse ideas, products or services.

Indeed there is growing interest in the potential of participatory methods to generate numerical and quantitative data (White & Pettit, 2007). Hence, participatory research methods could be used to identify appropriate criteria and questions, and to design better surveys, which can then be implemented in a conventional manner. This would benefit the design of more personalised subjective wellbeing questionnaires

Lastly, co-design is still a relatively new area and is only developing knowledge around how impact can be measured from its projects (Szebeko & Tan, 2010). In fact, this is an area where more research is required. How might one evaluate both objectively and subjectively the outcomes as well as the processes of co-design in the wellbeing of research participants and designers alike. In fact, research on the impact of design research projects on the wellbeing of researchers who may find themselves undergoing rather emotional processes (such as when working with people living with dementia) is lacking (Escalante et al., 2017).

Recommendations

The work presented above has demonstrated that there is a need for specific course of action for tackling the challenges associated with co-designing for wellbeing and encapsulating the values of participatory design. Below we present and discuss a set of recommendations developed from the literature and the two case studies presented in this chapter.

1. **Adapt and personalise co-design methods when working with people with cognitive disorders**

   Cognitive disorders may require that co-design techniques be modified to fit with individual abilities (Francis et al., 2009). A specific set of recommendations for co-designing interventions aimed at increasing the wellbeing of people with demen-

tia can be found in the work of Hendriks et al. (2015) and for co-designing wellbeing-related interventions with people with autism spectrum disorders, one can refer
to Francis et al. (2009).

2. **Reflection in co-design and on co-design to ensure researcher participant hierarchy balance**

   In tackling the challenge of the relationships established between researchers and
   research participants (White & Pettit, 2007), it is critical that the designer acts as a
   consultant to enhance outcomes rather than to control the process (Francis et al.,
   2009). Designers' assets of creative, visual and change-oriented thinking in co-design
   sessions should be focused purely as a motor of innovation or in driving ideas forward
   (Mattelmäki & Lehtonen, 2006) and not focused on the research agenda or specific
   concepts that emerge from the process. Here the facilitation role of the designer
   should be made clear to all co-designers right from the outset. The designer could
   employ Schon's (1984) reflective practitioner approach of 'reflection in action' and
   'reflection on action' both during and after each co-design activity to ensure that the
   co-design values have been followed. This is essential in ensuring that wellbeing is the
   focus of the co-design workshops that designers reflect in both during and after the
   workshop.

3. **Embed existing community-based participatory research ethical principles before the start of the co-design process**

   In tackling the ethical challenges of equal representation among co-designers,
   researchers should embed the ethical principles and practice for community-based
   participatory research, which have already been established by other researchers, such
   as the one by Banks and Manners (2012) at the Centre for Social Justice and Community Actions at Durham University. These will help ensure that any potential ethical
   challenges, such as representation, accountability and social responsiveness, have been
   considered and that there is a consistent and credible way of addressing them in the
   co-design process.

4. **Engage all key stakeholders prior, during and after the co-design process**

   Intended beneficiaries of the product, service or innovation to be co-designed should
   not be the only participants in the research process. Instead, participatory research
   may involve key officials as stakeholders within it. This is invaluable in order to help
   them own the findings, and hence influence knowledge and action at the levels of
   policy formulation and programme implementation, rather than simply relying on
   the research report to achieve results (White & Pettit, 2007).

5. **Consider whose wellbeing and how will it be integrated in the co-design process**

   Exploring how considerations of wellbeing can be integrated into design is a crucial
   step prior to the start of the co-design activities. If we want to integrate considerations
   of wellbeing into co-design, then we need to specify considerations of whose wellbeing the workshops focus on (Van de Poel, 2012). Typically co-design workshops may
   include diverse groups. For instance a co-design workshop aimed at exploring the
   subjective wellbeing of people living with a chronic condition, such as dementia, may
   include people living with dementia, professional caregivers and family members. It is
   therefore important that, at the start of the participatory design process, the research
   team has a clear view on whether the focus is placed on the wellbeing of one specific
   group or all of them. In terms of how, it is important to ask: Is the focus of the research
   methodology to co-design products or services aimed at improving or promoting the

wellbeing of people or is it more aimed at enhancing wellbeing through the social interaction benefits the co-design process affords? These are important questions that a designer would have to consider prior to starting a co-design activity.

6. **Employ co-design as an outcome of wellbeing in itself**

The literature as well as the case studies presented in this chapter, have demonstrated that the co-design process can be an outcome in itself. By focusing on social interaction as a key value, especially for seniors' wellbeing (Vaajakallio et al., 2013), co-design activities can mediate active social interaction and stimulate engagement. For more detailed and practical recommendations see the set of playful cards,[3] developed by the Ageing Playfully project, that offer guidance and ideas on how to run co-design workshops with wellbeing in focus and using playful activities.

Conclusion

This chapter has demonstrated that co-design and participatory research methods can actively contribute to the wellbeing of individuals and communities alike. We have presented two case studies and have discussed the challenges as well as the benefits of co-design research methods in the area of wellbeing. Moreover, this chapter has provided a number of recommendations for researchers who wish to embed co-design research methods in projects related to wellbeing. What has become clear is that creating a sense of control or perceived control forms one of the key benefits of participatory research methods that increases the wellbeing of people with chronic health conditions as well as in the workplace. In the current political climate, where increasingly more governments across the world pass more control to communities and individuals, co-design will have a significant role to play in the transformation of public services (Szebeko & Tan, 2010), and by extension in the wellbeing of individuals involved in this process and the recipients of such co-designed services. This chapter provides an insight into how one can contribute to wellbeing through co-design and participatory design research methods.

Notes

1 The Movement Disorder Society-Sponsored Revision of the Unified Parkinson's Disease Rating Scale (MDS-UPDRS), see https://www.parkinsons.org.uk/professionals/resources/unified-parkinsons-disease-rating-scale.
2 Top ten priorities in Parkinson's Research. Parkinson's UK. See https://www.parkinsons.org.uk/research/improving-life.
3 See http://imagination.lancs.ac.uk/outcomes/Ageing_Playfully_Cards.

References

Alzheimer's Research UK. (2018). Facts for the Media. https://www.alzheimers.org.uk/about-us/newsand-media/facts-media.
Alzheimer's Society. (2013). *Creating a Dementia-Friendly Workplace*. London: Alzheimer's Society.
Banks, S., & Manners, P. (2012). *Community-based Participatory Research: A Guide to Ethical Principles & Practice*. Durham, NC: Durham University Press.
Boyko, C. (2017). Urban design and wellbeing. In E. Tsekleves, & R. Cooper (Eds.), *Design for Health (Design for Social Responsibility)* (pp. 260–276). London: Routledge.

De Couvreur, L., Dejonghe, W., Detand, J., & Goossens, R. (2013). The role of subjective well-being in co-designing open-design assistive devices. *International Journal of Design*, 7(3), 57–70.

Crivello, G., Camfield, L., & Woodhead, M. (2009). How can children tell us about their wellbeing? Exploring the potential of participatory research approaches within young lives. *Social Indicators Research*, 90(1), 51–72.

Delaney, M., Simpson, J., & Leroi, I. (2012). Perceptions of cause and control of impulse control behaviours in people with Parkinson's disease. *British Journal of Health Psychology*, 17(3), 522–535.

Desmet, P.M., & Pohlmeyer, A.E. (2013). Positive design: An introduction to design for subjective well-being. *International Journal of Design*, 7(3), 2013.

Diener, E., & Chan, M.Y. (2011). Happy people live longer: Subjective well-being contributes to health and longevity. *Applied Psychology: Health and Well-Being*, 3(1), 1–43.

Diener, E., Oishi, S., & Lucas, R.E. (2002). Subjective well-being: The science of happiness and life satisfaction. In C.R. Snyder, & S.J. Lopez (Eds.), *Handbook of Positive Psychology*. Oxford and New York, NY: Oxford University Press.

Dolan, P., & Metcalfe, R. (2012). Measuring subjective wellbeing: Recommendations on measures for use by national governments. *Journal of Social Policy*, 41(2), 409–427.

Eccles, F.J., Murray, C., & Simpson, J. (2011). Perceptions of cause and control in people with Parkinson's disease. *Disability and Rehabilitation*, 33(15–16), 1409–1420.

Escalante, M.A.L., Tsekleves, E., Bingley, A., & Gradinar, A. (2017). 'Ageing Playfully': A story of forgetting and remembering. *Design for Health*, 1(1), 134–145.

Fozard, J.L., Bouma, H., Franco, A., & Van Bronswijk, J.E.M.H. (2009). Homo ludens: Adult creativity and quality of life. *Gerontechnology*, 8(4), 187–196.

Francis, P., Balbo, S., & Firth, L. (2009). Towards co-design with users who have autism spectrum disorders. *Universal Access in the Information Society*, 8(3), 123–135.

Freire, K., & Sangiorgi, D. (2010, December). Service design and healthcare innovation: From consumption to coproduction and co-creation. In *2nd Nordic Conference on Service Design and Service Innovation* (Vol. 5, p. 2011), Linköping, Sweden. Retrieved July.

Gaudion, K., Hall, A., Myerson, J., & Pellicano, L. (2014). Design and wellbeing: Bridging the empathy gap between neurotypical designers and autistic adults. *Design for Sustainable Wellbeing and Empowerment*, 2015(1), 61–77.

Giorgi, S., Ceriani, M., Bottoni, P., Talamo, A., & Ruggiero, S. (2013). Keeping 'InTOUCH': An ongoing co-design project to share memories, skills and demands through an interactive table. In *Human Factors in Computing and Informatics* (pp. 633–640). Berlin, Heidelberg: Springer.

Gordon, G. (2014). Well played: The origins and future of playfulness. *American Journal of Play*, 6(2), 234.

Graham, G. (2007). *Analyzing Qualitative Data. Qualitative Research Kit*. London: Sage.

Hagen, P., Collin, P., Metcalf, A., Nicholas, M., Rahilly, K., & Swainston, N. (2012). *Participatory Design of Evidence-based Online Youth Mental Health Promotion, Intervention and Treatment*. Young and Well CRC. Available from: www.youngandwellcrc.org.au

Hendriks, N., Huybrechts, L., Wilkinson, A., & Slegers, K. (2014). Challenges in doing participatory design with people with dementia. In *Proceedings of the 13th Participatory Design Conference: Short Papers, Industry Cases, Workshop Descriptions, Doctoral Consortium Papers, and Keynote Abstracts* (Vol. 2, pp. 33–36). Windhoek, Namibia: ACM

Hendriks, N., Slegers, K., & Duysburgh, P. (2015). Codesign with people living with cognitive or sensory impairments: A case for method stories and uniqueness. *CoDesign*, 11(1), 70–82.

Hendriks, N., Truyen, F., & Duval, E. (2013). Designing with dementia: Guidelines for participatory design together with persons with dementia. In *IFIP Conference on Human-Computer Interaction* (pp. 649–666). Berlin Heidelberg: Springer.

Howell, R.T., Kern, M.L., & Lyubomirsky, S. (2007). Health benefits: Meta-analytically determining the impact of well-being on objective health outcomes. *Health Psychology Review*, 1(1), 83–136.

Hubbard, G., Downs, M.G., & Tester, S. (2003). Including older people with dementia in research: Challenges and strategies. *Aging & Mental Health*, 7(5), 351–362.

Keinonen, T., Vaajakallio, K., & Honkonen, J. (2013). Design, wellbeing and design for wellbeing. In *Designing for Wellbeing*. Aalto: Aalto Arts Books.

Mattelmäki, T., & Lehtonen, K. (2006, January). Designing alternative arrangement for ageing workers. In Finn Kensing & Gianni Jacucci (Eds.), *Proceedings of the 9th Biennial Participatory Design Conference 2006: Expanding boundaries in Design* - Volume 2, August 1–5, 2006, (pp. 101–104). Trento, Italy: ACM Digital Library.

Muller, M.J., & Kuhn, S. (1993). Participatory design. *Communications of the ACM, 36*(6), 24–28.

Myerson, J., & Ramsen, G. (2017). Workplace health and wellbeing: Can greater design participation provide a cure? In E. Tsekleves, & R. Cooper (Eds.), *Design for Health (Design for Social Responsibility)* (pp. 357–357). London: Routledge.

Proyer, R.T. (2014). Playfulness over the lifespan and its relation to happiness. *Zeitschrift für Gerontologie und Geriatrie, 47*(6), 508–512.

Robert, G., Cornwell, J., Locock, L., Purushotham, A., Sturmey, G., & Gager, M. (2015). Patients and staff as codesigners of healthcare services. *BMJ, 350*, g7714.

Rotter, J.B. (1990). Internal versus external control of reinforcement: A case history of a variable. *American Psychologist, 45*(4), 489.

Sanders, E.B.N., & Stappers, P.J. (2008). Co-creation and the new landscapes of design. *Co-design, 4*(1), 5–18.

Sanders, E.B.-N., & Stappers, P.J. (2014). Probes, toolkits and prototypes: Three approaches to making in codesigning. *CoDesign: International Journal of CoCreation in Design and the Arts, 10*(1), 5–14.

Schon, D.A. (1984). *The Reflective Practitioner: How Professionals Think in Action* (Vol. 5126). New York: Basic Books.

Schuler, D., & Namioka, A. (1993). *Participatory Design: Principles and Practices*. Hillsdale, NJ: Lawrence Erlbaum Associates.

Simonsen, J., & Robertson, T. (Eds.) (2012). *Routledge International Handbook of Participatory Design*. New York: Routledge.

Simpson, J., Fletcher, I., Perpetuo, L., Chatzidamianos, G., & Eccles, F.J.R. (2016). *The Parkinson's UK Scale of Perceived Control: Further Validation*. Lancaster: Lancaster University.

Staempfli, Marianne B. (2007). Adolescent playfulness, stress perception, coping and well being. *Journal of Leisure Research, 39*(3), 393–412.

Stappers, P.J. (2006). Creative connections: user, designer, context, and tools. *Personal and ubiquitous computing, 10*(2–3), 95–100.

Szebeko, D., & Tan, L. (2010). Co-designing for Society. *Australasian Medical Journal, 3*(9), 580–590.

Tieben, R., Sturm, J., Bekker, T., & Schouten, B. (2014). Playful persuasion: Designing for ambient playful interactions in public spaces. *Journal of Ambient Intelligence and Smart Environments, 6*(4), 341–357.

Treadaway, C., & Kenning, G. (2016). Sensor e-textiles: Person centered co-design for people with late stage dementia. *Working with Older People, 20*(2), 76–85.

Tsekleves, E., & Cooper, R. (2017). *Design for Health (Design for Social Responsibility)*. London: Routledge.

Tsianakas, V., Robert, G., Richardson, A., Verity, R., Oakley, C., Murrells, T., … and Ream, E. (2015). Enhancing the experience of carers in the chemotherapy outpatient setting: An exploratory randomised controlled trial to test impact, acceptability and feasibility of a complex intervention co-designed by carers and staff. *Supportive Care in Cancer, 23*(10), 3069–3080.

Vaajakallio, K., Lee, J.J., Kronqvist, J., & Mattelmäki, T. (2013). Service co-design with the public sector: Challenges and opportunities in a healthcare context. In *7th Conference of Include Asia* (Vol. 30, p. 2015). Retrieved October.

Van de Poel, I. (2012). 21 Can we design for well-being? *The Good Life in a Technological Age, 17*, 295.

Van Vleet, M., & Feeney, B.C. (2015). Young at heart a perspective for advancing research on play in adulthood. *Perspectives on Psychological Science, 10*(5), 639–645.

Vink, P., Koningsveld, E.A., & Molenbroek, J.F. (2006). Positive outcomes of participatory ergonomics in terms of greater comfort and higher productivity. *Applied Ergonomics, 37*(4), 537–546.

Visser, F.S., Stappers, P.J., Van der Lugt, R., & Sanders, E.B. (2005). Contextmapping: Experiences from practice. *CoDesign, 1*(2), 119–149.

Wallace, J., Wright, P.C., McCarthy, J., Green, D.P., Thomas, J., & Olivier, P. (2013, April). A design-led inquiry into personhood in dementia. In *Proceedings of the SIGCHI Conference on Human Factors in Computing Systems* (pp. 2617–2626). Paris, France: ACM.

Weiss, L.A., Westerhof, G.J., & Bohlmeijer, E.T. (2016). Can we increase psychological well-being? The effects of interventions on psychological well-being: A meta-analysis of randomized controlled trials. *PloS One, 11*(6), e0158092.

White, S., & Pettit, J. (2007). Participatory approaches and the measurement of human well-being. In *Human Well-Being* (pp. 240–267). UK: Palgrave Macmillan.

9 Creative methods for sustainable design for happiness and wellbeing

Emily Corrigan-Kavanagh and Carolina Escobar-Tello

Introduction

Design for happiness and wellbeing is an emerging design approach that has been gaining traction for the past decade. It shifts the view of the user from passive consumer to active participator. It aims to engage users in more sustainable behaviours and interactions within society, the home and the local community, to appeal to their intrinsic values and/or to co-create happy everyday experiences through design and emerging collaboration, rather than the stand-alone physical consumption of objects. Consequently, this approach requires novel ways of prompting and supporting suitable design thinking to trigger relevant design propositions.

Creative methods are useful in encouraging ideation and divergent thinking in design research and practice (Cross, 2008). We define these for the purposes of this discussion as those that require prospective users to create something (e.g., artefacts, enactments) that supports the design process by providing inspiration, information or new understandings about relevant contexts for design ideas – allowing designers, potential users and target groups to *collaborate* on the development of design projects, such as products, services and systems. However, to date, it is hard to find specific creative methods to design for happiness and wellbeing. This is significant as happiness and wellbeing are notoriously difficult concepts to define (Veenhoven, 2010); their meaning differs for everyone, both culturally and personally, which presents challenges for designing corresponding moments.

Research on the themes of happiness and wellbeing suggests that there are key activities, such as setting goals, that allow individuals to achieve high levels of happiness and wellbeing – adaptable to each person's preferences, circumstances and cultural context (Seligman, 2002, 2011). Consequently, design artefacts that embed and/or support these actions could potentially present opportunities to improve individuals' and ultimately society's happiness and wellbeing. In this chapter, we present the Design for Happiness Framework (DfH) and the Designing for Home Happiness Framework (DfHH) as applicable specific creative methods for this purpose; they provide relevant processes and tools to design for happiness and wellbeing. This chapter presents a short summary of prevalent creative methods available to designers, such as probes, toolkits and prototypes. Following this, the DfH and DfHH are expanded upon, including tools, processes, relevant happiness concepts and how these are embedded in their application and resulting designs. The chapter then concludes with suggestions on how these methods might be implemented in future scenarios and includes guidelines for their use.

Overview of common creative methods for supporting design

The most common creative methods used by designers can be consolidated under the headings: *probes, toolkits* and *prototypes*. Notably, Sanders and Stappers (2014) use these categorisations when organising methods for co-designing – those enabling users to contribute ideas to design projects. Other prolific creative design methods can be discussed within these themes, and so they are employed here for discussion purposes. The following is not intended to be a comprehensive review of such, instead relevant aspects for designing for happiness and wellbeing are explored to demonstrate a need to specialise methods in this area.

Probes

The 'probe' method usually consists of a well-designed package with various materials and activities for participants to complete unobserved (Mattelmäki, 2006). Using self-documentation, data can be collected from multiple scenarios, as opposed to singular experiences, to create deeper understandings of individuals (DeLongis, Hemphill & Lehman, 1992). A probe can include (daily) logs, maps, cameras and video recorders for participants to express their emotions and experiences. Use of (daily) logs using video and/or photos outside the probe method are referred to as 'elicitation studies', where media recorded by participants are used to guide conversations during follow-up interviews (Carter & Mankoff, 2005) – photo elicitation (Harper, 2002) or video elicitation method (Henry & Fetters, 2012), depending on the material produced. Notably, sometimes video or imagery is supplied by the investigator.

Toolkits

Toolkits allow users to volunteer ideas and collaborate with designers on design projects (Sanders & Stappers, 2014). Toolkits can include props, cards, diaries, 3D materials (e.g., Lego, Velcro modelling) and 2D materials (e.g., word and picture sets). Collage-making, concept mapping and acting out scenarios are frequently used as techniques. Toolkits are created by designers and/or researchers with more intentional outcomes than probes (ibid.), tailored to each study's purpose. They can also include probes to sensitise users to relevant ideas in preparation for toolkit activities. Initial toolkit exercises might be aimed at activating feelings around the subject while later activities could involve visualising new possibilities. Resulting artefacts can then inspire discussion of underlying needs, values and future aspirations, or prompt further research and use of toolkits (ibid.).

Prototypes

Prototypes are artefacts created to evaluate a design proposition with prospective users (Sanders & Stappers, 2012). Generally, prototyping illustrates potential design objects and spaces to validate and refine emerging designs with relevant stakeholders. It could provide an approach for 'designing for happiness' by enabling tangible design propositions that can be tested in real-world scenarios with multiple users to develop solutions for collective happiness. Common tools used in prototyping include Lego (Lego Serious Play, 2002), Velcro modelling (Hanington, 2007) and props (Foverskov & Yndigegn, 2011).

Limitations in designing for happiness and wellbeing with probe-related creative methods, toolkits and prototypes

Designing for happiness and wellbeing requires holistic and systemic investigation. Using the methods mentioned, capturing happy experiences and how they relate to society more generally, such as home happiness, either retrospectively (e.g., toolkits) or during moments (e.g., probes) is difficult, as it is hard to motivate participants to complete tasks when deeply immersed in them. For example, a prompting probe activity could disrupt one's joy when receiving a gift. Additionally, probe results are usually incomplete, uncertain and biased (Gaver et al., 2004), making it difficult to choose relevant content to utilise in designs for happiness and wellbeing. Lastly, deep reflection on the systemic nature of subjective moments (i.e., sustainable happiness), how they are supported personally and communally, is not normally the main focus of toolkits. Creative toolkit activities are generally predefined with prepared materials (i.e., images and words), enabling participants to easily create compositions to support collaborative group work, creating culturally relevant solutions (Sanders & Stappers, 2012).

Relatedly, prototypes can provide stimulus for discussion on illustrated ideas, encourage users to consider other overlapping frames/theories/perspectives and challenge present social trends by illustrating alternative realities (Stappers, 2013). Their creation is therefore vital for ensuring valuable designs for happiness and wellbeing. However, generating appropriate prototypes is not possible without methods that are specific to designing for happiness and wellbeing, given its complexity.

To design for happiness and wellbeing, it is necessary to examine happiness in a collective sense – such as how design can support the happiness of multiple individuals concurrently. This is hard to achieve through individual probe exercises, or with toolkit group visualisation activities when happiness is different for everyone. Instead, specialised activities for introspection on happiness with a facilitator (Corrigan-Doyle, Escobar-Tello & Lo, 2016) and/or using visual stimulus material (e.g., happiness-evoking imagery) with related exercises (Stevens et al., 2013) may prove more suitable. The following sections thus elaborate on unique creative methods specialised for this.

Design for Happiness Framework

The DfH is a progressive design method, including a process and toolkit, that focuses on building sustainable happier societies. When it was first developed, most of the sustainable design methods, tools or approaches focused on the environmental and economic dimension of sustainability (Thorpe, 2012). A few focused on the social dimension of sustainability, but none on happiness and wellbeing.

The unique design process of DfH combines for the first time elements of holistic sustainable design plus happiness characteristics (Escobar-Tello, 2016b). It invites a reinterpretation of the traditional relationship between artefacts and users to a people-centric approach where the characteristics of what is meaningful for people sits at the heart of our material culture (e.g., experiences delivered through products, services and systems that contribute towards happiness and wellbeing). It embodies these key fundamentals to bridge the social gap in design (Escobar-Tello, 2016a), and understands sustainability as a symbiotic system that is continuously updated because of the dynamic conditions of its dimensions. It involves addressing all dimensions (social, economic, environmental and cultural) in a balanced interlocking way, where people are a piece of a collective wider system as opposed to the centre of it; appealing to a timescale that is neither immortalising nor market-driven.

The nature of the DfH is organic, iterative and systemic. However, for the purposes of explaining DfH in a clear manner, the following sections split it into three separate foundations: design approach; design process; and the toolkit. In practice, these have been combined, hence assembling a framework to design for happiness (*approach*), and they are delivered in an integrated manner (*workshop*), as illustrated in Figure 9.1 (Escobar-Tello, 2016a).

DfH approach

Within the context of DfH, happiness is understood as 'a state of deep contentment (serenity and fulfilment) with one's life which results from the combination of three variables: feeling positive, life satisfaction, and genetics' (Escobar-Tello, 2016a, p. 95). It is triggered by, and found in, activities that individuals can engage with and that correspond to personal intrinsic values. Furthermore, it holds fantastic potential to drive behaviours towards sustainable lifestyles as its key characteristics overlap with sustainable society's characteristics (Escobar-Tello & Bhamra, 2009). DfH takes advantage of this and, by using happiness as a leverage, it approaches design in a systemic manner: addressing and changing urgent needs of the world today, uncovering opportunities for innovation, and enabling the design of sustainable artefacts that engage individuals in 'bigger-than-self' problems. In this way, its success does not rest only in the tangible characteristics of the framework,

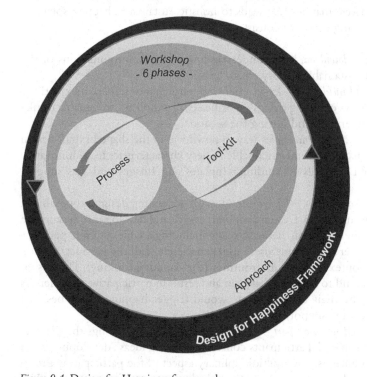

Figure 9.1 Design for Happiness framework.

Source: Escobar-Tello, 2016.

namely its design process and toolkit, but also in its capacity to challenge the possible evolution of the design discipline and its (possible) subsequent theoretical development. The approach gives way to bottom-up solutions that deliver a collection of experiences that contribute to the proliferation of happiness, not only because of themselves (i.e., happiness and sustainable society values embedded at the core of the *design* and the *design process* of products, services or systems) but also because of the systemic shifts it triggers by encouraging people to behave and live in more sustainable ways (i.e., happiness and sustainable society values embedded at the core of the *delivery* of products, services or systems).

DfH process

Carried out through a workshop scenario, with the designer as facilitator, DfH brings multidisciplinary stakeholders together to generate design proposals that, via design, contribute to happier and more sustainable societies. It is open to all members of society and can be applied to any challenge.

Through a bespoke design process and toolkit, each DfH workshop session takes participants through six phases of in-depth exploration of a problem to be mitigated. Uncovering its core function or need, this journey opens up a wide canvas for innovative design solutions to emerge at a sustainable product–service system (sustainable PSS) level. Distinctively, the combination of social innovation design methods, service design methods and principles of creativity and sustainability underpin the journey's guiding narrative (Escobar-Tello, 2016a). This enables participants to really understand the 'world' as a co-sustained system. In this way, new thinking is triggered where co-designed solutions are framed in a transformative manner that leads to holistic, sustainable, happier societies. In detail, the journey's guiding narrative consists of:

- Phase 1. *First insight – download*, levels understanding of the key foundations of the DfH: 'happiness' and 'sustainable society characteristics'.
- Phase 2. *Preparation and incubation – let go*, opens up participants' senses and creativity to contemplate new ways of 'doing things', specifically, new holistic, sustainable thinking regarding the problem at hand during the session.
- Phase 3. *Incubation part 2 – presence*, gives way to new ideas in the shape of draft design concepts that embed happiness and sustainable society characteristics in an innovative manner. The bespoke DfH tools 'Recording templates' and 'Images cards sets' support this phase.
- Phase 4. *Illumination and reflection – let come*, focuses on generating design proposals out of the initial concepts in Phase 3. Design proposals evolve and develop into sustainable PSS characterised by their systemic nature; usually including a wide systemic perspective that includes the user's behaviour, user's use/experience with the product/service, and their associated contexts of use and routines (e.g., laundry, cooking). The design proposals at this level tend to be service-driven and result in participative experiences in communities that, by their design nature, would trigger happiness. The bespoke DfH 'Recording templates' support this phase.
- Phase 5. *Illumination and reflection part 2 – co-design and co-creation*, brings the generation of design ideas to an end. Participants collate 'incubating ideas', developing them into one or two full concepts. The multidisciplinary aspect of the participating group continues to enrich and grounds them within viable contexts of everyday life. The bespoke DfH tools 'Recording templates' and 'Idea catalyst web' support this phase.

- Phase 6. *Evaluation*, focuses on assessing the outcomes of the session after it has finished. Particular attention is given to the evaluation of the design proposal/s against the DfH triggers. This phase is led by the session facilitator. The bespoke DfH 'Range-scale' tool supports this phase.

DfH toolkit

The inherent nature of happiness, wellbeing and sustainability makes it difficult to understand them, let alone embed them in a holistic manner within new design proposals. Consisting of a set of 'Recording templates', 'Images cards sets' and 'Idea catalyst web', the DfH toolkit aims to facilitate this and successfully achieves this aim by making them tangible, breaking down complex values into simple bites of information. In synthesis:

- The 'Recording templates' consist of four sets, each tailored and used in a different workshop phase. They are structured sheets where participants' thinking, ideas and sketching are recorded. They also provide a useful format to record the workshop outputs.
- The 'Images cards sets' consist of nine sets of colour-coded DfH cards, corresponding to the nine triggers of happiness and sustainable lifestyles. They are used to inspire and broaden participants' creative thinking.
- The 'Catalyst web puzzle' helps progress the design ideas into innovative co-designed concepts. It helps to visualise, discuss and reflect on how the 'happiness' and 'sustainable society' triggers connect to each other and result in a complex, holistic, interactive system.

Making use of synectics, the tools encourage participants to see parallels or connections between apparently dissimilar topics. Overall, they enable and inspire creative dialogues between designers and multidisciplinary stakeholders when exploring new design solutions. Figure 9.2 (Escobar-Tello, 2016a) summarises the five collaborative tools that compose such a toolkit, illustrating the phase and the guiding narrative underlying its deployment within the DfH.

DfH outputs

The DfH serves to trigger the proliferation of happiness through the design of sustainable PSS, to achieve deep, cultural, systemic shifts and to enable a transition at a broad societal system level. Outputs so far demonstrate that sustainable products, services and systems

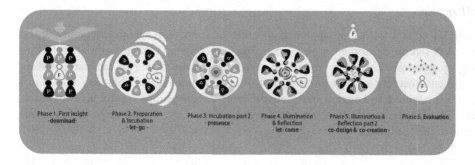

Figure 9.2 Design for Happiness framework, phases and guiding narrative.

Escobar-Tello, 2016.

can enable material changes to take place without having to leave behind social networks that feed our happiness and wellbeing. SLEUTH Project (Escobar-Tello & Bhamra, 2013), for example, is a complex PSS which aims to go beyond saving energy at universities by building on students' happiness and sustainable lifestyles issues such as 'communities', 'proactive citizenship', 'skills development', 'sharing PSS' and 'low material consumption'. In this way, DfH can assist the development of new processes of designing that enable greater potential for driving sustainable change in business, organisations and society. Its outputs show promise in encouraging a wide array of multidisciplinary practitioners and designers to approach design from a holistic sustainable perspective.

Designing for Home Happiness Framework

The DfHH is a creative method, also following a workshop format, that focuses on enabling the generating of home happiness service designs and/or sustainable PSS. It adheres to the long-term happiness perspective taken by the DfH but also incorporates Seligman's (2002) 'authentic happiness' theory. This concept suggests that *long-term* happiness consists of three levels, *pleasure, engagement* and *meaning,* that tend to occur sequentially in this order. Pleasure ('The Pleasant Life') refers to positive emotions, such as joy, most immediately felt from satisfying basic needs (e.g., food) but can also occur from other interactions, such as viewing a beautiful painting for example. Engagement ('The Good Life') denotes utilising and/or developing personal strengths. Finally, meaning ('The Meaningful Life') results from using these strengths towards the happiness of others, such as helping a charity. Employing this concept allows designs for happiness and wellbeing to be conceived by creating designs that facilitate actions for *pleasure, engagement* and *meaning* concurrently. Finally, the DfHH focuses on home because it is very influential in everyone's happiness, affecting almost all areas of life (e.g., levels of social engagement, security and sleep) (UK Green Building Council, 2016). Relatedly, the 'essential qualities' of home can be seen to satisfy basic and psychological needs collectively; for example, the home should provide a space to rest and sleep (basic needs) and to personalise and express love towards family (psychological needs) (Smith, 1994). Furthermore, the home can regulate behaviours by the actions it affords or does not support. Kitchen set-ups with countertops and cooking facilities motivate food preparation, for example, supporting basic needs. Homes can hence be shaped through design to encourage happier and more sustainable lifestyles by supporting alternative activities, such as positive social experiences through the provision of comfortable communal spaces.

DfHH approach

The DfHH takes a workshop approach to create a context in which designers can be sensitised to significant home happiness concepts and come up with appropriate solutions during group work. Designers undertake collective brainstorming to facilitate concept development, enabling a wider discussion of issues and more marketable outcomes. Final outcomes presented and shared between different design groups receive live feedback, fostering further design ideation through the discussion of alternatives or potential modifications to propositions.

DfHH process

Designing for home happiness requires a process that facilitates empathy, allowing designers to understand users' home moments by relating these to their own. This is achieved through nine sequential design activities. A summary of these, named by the corresponding task and organised in relation to the Double Diamond Design Process (Design Council, 2005), can be seen in Figure 9.3.

DfHH design tools and techniques

A presentation of home happiness concepts and real-life examples is used to introduce the workshop to provide relatable content for the designers to 'design for home happiness'. A preparatory exercise (the sharing of positive family experiences) is also employed prior to the workshop where designers are asked to reflect on previous positive home experiences, such as who and what artefacts were involved in making it significant. After the workshop's introduction, designers are invited to share these. This encourages reflection on significant aspects of positive family experiences before the session, helping designers to make connections between these and those of potential users during the workshop. A persona is then introduced. Personas can support user empathy (Miaskiewicz & Kozar, 2011) by offering an archetype of multiple user characteristics in one or more fictional characters (Marshall et al., 2015), that engage associated memories and encourage greater ideational creativity (So & Joo, 2017). Consequently, the persona is dependent on the target group and should be conceptualised accordingly in relation to each group's needs and varying scenarios.

Home happiness design tools (HHDTs)

The HHDTs, employed after introducing the persona, are used to facilitate designs encompassing key components of positive family experiences: *physical binders* and *emotional binders*. 'Family' is used here to reference all cohabiting situations that include close relationships, which can extend to friendships as well as biological relations and intimate partnerships. *Physical binders* are the object(s) and/or environments that create the right context for activities within positive family experiences as they physically bind individuals

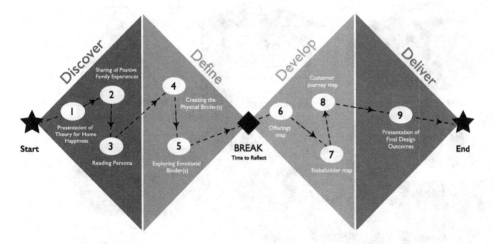

Figure 9.3 Designing for Home Happiness framework, stages and process within the Double Diamond Design Process.

Original work by authors.

to the moment. *Emotional binders* are those activities that emotionally bind participants to positive family experiences. Design, such as service designs and sustainable PSS, can act as a physical binder for such home moments by facilitating emotional binders that support basic and psychological needs simultaneously. Considering Seligman's 'authentic happiness' theory, it is suggested that unhappy homes are as such because of an overreliance on *pleasure* activities, such as satisfying basic needs, while those for psychological needs (engagement and meaning) are neglected, as the former cannot be ignored long-term, unlike the latter. Therefore, designs for home happiness need to entice interactions from unhappy homes by advertising the ability to satisfy basic needs and amplify home happiness by fulfilling psychological needs concurrently.

To support this design process, the HHDTs include: Design Tool 1: 'Creating the physical binders', consisting of a template, Essential and non-essential home happiness cards (ENHAC) and the Essential and non-essential home activities sheet (ENHAS); and Design Tool 2 'Exploring emotional binders', comprised of a template and three emotional binder sheets (see Figure 9.4).

Essential home activities are termed as such as they satisfy basic needs, eating for example, which cannot be left unfulfilled long-term. Non-essential home activities refer to those for maintaining psychological needs, such as time with family, and those not necessary for living, which can be neglected for extended periods. The Design Tool 1 template (see top left-hand side of Figure 9.4) prompts users to explore how different essential and non-essential home activities can be combined and collectively facilitated through design, supporting positive family experiences suitable for unhappy homes. The ENHAS (see top middle of Figure 9.4) then provides a graphical illustration of essential and non-essential home action examples that can be considered in this. These are categorised and colour-coded in relation to Maslow's (1943) Hierarchy of Needs pyramid (see top right-hand side of Figure 9.4) – for example, physiological needs on

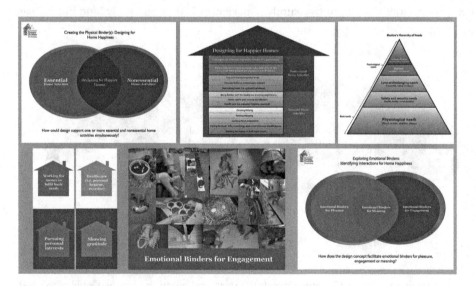

Figure 9.4 Snapshot of home happiness design tools: Design Tool 1 and Design Tool 2.
Original work by authors.

Maslow's pyramid and corresponding essential home activities (e.g., cleaning/tidying) are depicted in the same shade. Maslow's Theory of Motivation states that everyone has universal human needs, the most basic of which, for example food, tend to be pursued before those necessary for psychological wellbeing – love and belonging for example. Organising essential and non-essential home activities in this way allows designers to select home activities from each need grouping (e.g., physiological) to be included in final concepts, improving their potential happiness impact. Homes that are lacking in one need area will be able to benefit from a design proposition that supports home activities for all, or most, needs collectively. The ENHAC supports this process further by illustrating each essential and non-essential home activity individually on cards in the same colour coding as the ENHAS (see bottom left-hand side of Figure 9.4). This enables designers to quickly pair up different combinations of essential and non-essential home activities from each need classification, motivating rapid ideations. The Design Tool 2 template then motivates designers to consider the *types* of emotional binders (activities within positive family experiences) their emerging concepts support and could facilitate (see bottom right-hand side of Figure 9.4). Design Tool 2 emotional binder sheets then aid this by depicting pictorial and word examples of varying emotional binder categories on either side, such as *emotional binders for pleasure, engagement* and *meaning*. The bottom middle of Figure 9.4 displays an example of the image side for the emotional binder sheet for engagement.

These emotional binder types relate specifically to Seligman's 'authentic happiness' theory, as emotional binders (i.e., activities within positive family experiences) can be related directly to the different levels of happiness and be named accordingly. For example, emotional binders for pleasure can include activities for basic needs, providing *pleasure*; emotional binders for engagement can include developing strengths, supplying *engagement*; and emotional binders for meaning can involve using one's strengths for others, supporting *meaning*. The emotional binder sheets therefore provide visuals and annotations of different activities that can be included in each emotional binder type, allowing designers to understand how their concept could facilitate long-term happiness.

Service design tools

Service design tools are then employed to realise preliminary propositions further, such as an offerings map, stakeholder map and customer journey map. Offerings maps can take many forms. In this case, the offerings map consists of a template comprising three different columns in order to list: (1) existing relatable designs (e.g., services and/or sustainable PSS); (2) their offerings (e.g., limitations and selling points); and (3) those of the home happiness designs in comparison to these. A stakeholder map is employed subsequently to identify the 'direct', 'indirect' and 'possible' stakeholders that could support the design. Its template is kept relatively simple, consisting of three circles that build on top of each other and increase in size, labelled with the previous headings in the same order. A customer journey map is then utilised to understand how future users will interact with designs, incorporating all results from subsequent tools. The customer journey map template illustrates all the generic user steps that can happen with any new design, such as *discovery, purchase/join, interaction, continued use* and *refer*. It enables designers to consider and document the practicalities of their home happiness designs: how they are advertised, how and where they are bought or joined, how and why they are interacted with, and why they continue to be used and are recommended to others.

DfHH outputs

So far, design concepts from the DfHH suggest that it could potentially facilitate the creation of sustainable home happiness designs supportive of happiness for various people and homes simultaneously. Emerging propositions all appear to be adjustable to needs and preferences of users because they support generalised activities for essential and non-essential home activities collectively. Examples include a PSS, a 'Giggleometer', which gamifies household chores, merging the concepts of essential (e.g., chores) and non-essential home activities (e.g., games); it appears as a physical artefact that is connected to the central smart home system in which timed household tasks can be inputted and their perceived enjoyment recorded, allocating points to different family members upon completion. Activities that can be personalised to each household's needs and family scores (e.g., from recording feelings and household tasks finished) are accessible through smart devices, such as a mobile app or smart television, encouraging the sharing of emotions, equal delegation of activities and friendly competition.

Discussion

The DfH and DfHH present exciting opportunities for designers, service designers, social innovators and agents of change from any discipline to create propositions for positive systemic transitions that lead to sustainable social initiatives.

The DfH inspires and enables creative dialogues between multiple stakeholders, allowing for the co-design of sustainable PSSs, services and systems for happiness and wellbeing. It is transferable to multiple contexts and situations, including businesses and organisations. Through this, it generates a context for societal transformation through discussions and evolutions of thought as varying groups engage with its toolkit and process.

The DfHH takes a more expert-led perspective, where mixed or focused design teams (e.g., service designers) are assembled to utilise design tools supportive of empathy and designs for home happiness. Design outputs are guided by a persona, personalised to the scenario in question, in order to develop a deep understanding of the most significant needs of related households. The DfHH is therefore context-specific, specialised for designing for the happiness and wellbeing of homes and communities. Consequently, although the DfHH does not directly include co-design methods, these (e.g., toolkits) can be employed to either create the persona or to begin prototyping initial concepts with relevant stakeholders after using the DfHH. In this way, it is anticipated that the DfHH, with continuous refinement and development, will provide a valuable resource for social design studios, think-tanks, councils and community groups to create new and/or improve existing services and sustainable PSSs for home happiness and wellbeing.

Collectively, the DfH and the DfHH appear to be facilitators of social innovations, defined here as solutions to social problems that are initiated, sustained and managed by members of local communities for the wellbeing, happiness and sustainability of specific groups and/or of society more generally. The characteristics of happy societies and those that are sustainable seem to be complementary (Escobar-Tello & Bhamra, 2009), therefore supporting social innovations towards these goals provides a promising route to creating self-maintained happy and sustainable communities. By supporting the development of social innovations, specifically for happiness and more sustainable behaviour, the DfH and DfHH could be used to help build resiliency, independence and sustainable capabilities within different social contexts through design.

In the last ten years the DfH has been used in several academic and non-academic environments, refining its capacities, skills and capabilities. Examples have included projects in and outside the UK, including Colombia and Mexico, confirming its capacity to trigger bottom-up initiatives that proliferate happiness through sustainable PSS. A particularly successful project – in collaboration with Escobar-Tello (2016b) – resulted in four different sustainable PSS solutions that came out of a national initiative to promote healthier nutrition habits in Mexico. These have been historically shaped by the local eating habits and behaviours within the family. Nevertheless, nowadays they are strongly influenced by media (e.g., television, the internet) and 'globalised' food choices and lifestyles. Although this is positive in many ways, the lack of knowledge about and time and/ or financial resources for healthy diets can affect people's wellbeing. Consequently, the number of overweight children and adults and lifestyle-related deaths in the population has increased. This project allowed new ways of mitigating this economic and sociocultural issue through design. Design outputs included: (a) a board game for low socioeconomic status families lacking knowledge about healthy eating habits, time to cook healthily and family shared time to teach younger generations about these; (b) a university-led initiative to enable employees to learn, cook and eat healthy lunches; and (c) a student-led initiative to educate and track healthy eating habits while at university. Through the analysis of the empirical evidence it was possible to identify that happiness triggers and sustainable lifestyle characteristics were significant themes that emerged during the project. As in previous case studies, the DfH was welcomed and perceived as a valuable novel approach that enabled the generation of sustainable PSSs.

The DfHH shows promise in facilitating social innovations, either directly through its outputs or the activities they encourage. For example, a previous design resulting from the DfHH included a community-driven organisation. It facilitated the creation and sharing of goods, such as food and crafts, between neighbours by organising exchanges and the supply of information and ideas for related activities to interested households through an online forum, an app and a downloadable information pack. This initiative was intended to act as a mediator for people to understand the true needs of their community as it created a platform (e.g., through sharing goods) for neighbours to communicate other ways in which they could help each other. Evidently, the DfHH presents a potential means of creating future solutions that empower local communities in achieving and maintaining their own happiness and wellbeing. We now end this chapter with some guidelines for best practice for designers when using the DfHH and DfH.

Best practice guidance for designers

Having a predominantly participatory design approach, the DfH requires a cross-disciplinary team to gain maximum benefits from resulting knowledge exchanges and to encourage 'innovative experiences'. The workshop setting is used to recreate a welcoming and familiar environment where ideas can thrive, the status quo can be challenged and boundaries are blurred. The DfH process, its narrative and toolkit should anchor this environment.

DfH's nature is flexible, therefore the workshop's structure – including its narrative and use of the toolkit – can be tailored to meet the aim and the participants' needs and requirements as needed. For best practice it is recommended to allow a minimum of three hours to complete the workshop, and to use the complete toolkit, enabling a holistic exploration of the triggers and characteristics of happiness and sustainable lifestyles. However, if desired, just one or a selected array of sets of the 'Images cards', the most relevant to the brief at hand, could also be used.

Importantly, the toolkit is meant to inspire, surprise and provoke. It is to be used in a playful manner, not too literally, making the strange familiar and vice versa.

The DfHH aims to facilitate designs that are collectively supportive of happiness for various households and the locality. To that end, personas should be created from participatory design activities (e.g., toolkits and/or in-depth interviews) that illustrate connected issues (e.g., lack of security and social relationships) within the home and in the community to direct design outcomes supportive of essential and non-essential home activities simultaneously. Using the ENHAC (Design Tool 1) (see bottom right-hand side of Figure 9.4), designers should aim to develop concepts that support an activity from each need level on the ENHAS (e.g., physiological, security, love, esteem and self-actualisation) (see top middle of Figure 9.4) in order to facilitate long-term home happiness as holistically as possible. Furthermore, this tool, given the multiple card combinations possible, should be explored for at least one hour to maximise its ideational outputs. Finally, the emotional binder sheets (Design Tool 2) (see bottom middle of Figure 9.4) that follow this activity should be treated as prompters to examine how emerging concepts could support home happiness, using insights to select those with the greatest possible benefit to households and their community collectively.

References

Carter, S., & Mankoff, J. (2005). When participants do the capturing : The role of media in diary studies, *CHI*. Pittsburgh: Carnegie Mellon University, pp. 899–908.

Corrigan-Doyle, E., Escobar-Tello, C., & Lo, K.P.Y. (2016). Using art therapy techniques to explore home life happiness. In *Happiness: 2nd Global Meeting*. Budapest: Interdisciplinary Press, p. in press.

Cross, N. (2008). *Engineering Design Methods: Strategies for Product Design* (3rd edition). Chichester, New York, NY, Weinheim, Brisbane, Singapore, Toronto: John Wiley & Sons, Ltd.

DeLongis, A., Hemphill, K.J., & Lehman, D.R. (1992). A structured diary methodology for the study of daily events. In Bryant et al. (Eds.), *Methodological Issues in Applied Psychology* (pp. 83–109). New York, NY: Plenium Press.

Design Council (2005). *The Design Process: What is the Double Diamond?* Available from: https://www.des igncouncil.org.uk/news-opinion/design-process-what-double-diamond (Accessed 6 December 2017).

Escobar-Tello, C. (2016a). A design framework to build sustainable societies: Using happiness as leverage. *The Design Journal*, 19(1), 93–115.

Escobar-Tello, M.C. (2016b). Design for Happiness and Social Innovation Course. Universidad de Guadalajara, Mexico

Escobar-Tello, C., & Bhamra, T. (2009). Happiness and its role in sustainable design. In *8th European Academy of Design Conference* (pp. 1–5), Aberdeen.

Escobar-Tello, C., & Bhamra, T. (2013). Happiness as a harmonising path for bringing higher education towards sustainability. *Environment, Development and Sustainability*, 15(1), 177–197.

Foverskov, M., & Yndigegn, S.L. (2011). Props to evoke 'The New' by staging the everyday into future scenarios. In J. Burr (Ed.), *Participatory Innovation Conference* (pp. 2208–2214). Sønderborg: University of Southern Denmark. Available from: http://research.kadk.dk/files/34564313/PINC_proceedings Foveskov2011.pdf

Gaver, W.W., et al. (2004). Cultural probes and the value of uncertainty. *Interactions*, XI(5), 53–56.

Hanington, B.M. (2007). Generative research in design education. In *International Association of Societies of Design Research*, IASDR 2007 (pp. 1–15), Hong Kong.

Harper, D. (2002). Talking about pictures: A case for photo elicitation. *Visual Studies*, 17(1), 13–26.

Henry, S.G., & Fetters, M.D. (2012). Research method for investigating physician-patient interactions. *Annals of Family Medicine, 10*(2), 118–126.

Lego Serious Play (2002). *The Science of LEGO ® SERIOUS PLAYTM.* Enfield, London. Available from: http://www.strategicplay.ca/upload/documents/the-science-of-lego-serious-play.pdf

Marshall, R., et al. (2015). Design and evaluation: End users, user datasets and personas. *Applied Ergonomics.* Elsevier Ltd, *46*(Part B), 311–317.

Maslow, A.H. (1943). A theory of human motivation. *Psychology Review, 50,* 370–396.

Mattelmäki, T. (2006). *Design Probes.* Helsinki: University of Art and Design Helsinki. Available from: https ://aaltodoc.aalto.fi:443/handle/123456789/11829

Miaskiewicz, T., & Kozar, K.A. (2011). Personas and user-centered design: How can personas benefit product design processes? *Design Studies.* Elsevier Ltd., *32*(5), 417–430.

Sanders, E.B.N., & Stappers, P.J. (2012). *Convivial Toolbox: Generative Research for the Front End of Design.* London: BIS Publishers.

Sanders, E.B.N., & Stappers, P.J. (2014). Probes, toolkits and prototypes: Three approaches to making in codesigning. *Codesign: International Journal of Cocreation in Design and the Arts.* Taylor & Francis, 5–14.

Seligman, M.E.P. (2002). *Authentic Happiness.* New York, NY: Atria Paperback.

Seligman, M.E.P. (2011). *Flourish: A New Understanding of Happiness and Well-Being.* London and Boston, MA: Nicholas Brealey Publishing.

Smith, S.G. (1994). The essential qualities of a home. *Journal of Environmental Psychology, 14*(1), 31–46.

So, C., & Joo, J. (2017). Does a persona improve creativity? *The Design Journal.* Routledge, 1–17.

Stappers, P.J. (2013). Prototypes as central vein for knowledge development. In L.Valentine (Ed.), *Prototype: Design and Craft in the 20th Century* (pp. 85–98). London: Bloomsbury.

Stevens, R., Petermans, A., Vanrie, J., & Van Cleempoel, K. (2013). Well-being from the perspective of interior architecture : Expected experience about residing in residential care centers. *IASDR13,* pp. 26–30.

Thorpe, A. (2012). *Architecture & Design versus Consumerism: How Design Activism Confronts Growth.* London: Routledge.

UK Green Building Council (2016). *Health and Wellbeing in Homes.* London: UK Green Building Council.

Veenhoven, R. (2010). How universal is happiness? *International Differences in Well-Being,* 1–27.

10 Building Storey/ies

A scenario card game to architecturally design for human flourishing

Ruth Stevens and Pieter M.A. Desmet

Introduction

This chapter presents the development of a scenario-based game that supports architectural designers in their efforts to design for human flourishing. In positive psychology, human flourishing is generally defined as fulfilling one's psychological needs in a way that one can become the best person one can be (Ryan & Deci, 2001; Keyes, 2005; Ryff & Singer, 2008). Design for human flourishing (DfHF) has been operationalised as design that supports people in engaging in meaningful activities, that is, activities that fulfil their psychological needs and stimulate them to use and cultivate their personal talents (Desmet & Pohlmeyer, 2013). Correspondingly, in the domain of architecture, DfHF involves the design of spatial environments that support the end-users in undertaking meaningful activities. Stevens (2018) developed a systematic approach to architectural DfHF, see Figure 10.1. The fundamental of this approach is a so-called *enriched programme* that explicates what kind of meaningful activities are leading in the design process. This enriched programme is based on an understanding of the target group's psychological needs and gives direction to the development of the physical, material reality of architectural elements. An enriched programme is developed with 'programmatic writing' and activity that creatively designs social stories in a spatial environment.

In the application of this systematic approach, we found that designers who aim to use an enriched programme face three main challenges. The first is that most architects are not yet acquainted with the state-of-the-art knowledge about DfHF. As a consequence, many architects do not know *how* to systematically create an enriched programme. The second is the challenge of operationalising the enriched programme in the programme-phase of the architectural process.[1] Currently, architects' relation with the programme-phase can be seen as twisted (Stevens, 2018), as the programme is a multi-layered aspect and architects often start working based on incomplete information received from clients, which results in a rather narrow interpretation (Yu et al., 2010). Moreover, architects spend a relatively short amount of time on programming compared with the entire design process (e.g., Chapin, 2006). The third challenge is related to process-relevant communication. Successful DfHF also relies on an effective integration of expert knowledge of relevant stakeholders in the design process, since, often, architects themselves have little knowledge about the psychological needs of their user clients (Van der Linden et al., 2016; Cardoso et al., 2005; Eisma et al., 2003). Even though these psychological needs are universal, their manifestations in actual activities are strongly influenced by contextual factors, such as situation and social context. In a series of case studies, Stevens (2018) found that while constructive collaborations between designers and commissioners can take place,

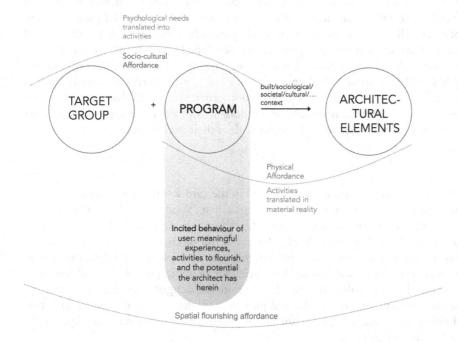

Figure 10.1 A theoretical trajectory to design for human flourishing in architecture.

discussing psychological information is often challenging and time-consuming, partly due to a lack of common language about the subjective phenomenon of human flourishing (HF). Moreover, because the architect is required to filter flourishing–relevant insights from the stream of communication, he or she may fail to notice or may misinterpret essential information.

Building Stor*ey/ies* was developed to support architects in overcoming these three challenges. Architectural designers can use the scenario-based card game together with the relevant stakeholders in their design process. In line with the key challenges, the tool has the threefold purpose of (i) transferring knowledge about what HF means and what its ingredients are in an architectural context, (ii) supporting designers in operationalising this knowledge in their design processes and (iii) facilitating the required communication between the designer and relevant stakeholders. First, we report the game's development. Some key considerations are discussed that motivated the choice for a scenario-type game. Next, we introduce the game components and scenario, illustrate the test phase and reflect on the degree to which the game fulfils the intended purposes. Finally, a general discussion reflects on the tool's value for DfHF practice.

A suitable format

Today, information that needs to be implemented in architectural design processes is typically communicated with descriptive checklists (e.g., for accessibility) or normative measurements (e.g., for ventilation or insulation). While such checklists have advantages (i.e., they are instructive, objective and measurable), they also have important disadvantages.

First, due to the complex character of an architectural design project, architects are often already overloaded with regulations and guidelines. Second, the enriched programme in DfHF includes holistic scenarios that cannot adequately be captured with straightforward checklists. And third, checklists are typically not developed to stimulate creativity – and they can even inhibit a designer's creativity or endanger the creative collaboration. Sleeswijk Visser (2009) stressed the importance of using *inspiring* forms of communication to support effective design processes. Finally, a tool format is required that incites collaborative design creativity, that is malleable to the designer's professional approach, and does not limit or frustrate the designer but instead widens their perspective.

Card sets

To find a suitable format, inspiration was found in the card sets that have been developed to transfer knowledge in 'positive design' research (e.g., Yoon et al., 2016; Casais et al., 2016). The card-set format has several advantages (see e.g., Lucero & Arrasvuori, 2013; Bekker & Antle, 2011; Friedman & Hendry, 2012; Yoon, Desmet & Pohlmeyer, 2013). First, cards are effective in communicating insights with multiple modes of information in a compact and concise physical format. A card can, for example, provide a visual context, a design theme and some explanatory words to inspire the designer. Second, cards have the ability to break down complex topics and provide particles of information in an accessible and visible way. And third, they can be interpreted more creatively and support the designer's freedom of usage.

Inspired by these successes, a card format was used in an initial attempt to develop a DfHF tool. Tests with student designers were promising, but also revealed limitations. First, the cards were effectively communicating insights about the phenomenon of HF, but they were not well equipped to support the designer in connecting these insights to the design briefs' contextual parameters. Second, the cards did not stimulate creative discussions, but rather encouraged the designers to copy or integrate what was displayed on the cards. Given these findings, we decided to explore possibilities to combine the card-set format with a more dynamic and proactive format: a design game.

Design games

The choice for a game-based format in architecture is not totally new, and the relation between architecture and games has recently been explored by a number of scholars, for example Walz et al. (2005), Bories et al. (2007) and Sofronie (2014). Walz (2010, p. 15) has pointed at the possibility of viewing games as 'dynamic, innovative, and challenging architectural outlets that can be design results or components of the design process'. From these sources, four promising qualities of game-based knowledge transfer can be distilled: (1) motivation, (2) interaction, (3) tangibility and (4) narration.

(1) Motivation

Schell (2008, n.p.) defined games as: 'a problem-solving activity, approached with a playful attitude'. The entertaining qualities of games provide intrinsic motivation, which can help architects to maintain their enthusiasm for DfHF during their design process. The playful nature of the game format matches the need for a creative form of knowledge transfer that inspires and enthuses rather than induces architects to work with specific information.

(2) Interaction

Flanagan and Nissenbaum (2007) and McGonigal (2010) found that gameplay can neutralise collaboration difficulties caused by social and cultural interpersonal differences. In her research on participatory urban planning games, Sofronie (2014) experienced that games can give people from different backgrounds a platform to decide on the planning of their environment. While playfulness lowers the threshold for communication and participation, the interactive character of a game allows *everyone* to be a player, encouraging the inclusion of stakeholders in the DfHF process, such as 'sponsor clients', managers and staff, as well as possible 'user clients', who carry useful information and who can participate or simply contemplate and reflect on design ideas 'built' in the game.

(3) Tangibility

The architectural design process involves a wide variety of iterative creative and communicative actions, such as drawing lines, writing keywords, sketching, discussing with colleagues and stakeholders and group brainstorming. The physical and tangible format of games is compatible with this way of working. Gameplay can allow players to visually 'build' reasoning and argumentation in a 'coded' way, instead of only visualising (intermediate) results via sketches. That way, the iterative character of a design process is facilitated. It then also becomes easier to safeguard the HF mindset and stay put regarding important decisions made throughout the design process.

(4) Narration

Games enable the incorporation of storytelling, which is particularly relevant for the current knowledge transfer objective. Heylighen (2005) indicated that stories provide a dense, compact way to deal with and communicate complex information in a short time. In the words of Arendt (1968, p. 105), 'storytelling reveals meaning without committing the error of defining it'. Storytelling helps when conveying the holistic DfHF knowledge in a manner that enables architectural designers to adopt relevant insights and adapt them to fit their design process.

Building Store*y/ie*s

Building Store*y/ie*s is a scenario-based card game for architectural designers and stakeholders that supports the practice of DfHF. The game helps designers to create an enriched programme by creatively exploring and combining the necessary ingredients, such as psychological needs of the target group, social and spatial opportunities in the context, other users, interesting themes for activities and actions related to these themes (see Stevens, 2018).

The sociologist Caillois (1961) placed forms of play on a continuum from *ludus*, structured activities with explicit rules that lead to winners and losers (games), to *paidia*, unstructured, enjoyable and spontaneous activities that do not lead to a 'winning versus losing scenario' (playfulness). Games with a *paidia* set-up have the goal of letting players explore, with no regulations or specific end-goal, while games from a *ludus* set-up motivate players to win in a competitive structure with rules and end-goals. Building Store*y/ie*s was based on a hybrid between a *paidia* and *ludus* game design: an overall *paidia* structure is used to give the phenomenon of HF the central stage and to stimulate players to creatively explore the phenomenon. *Ludus* elements are added to enable players to progress towards the aim of developing an enriched programme, including some rules and boundaries within the design process that prevent the designer from wandering off and getting stuck in the conceptual phase. The heart of the game is based on the act of *storytelling* in the form of narration and scenario writing that combines to the overall programmatic writing (see Introduction). The game consists of the following contents:

1. an inspiration poster;
2. a deck of 12 information cards;
3. a stack of 79 hexagon-shaped ingredient tiles;
4. 3 methods fans containing 29 techniques.

The game progresses in two phases and results in an enriched programme. The first phase is called 'get in the mood', which familiarises the designer with the game and with the general topic of DfHF. The second phase is playing the game, in *single-player* mode or in *multi-player* mode with stakeholders.

First phase: Get in the mood

The first phase, 'getting in the mood', provides an introduction to DfHF with three ingredients: stimulating a fitting mindset, inspiring designers and making them acquainted with the content in the game and the possible avenues in designing. This first phase was included because DfHF requires one to embrace a different way of thinking and designing. Hence, 'getting in the mood' aims to provide some mental groundwork. Evidently, this will start taking less time when the designer gains experience and becomes more seasoned in DfHF.

An appropriate mindset is stimulated with the mindset card (see Figure 10.2, left), which is ideally kept within sight during the game. The front provides three 'state-of-mind' tips, and the back provides three 'to strive for' tips. Together, these six tips aim to help the designers keep their focus on the overarching design goal of supporting the HF of user clients. The front tips stress the need for empathy and a willingness to fully immerse in the topic of HF and the life atmosphere of the user clients. In addition, they remind the designer that enriching everyday activities offers a wider range of possibilities than adding exceptional once-in-a-lifetime-experiences. The back addresses the relevance of the surrounding environmental fabric, stimulating designers to socially and spatially root their design in this fabric. Moreover it stimulates to strive for continuity on the site, and to focus on the realm of everyday life.

To inspire the designer, the first phase also includes an inspiration poster (21 by 29.7 cm; see Figure 10.2, right) that gives an example of what is meant by the concept of an enriched programme. The infographic visualises a designed scenario as a full-page comic book story.[2] The story is divided over twelve frames but also represents one coherently designed environment. Each frame depicts (at least) one unique designed (social or individual) meaningful activity and explains how this activity contributes to the potential flourishing of the users. The decision to combine a full-page visual with separate frames was motivated by the aim to communicate both the architectural coherence of the designed physical environment and the multiple action possibilities it offers. Ideally, the frames inspire designers with a wide variety of meaningful activities, and, at the same time, the overall visualisation communicates the importance of designing a coherent spatial

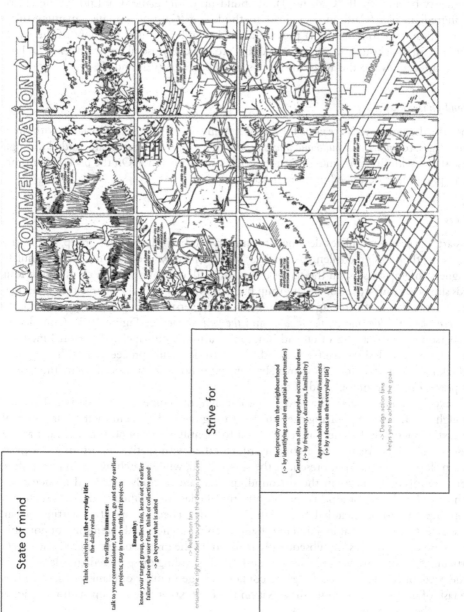

Figure 10.2 Mindset card (left) and an inspiration poster with the theme 'commemoration' (right) – not to scale.

environment. For a novice DfHF designer, the poster is informative, and for more experienced designers, the poster can serve as a mnemonic.

In addition to the mindset card and poster, the 'get in the mood' phase uses seven introduction cards that provide gameplay instructions. Four cards (Figure 10.3) explain the theory behind DfHF (Card no. 1), the build-up of the game (Card no. 2), the use of the ingredient tiles (Card no. 3) and the methods fans (Card no. 4). The remaining three introduction cards (Figure 10.4) provide a 'guided walk' through the flow of the game (Card no. 5), tips about how to get started that are especially useful for *newcomers* (Card no. 6), and tips for advanced playing for more seasoned players (Card no. 7).

Second phase: Play

Once the designers are *in the mood* for DfHF, it is time to play the scenario game with three main stages: To *immerse*, to *build and intensify*, and to *communicate*. Players are guided through these stages with the pink lines on introduction Cards 5, 6 and 7. On the back of Card no. 5, this pink line is described in more detail.

Immerse

To start, the game stimulates designers to immerse in both their target group, and in the context of their design challenge, socially as well as spatially (see Card no. 5). To stimulate designers to empathise with the target group, they fill out four persona cards. These four cards showcase four 'types' of target group persons, who differ in the degree to which they are attracted to stimuli that are either more socially versus more personally oriented: *the busy bee, the quiet life enjoyer, the socialite* and *the focused one* (see Figure 10.5). Completing the persona cards is an act of empathising, since a more 'humane' and personal image is created, thus the designer can bond with the personas while proceeding with the game and taking design decisions. Moreover, by varying private- versus social-focus, the personas prevent fixation on one end of the spectrum.

Next, the game requests the designers to analyse the context of the design challenge through an HF-lens, supporting them in anchoring the end-users in their environmental context. Concretely, designers are challenged to identify social opportunities, such as the presence of a kindergarten or a churchyard, together with spatial opportunities, such as a steep slope or an old ruin present at the site. Indeed, while searching for opportunities, even controversial aspects in the surroundings that are typically perceived as 'negative', such as a churchyard, or aspects that are mostly labelled as a 'difficulty on site', such as a steep slope, are to be included. Since DfHF is characterised by a positive starting vision, these aspects are looked at in a different light, opening up new and interesting opportunities. These opportunities are subsequently mapped on the green context ingredient tiles (a particular type of ingredient tile, see Figure 10.3). Regarding these ingredient tiles, next to some predefined suggestions, the game contains a large number of blank cards, since it is the task of designers to identify these within the context, or to come up with more ideas through their previous experiences.

Build and intensify

This stage represents the essence of the scenario card game. Building is done by linking and combining the hexagon-shaped ingredient tiles (displayed on Card 3, Figure 10.3), with the help of the techniques in the methods fans (displayed on Card 4, Figure 10.3).

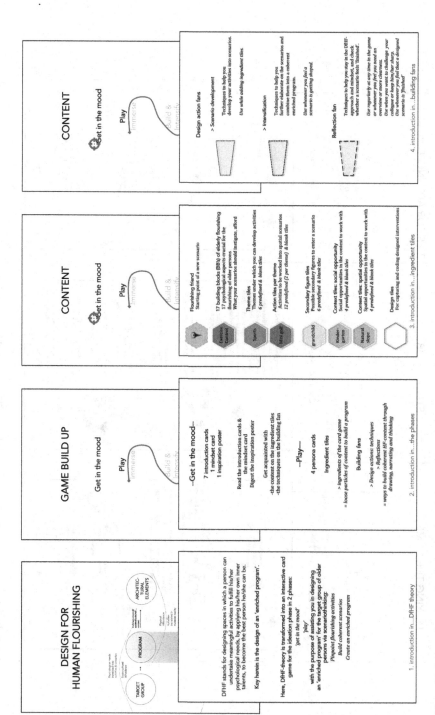

Figure 10.3 Introduction Cards 1 to 4, from left to right: (1) DfHF theory, (2) the build-up of the game, (3&4) the content

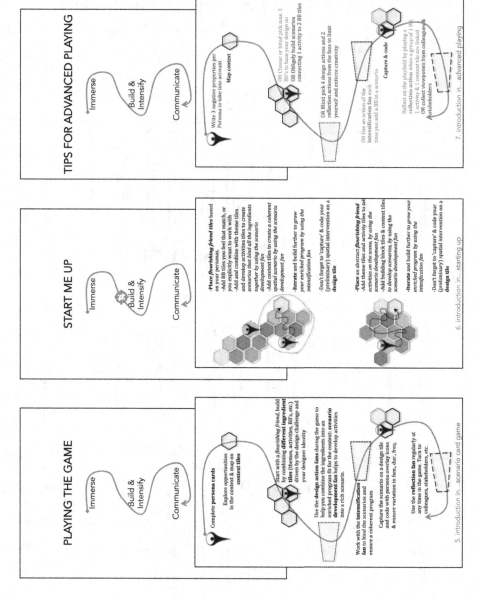

Figure 10.4 introduction Cards 5, 6 and 7 handling instructions and tips to play.

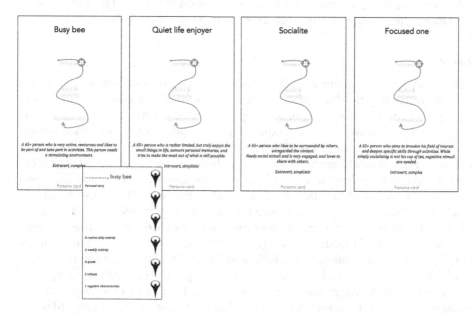

Figure 10.5 The four persona cards.

To support the *paidia*-type play, the main idea is to explore the different ingredient tiles and to creatively build associations. There are no rules about the order in which ingredient tiles are to be placed to form a play-field. It is however necessary to insert all the different types of ingredient tiles, in order to build a complete enriched programme.

To help novice players, the tips displayed on Card 6 (Figure 10.4) hint at starting with the 'flourishing friend' ingredient tile, the protagonist of the scenario card game, representing the target group of the future building and standing for one or all four of the personas that were created in the 'get in the mood' phase of the game. Then, the other ingredient tiles can be placed adjacent to the flourishing friend, to create a story, and thus to start designing meaningful activities that will be enabled in the future building. Activities are created by combining ingredients and making associations in a narrative way with tiles of five different colours: blue *building block tiles*, representing psychological needs; green *context tiles*, capturing the social and spatial opportunities; light red *theme tiles*, giving an overview of general themes and topics around which activities can be shaped; dark red *action tiles* per theme, capturing concrete actions and activities that one has come up with; and light yellow *secondary figure tiles*, representing other persons present at the site, or people that can be attracted to join in the designed activities.

An overview of 29 unique techniques is available throughout the game that can stimulate creativity in combining and associating the tiles and developing scenarios. These techniques, which were derived from a qualitative case-based study and design exercises on the topic of DfHF (see Stevens, 2018), are arranged into three 'fans': 'design action fan > scenario development', 'design action fan > intensification' and 'reflection fan'. Respectively, the first fan contains techniques that are best applied when a meaningful activity idea is shaped and is to be elaborated into different scenarios. The second helps to combine the scenarios and transform them into a coherent enriched programme. The latter provides techniques to reflect on the designed enriched programme in all its facets, to validate the HF-potential, to explore opportunities to further enrich, and to safeguard the overall HF-mindset while playing. During the game, players are encouraged to try to use these freely.

Communicate

The game facilitates communication between designers and stakeholders by making physical and visualising the 'think process' that occurs through combining the ingredient tiles. The play-field in itself is a sort of time-lapse of potentially interesting ideas that are formed, allowing others to join in and explore more opportunities or uncharted territories as a way to advise the designer or to actively co-design. It enables designers and stakeholders to exchange knowledge, since all the ingredients are on the table, and players can add ingredients linked to their own vision. This is a more creative way to exchange information, which is advocated by different scholars (e.g. Bogers et al. 2008). Also, being able to literally 'see' where a design idea has come from, and what its ingredients were, helps to convince stakeholders about the relevance of particular ideas. Moreover, between designers reciprocally, the visual play-field and particular techniques found in the 'reflection fan' help to check ideas, for example, 'get challenged by a colleague on a specific activity/ scenario'. Moreover, within each 'fan', some techniques particularly address the aspect of communication, stimulating players to make things tangible and share ideas and visions, for example 'draw flow charts for people to visualize the scenarios'. (See Figure 10.6.)

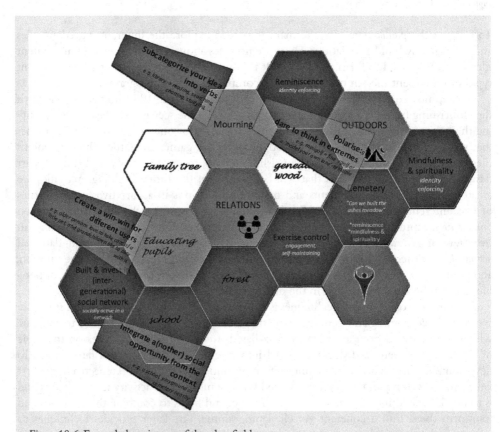

Figure 10.6 Example box: image of the play-field.

During one of the workshops, a designer first combined the yellow <u>flourishing friend tile</u> with two triggering opportunities he had identified in the environment: '<u>cemetery</u>' (predefined tile) and '<u>forest</u>' (written on a blank context tile). He then selected the building block tile '<u>mindfulness and spirituality</u>', due to its affinity with '<u>cemetery</u>'. This primary play-field sparked '*genealogy*' as a conceptual idea with the designer.

He then added the red theme tile '<u>outdoors</u>', nudged by the technique '*polarise – dare to think in extremes*' (in 'design action fan < scenario development') to take a more extreme course, as he felt people would expect so-called genealogy family trees to be a written or digital document. In true designer-fashion, he opted for a physical 3D-version, and aimed to transform the existing forest into a *genealogy wood*, envisioning trees to serve as a literal 'family tree' for each family to place the names of their relatives on, and to care for.

To further this line of thinking, the designer used the technique '*subcategorize your idea into verbs*' (in 'design action fan > scenario development') to add the action tile of '<u>mourning</u>', an activity he felt could be uplifted to a more positive experience via the natural atmosphere of the forest, and via shaping an appropriate physical space around the *family trees*. That way, the trees could also become a place for '<u>reminiscence</u>' (blue building block tile).

Driven by the hope that the genealogy wood could not only strengthen family ties but also fortify relations between villagers, the designer added the red theme tile '<u>relations</u>', as an additional avenue for flourishing design interventions. Concretely, he felt the genealogy wood could help villagers to '<u>build and invest in (intergenerational) network</u>' (blue building block tile), by claiming trees to dedicate to members of a hobby club. Placing names or pictures on the tree, literally brings different people together. Furthermore, prompted by the technique '*integrate a(nother) social opportunity from the context*' (in 'design action fan > intensification'), the designer mapped and added the opportunity tile '<u>school</u>' to the play-field. To build a flourishing scenario, the designer used the technique '*create a win-win for different users*' (in 'design action fan > scenario development'), that led to a situation in which older villagers can educate pupils on the village history, via trees that cover and honour village war veterans or carry pictures of former majors. This also benefits pupils, since they can learn in the outdoors, instead of in a typical classroom.

All in all, the genealogy wood tells personal tales of family ancestry, hints at the village social life and informs on the local history, in a way that contributes to the flourishing of different villagers by affording them opportunities to reminisce, build social contacts, exercise control, learn, etc.

This example shows how quickly *design ideas* can spark during instinctive and reflective mapping with the use of the techniques, combined with the player's design-based creativity. It also illustrates that next to elaborating on existing activity ideas and building scenarios around these, fresh avenues for new scenarios are easily found and started.

A short description of the testing phase of the scenario card game

To date, a testing phase with three exploratory workshops has been conducted to evaluate and refine the card game. These workshops were organised to explore: (i) if the participants were able to get acquainted with the novel principle of DfHF (and thus if the game could transfer information regarding DfHF); and (ii) how the format was welcomed and handled in the design practice of architectural designers (thus how participants adopted the game in their practice and could reach a result). These objectives correspond to the first two key challenges presented in the introduction.[3]

Figure 10.7 Two instinctive play approaches of two design groups in the workshops.

The workshops consisted of an informative introduction followed by presenting a fictional design challenge handled by playing the scenario card game. Each time, designers were asked to present their enriched programme design result at the end of the 2-hour sessions using the play-field they had created via the game, and to deliver sketches as hints of spatial translations of the enriched programme design. The workshops were recorded, observed and captured via field notes on design approaches, discussions and design/play processes. Also, feedback on the players' experiences was collected via questionnaires.

Figure 10.6 shows an impression of the workshops through time lapses, resulting in a *patchwork-like* (above) and a *concentric* (below) play-field, of which the design results appeared equally complex, incorporating a large variety of all the different ingredient tiles. More detailed information on the set-up, results and insights gained via the workshops can be read in Stevens (2018). (See Figures 10.7a and 10.7b.)

General discussion

The main goal of this chapter was to introduce a design tool, based on the knowledge developed regarding DfHF, which can assist architectural designers to design an enriched programme as a way to DfHF. To do so, the tool had to (i) transfer knowledge on what (Df)HF is, (ii) operationalise this knowledge in the architectural design process and (iii) facilitate the communication between designers reciprocally, and between designers and stakeholders in the design process. After screening benefits and difficulties in existing tool formats, a game-based format was used, and the scenario card game 'Building Stor*ey/ies*' is the end result. Concretely, the scenario card game helps designers to create an enriched programme by exploring and combining necessary 'ingredients' in a creative matter using techniques provided by the game, such as, psychological needs of their target group, the social and spatial opportunities in context, other users, interesting themes for activities and actions related to these themes. Via this approach, architectural designers can be assisted to create a dynamic coexistence of activities on site in a way that it helps a specific target group to flourish.

Exploratory tests in which the scenario card game was used to design a HF intervention in a fictional setting for older persons showed promising results in both leading to a designed environmental intervention that – theoretically – supports the flourishing of users.

To date, the scenario card game has only been tested a limited number of times with a limited number of participants, all architectural students and designer/researchers. This indicates that the game has not yet been used in a realistic setting, namely a design office handling a concrete design challenge for which stakeholders can be invited to participate in the playing. There is also a considerable difference between novice and student designers and experienced designers. According to Christiaans (1992), a designer's creative space increases with his increased design experiences. Thus, at this moment, the applications we currently foresee for the scenario card game, are directed at design students. Using the game in design education can make students aware of what DfHf is, and teach them how they can take a specific human-centred design approach by integrating HF as an important affordance of the designed environment. Integrating the scenario card game in design education is a crucial step in the dissemination strategy of the game.

To further widen the game's applicability, some strategies can be mentioned. First, more research needs to be performed to be able to broaden the width and depth of the use of the scenario card game in a professional setting. Part of the dissemination strategy can be to research how novice and experienced designers approach the game in order to tailor the game's functioning. Moreover, it can also be worthwhile to research if the game can be played *without* designers for screening purposes, for instance in situations when a design project of a public building (such as a library) is proposed by a local government, and a first task is exploring opportunities with neighbourhood residents for revealing other activities. A designer could moderate workshops such as these, and potentially interesting results could be inserted in the scenario card game, as a fixed first map. Then, the fixed map together with the scenario card game could be given to the architect who is appointed to design the building, as a new type of more 'human-centred' design brief.

Second, the game is currently directed at designing environments that support older people in flourishing, however, by replacing the Building Block tiles (the dark blue ones) – that contain the psychological needs linked to a specific target group – by a different set, the range of application can be expanded substantially. In that context, on a more general level, the aspect of expandability and updateability is crucial as well in the application and dissemination strategy of the scenario card game.

On a more general level, a specific limitation with regard to the impact of the scenario card game should be mentioned. The scenario card game in itself is developed in a way that psychological knowledge of the target group is already included and ready-to-use (via the BB-ingredient tiles), and additional empathic information on the target group is to be entered by the players via the persona cards. As DfHF theory stresses, it remains important for architects to empathise and receive information directly from their clients.

Notes

1 The programme-phase in an architectural process, is a phase in the design process in which the architect develops all the functions the future design has and the activities that can take place in the future building or other type of architectural design.
2 The one-page image format was inspired by the painting *De Kinderspelen* of Bruegel de Oude and the innovative all-over background page design of Frank King's *Gasoline Alley*, a comic strip dating from the early 1900s. Bruegel aimed to inform viewers on the specific topic of 'entertaining and playing of children' by portraying the many different (playful) activities that children could possibly undertake to entertain themselves, in an almost exhaustive way, albeit displayed against an *incorrectly* represented spatial background. *Gasoline Alley*, on the other hand, seems to view the meticulously portrayed architectural surroundings as the visual glue in the main story. The comic book showcases clearly what can be done or undertaken in that one spatial environment, however the activities do not necessarily serve a particular purpose or lead to something 'bigger', such as the goal of 'flourishing' of the actors. What is done is not always linked to what people in the comic book 'say', or 'think', therefore the portrayed activities seem rather freestanding.
3 The third key challenge (i.e., communication with stakeholders) has not yet been explored, since no commissioners took part so far, but will be the focus of future research.

References

Arendt, H. (1968). *Between Past and Future: Eight Exercises in Political Thought.* Harmondsworth, England: Penguin.

Bekker, T., & Antle, A.N. (2011). Developmentally situated design (DSD): Making theoretical knowledge accessible to designers of children's technology. In *Proceedings of the SIGCHI Conference on Human Factors in Computing Systems*, Vancouver, Canada: ACM, (pp. 2531–2540).

Bogers, T., Van Meel, J.J., & Van der Voordt, T.J.M. (2008). Architects about briefing: Recommendations to improve communication between clients and architects. *Facilities, 26*(3/4), 109–116.

Bories, F., Walz, S., Böttger, M., Davidson, D., Kelley, H., & Kücklich, J. (2007). *Space Time Play: Computer Games, Architecture and Urbanism. The Next Level.* Basel: Birkhäuser.

Caillois, R. (1961). *Man, Play, and Games.* Champaign, IL: University of Illinois Press.

Cardoso, C., Clarkson, P.J., & Keates, S. (2005). Can users be excluded from an inclusive design process? In *Proceedings of HCII 2005*, Las Vegas.

Casais, M., Mugge, R., & Desmet, P.M.A. (2016). Developing meaning as a means for design for happiness: Development of a card set for designers. In *Proceeding of the 2016 Design Research Society 50th Anniversary Conference* (pp. 1553–1570).

Chapin, M. (2006). Creating innovative places: Organizational and architectural case studies of the culture change movement in long-term care. Southern Gerontological Society Annual Meeting, Lexington, KY.

Christiaans, H. (1992). *Creativity in Design: The Role of Domain Knowledge in Designing.* Lemma: Utrecht, The Netherlands.

Desmet, P.M.A., & Pohlmeyer, A.E. (2013). Positive design: An introduction to design for subjective well-being. *International Journal of Design, 7*(3), 5–19.

Eisma, R., Dickinson, A., Goodman, J., Mival, O., Syme, A., & Tiwari, L. (2003). Mutual inspiration in the development of new technology for older people. In *Include 2003* (pp. 7:252–7:259). London: Helen Hamlyn Research Centre.

Flanagan, M., & Nissenbaum, H. (2007). A game design methodology to incorporate social activist themes. CHI: San Jose, California, USA.

Friedman, B., & Hendry, D.G. (2012). The envisioning cards: A toolkit for catalyzing humanistic and technical imaginations. *Proceedings of the SIGCHI Conference on Human Factors in Computing Systems (CHI'12)*, New York, NY: ACM, pp. 1145–1148.

Heylighen, A. (2005). Knowledge sharing in the wild; building stories' attempt to unlock the knowledge capital of architectural practice. *Proceedings of the CIB W096 Architectural Management 'Special Meeting' on Designing Value: New Directions in Architectural Management*, Denmark. Lyngby: Technical University of Denmark, pp. 17–425.

Keyes, C. (2002). The mental health continuum: From languishing to flourishing in life. *Journal of Health and Behavior Research, 43*, 207–222.

Lucero, A., & Arrasvuori, J. (2013). The PLEX card and its techniques as sources of inspiration when designing for playfulness. *International Journal of Arts and Technology, 6*(1), 22–43.

McGonical, J. (2010). *Gaming Can Make a Better World.* TED talk February 2010. Retrieved from: http:// www.ted.com/talks/jane_mngonical_gaming_can_make_a_better_world.html

Ryan, R.M., & Deci, E.L. (2001). On happiness and human potentials. A review of research on hedonic and eudaimonic well-being. *Annual Revue of Psychology, 52*, 141–166.

Ryff, C.D., & Singer, B.H. (2008). Know thyself and become what you are: A eudaimonic approach to psychological well-being. *Journal of Happiness Studies, 9*(1), 13–39.

Schell, J. (2008). *The Art of Game Design: A Book of Lenses.* Burlington, MA: Elsevier/Morgan Kaufman.

Sleeswijk Visser, F. (2009). *Bringing the Everyday Life of People into Design.* PhD Dissertation, TU Delft.

Sofronie, S. (2014). *A Location-based Game to Visualize Spatial Tactics.* Unpublished doctoral dissertation, Hasselt University, Hasselt, Belgium.

Stevens, R. (2018). A launchpad for design for human flourishing in architecture. *Theoretical Foundations, Practical Guidance and a Design Tool.* Unpublished doctoral dissertation, Hasselt University, Hasselt, Belgium.

Van der Linden, V., Annemans, M., & Heylighen, A. (2016). Architects' approaches to healing environments in designing a Maggie's Cancer Caring centre. *The Design Journal, 19*(3), 511–533.

Walz, S.P. (2010). *Towards a Ludic Architecture: The Space of Play and Games.* Pittsburgh, PA: ETC Press.

Walz, S.P., Schoch, O., Schaerer, P., Gmelin, S., Bonwetsch, T., Hillner, B., Schmidt, R.G., Mermans, B., Przerwa, J., & Schlueter, A. (2005). Serious bioplay: A computer integrated building service game applying psychophysiological input. In *Extended Proceedings of UbiComp 2005 – The 7th International Conference on Ubiquitous Computing,* Tokyo, Japan.

Yoon, J., Desmet, P., & Pohlmeyer, A. (2016). Developing usage guidelines for a card-based design tool: A case of the positive emotional granularity cards. *Archives of Design Research, 29*(4), 5–19.

Yoon, J., Desmet, P.M.A., & Pohlmeyer, A.E. (2013). Embodied typology of positive emotions: The development of a tool to facilitate emotional granularity in design. Presented at the 5th International Congress of International Association of Sciences of Design Research (pp. 1195–1206), Tokyo, Japan.

Yu, A.T.W., Chan, E.H.W., Chan, D.W.M., Lam, P.T.I., & Tang, P.W.L. (2010). Management of client requirements for design and build projects in the construction industry of Hong Kong. *Facilities, 28*(13/14), 657–672.

11 Mind the gap

A social practice approach to wellbeing-driven design

*Holger Klapperich, Matthias Laschke, Marc Hassenzahl,
Melanie Becker, Diana Cürlis, Thorsten Frackenpohl,
Henning Köhler, Kai Ludwigs and Marius Tippkämper*

Understanding wellbeing is not enough

Human–Computer Interaction (HCI) and Interaction Design (ID) focus increasingly on designing technology in ways to increase users' subjective wellbeing through interaction (see Diefenbach, 2017). Consequently, a number of models attempt to describe 'wellbeing' and 'positive experiences'. For instance, Desmet and Pohlmeyer (2013) provided a 'framework for positive design [...] that includes three main components of subjective wellbeing: pleasure, personal significance and virtue'. Jordan (2000) distinguished four types of pleasure: physio-, socio-, psycho- and ideo-pleasure. Hassenzahl et al. (2013) introduced an approach based on psychological needs, such as autonomy, relatedness, competence, stimulation, and popularity, which provide 'potential "sources" of positivity, meaning – and ultimately – happiness, when fulfilled'. Those approaches mainly provide a general mindset, that is, a high-level model of how wellbeing might be best understood in the context of technology design. However, in design the devil is in the details. While understanding positive experience is a good start, this alone does not provide sufficient support to design for wellbeing. In other words, there is a substantial gap between the abstract models of wellbeing in HCI/ID and the concrete design of wellbeing-driven technology.

In this chapter, we suggest a practice-oriented approach to begin to bridge the gap between abstract experiential design objectives and specific products and interactions. We start with a short introduction to our theoretical understanding of wellbeing-driven design and show how elements of social practice theory can inspire a set of practical design-supporting activities. Then, we present and discuss a case study to highlight challenges and opportunities of the suggested approach. Finally, we discuss potential future work and some ethical challenges.

Linking wellbeing and social practice theory

Subjective wellbeing (i.e., happiness) is essential to people. Lyubomirsky (2007) describes happiness as the 'experience of joy, contentment, or positive well-being, combined with a sense that one's life is good, meaningful and worthwhile' (p. 32). Obviously, this description is too unspecific for design. Furthermore, it is a pressing question how positive experiences are formed, and what role technology might play in this process.

Sheldon and Lyubomirsky (2006) argued that intentional activities are an important source for wellbeing. What people do and how they do it can increase or decrease wellbeing in everyday life (see also Diefenbach et al., 2017). While Sheldon and Lyubomirsky

Autonomy
Feeling like you are the cause of your own actions rather than feeling that external forces or pressures are the cause of your actions.

Competence
Feeling that you are very capable and effective in your actions rather than feeling incompetent or ineffective.

Stimulation
Feeling that you get plenty of enjoyment and pleasure rather than feeling bored and under-stimulated by life.

Security
Feeling safe and in control of your life rather than feeling uncertain and threatened by your circumstances.

Popularity
Feeling that you are liked, respected, and have influence over others rather than feeling like a person whose advice or opinions nobody is interested in.

Relatedness
Feeling that you have regular intimate contact with people who care about you rather than feeling lonely and uncared for.

Physicalness
Feeling that your body is healthy and well taken care of rather than feeling out of shape or unhealthy.

Figure 11.1 Overview of a set of needs.

Hassenzahl et al., 2010; based on Sheldon et al., 2001.

(2006) focused on carefully arranged, intentional, therapeutic activities, such as reflecting on personal strengths or being grateful, we assume that wellbeing is also made through mundane everyday activities (see Huta & Ryan, 2010), such as preparing coffee.

Hassenzahl et al. (2010) introduced a set of needs into HCI and ID (see Figure 11.1). They understand this particular set as a multifaceted lens increasing the comprehensibility of the sources for positivity in everyday activities. Needs offer a valuable way to characterise and categorise positive experiences. They constitute a starting point as well as an objective for design.

Conceptually, in order to provide greater need fulfilment, it seems to be a small step to design for wellbeing by arranging and crafting mundane everyday life activities deliberately (Hassenzahl et al., 2013). Practically, the gap between possibilities for need satisfaction and actually creating specific activities in a fulfilling way is substantial. Moreover, HCI and ID focuses primarily on things such as artefacts and technology. The emerging interaction of people with technology and artefacts could be seen as a way to shape the activity and ultimately the experience. What is needed is an action-oriented framework, which explicitly includes the material as an important constituent of action.

To this end, social practice theory (Reckwitz, 2002) provides a number of ideas which help to bridge the gap between abstract need fulfilment and concrete, situated, everyday use of technologies (Hassenzahl, 2018). First of all, a social practice can be understood as:

> a routinized type of behaviour which consists of several elements, interconnected to one another: forms of bodily activities, forms of mental activities, 'things' and their use,

a background knowledge in the form of understanding, know-how, states of emotion and motivational knowledge.

(Reckwitz, 2002, p. 294)

'A practice forms a 'block' whose existence necessarily depends on the existence and specific interconnectedness of these elements, and which cannot be reduced to any one of these single elements' (Reckwitz, 2002, p. 250). In this sense, practice theory is an action theory that focuses on the constitution of routine everyday behaviour through 'shared knowledge, which enables a socially shared way of ascribing meaning to the world' (Reckwitz, 2002, p. 246).

Based on Reckwitz (2002), Shove et al. (2012) further simplify the notion of a social practice. To them, the practice as a unit of analysis consists of *competence* (e.g., skill, know-how and technique), *meaning* (e.g. symbolic meanings, ideas and aspirations) and the *material* (e.g. objects, tools and infrastructures). Forming a practice is understood as establishing new links between these elements. In addition, if any of those three elements changes or is changed, the remaining elements will change, too.

Shove et al.'s structure is especially helpful from a design perspective. First, it highlights the integral role of the *material* (e.g., technology in the context of HCI/ID) and asserts that practice and material are inseparable. Whether intended by design or not, the particular form of the material will inevitably shape the practice, in the same way the practice shapes the material. A close interdependence of action and the 'tools for action' are decisive factors to which extent the material has an impact on a practice. Second, *competence* in the sense of 'technique' underlines bringing in knowledge and skills by incorporating technology (İhde, 1990). We have to bear in mind, that today's technology design mainly attempts to 'move' competence into the material in order to enable the user to fulfil a task. For instance, almost every car is equipped with a navigation system. Skills of wayfinding (competence) are moved into the car (material) in the form of navigation systems. Wayfinding as a practice changes dramatically or even disappears (e.g., Aporta & Higgs, 2005). Third, thoughts, emotions and motives are subsumed under the notion of *meaning*. Shove et al. (2012, p. 23) argue that meaning is 'tricky territory in that those who write about social practices are in much less agreement about how to characterize meaning' and therefore it should be dealt with cautiously.

We suggest that the notion of needs helps to clarify the 'tricky territory' of meaning. The fulfilment of certain needs is the basis of the motivation to perform an activity, i.e., to engage in a practice. Although there are only a few needs, there are numerous ways in which they are fulfilled. We believe that this link between social practices and need fulfilment outlines a comprehensible approach which helps to bridge the gap between abstract notions of wellbeing through need fulfilment and general and concrete ways of the same (see Figure 11.2).

Finally, Shove et al. (2012) distinguish 'practice-as-performance' from 'practice-as-entity'. Practices constitute themselves, change and dissolve through individual performances: '[…] Through performance, through the immediacy of doing, […] the "pattern" provided by the practice-as-an-entity is filled out and reproduced' (Shove et al., 2012, p. 7). The practice-as-entity is thus more normative, a potentially idealised representation of a practice. For example, if talking with other people about practices of riding a bike, most people will know that the material is a bike, that particular competencies are required in order to be able to ride the bike. The potential meanings might be resource-saving, weather-dependent, slow, healthy, exhausting or dangerous. This practice pattern

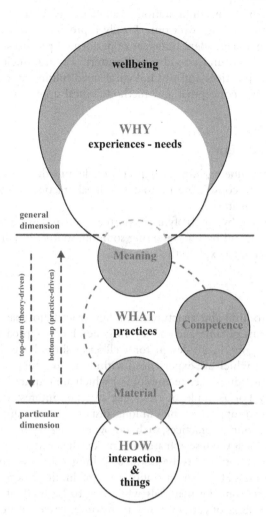

Figure 11.2 How practices link the particular dimension of 'How' (e.g., design) and the general
dimension 'Why' (e.g., research).

is constituted through single performances and experiences but provides a more abstract
blueprint of what it means 'to ride a bike'. At the same time the pattern impacts the way
the practice is performed. Changes in practices happen through deviations in performances, which eventually alter the pattern. For example, people who grew up in a time
when it was still unusual to own a car, used bikes frequently, making it the dominant mode
for individual transportation. The practice was related to feelings of autonomy and freedom. Later, the car took over and today, in the Western world, riding a bike is more closely
related to leisure time, health and sustainability than to getting from A to B. As a result, it is
important for designers to understand that they are able to modify practices by changing
the material, the meaning and also the competence involved.

   In sum, practice theory provides a relevant theoretical frame, which links action,
knowledge, material and meaning with each other and suggests a reciprocal relationship.
Design artefacts (i.e., material) provide opportunities for action, and the performance of a

practice creates meaning through the particular configuration of all elements. Moreover, practice theory addresses the way practices change over time. Finally, it provides a way to understand single, situated, highly context-dependent instances of performed practices as part of a more abstract, culturally shared and understood overall pattern. By introducing a link between the meaning of specific practices and psychological need fulfilment, the present approach constitutes a reasonable conceptual and methodological approach to wellbeing-driven design.

The practice of wellbeing-driven design

We divide our approach to design for wellbeing into six steps: (1) to delimit the design space, (2) to gather positive practices, (3) to consolidate, (4) to design ideal practices, (5) to specify the material and (6) to realise the material.

In the following, we introduce each step by (a) clarifying its purpose, by (b) describing the main activity to achieve this purpose and by (c) presenting some illustrative insights from one of the case studies we conducted to explore the approach.

Step 1: Delimit the design space

Most practical design projects require to limit and structure the design space beforehand, mainly due to limited resources in terms of time and money. In general, our approach assumes a *top-down* perspective (see Figure 11.2): design for wellbeing should ideally begin with 'designing' positive moments which are experienced within meaningful practices, and only later should it address the 'things' (i.e., technologies) which are required in order to shape the practice accordingly. For example, one can take a certain interest as a starting point, such as looking for ways to support couples in long-distance relationships. Such a 'theme' will help to focus on a group of practices, such as how couples try to feel close over a distance. This limitation reduces the research area and makes the design work more manageable. The 'theme' itself does not need to be justified, as long as the designers who are involved agree on its relevancy. However, in reality many technology design projects are *bottom-up*, that is, they start from the materials which are to be used later. For example, when designing in the context of cars, one may focus on practices related to cars. When designing a coffee machine, one may focus on practices of brewing coffee (as in our case study). In general, there is a danger of setting the limits too narrow. Thus, we always recommend broadening the scope a little further than one would typically consider given the material at hand. For example, in the context of brewing coffee, one may focus on broader practices, such as the 'coffee klatsch' (a spontaneous get together for having a coffee and a chat), rather than on narrow issues of, for instance, operating the coffee machine.

To familiarise oneself with the theme, initially, a number of practices from one's own everyday life experience should be compiled, in order to get a feel for the design space. Of course, it is possible that the research area at hand is not ubiquitous and there is no connection to the designer's personal experience. For instance, it may be difficult to name practices of parenting without the experience of being a parent. However, even in this case, culturally shared notions of practices exist. They may lack detail and may even be overly stereotypical; nevertheless, they can and should serve as a starting point for future research. If resources allow for it, a number of additional open conversations with other people outside the team may add further depth to the initial design space. Another source .

for practices can be found in movies or literature (Blythe & Wright, 2006). In general, the practices gathered in this first step should be as authentic as possible.

Step 2: Gather positive practices

Typically, empirical explorations of tasks and contexts which support design, attempt to answer the question of what people do and what types of problems they experience – on average. Design is then used to supposedly 'solve' these problems. In fact, the gap between the knowledge which is gathered through this type of analysis (e.g., average notions about the problems people have with brewing coffee) and potential solutions (e.g., new ways of brewing coffee) is wide, potentially leading to the disconnection of 'data' and 'idea' (design gap, Wood, 1997). We advocate a different strategy, namely to analyse people, we call them 'positive practitioners', who particularly take joy from a practice within the limits of the given theme (Step 1). Those instances of outstanding performances of positive practices in terms of need fulfilment will serve as further inspiration for the deliberate (re)design of practices.

We explore the main elements of a positive practice through applying a semi-structured interview and an in situ (re-)performance of the positive practice. To this end, we developed the positive-practice canvas (PPC) as a design-oriented, visual interview guide (see Figure 11.3). The PPC is printed on an A3 paper size format. On the one hand, it provides an overview of all relevant elements and key questions. On the other hand, it works as a notepad to document answers. As a first step, we ask participants to 'pick a positive everyday practice, associated with the [theme]'. We then ask participants to perform the positive practice they have picked. Ideally, researchers would find themselves in the right place at the right time. As this is only rarely possible, we encourage the interviewee to act out the practice as close to the original performance as possible. Subsequently, we ask participants to go through the practice just performed before step-by-step using the PPC. In each step we ask participants to elaborate on the meaning (e.g., 'Take a minute to think about the selected practice', 'Tell me why you are engaging with this practice', 'What is your motivation?'), the competencies (e.g., 'What kinds of skills and knowledge are necessary to perform your practice?'), and the material (e.g., 'What kinds of objects do you use to do this?'). From a wellbeing perspective, it is important to gather the specific meaning of a given practice which is provided by the participant. While practices can be comprised of similar materials and competencies, they can differ in the way they are performed. For instance, the act of riding a bike requires a bicycle and the skills to ride it. However, an especially competence-oriented way to ride a bike (e.g., a BMX) certainly differs from a, say, socially-oriented way (e.g., touring with friends). When trying to pinpoint the needs which are involved proves to be difficult, the guideline offers clarifying questions (based on Sheldon et al., 2001), such as: 'When you engage in this practice, do you feel close to people important to you?' (relatedness), or '… do you feel like experiencing something new?' (stimulation). Through these questions, different types of motivations can be brought up and they may help to characterise the meaning which is experienced by the interviewee. It is advisable to first find out about the motivation which stands behind the motivation to perform a certain practice (i.e., meaning) as it helps immensely to gather information on the competencies and the materials which are needed. When talking about the materials, the interviewer must not only take material objects (e.g., tools) into focus, but also the context (e.g., location, time). In each step all three elements are present and remain connected. Thus, the PPC helps to organise, structure and elaborate all elements of a practice.

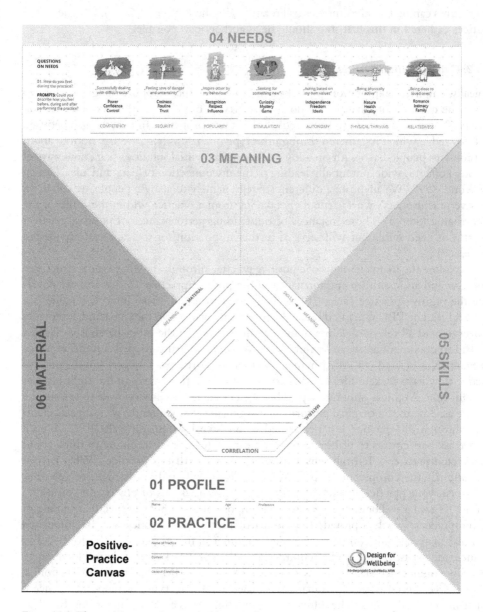

Figure 11.3 The positive-practice canvas (abstracted).

The interviewer should ensure that important information and insights are noted on the canvas (see Figure 11.4). Furthermore, the PPC is accompanied by a more traditional written guideline; both can easily be used together or as separate tools. The PPC's overall goal is to capture the unfolding of a particularly positive performance of a practice over time, organise its content and select verbatim quotes, to make it accessible for design. It needs to be pointed out that from our experience, it is better to let participants describe different practices one after the other rather than mixing them up in one description.

Figure 11.4 A handwritten positive-practice canvas used in an interview.

In our case study we interviewed eight people who enjoy brewing coffee and gathered 17 single positive practices. P1, a 29-year-old male civil engineer, enjoys 'coffee brewing for guests'. He wants to be a good host: '[…] I want to demonstrate hospitality by giving only the best to my guests.' He creates an atmosphere of comfort and cosiness through the warmth and smell of the freshly brewed coffee. This practice is driven by the need of *relatedness*: he takes care of his guests, as they are important to him. For example, it is important for him not to lose contact with his guests during the practice of brewing coffee. As a result, he gives a detailed explanation, attempts to keep them in a loop and tries to make the coffee brewing process more transparent. P2, a 35-year-old female student, engages in a 'ritualised coffee brewing'. For her, the manual coffee grinder is the most important tool in the kitchen. Grinding the beans, taking care of the coffee is a sign of taking a moment off on a busy day. P2 enjoys the ritual and the security it provides: '[…] it is like a holiday from daily life, a break.' These examples show how practices can be distinguished by the major needs they fulfil. Although both practices involve the preparation of coffee, their purpose is quite different, which in turn impacts the way the practice is performed.

Step 3: Consolidate positive practices

Gathering positive practices results in a collection of distinct, individual, positive performances of practices. Depending on the number of 'positive practitioners' interviewed and their practices, the collection of positive practices can become large. On the one hand this is good, as it represents a substantial pool to be inspired by; on the other hand, this pool might need to be consolidated. We suggest two different strategies. One is to take the most inspiring positive practice (with a clear need fulfilment and a strong connection between all elements) and to use it as anecdotal input for design. The other is to further consolidate the gathered positive practices.

We suggest the above can be consolidated by grouping practices which are similar in terms of their meaning (i.e., needs fulfilled) (see above). This results in bundles of practices with the same meaning populating the same design space (in our case, to brew coffee). Similar practices are not 'averaged', but rather accumulated to enrich the designer's understanding through different combinations of competencies and materials leading to a similar meaning. The overall aim is to gain an understanding of the underlying pattern of a practice. A tool that may assist in consolidating is an accumulation chart, a simple table. The idea of the chart is to compare the individual PPCs and their elements. Each row of the table represents an individual positive practice, since the unit of the analysis is the practice and not to be confused with the individual practitioner. Columns of the chart start with the title of the practice, the name or code of the contributing participant, the meaning and the ascribed need, the competencies and finally the materials which are involved. Here it is helpful to highlight needs by using different colours. The difference between raw data and processed data needs to be apparent (see Figure 11.5 for an exemplary accumulation chart).

In our case study of brewing coffee, 17 positive practices were copied into an accumulation chart and sorted into three bundles of shared meaning. The first bundle, labelled 'brewing a coffee as a ritual', describes practices that fulfil the need of security and highlights the actual process of brewing a coffee and the positivity of a repetitive action. For instance, P1 characterises brewing coffee as a morning routine, that is, a fixed procedure that ensures that every day starts with a good coffee. For him, timing plays an important role. He mentioned: 'I boil water while taking a shower. Thus, I can make a coffee right after showering.' P1 experiences the efficiency, the interlocking of different activities, as positive. P3 describes a further security practice. She likes to brew a coffee in a way to always achieve the same quality: '[…] without my [particularly] coffee it is not a real start of the day.' The second bundle of shared meaning is to 'brew a coffee in a professional way'. It addresses the need for competence. A third bundle is 'brewing a coffee for others' (a relatedness practice).

Examining practices with similar meanings in a similar design space focuses as well as broadens the perspective on what people do and feel within a practice. In all of the three examples, the practice of preparing coffee helps the participants to feel competent, to feel safe and to feel related. Moreover, the particular needs stay the same, but the ways to fulfil these needs vary. The different practices of preparing coffee with the same goal of satisfying needs provide inspiring ways to design for different competencies and materials.

Step 4: Design ideal practices

Practices have a narrative structure: they unfold linearly over time through their performance. However, even very positive performances are not always ideal. The purpose of this step is to write a story about how an *ideal* performance of a practice in terms of need fulfilment may unfold over time. Furthermore, Step 4 offers the possibility of including authentic research findings in the design process and making those insights traceable at the same time.

social practice	Happy User	meaning: bulletpoints and quotes from the interview	competencies: bulletpoints and quotes from the interview	material: bulletpoints and quotes from the interview	satisfied need
Daily preparation of Latte Macchiato using Portafilter coffee machine	P2, F, freelance Fashion designer	Coffee making as a daily morning ritual / daily ritual which must not be changed	Knowing how the machine works	Well performing coffee maker (Portafilter coffee machine by Gastroback)	Safety
		Consistently high quality of coffee taste & perfect milk foam	Choosing the right Espresso coffee beans	Latte Macchiato glasses + Long spoons	
		Pleasure	Frothing the milk: Choosing the right temperature for the right milk	Milk frother (Frother for the stove / Battery-operated handheld device)	
		Waking up ("I need my coffee in the morning for a good start to the day")	Understanding the features and finding the correct settings	Choosing the right Espresso coffee beans	
		Part of common life / every-day life	Right interplay of grinding degree, water pressure and coffee form	Coffee grounds container for easier emptying	
		Taking a break with husband in the kitchen	Continuously trying out in order to get the perfect individual coffee taste	Accessories: rubber mat for setting aside hot milk, small cups, spoons, different filters	
		Ability to offer very good coffee to family / friends / acquaintances and neighbours (Being known for serving very good coffee)	Finding out about the correct settings with the aid of youtube videos	Stove	
Preparation of coffee using Hario V60 Drip kettle (Hand filter) in the morning on weekends for family and friends	P3, M, UX Designer	Preparing a special coffee for family and friends	Knowledge about the right preparation method (Amount of beans, grinding degree, Ratio of water and coffee, right way of pouring brewing, specifics)	Hario V60 Bueno Drip Kettle (Especially built to optimise the process of pouring over hot water)	Relatedness
		Sharing with others	to keep the others in the loop of brewing coffee	Hario V60 Bueno Drip Kettle (Especially built to optimise the process of pouring over hot water)	
		"His specialty" – He is experienced and his skills will ensure a good outcome	Preparation off the top of your head	Paper filter of Hario V60	
		Welfare of his family	Mental preparation: especially when handling may require more attention / visualising the proceedings	Old jug made from ceramic with insulating cover	
		Time and effort for others ("Providing more than just a cup of coffee")	Rapid recognition of different results (colour, taste, smell)	Electric coffee grinder (Gastroback) / manual coffee grinder (Hario)	
		Being part of the process from the beginning until the end - superiority to control the process	Choosing a specific coffee bean (in-depth knowledge of origin, growing region, taste, particularities of the coffee bean; i.e. he once tried a coffee made from Indian coffee beans, which supposedly is very rare)	Scale	
		Understanding the process and the science behind it	Keeping a steady level	Timer / mobile phone	
		Continually challenging and improving oneself	Experimenting with various determinants		
		Honest and authentic preparation of coffee	Constantly improving his tools ("MacGyver of Coffee")		
Preparing espresso coffee for himself in the morning using Portafilter machine	P4, M, 38, Sales manager in a medium-sized company, married, 2 children	"I am treating myself"	"single work steps are not difficult"	"The coffee maker indicates the right amount of coffee beans"	Autonomy
		"I am treating myself with the perfect coffee. I am taking the time"	Grinding the coffee correctly	»25 seconds for this activity are untouchable«	
		"I am always looking for the best espresso (Geschmack)"	15 kg steady pressure	100 % Robusta coffee bean 23 €/kg · 1 kg / Month obtained from a coffee roastery from Cologne	
		"I am glad that everything went well"	Operating a machine	Rocket Cellini Classic (Portafilter coffee machine, 2 Kreiser) approximately 1100 €	
		"Preparing the coffee and enjoying it afterwards. With guests others have prepared the coffee for me 5/10, but only if it is the perfect espresso"	Cleaning a machine	Tamper	
		"Challenging myself"	Pinning the cup in order to be able to drink all of the coffee crema	Customised cup (Ristretto cup, heated)	
		"Relaxing and enjoying something just for myself"		Vision: »better machines, more barometers, more manometers«	
Espresso und Milchkaffee / Cappuchino kochen für andere / Gäste	P4, M, 38, Sales manager in a medium-sized company, married, 2 children	"Allowing others to prepare an espresso with my coffee maker"	As already mentioned above: foam milk	As mentioned above, minus Olive oil, plus milk and a small milk jug plus: Nespresso machine in case that there are more guests visiting	Popularity
		Inspiring others – evoke interest for espresso coffee			
		Passing on gathered know-how, sharing knowledge and opinions about taste			
		I enjoy preparing coffee for others (6/10)			
		"Treating others"			
Energetic preparation of coffee	P1, M, 29, Civil engineer	Morning ritual		A sufficient amount of time	safety
		Waking up and starting the day off right		Resources: Coffee beans, milk, water	
		Taste and smell revive the senses	Everything is happening simultaneously / everything is interlinked	Manual coffee grinder, cafetière, cups, kettle, gas stove	
		Joyful anticipation / Drinking coffee in the morning as motivation	Choosing the right coffee beans		
		the outcome needs to be right: preparing coffee on my own hands	Anticipating prospective duration of processes / Bearing in mind variables (Amount of water, Amount of coffee, grinding degree, etc.)	Fixed sequence of actions	
Preparing coffee when people are visiting	P1, M, 29, civil engineer	Hospitality: "I would like to offer something special"	"Made with love" / you need to take time / "I know some of my guests' preferences when it comes to drinking coffee"	A sufficient amount of time	feeling connected to family and friends
		My guests are supposed to feel at home / at ease		Cosy surroundings	
		Being able to have something special to offer to my guests/ Sharing knowledge	Welcoming my guests/ lucid communication/ Maintaining a friendly atmosphere	Manual coffee grinder, Bialetti, cups, kettle, gas stove	
		The best way to be able to serve very good coffee for a large group of people	Choosing the right coffee beans	Resources: Coffee beans, milk, water	
		Demonstrating know-how	Skills: course of action / using the coffee maker the right way	Cup (depending on the beverage)	
Cold brewing of coffee	Daniel, 29, Civil engineer	"I am well-prepared, like a well appointed laboratory" / feeling competent & self-confident	Organisational skills, Preparation, estimation of time/parameters: How long does it take? How much will I need?	a sufficient amount of time	Feeling competent
		I like to experiment / I have always wanted to try things out	Being inspired/ searching for new methods/ staying up-to-date	Resources: Coffee beans, Water	
		I don't know what people think about my actions, I am rather focusing on myself	you need to get a feeling for the right coffee "I need to be up for it"	Manual coffee grinder, fridge, jars, scale, measuring jug	
		I have a special interest in it, it is interesting as things could also go wrong		Recipe / Inspiration	
		Expanding my horizon			
		I like to share what I have found out with my friends			
Manual preparation of coffee serves as a ritual	Tanja, 35, Student	My coffee grinder serves as a pragmatic statement and not just mere decoration		My coffee grinder is the most important tool in my kitchen/ I always have to be able to have it at hand	Autonomy
		I love antiques ("a big soul") Feeling at home		Resources: coffee beans, water	
		To make time / like taking a break in the afternoon "I decide when I take a break"	Being willing to take time / time-out from every-day life / no rules apply	cafetière (Bodum), my favorite coffee cup	
		Gourmet, superior quality is desired	Estimating amount "you need to be daring, especially in the beginning" / Trying out, curiosity to try out something new		
		Looking forward to the product while preparing it / joyful anticipation starts while preparing the coffee			

Figure 11.5 An exemplary accumulation chart.

Take an anecdotal practice or an accumulated positive practice bundle as a starting point for the story. Do not simply recount what was gathered in Step 2 but create your own envisioned practice out of the existing material. Start adding ideas of how to improve psychological need fulfilment which fit the elements given. To be clear, this is not a further step of analysis, but already an act of design. The ideal practice narrative's purpose is to envision practices that should emerge through using the yet-to-be-specified products and/or services with the help of insights from the gathered positive practices. At best, the resulting narratives represent a realistic and rich description of how a future positive practice should unfold in everyday life.

The ideal practice serves as a reference for the later specification of the 'material'. It allows revisiting the initial idea (as a reference) as well as giving to answer the crucial question of whether the created product or service is able to shape the envisioned practice and experiences.

The following guideline helps to structure the narrative and to keep all necessary elements in view:

- *Context.* Describe the situation in which the practice is placed through time, location and related previous and following events.
- *People.* Introduce the acting practitioners who engage in the practice by age, gender, profession (if necessary), personality and other relevant elements of their life-world.
- *Motivation.* State why the practitioner engages in the practice. Clarify the personal meaning of the practice and describe how the practice fulfils the needs.
- *Interaction.* Describe in detail how the practice unfolds over time. Describe all single activities and meaningful moments. Emotions and thoughts of your practitioner should be as detailed as possible. Use quotes from Step 2 to make it as authentic as possible. Keep the material vague. The narrative should focus on the interaction as if the material already existed.
- *Happy ending.* Summarise the whole practice and make sure that your practitioner is happy and satisfied because of performing the practice. Describe the final state of the practitioner.

The author should stay positive throughout the whole narrative. A narrative of an ideal practice avoids all traces of a pejorative undertone and should not be negative or sarcastic. The story makes the practice accessible to others. To be sure, the narrative does not have to be a written story. Animated cartoons, storyboards (see Figure 11.6), theatre plays or videos are also ways to tell a story. They help people to understand the narrative based on additional visual information. Another advantage of, for example, video as a format, is that the speed and duration of the narrative can be better controlled. However, videos and cartoons need time and resources to prepare. This extra portion of effort does not automatically make a difference and can even make it more complicated. For example, video will inevitably show details unimportant to the story but nevertheless likely to grab attention, while written stories generally allow for a much better control of distracting detail (also see Diefenbach et al., 2010).

For our case study, three narratives were created. *Coffee-Love* is a narrative based on *brewing a coffee as a ritual*, predominantly fulfilling a need for routine and relaxation (i.e., security). The second narrative, called *Experto*, is based on *brewing a coffee in a professional way* and addresses the need for competence. The third narrative, called *Share-Co*, is based on *brewing a coffee for others* and tells the story of experiencing relatedness. Undeniably, the

After the alarm clock rings Julia awakes and turns it off. The first rays of the sunshine through the window.

Julia stretches out and starts to think about the forthcoming day. But her first thought is: "First, I need a coffee". The sound of Co-Lo heating-up shows Julia that Co-Lo is ready to start the day.

Now Julia is in her element. She knows the process of brewing coffee by heart although it is complex. Instead of doing everything automatically Co-Lo leaves many steps to Julia. For Julia it is already some kind of routine to cooperate with Co-Lo.

After everything is prepared, Co-Lo shows in detail how the coffee is brewed. The whole brewing process is very transparent.

Julia is still following it every morning again and again. Co-Lo spreads coffee aroma through the whole kitchen. More intensive than the machine Julia used before.

With a cup of coffee in her hand Julia is ready to start the day – even before she took the first sip.

Figure 11.6 Excerpt of the Coffee-Love narrative. Note that the original story is more extensive, and more images are included in the storyboard.

number of narratives and the number of bundles of shared meaning match unintentionally. Based on the three bundles of shared meanings, more narratives would be possible and even beneficial. For a brief example of an ideal practice narrative, see Figure 11.6.

Narratives of ideal practices can be evaluated easily by potential users. Positive practitioners from the interviews can be revisited and asked to comment on the stories. This input can be used to improve the narrative further.

Step 5: Specify the material to shape the ideal practice

So far, the material that was used to formulate the ideal practice narratives was deliberately left vague. In the fifth step, the material is specified, based on the narratives. In other words, the 'design problem' is specified by the material (i.e., product, service) in a way that it will evoke and shape the practice through the functionality and interaction offered.

To generate concepts for analogue or digital products and services is the heart of the design practitioners' work. Most design agencies or companies follow their own processes of how concepts should be generated. Thus, this step does not include a formal guideline or tool. We believe that designers and developers are far better off using their own processes and the procedures they are experienced with. However, we suggest that people involved in the creative process should familiarise themselves with the narratives and understand them as the objective and reference for their design work. At best, people participate in the design, who also conducted the interviews and developed the narratives. All in all, designers involved in this step should be able to relate to the narratives and use their capacity for empathy to create a 'material' able to evoke the practice.

In our case study, six coffee machines were created. Figure 11.7 presents the concepts and a short description of the design rationales and intended need fulfilment.

Ideal practice narrative: Coffee Love

A machine that still has many manual steps.
A transparent water tank, coffee decanter and an hourglass like shape
embody the process and let users participate.

The machine is very transparent so that users can participate
in the process. Moreover, the distance between filter and water supply allows the coffee's smell to spread.

Ideal practice narrative: Experto

A machine that is like a laboratory. Users can manipulate parameters
such as grinding, water temperature and amount of water precisely.
This degree of freedom increases the influence users
can take on the actual coffee. Moreover, most components are
attached manually that is based on a workmanlike manner.

The machine provides separate parts for each step of the
brewing process. Coffee grinder and water tank are side by side
and offer marks to measure all required components.
Before the coffee is brewed the grinded coffee can be
checked in the filter a second time.

Ideal practice narrative: Share-Co

A machine that is placed on the table to serve coffee to others.
Having the machine on the table no one has to leave the table and
the social interaction remains stable. When the coffee is ready the
host could show his hospitality by offering sugar and milk
to her guests.

The two-sided brew-station provides space for four cups.
The host can fine-tune the coffee for each cup from one side of the
machine and guests could see how the coffee is prepared
individually from the other side.

Figure 11.7 Six concepts (two per narrative) that try to fit into and evoke the corresponding narrative.

Step 6: Realise the material

In the previous steps, meaning and competence (Step 4) and the material (Step 5) were combined in a particular way to create an ideal practice. In the final step, the actual material is realised. This requires a specialised set of design skills, depending on the used material (e.g., particular technologies), which is beyond the scope of the present chapter. Keep in mind, that the design narrative itself no longer matters, as the material has to tell the narrative through its experiential qualities, functionality and detailed interaction – i.e., on its own. Step 5 represents the bridge between wellbeing and products/services we were looking for. The second version of the ideal practice narrative presents an integrated story, material, emerging practices and experiences together, as one interdependent unit. But while the material remains tangible and consistent, the practices and experiences are intangible and need to be reproduced through situated performances in everyday life. We believe that the process that is described in this chapter supports the inscribing of the practice and especially its meaning into the material. If the material is used in an intended situation, it will help to achieve a result which is as close as possible to the desired ideal in a practice-as-performance situation. As a result, this process can be supported by additional information given to potential users about the envisioned practice. In this respect, the ideal practice narrative can be used further as a reference document for marketing or any related purpose in an industrial setting.

Conclusion

Nowadays, to explicitly design for subjective wellbeing is an accepted objective of HCI and ID. Nevertheless, a very large part of this work in this area is still concerned with clarifying what wellbeing, meaning and enjoyment is. Up to now, design practice remained more or less unaffected by the research on subjective wellbeing. We believe this to be due to a gap between the abstract, intangible notion of wellbeing, needs and experiences and the concreteness of digital or analogue products. It seems easy to proclaim that it is 'all about experiences', without addressing the question of *how* concrete products and services can be designed to create those experiences any further.

The presented approach to design for wellbeing intends to bridge the gap between abstract and concrete. It uses Hassenzahl's approach to experience design, i.e., to provide need fulfilment and positive experience through particular functionality, interaction and form bundled into a technology (Law et al., 2009) and combines it with social practice theory to connect meaning with the material. The step-by-step approach is meant as a sufficiently detailed, but still adaptable, process for practitioners. It is a starting point rather than a fixed process. It seeks to inspire a more systematic approach to the design of wellbeing, without being overly prescriptive and rigid.

We believe that the described process is able to provide a more explicit grounding of products and services in wellbeing. Gathering positive practices, understanding them, combining them, idealising them, turning them into a narrative and finally inscribing them into material is a highly reflective process. It helps to bridge the gap between theory and material (in our case a product/technology). As Dalsgaard and Dinger put it: 'It is exactly this process of grounding, re-grounding, articulation and re-articulation that facilitates exchanges and thus reflections on the ties between theory and practice' (Dalsgaard & Dindler, 2014, p. 1643).

In the end, design is always normative. Any new product will change existing practices – whether intended by the designers or not. Thus, designers carry responsibility not only for the material and its quality, but also for the practices it encourages and experiences that are mediated. Naturally, designers try to anticipate possible side-effects and misuses of the envisioned product or service. This, however, appears quite passive. With the present process we encourage designers to take a more active role by explicitly addressing wellbeing and envisioned practices *before* a product is designed.

Acknowledgements

All presented tools and case studies are outcomes of the project Design for Wellbeing. NRW. This work has been funded by Leitmarkt Agentur NRW and the European Regional Development Fund (EFRE-0800005). For more information see www.design-for-wellbeing.org.

References

Aporta, C., & Higgs, E. (2005). Satellite culture. *Current Anthropology*, *46*(5), 729–753.

Blythe, M.A., & Wright, P.C. (2006). Pastiche scenarios: Fiction as a resource for user centred design. *Interacting with Computers*, *18*(5), 1139–1164.

Dalsgaard, P., & Dindler, C. (2014). Between theory and practice: Bridging concepts in HCI research. In *Proc. CHI 2014* (pp. 1635–1644).

Desmet, P., & Pohlmeyer, A.E. (2013). Positive design: An introduction to design for subjective wellbeing. *International Journal of Design*, *7*(3), 5–19.

Diefenbach, S. (2017). Positive technology – A powerful partnership between positive psychology and interactive technology. A discussion of potential and challenges. *Journal of Positive Psychology and Wellbeing*, *2*(1), 1–22.

Diefenbach, S., Hassenzahl, M., Eckoldt, K., Hartung, L., Lenz, E., & Laschke, M. (2017). Designing for well-being: A case study of keeping small secrets. *The Journal of Positive Psychology*, *12*(2), 151–158.

Diefenbach, S., Hassenzahl, M., Eckoldt, K., & Laschke, M. (2010). The impact of concept (re) presentation on users' evaluation and perception. In *Proceedings of the 6th Nordic Conference on Human-Computer Interaction: Extending Boundaries* (pp. 631–634).

Hassenzahl, M. (2018). The thing and I (Spring of '17 remix). In M. Blythe, & A. Monk (Eds.), *Funology 2 – From Usability to Enjoyment* (pp. 301–313). Cham: Springer International Publishing.

Hassenzahl, M., Diefenbach, S., & Göritz, A. (2010). Needs, affect, and interactive products – Facets of user experience. *Interacting with Computers*, *22*(5), 353–362.

Hassenzahl, M., Eckoldt, K., Diefenbach, S., Laschke, M., Lenz, E., & Kim, J. (2013). Designing moments of meaning and pleasure. Experience design and happiness. *International Journal of Design*, *7*(3), 21–31.

Huta, V., & Ryan, R.M. (2010). Pursuing pleasure or virtue: The differential and overlapping well-being benefits of hedonic and eudaimonic motives. *Journal of Happiness Studies*, *11*, 735–762.

Ihde, D. (1990). *Technology and the Lifeworld: From Garden to Earth*. Indianapolis, IN, USA: Indiana University Press.

Jordan, P.W. (2000). *Designing Pleasurable Products : An Introduction to the New Human Factors*. London, UK: Taylor & Francis.

Law, E.L.-C., Roto, V., Hassenzahl, M., Vermeeren, A.P.O.S., & Kort, J. (2009). Understanding, scoping and defining user experience. In *Proceedings of the 27th International Conference on Human Factors in Computing Systems – CHI 09* (p. 719).

Lyubomirsky, S. (2007). *The How of Happiness: A New Approach to Getting the Life You Want*. New York, NY, USA: Penguin Books.

Reckwitz, A. (2002). Toward a theory of social practices: A development in culturalist theorizing. *European Journal of Social Theory*, *5*(2), 243–263.

Sheldon, K.M., Elliot, A.J., Kim, Y., & Kasser, T. (2001). What is satisfying about satisfying events ? Testing 10 candidate psychological needs. *Journal of Personality and Social Psychology*, *80*(2), 325–339.

Sheldon, K.M., & Lyubomirsky, S. (2006). Achieving sustainable gains in happiness: Change your actions, not your circumstances. *Journal of Happiness Studies*, 7(1), 55–86.

Shove, E., Pantzar, M., & Watson, M. (2012). *The Dynamics of Social Practice: Everyday Life and How It Changes*. London, UK: SAGE Publications Ltd.

Wood, L.E. (1997). *User Interface Design: Bridging the Gap from User Requirements to Design*. Boca Raton, FL: CRC Press.

12 Dilemma-thinking as a means to enhance criticality in design for wellbeing

Deger Ozkaramanli

Design for wellbeing is intricately linked to handling complex societal challenges through design. Wellbeing-oriented design approaches, such as social design (Tromp, 2013), persuasive technologies (e.g., Fogg, 2003) or positive design (Desmet & Pohlmeyer, 2013), are often applied in domains such as social exclusion, obesity, mental ill-health, online privacy or the refugee crisis. However, societal challenges are unanticipatedly complex requiring interdisciplinary expertise, as well as the ability to bridge and make sense out of such interdisciplinary expertise. As a result, an increased attention to the notions of critique and criticality is needed when tackling societal challenges in the context of design for wellbeing. Following Butler (2001), critique can be defined as the mode of purposive and reflective questioning that seeks to identify the familiar and unchallenged thoughts and assumptions that underlie accepted practices, i.e., seeing what lies beneath the surface.

A number of design approaches have recently emerged that place criticality at the centre of their activities – they will be referred to as 'critical design approaches' in this chapter. Among these are critical and speculative design (Dunne & Raby, 2013), adversarial design (DiSalvo, 2012) and reflective design (Sengers et al., 2005). These approaches, despite important nuances in their practices, converge at the main aim of raising questions and stimulating critical reflection and debate, among designers and users alike, about the implicit values and assumptions that drive the agenda of existing design practices. Because of this, they act as an 'inward-looking' mechanism that question and critique the state of existing design practices, i.e., the 'status quo' (Malpass, 2017; Bardzell & Bardzell, 2013; Dunne & Raby, 2013). The ideologies underpinning these approaches can in fact be traced back to radical design practices that originated in Italy in the 1950s (Malpass, 2017). However, only recently have critical design approaches started receiving scholarly attention (see Bardzell & Bardzell, 2013). This arguably reflects the increasing need for critique in the socially and ethically expanding landscape of design research.

The way critical design approaches place criticality at the heart of their practices can inform and enhance design for wellbeing approaches, particularly approaches that aim for societal wellbeing by influencing people's experiences, attitudes and behaviour. The aim of this chapter, therefore, is to expand on the value of critique in the context of designing in order to address societal challenges and to propose three *criticality skills* that can support framing societal challenges in design. The proposition here is that developing a critical design practice can support handling the complexity of societal challenges, and, thus, increase the chance of designing meaningful interventions that contribute to wellbeing. The first part of this chapter aims to position criticality as a way of thinking that can pervade all design activities instead of being considered an isolated method or style of designing. The second part focuses on the need for criticality when addressing societal challenges. Finally, the third part explores the intimate link between criticality and dilemmas, proposing that dilemma-driven design can be used as an approach to catalyse criticality in design. Based on this understanding, three skills are proposed to enhance criticality in design activities.

This chapter builds on previous work in which three ideation strategies (i.e., embodying symbols, forced choices and behavioural barriers) were proposed that could be used to trigger emotional dilemmas as a means to design for provocation (Ozkaramanli & Desmet, 2016). Implementing these strategies in idea generation revealed that designers, who are trained in a creative problem-solving type of tradition, may find it challenging to adopt the nature of reasoning necessary to design for provocation (Ozkaramanli & Desmet, 2016). This outcome indicates that critical design approaches require a distinct mindset and skills, as suggested by Dunne and Raby (2013, p. 34): 'It [critical design] was more of an attitude than anything else, a position rather than a methodology'. This chapter is a step towards uncovering what that critical mindset can be and the role of dilemmas in supporting it.

Critical design vs criticality in design

Critical design, a term originally coined by Dunne and Raby (2013), emphasises a distinction between 'affirmative' design practices that reinforce the status quo defined by global capitalism and 'critical' design practices that subvert this status quo. The main intention of critical design is to examine and critique design through design, i.e., to critique market thinking that dominates existing design practices through hypothetical design concepts that embody this critique. This is a noble and valuable intention that can be expanded upon in a number of ways.

First, the emergence of wellbeing-oriented design approaches has blurred the affirmative/critical divide. Many examples of wellbeing-oriented design prioritise individual and societal wellbeing over profitability (see Desmet, Pohlmeyer & Forlizzi, 2013). In that sense, design for wellbeing practices can be considered critical to the extent that they reassess design's priorities, and affirmative to the extent that they can be commercialised and adopted by the masses. Related to this, Bardzell and Bardzell (2013, p. 8) noted: 'A design is critical inasmuch as some aspect of it critiques the status quo, and it is affirmative inasmuch as it affirms the status quo; that is, any given design may be both affirmative and critical.' Second, criticality consists of a multitude of perspectives that go beyond global capitalism. When reformulating critical design approaches, Bardzell and Bardzell (2013) proposed a more holistic understanding of critical thought, borrowing from critical theory and literary criticism. Among these are matters of gender, race, class, sexuality, religion, education and other social dynamics (Tyson, 2014). These critical perspectives can be leveraged to a wide range of design practices, including those in design for wellbeing. As a result, criticality is a way of thinking that can infuse and enhance any design activity (versus being a specific method or a style of designing).

The need for criticality in design for wellbeing

Every intellectual endeavour that aspires to 'change the social world for the better', which essentially applies to design for wellbeing, can benefit from 'inward-looking' mechanisms to critically examine the values and assumptions underlying its activities. In humanities and social sciences, critical theory-based approaches have a long history. For example, critical approaches to international law focus on the possible biases and blind spots of international law and its role in propagating unequal global power relations (see Schwöbel-Patel, 2014).This debate is not as far off from critical design approaches as one may think. In 'International Law's Objects', Schwöbel-Patel and Werner (2017) investigate *the screen* as an object that symbolises how media displays societal challenges (e.g., the refugee crisis) in a way that hides aspects of the problem presumably unsuited for public debate. In addition, critical marketing challenges institutional relationships that solely focus on the satisfaction of the customer (see Saren et al., 2007).These critical standpoints welcome the discomfort of dealing with societal tensions, unexamined power relationships and disputed interests. Having such perspectives in design can help establish an intellectual space motivated by the need for critique (versus the need for monetary gain or for technological advancement that often dominate existing design practices, see Malpass, 2017).When applied to design for wellbeing, such an intellectual space can create room for questioning various conceptualisations of wellbeing (e.g., from the perspectives of age, gender, sexuality and so on) and how these conceptualisations inform design practices.

In addition, design has become increasingly more sensitive to complex societal challenges, such as the refugee crisis (see Margolin & Margolin, 2002;Tromp, 2013). Handling this complexity can greatly benefit from critical perspectives that help questioning design decisions and the implications of proposed design interventions for societal wellbeing. Societal challenges are often unanticipatedly complex. They have historical roots and unforeseen consequences that influence society at many levels. In addition, they often involve political agendas, power struggles and emotional tensions. As a result, approaching these challenges in the same way one would traditionally approach a design brief may prove to be a futile, or even damaging, effort unless creative problem-solving skills are coupled with criticality skills.This is evidenced in Pater's (2016) reaction to a design competition launched to address the refugee crisis, which stated:

> By emphasising the problem-solving capabilities of design, the WDCD [What Design Can Do] Refugee Challenge supports the idea that the free market is much better at solving the world's crises than governments are. Design may be able to come up with clever products or enlightening ideas, but only governments and NGOs can provide refugees with the resources, infrastructure and laws that are needed in the long run.

Pater's (2016) reluctance to position design as the 'solution' to such a complex societal issue deserves attention for several reasons. First, addressing societal challenges through design requires holistic/systems thinking and collaboration among governments, non-profit organisations and experts across a variety of disciplines.This point has also been articulated by Siegel and Beck (2014) when outlining a theory of slow change in interaction design. Siegel and Beck (2014) stated that problems have histories and futures, and they relate to other problems that permeate individual, community and global levels. Second, left to their own devices, novice designers may fall short of responses to various political, economic, ethical and cultural questions that arise in the context of such issues. These questions require critical thinking, which is not always sufficiently emphasised in educational contexts as is, for example, market thinking. Third, societal challenges are often morally loaded subjects. The refugee crisis, for instance, receives wide media coverage; it often gets associated with even more morally loaded subjects such as terrorism, and it affects the political landscape of many countries in shocking ways. Because of this, falling into ethical biases when designing to address such challenges seems inevitable.

Figure 12.1 Photo of 25 m² Syria project.
Photo: courtesy of POL.

The aforementioned challenges indicate that much is left to designers' intuition, empathic capacity and worldview when striving to adopt a viable approach to contribute to societal wellbeing. Should industrial design avoid addressing complex societal challenges then? An example may help to answer this question. In November 2016, the replica of a Syrian home was set up in an IKEA store to create a stark contrast between the cosy idea of a Western house and a house affected by the horrors of war (see Figure 12.1). The set-up was part of a Red Cross fundraising campaign in Norway. One can imagine that, upon an unexpected encounter with the Syrian home, a shopper would be confronted with their own privileged position. The execution of this idea (e.g., whether stereotypical representations of refugees were used or the vulnerability of women and children was exploited) is as crucial as its intention in qualifying it as critical design. If we strictly focus on the context of the intervention, however, encountering this intervention at the heart of commercial design (i.e., an IKEA store) may be considered a clever choice in stimulating critical reflection. As the example illustrates, design can (and should) aim to tackle societal challenges and, in doing so, every effort should be made to remain critically engaged with the process and outcome of designing.

Dilemma-driven design as a catalyst for criticality

Engaging in critical design practices can be very challenging for those who are inspired by it, but do not have a background or training in realising their intentions. The work on critical design offers little information about the process of designing critically. For instance, Dunne and Raby (2013) clarify the main goals of critical design and provide many inspiring design examples, but they rarely provide reference to the theory and decisions that informed these examples. In fact, the focus of critical design mostly lies with the subject of design rather than the process of designing (Bardzell & Bardzell, 2013). This is unfortunate considering the value of criticality for design practice: to make people, including product users and designers, more critical about the values, norms, assumptions and power relationships that shape products and services used in everyday life. As a result, conceptual and methodological handles are needed to engage with critical design processes.

One way of engaging in critical design practices is to explicitly focus on *triggering dilemmas* (Ozkaramanli & Desmet, 2016). In fact, examples of critical design often stimulate dilemmas to encourage reinterpretation of sociocultural norms and practices (see Malpass, 2012, p. 186; Dunne & Ruby, 2013, p. 89; Bardzell et al., 2012). This shared appreciation of the dilemma phenomenon links critical design practices to dilemma-driven design (DDD). DDD considers the emotional dilemmas of end-users as fruitful starting points for user-centred design activities (Ozkaramanli, 2017). In the context of DDD, dilemmas are defined as the realisation that one cannot simultaneously engage in two behavioural alternatives, which are guided by contradictory desires, motives or personal values (Ozkaramanli, Desmet & Özcan, 2016). Dilemmas often produce discomfort as they evoke difficult emotions such as doubt, anxiety or anticipated regret. This discomfort, however, serves an important function: it slows down mental processes to collect information for making informed choices (Fleming, 2014). In transformative learning theories, experiencing a dilemma is considered a crucial starting point for critical reflection (Mezirow, 1990). On this, Mezirow (1990, p. 2) notes:

> Much of what we learn involves making new interpretations that enable us to elaborate, further differentiate and reinforce our long-established frames of reference or to create new meaning schemes. Perhaps even more central to adult learning than elaborating established meaning schemes is the process of reflecting back on prior learning to determine whether what we have learned is justified under present circumstances.

Here, the distinction between reflection and critical reflection is important, as the latter emphasises an element of critique as in 'challenging the validity of *presuppositions* in prior learning' (Mezirow, 1990, p. 4). Due to this relationship between dilemmas and criticality, DDD can provide methodological guidance on critical design processes.

Based on the relationship between dilemmas and criticality, triggering dilemmas through products can be a means to *doing* critical design (Ozkaramanli & Desmet, 2016). A good example of critical design that surfaces dilemmas is 'New-born Fame' by Laura Cornet in Figure 12.2a. It is a set of toys, which is attached to a baby's crib, takes random photos of the baby and posts them on social media platforms. The function of 'New-born Fame' goes beyond the practical functionality of a playful object. Although it exhibits the properties of a regular toy, it deploys these properties to invite the viewer to think critically about the matter of online privacy. In doing so, 'New-born Fame' reveals various dilemmas such as:

> I want [to] protect the privacy of my family (at the cost of feeling isolated), and at the same time, I want to conveniently share my family joys with others (even though I cannot control who has access to what I share).

Figure 12.2b illustrates this example dilemma using the framework of dilemmas for designers (see Ozkaramanli, 2017). This framework serves as an analytical tool to structure and reflect on the deeply held motivations and emotions that underlie a dilemma, and, thus, it encourages reflection and discussion about the implications of design decisions (Ozkaramanli, 2017).

The reflective questioning facilitated by analysing dilemmas can enhance criticality when tackling societal challenges. This way of reflective questioning is particularly relevant

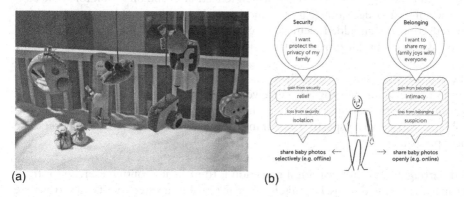

Figure 12.2 a. Photo of 'New-born Fame'. b. Framework of dilemmas for designers illustrating the dilemma of security vs belonging.

Source: a) photo courtesy of the designer; b) adapted from Ozkaramanli, 2017.

for the problem-framing phase of the design process. Traditionally, the evolution of the problem and the solution go hand-in-hand, where the development of solutions adds to the understanding of the problem until 'the feeling of having grasped the core of the problem' is reached (Dorst & Cross, 2001, p. 436). As critique is about raising questions instead of finding solutions, the interest in critical design practices lies with *lingering* in the problem space. The goal here is to approach the problem from different perspectives and to find alternative ways of framing the problem through critical thinking and reflective questioning (e.g., *Does the problem involve hidden agendas and power struggles among different stakeholders? Am I interpreting this problem, knowingly or unknowingly, in an elitist way?*). These questions are likely to evoke numerous dilemmas, which may generate discomfort – the feeling of grasping the core of the problem, as suggested by Dorst and Cross (2001), may never be achieved. As a result, lingering in the problem space can be characterised by finding comfort in the discomfort of dilemmas. Three main *criticality skills* can be learned and nurtured to fuel this process, namely:

(1) critical reflection;
(2) systemic thinking;
(3) suspending moral judgement.

The following paragraphs explain these skills and suggest preliminary practices through which they can be cultivated.

Critical reflection

Reflection is a core element of critical design approaches. In critical design, critical thinking is about 'not taking things for granted and always questioning what is given' (Dunne & Raby, 2013, p. 35). In reflective design, reflection is defined as 'bringing unconscious aspects of experience to conscious awareness, thereby making them available for conscious choice' (Sengers et al., 2005, p. 50). Slow technology is a design philosophy that places increased emphasis on time and presence in interaction as a means to engage users in reflection (Hallnäs & Redström, 2001). These definitions align with the reflective practice paradigm pioneered by Schön (1991), in which reflection in and on action form the basis of all types of design decisions (e.g., technical, creative, aesthetic and so on). In critical design, reflection has an added element of critique, which shifts the attention to *critical* reflection as defined by Mezirow (1990, p. 14):

> the process of becoming critically aware of how and why our presuppositions have come to constrain the way we perceive, understand and feel about our world; of reformulating these assumptions to permit a more inclusive, discriminating, permeable and integrative perspective; and of making decisions or otherwise acting on these new perspectives.

A good starting point to foster critical reflection is to make it a routine exercise to structurally analyse existing designs. For this, Ferri et al. (2014) suggested four tactics to analyse critical designs based on semiotic analysis, namely thematic blending, semantic shifts, social transgression and body modification. In addition, Bardzell et al. (2014) proposed a matrix of common argument types, which is composed of six dimensions of interaction design (i.e., topic, purpose, functionality, interactivity, form, materiality) and four dimensions of criticality (i.e., changing perspectives, proposals for change, enhancing appreciation and reflectiveness). This matrix is intended to bring clarity in the form of justifiable arguments as to what makes a specific design an example of critical design (see Bardzell et al., 2014). Finally, Tyson (2014) suggested a set of reflective questions for each of the leading theoretical frameworks in literary critical theory (e.g., psychoanalytic criticism, Marxist criticism and postcolonial criticism), which can be used to analyse and unpack the hidden values and assumptions in literary texts. Some of these critical lenses can be adapted to reading existing designs in order to fine-tune criticality skills. Presumably, this starts as a conscious and effortful process, and gradually becomes embedded in everyday practice. Developing a critically reflective design practice can consequently support handling the complexity of societal challenges and increase the chance of designing meaningful interventions that enhance societal wellbeing.

Systemic thinking

Design problems are defined as wicked problems, characterised by unclear formulations, malleable goals and multiple possible solutions and solution paths (Simon, 1973). This 'wickedness' becomes even more challenging in the context of addressing complex societal issues. This is because any design intervention proposed to alleviate the problem eventually has to fit back into an interdisciplinary system in which the problem is situated. For instance, 'Reframe Refugees' is an intervention that was one of the five shortlisted designs of the 2016 What Design Can Do's Refugee Challenge.[1] It is an online platform that enables refugees to sell their own photographs to media companies to raise money for selected charities. The designers of 'Reframe Refugees' have placed self-representation and empowerment at the core of their design concept. The design concept has attracted many positive comments from the public, including refugees themselves. Although self-representation can be a powerful stance in combatting stereotypical representations of refugees, the hidden assumption here seems to be that refugees are aware of and ready to challenge their own stereotypical representations in powerful media channels – which may or may not hold true for distressed communities. The intention here is not to claim that 'Reframe Refugees' is unaspiring or unhelpful. A point to be taken is that, when faced with complex issues such as the refugee crisis, designers should seek to understand different parts of the system in which the problem is situated and how these parts relate to the whole of the system (e.g., how media companies benefit from using stereotypical images of refugees). This skill is an integral part of systemic thinking (Siegel & Beck, 2014).

As critical design approaches are interested in exposing the hidden relationships among different parts of the system, embracing and unpacking the complexity of systemic problems becomes a useful skill. A valuable starting point to foster this skill is to adopt participatory design principles and collaborative interdisciplinary practices. Open collaborations potentially raise conflicting needs and interests (i.e., dilemmas) within and between stakeholders. If managed productively, these dilemmas can generate a nuanced understanding of multiple, and potentially conflicting, perspectives of the stakeholders. For this, 'framework of dilemmas' (see Figure 12.2b) can serve as an analytical tool to reflect on these dilemmas (Ozkaramanli, Desmet & Özcan, 2016). Such reflection involves identifying the needs, goals and values underpinning the dilemmas in the context of the collaboration and reframing the design problem from multiple perspectives. Although the framework of dilemmas was developed in the context of intrapersonal dilemmas (e.g., health vs indulgence, belonging vs autonomy), it can be adapted to analysing interpersonal dilemmas (e.g., dilemmas among various stakeholders). The critical design objects can consequently be physical manifestations of this dialogue and its dilemmas.

Suspending moral judgement

The process of designing involves making ethical decisions (Lloyd, 2009; Verbeek, 2006). These decisions can be made implicitly when they are intertwined with other decisions, such as technical or aesthetic considerations that shape the design outcome (Lloyd, 2009). With the growing complexity and interdisciplinarity of design problems, however, the need to facilitate *explicit* ethical decision-making has increased (Lloyd & Poel, 2008). For instance, in the context of design for behaviour change, the designer makes an explicit decision to adopt an ethical stance right from the outset of the design process (e.g., to motivate responsible driving) (Tromp, 2013, p. 33). This stance is reflected in the product–person relationship in the form of a 'script' (Verbeek, 2006; Tromp 2013, p. 30). To cite an often-used example, a speed bump has the script, 'slow down when you approach me' (Verbeek, 2006, p. 366). As a result, ethical considerations of designers get materialised in products in a manner that influences how people act and feel in everyday environments.

In critical design practices, similar to designing for behaviour change, the ethical stance of the designer is often clear from the outset. However, unlike behaviour-change interventions, critical designs intend to *inform* behavioural choices instead of *steering* them in a socially desired direction (Ozkaramanli & Desmet, 2016). For instance, the designer of 'New-born Fame' (Figure 12.2a) intended to raise awareness about the issue of online privacy, without suggesting either behavioural choice (*sharing* vs *not sharing* baby photos on social media) as the desired alternative. The challenge here is to remove one's own intuitive sense of 'right or wrong' from the way the design is executed. In this way, the designer exposes the reasoning behind each behavioural alternative to create space for a discourse that can accommodate multiple behavioural choices and, thus, multiple viewpoints. This means that the design needs to afford behavioural choices that the designer may not morally agree with, which requires suspending one's moral judgement on the topic. For instance, 'New-born Fame' (Figure 12.2a) may in fact be used to share baby photos by extreme social media users. Although this does not seem to align with the moral starting point of the designer, it serves to accommodate the viewpoint of extreme social media users in the dialogue 'New-born Fame' intends to stimulate.

Conclusion

The purpose of this chapter was to establish the value of critique and critical design approaches in the context of designing to address societal challenges. Addressing issues of societal relevance, such as mental health issues, online privacy or the refugee crisis, is an integral part of design for wellbeing. Handling the complexity of societal challenges requires a skilful blending of interdisciplinary expertise, which can be supported by a critical mindset. The *first part* of this chapter provided an expanded definition of the term 'critical' in design, positioning criticality as a skill that can be learned and nurtured rather than a specific way or style of designing. The *second part* of the chapter elaborated on the benefits of critique in addressing societal challenges, suggesting that designing wellbeing-relevant interventions requires a combination of creative problem-solving and criticality skills. The *third part* of this chapter introduced dilemma-driven design as an approach to embed criticality in design activities through analysing the connection between criticality and dilemmas. Drawing from this connection, three *criticality skills* have been proposed, namely, critical reflection, systemic thinking and suspending moral judgement, in order to support criticality in design. These skills indicate that the development of criticality relies heavily on interdisciplinary thinking. Therefore, this chapter can be regarded as an invitation to increase interdisciplinary collaboration in design research and practice, and, in doing so, maintaining a critical attitude.

Acknowledgements

Special thanks to Dr Christine Schwöbel-Patel for her valuable feedback on earlier versions of this chapter, the designers who kindly shared the images of their work, and the delegates and organisers of Critical By Design conference who, through valuable discussions and lectures, contributed to the insights in this chapter.[2]

Notes

1 https://refugeechallenge.unhcrideas.org/Page/ViewIdea?ideaid=4926.
2 https://criticalbydesign.ch/.

References

Bardzell, J., & Bardzell, S. (2013). What is critical about critical design? In *Proceedings of the SIGCHI Conference on Human Factors in Computing Systems* (pp. 3297–3306), Paris. New York, NY: ACM Press.

Bardzell, J., Bardzell, S., & Stolterman, E. (2014). Reading critical designs: Supporting reasoned interpretations of critical design. In *Proceedings of the SIGCHI Conference on Human Factors in Computing Systems* (pp. 1951–1960), Toronto. New York, NY: ACM Press.

Bardzell, S., Bardzell, J., Forlizzi, J., Zimmerman, J., & Antanitis, J. (2012). Critical design and critical theory: The challenge of designing for provocation. In *Proceedings of the Designing Interactive Systems Conference: In The Wild* (pp. 288–297), New Castle. New York, NY: ACM Press.

Butler, J. (2001). *What is Critique? An Essay on Foucault's Virtue*. European Institute for Progressive Cultural Policies. Available from: http://eipcp.net/transversal/0806/butler/en [Accessed 29 May 2018].

Desmet, P.M.A., & Pohlmeyer, A.E. (2013). Positive design: An introduction to design for subjective well-being. *International Journal of Design*, 7(3), 5–19.

Desmet, P.M.A., Pohlmeyer, A.E., & Forlizzi, J. (2013). Special issue editorial: Design for subjective well-being. *International Journal of Design*, 7(3), 1–3.

DiSalvo, C. (2012). *Adversarial Design*. Cambridge: MIT Press.

Dorst, K., & Cross, N. (2001). Creativity in the design process: Co-evolution of problem–solution. *Design Studies*, 22(5), 425–437.

Dunne, A., & Raby, F. (2013). *Speculative Everything: Design, Fiction, and Social Dreaming*. Cambridge: MIT Press.

Ferri, G., Bardzell, J., Bardzell, S., & Louraine, S. (2014). Analyzing critical designs: Categories, distinctions, and canons of exemplars. In *Proceedings of the 2014 Conference on Designing Interactive Systems* (pp. 355–364), Vancouver. New York, NY: ACM Press.

Fleming, S. (2014, 8 January). Hesitate! *Aeon Magazine*, [online]. Available from: https://aeon.co/essays/forget-being-boldly-decisive-let-your-brain-take-its-time [Accessed 19 December 2017].

Fogg, B.J. (2003). *Persuasive Technology: Using Computers to Change What We Think and Do*. Boston, MA: Morgan Kaufmann Publishers.

Hallnäs, L., & Redström, J. (2001). Slow technology – designing for reflection. *Personal and Ubiquitous Computing*, 5(3), 201–212.

Lloyd, P. (2009). Ethical imagination and design. *Design Studies*, 30(2), 154–168.

Lloyd, P., & Van De Poel, I. (2008). Designing games to teach ethics. *Science and Engineering Ethics*, 14(3), 433–447.

Malpass, M. (2012). *Contextualising Critical Design: Towards a Taxonomy of Critical Practice in Product Design*. Unpublished doctoral dissertation. Nottingham Trent University, Nottingham, UK.

Malpass, M. (2017). *Critical Design in Context: History, Theory, and Practices*. London: Bloomsbury Publishing.

Margolin, V., & Margolin, S. (2002). A 'social model' of design: Issues of practice and research. *Design Issues*, 18(4), 24–30.

Mezirow, J. (1990). How critical reflection triggers transformative learning. *Fostering Critical Reflection in Adulthood*, 1(20), 1–6.

Ozkaramanli, D. (2017). *Me Against Myself: Addressing Personal Dilemmas through Design*. Unpublished doctoral dissertation. Delft University of Technology, Delft, The Netherlands.

Ozkaramanli, D., & Desmet, P.M.A. (2016). Provocative design for unprovocative designers: Strategies for triggering personal dilemmas. In *Proceedings of DRS 2016, Design Research Society 50th Anniversary Conference*, Brighton, UK, 27–30 June.

Ozkaramanli, D., Desmet, P.M.A., & Özcan, E. (2016). Beyond resolving dilemmas: Three design directions for addressing intrapersonal concern conflicts. *Design Issues*, 32(3), 78–91.

Pater, R. (2016). Treating the refugee crisis as a design problem is problematic. *Dezeen*, [online]. Available from: https://www.dezeen.com/2016/04/21/ruben-pater-opinion-what-design-can-do-refugee-crisis-problematic-design/ [Accessed 19 December 2017].

Saren, M., Maclaran, P., Goulding, C., Elliott, R., Shankar, A., & Catterall, M. (Eds.) (2007). *Critical Marketing: Defining the Field*. Amsterdam: Butterworth-Heinemann.

Schön, D. (1991). *The Reflective Practitioner: How Professionals Think in Action*. New York, NY: Basic Books.

Schwöbel, C. (Ed.) (2014). *Critical Approaches to International Criminal Law: An Introduction*. New York, NY: Routledge.

Schwöbel-Patel, C., & Werner, W. (2017). The Screen as an object of international law. In Jessie Hohmann, & Daniel Joyce (Eds.), *International Law's Objects*, OUP, Forthcoming. Available from: SSRN: https://ssrn.com/abstract=2966027

Sengers, P., Boehner, K., David, S., & Kaye, J.J. (2005). Reflective design. In *Proceedings of the 4th Decennial Conference on Critical Computing: Between Sense and Sensibility* (pp. 49–58), Aarhus. New York, NY: ACM Press.

Siegel, M.A., & Beck, J. (2014). Slow change interaction design. *Interactions*, 21(1), 28–35.

Simon, H.A. (1973). The structure of ill structured problems. *Artificial Intelligence*, 4(3–4), 181–201.

180 *Deger Ozkaramanli*

Tromp, N. (2013). *Social Design*. Unpublished doctoral dissertation. Delft University of Technology, Delft, The Netherlands.

Tyson, L. (2014). *Critical Theory Today: A User-Friendly Guide*. New York, NY: Routledge.

Verbeek, P.P. (2006). Materializing morality: Design ethics and technological mediation. *Science, Technology, & Human Values*, *31*(3), 361–380.

Part IV

Future challenges for design for wellbeing

13 Mapping research at the intersection of design and mental health

Sarah Kettley and Rachel Lucas

Mental health

It is widely acknowledged that one in four people in the UK will experience a mental health problem each year (Mind, 2017), and that there is a need to take a far more proactive and preventative approach to reduce the long-term impact for people experiencing mental health problems, for their families, and to reduce costs for the National Health Service (NHS) and emergency services (NHS Independent Taskforce, 2016). Pressures on the system include an ageing population and an overreliance on informal carers, who have in turn become a socially excluded group (Gray et al., 2010). Mental health difficulties can be highly complex and less easily perceived and explained than physical health issues, and, despite an estimated cost to the economy of £105 billion a year, roughly equivalent to the cost of the entire NHS, the sector remains under-prioritised, receiving 13 per cent of NHS funding (Centre for Mental Health, 2014). Those affected by long-term mental health issues report feeling overlooked and hurried through a health system, at a time when they feel at their most vulnerable; accustomed to having no voice and little say in their recovery process, many are left feeling powerless, unheard and marginalised. Costs are compounded by the high levels of social exclusion experienced by people with mental health problems, and the relevance of social factors in supporting mental health is well-recognised (Benjamin 2014; Fostvedt & Alasker 2014; Holttum 2014; Jones et al., 2013; Oh, 2014). Crisis intervention and home treatment teams have been introduced across the UK, with informal carers recognised as a fundamental element of mental health service provision (Bradley 2015). In May 2013, the 66th World Health Assembly adopted the World Health Organisation's (WHO's) Comprehensive Mental Health Action Plan, recognising the essential role of mental health in achieving health for all people, calling for more effective leadership and governance for mental health, and calling for better integrated mental health and social care services in community-based settings (World Health Organisation, 2013). In the same year, the UK National Health Service mandated action towards parity of esteem between mental and physical health, as set out by the government in the Health and Social Care Act in 2012 (Centre for Mental Health, 2013).

The range of mental health conditions people live with is extensive, and in the UK it is typically organised around a three-tier system. Individuals presented to their local general medical practice (primary care), are referred for specialist assessment for treatment (secondary care), and may access social and third sector (charity) services alongside or after treatment (tertiary care). Services are not well integrated, are funded differently, and, particularly in the third sector, can be fragile and temporary (see Cottam, 2018, for accessible case studies on the complexity of care services in the UK). We do not have space in this chapter to detail conditions, but it is worth noting that different theoretical models lead to different views on the usefulness of diagnosis and also to different professions (i.e., psychiatry, psychology and psychotherapy).

Design research and authors' motivation

Design research increasingly collaborates across disciplines, drawing methodology, practice and theory from fields such as psychology, sociology and anthropology, and strengthening relationships between academic institutions and industry. Environmental, social and cultural challenges can be helped by design innovation and by opening up the design process and increasing transparency. Service and Transformation Design approaches continue to develop, enhancing shared capacity to facilitate change across organisational and community contexts. The potential for these design methods within mental health is evident (Cottam 2018; Sangiorgi 2011), and recent conferences illustrate growing interest in the potential for new forms of design to respond creatively: see for example Christer et al. (2018), the Design Research Society SIGWELL tracks at Design Research Society (DRS) conferences (2016, 2018) and the Arts and Humanities Research Council (AHRC) Does Design Care symposium at Lancaster University (2017).

Our own motivation for carrying out this literature review came from our efforts to put the theory of humanist Carl Rogers into practice as a participatory design research framework (Kettley et al., 2016), and our increasing consternation when other design efforts did not, or could not, tell us what theoretical model or framework informed their work. We became increasingly aware that, particularly in multi-sector and multidisciplinary projects, individual stakeholders and team members may also have been trained in diverse and sometimes incompatible theoretical models, giving rise to managerial and personal difficulties, as well as potentially compromising the ethical processes of the projects. The goal of this review is therefore to describe where design research meets mental health, and we hope it will encourage further discussion and knowledge exchange across design, mental health and research contexts.

Scope and methodology

The six-month review[1] included academic publications between 2010 and 2016, limited to UK and European research. An analysis of the grey literature was beyond the scope of this review.[2] Ten databases were identified as the core search locations: Art Bibliographies Modern (*Proquest*), Design and Applied Art Index (*Proquest*), International Bibliography of Art (*Proquest*), SCOPUS (*Elsevier*), PsychINFO (*Proquest*), Web of Science (*Thomson Reuters*), International Bibliography of Social Sciences (*Proquest*), Applied Social Sciences Index and Abstracts (*Proquest*), PsychARTICLES (Proquest), and the British Humanities Index. Further search areas, primarily academic institutions and research professionals, were located via the Service Design Research UK Network (2018). A search strategy was developed using single terms and combinations of terms, to locate the intersections of the two subject areas. This was an iterative process, with search terms developed around the domains of both mental health and design. An initial search undertaken using SCOPUS indicated terms that were overly general in locating the specific intersection of the two subject areas, and keywords were identified through emergent themes.[3] This led to a final search string, which was then run across each database.

(TITLE-ABS-KEY ("co-design") OR TITLE-ABS-KEY ("experience-based co-design") OR TITLE-ABS-KEY ("participatory design") OR TITLE-ABS-KEY ("user-centred design") OR TITLE-ABS-KEY ("practice-based design") OR TITLE-ABS-KEY ("human-centred design") OR TITLE-ABS-KEY ("collaborative design") OR TITLE-ABS-KEY ("co-production") OR TITLE-ABS-KEY ("inclusive design") OR TITLE-ABS-KEY ("empathic design") AND TITLE-ABS-KEY ("mental health") OR TITLE-ABS-KEY ("emotional wellbeing") OR TITLE-ABS-KEY ("mental illness") OR TITLE-ABS-KEY ("psychiatric care")) AND PUBYEAR > 2009

There were 1,731 results returned, which were screened to assess whether they were in scope by asking the following question:

> Does the paper include description of design processes or thinking, alongside consideration of mental health or wellbeing issues, or specifically refer to design methodology or practice within a mental health context?

Papers were excluded if found to be non-European in origin and/or focus, written in a language other than English or published before 2010. This resulted in 179 publications found to be in scope.

A further 134 results were contributed from an expert review with the research team of the *Internet of Soft Things Project* project, giving 313 results. An extensive review of these full papers left a final 131 publications considered to be accurately located at the intersection of *both* domains (Figure 13.1).

Emergent themes

The 131 results were read and iteratively categorised. This manual open coding process gave us the four major themes discussed here: lived experience; collaboration; experiential engagement and creative practice; and the theoretical framing of technology. This discussion does not go so far as to present a category map of relationships between the publications or analytical themes, but it uses key illustrative examples from the results to describe the landscape of research approaches at the intersection of mental health and design research.

Lived experience

It is evident from the literature compiled through this review, that increased recognition of the 'service-user experience' is beginning to emerge in mental health service provision. For instance, Bradley (2015) provides a brief overview of the literature to date which has focused on 'co-production' within mental health care in the UK, including service-user and carer involvement and collaboration. The paper identifies a distinct gap in communication between the carer community and mental health professionals and questions whether co-production approaches can address this chasm. The paper further questions the cultural and ideological shift required from staff, service-users and family members to undertake co-produced care and acknowledges the challenges to service redesign and new roles in practice. The same publication highlights the danger of increasing expectations on service providers to undertake shared decision-making and co-production in the absence of practical guidance. Co-production of care, although reflective of an intention to work empathically with service-users and families, requires attentiveness and commitment to the 'triangle of care' – with carers and service-users actively contributing personal skills, resources and expertise. Locock et al. (2014) suggest improving patient experience to be a priority for the government and the NHS, emphasising the need for greater understanding of service-user experience and opportunities to directly affect care planning. Carer and service-user involvement in co-production can help contribute to a wider perspective of mental health difficulty, beyond symptom reduction, and experience-based approaches make room for a greater understanding of those engaged in the process of both design and research (Cooper, Gillmore & Hogg, 2016, Russ et al., 2013).

The potential of participation in creative activity and arts engagement in terms of recovery processes and wellbeing, is evident (Abbotts & Spence, 2013; Crawford et al., 2013; McKeown et al., 2016; Pöllänen, 2015; Stacey & Stickley, 2010; Stickley & Eades, 2013) and collaborative approaches to service development, which look to incorporate the lived experience of service-users, are beginning to emerge (Arblaster et al., 2015; Bradley, 2015; Bredski et al., 2015; Larkin et al., 2015; Peterson et al., 2012). However, the use of experience-based approaches is still relatively novel in mental health settings (Larkin et al., 2015).

Collaboration

The concept of collaboration and 'working with', is increasingly evident within UK health services. The NHS 'Five Year Forward View' refers to new relationships with patients and communities (NHS England, 2016), and an NHS independent taskforce report (February 2016) highlights the specific need to re-energise and improve mental health care across the NHS through innovative approaches in order to meet increased

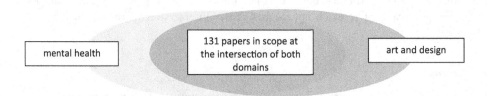

Figure 13.1 Final papers in scope.

demand and improve outcomes. In this respect, Larkin et al. (2015) consider inpatient mental health services in the UK to be unsatisfactory for both service-users and staff, reporting on three qualitative research studies concerned with stakeholder experiences of hospitalisation during early psychosis, as a starting point for translation into service improvements developed in collaboration with service-users, carers, community, inpatient staff and management. The paper considers an adapted form of experience-based co-design (EBCD), a participatory action-research method for collaboratively improving health care services. The use of EBCD is still relatively novel in mental health settings; Goodrich and Stanley (2014) include a successful case study of an initiative at Oxleas Foundation Trust, while Larkin et al. (2015) discuss adaptations to the methodology and the implications of using EBCD with vulnerable populations in complex services. Carr et al. (2011) investigate connections between evidence-based and experience-based methods in the redesign of services.

Experiential engagement and creative practice

Our review revealed a large number of papers concerned with the benefits of creative practice and engagement in participatory arts to mental health. The potential of participation in creative activity to support wellbeing improvement and 'recovery' is highlighted in mental health policy and commissioning guidance such as the Department of Health's *No Health without Mental Health: A Cross-Government Mental Health Outcomes Strategy for People of All Ages* (2011) and Health Scotland's *Good Mental Health for All* (2016). This theme includes both engagement in activity, where a focus on creative 'doing and making' are seen as therapeutic in themselves, as well as social inclusion and group support. Group engagement in craft activities is perceived as highly supportive of mental health and wellbeing, and there is a prevalence of creative activities within occupational therapy in Sweden (Müllersdorf & Ivarsson, 2012). However, there is limited empirical research on the intervention of creative activities within mental health and extended health services (Fostvedt & Alasker, 2014). Caddy et al. (2012) respond to a call for quantitative outcome evidence about the therapeutic relationship between creative activity and mental health. The study examines the mental health outcomes of inpatients participating in art-and-craft-based creative therapies at a private psychiatric hospital over a five-year period. Research findings established that participation in creative activity holds potential benefits for those experiencing mental health problems. Crawford et al. (2013) examine the value of approaches to mental health that are based on creative practice in the humanities and arts, and their potential contribution to mutual recovery. Further qualitative evidence can be found in those papers concerned with the role of community centre-based arts, leisure and social activities in promoting adult wellbeing and healthy lifestyles (Jones et al., 2013), engagement in crafts as a coping mechanism, stress reduction and enhancement to wellbeing (Pöllänen, 2015a, 2015b; Argyle & Winship 2015). Burt and Atkinson (2012) consider the relationship between quilting and wellbeing for the wider population without taking a 'problem-based' approach. Their qualitative, interview-based study, uncovered social, emotional and cognitive processes identified as being connected to emotional wellbeing. Benjamin (2014) is unusual in explicitly stating a humanistic Rogerian theoretical framework when reporting on the therapeutic benefits of a creative artists support group, connecting creativity with mental health. A further uncontrolled study, commissioned to address concerns about lacking evidence of the effectiveness of participatory arts engagement, indicated those with mental health needs found participation (in the arts) highly beneficial to recovery, reporting an increased sense of empowerment and social inclusion. Interest in the positive results from this study among senior managers at the South Essex Partnership University Foundation NHS Trust led directly to the establishment of Open Arts in 2008. The aim of Open Arts has been to promote well-being and social inclusion by providing relaxing, welcoming art groups in community venues for people with mental health needs. Their approach embraces concepts derived from the field of art therapy, complemented by Rogerian principles of facilitated learning (Margrove et al., 2013).

McKeown et al. (2016) examine the experiences of mental health service-users in a community-based arts programme at Tate Modern; the study combined object handling and museum visits with arts and craft activities. Morse et al. (2015) examine the effects of museum outreach sessions on confidence, sociability and wellbeing measures for mental health. Dijana and Sasa (2010) address creative expression as means of assisted communication for Alzheimer's disease patients, offering a brief overview of the influence of creative media on the development and maintenance of communication skills, and thus on the development of patients' social interactions. Although diagnosis-based, they take a relational rather than problem-based approach. In 2011 the UK Crafts Council responded to a government agenda to determine and measure the nation's wellbeing as a basis for future policy. Their report acknowledges the absorption experienced in making activities as clinically proven to increase levels of mood-enhancing serotonin, inducing relaxation and promoting mindfulness. The benefits for 'wellbeing' and emotional health are presented, highlighting improvements to chronic stress and reduction in feelings of isolation and depression, facilitated through participation with others (Yair, 2011).

Technology, user-centred design and theoretical framing (modality)

In the literature that was studied, we could distil a range of approaches to technology in mental health, but point to the wealth of published research that finds a natural resonance between problem-solution models in design and the medical model of symptom reduction. It appears that computer-based psychotherapeutic interventions for mental health difficulties often work to a diagnostic label, and we are concerned that user-centred design essentially asks for a medical model. This is not an issue in itself, and we have already mentioned our own bias towards the humanistic; what is concerning is a more general lack of explicit theoretical framing or modality. A distinct number of related publications also point to the repeated limitations of research in the literature, including modality (or 'models') of care (Doherty et al., 2010; Orlowski et al., 2015; Wykes & Brown, 2016). The implications of the lack of theoretical framing should not be underestimated; consider the recent discussion in the *British Medical Journal* on its policies regarding reportage of studies using qualitative methodologies (Greenhalgh et al., 2016).

For instance, Wykes and Brown focus on e-therapy rather than electronic patient records and discuss the potential issues for implementation of e-health in mental health, including 'considering models of therapeutic support' (2016, p. 3). So, too, do Doherty et al. (2010), although related research continues to be categorised by diagnosis or type of technology; Doherty et al. advise that the researcher refrain from getting involved with the relative benefits of diverse theoretical models, without explicating the link between the design research methodologies and such models (2010). Those publications that do mention modality tend to do so implicitly through terminology and research expectations: Bauer and Moessner (2012) unreflexively adhere to the medical model, seeking to support data collection for optimisation of interventions, and the concept of 'traditional' care becomes aligned with face-to-face therapies; while Hilgart et al. (2012) acknowledge there is little research to inform design and development of internet interventions that support 'behavioural change 'and 'symptom reduction'; and Valenza et al. (2014) focus on the applicability of wearable technology to monitoring, diagnosis and treatment, all of which align with a medical model. Others focus on the behavioural model (e.g., Lin et al., 2013) or work from populations defined by diagnosis (Ellis et al., 2015). Dual diagnosis describes a deliberate focus on more than one presenting pathology, assuming a relation between them; Elison et al. (2014) consider e-therapy in terms of supporting alcohol-related dual diagnoses; Kim and Cho (2013) study a personalised e-textile-based smart health care glove for the wellbeing of an older female through analysis of cardiovascular dynamics within a bipolar population. Physiological responses are understood in connection to a *psychiatric* difficulty. Others focus on the regulation of emotion or mood, often as part of managing behaviour change, as helpfully reported as part of a wider theoretical discussion by Desmet (2015).

Methodological explorations of participatory practices are also evident in studies with people living with cognitive and sensory impairments, on the autistic spectrum, or living with dementia: Frauenberger et al. (2011) and Parsons et al. (2011) seek to include children and young people in the design process of technologically enhanced learning environments, using storytelling to bridge the gap between system design and the 'imaginary' world of the child. Malinverni et al. (2017) study the need for high-quality inclusive interdisciplinarity in the design of games for children on the autistic spectrum to support social initiation behaviours. Adults with communication difficulties are often excluded from design research, but Gaudion et al. (2015) look at collaborative methods to support this population, to allow their unique perceptions to be included. In participatory work with people living with cognitive or sensory impairments (as distinct from mental ill-health), others are examining the need for unique, individual methods development in response to highly individual participants (Hendricks et al., 2015) and considering the wellbeing of dementia patients whose identity is scripted through standardised design, including clothing (Iltanen-Tahkavuori et al., 2011). Qualitative studies of user experience and involvement in the development of assistive technologies are also undertaken from the perspectives of mental health service-users (Goodwin et al., 2016; Godwin, 2012); these could be considered at the person-centred end of a continuum of theories of care and the person.

Key findings, recommendations for design research and future challenges

In this section we provide an overview of the current key findings from this literature review.

First, the philosophical modalities (theoretical framings) underpinning different services are not immediately visible within the literature. Categorising papers via modality is a complex process due to the lack of acknowledgement from design sectors. Second, the potential for personal impact for the designer/researcher when working within the mental health sector is an ethical issue which remains predominantly unspoken. There is much in regard to ethical practice that is not made transparent within the research methodologies, including practical issues such as informed consent. Third, technological developments and the design of assistive digital devices for mental health represented the largest category of papers. The design approach within these studies is predominantly user-centred and problem-based, which effectively asks for a medical or disease model by engaging in design for a diagnostic label or disorder (a needs-based, or lack-based approach). Fourth, there is a growing acknowledgement of the mental health and wellbeing benefits of participatory arts and creative practice. These activities, when undertaken as group practice, also present opportunities for increased social inclusion and engagement. Outside the UK, Norwegian Mental Health reforms have incorporated 'inclusion in society' as necessary and supportive of emotional wellbeing. Fifth, language can be very misleading, and meanings can vary across context and subject area. In particular, the term 'person-centred' is widely used across design and varied mental health settings. Similar terms are used to promote diverse fundamental care philosophies. Widely used or generic terminology can make precise searches difficult.

This review was constrained to Europe and the UK between 2010 and 2016 and did not include an analysis of the grey literature. It is therefore limited in its scope and a significant amount of research remains to be done in mapping and developing design's relationship with mental health. Doherty et al. (2010) point out that there may be over 550 models of therapy in use, but the 'big three' could be usefully added to design's vocabulary through existing frameworks, such as Sanders and Stappers' map of human-centred design practices (2008). These three models are: cognitive/behavioural models, relational/social/humanistic models and disease/medical models.

In this way we argue that a design researcher does not need to become 'an expert' in any one theoretical model of mental health care, but can, and should, develop a reflexive overview of the key underlying theories that shape attitudes, methodologies and diverse ethical practices. It is our hope that our review of literature can contribute in this respect.

Notes

1   The second author was funded as a research fellow for six months through quality related funding by Nottingham Trent University, UK, to undertake the work.
2   Grey literature is unpublished material, e.g., technical, annual and government reports, conference papers or newsletters. A Google search using the following string was used: 'experience-based co-design' OR 'co-design' OR 'participatory design' OR 'collaborative design' OR 'practice-based design' AND 'mental health' OR 'mental illness' OR 'emotional wellbeing' OR 'psychiatric care'. The top 100 results were taken, and duplicates were removed leaving 28 papers in scope.
3   *Design* methodology: predominantly indicating relational and experiential aspects, e.g., 'co-design', 'experienced-based design', 'user-centred design' and variations; *design* practice: acknowledging creative engagement, e.g., 'craft', 'making', 'participatory arts', 'textiles'; *mental health* experiencing, e.g., 'wellbeing', 'emotional', 'relational', 'person-centred', 'awareness'; *mental health* in terms of medical/disease model, e.g., 'diagnosis', 'psychiatric', 'mental illness' and various diagnostic labels (dementia being the most prevalent); *stakeholders* in terms of populations, e.g., 'service-users', 'mental health communities', 'patients', 'health care professionals', 'carers'; *stakeholders* in regard to outcomes, e.g., 'empowerment', 'recovery', 'engagement', 'wellness', 'social inclusion'.

References

Abbotts, J., & Spence, W. (2013). Art and wellbeing in a deprived Scottish community. *Journal of Public Mental Health, 12*(2), 58–69.

An Internet of Soft Things (2016). *Participatory Design of Networked e-Textiles for Mental Health and Wellbeing.* https://aninternetofsoftthings.com/project/

Arblaster, K., Mackenzie, L., & Willis, K. (2015). Service user involvement in health professional education: Is it effective in promoting recovery-oriented practice? *Journal of Mental Health Training, Education and Practice, 10*(5), 325–336.

Argyle, E., & Winship, G. (2015). Creative practice in a group setting. *Mental Health and Social Inclusion, 19*(3), 141–147.

Bauer, S., & Moessner, M. (2012, August). Technology-enhanced monitoring in psychotherapy and e-mental health. *Journal of Mental Health, 21*(4), 355–363.

Benjamin, E. (2014). The creative artist support group: A case study. *Journal of Public Mental Health, 13*(3), 142–145.

Bradley, E. (2015). Carers and co-production: Enabling expertise through experience? *Mental Health Review Journal, 20*(4), 232–241.

Bredski, J., Forsyth, K., Mountain, D., Harrison, M., Irvine, L., & Maciver, D. (2015). What in-patients want: A qualitative study of what's important to mental health service users in their recovery (Wayfinder Partnership). *Mental Health Review Journal, 20*(1), 1–12.

Burt, E.L., & Atkinson, J. (2012). The relationship between quilting and wellbeing. *Journal of Public Health, 34*(1), 54–59.

Caddy, L., Crawford, F., & Page, A.C. (2012). 'Painting a path to wellness': Correlations between participating in a creative activity group and improved measured mental health outcome. *Journal of Psychiatric and Mental Health Nursing, 19*(4), 327–333.

Carr, V.L., Sangiorgi, D., Büscher, M., Junginger, S., & Cooper, R. (2011). Integrating evidence-based design and experience-based approaches in healthcare service design. *Health Environments Research and Design Journal, 4*(4), 12–33.

Centre for Mental Health (2013). *Briefing 46: The NHS Mandate.* Available from: https://www.centreformentalhealth.org.uk/Handlers/Download.ashx?IDMF=631f1fb7-df5a-4dc4-839c-8cfc25ba5a6f. Retrieved 12 September 2018.

Centre for Mental Health (2014). *Parity of Esteem.* Available from: https://www.centreformentalhealth.org.uk/parity-of-esteem. Retrieved 12 September 2018.

Chamberlain, P., Wolstenholme, D., Dexter, M., & Seals, E. (2015). *The State of the Art of Design in Health: An Expert-led Review of the Extent of the Art of Design Theory and Practice in Health and Social Care.* Sheffield: Sheffield Hallam University.

Christer, K., Craig, C., & Wolstenholme, D. (Eds.) (2018). *Proceedings of the 5th International Conference on Design4Health,* Sheffield, UK, 4th–6th September 2018.

Cooper, K., Gillmore, C., & Hogg, L. (2016). Experience-based co-design in an adult psychological therapies service. *Journal of Mental Health, 25*(1), 36–40.

Cottam, H. (2018). *Radical Help.* London: Virago.

Crawford, P., Lewis, L., Brown, B., & Manning, N. (2013). Creative practice as mutual recovery in mental health. *Mental Health Review Journal, 18*(2), 55–64.

Department of Health and Social Care (2011). *No Health without Mental Health: A Cross-Government Mental Health Outcomes Strategy for People of All Ages.* Report. Available at: https://www.gov.uk/government/publications/no-health-without-mental-health-a-cross-government-outcomes-strategy. Retrieved 6 September 2019.

Desmet, P.M.A. (2015). Design for mood: Twenty activity-based opportunities to design for mood regulation. *International Journal of Design, 9*(2), 1–19.

Dijana, Š., & Saša, R. (2010). Creative expression as means of assisted communication in Alzheimer's disease patients. *Ljetopis Socijalnog Rada, 17*(2), 263–279.

Doherty, G., Coyle, D., & Matthews, M. (2010). Design and evaluation guidelines for mental health technologies. *Interacting with Computers, 22*(2010), 243–252.

Elison, S., Ward, J., Davies, G., Lidbetter, N., Hulme, D., & Dagley, M. (2014). An outcomes study of eTherapy for dual diagnosis using Breaking Free Online. *Advances in Dual Diagnosis, 7*(2), 52–62.

Ellis, L.A., Mccabe, K., Davenport, T., Burns, J.M., Rahilly, K., Nicholas, M., & Hickie, I.B. (2015). Development and evaluation of an Internet-based program to improve the mental health and wellbeing of young men. *Interactive Technology and Smart Education, 12*(1), 2–13.

Fostvedt, B., & Alsaker, S. (2014). Craft activities in groups at meeting places: Supporting mental health users' everyday occupations. *Scandinavian Journal of Occupational Therapy, 21*(2), 145–152.

Frauenberger, C., Good, J., & Keay-Bright, W. (2011). Designing technology for children with special needs: bridging perspectives through participatory design. *CoDesign: International Journal of CoCreation in Design and the Arts, 7*(1), 1–28.

Gaudion, K., Hall, A., Myerson, J., & Pellicano, L. (2015). A designer's approach: How can autistic adults with learning disabilities be involved in the design process? *CoDesign, 11*(1), 49–69.

Godwin, B. (2012). The ethical evaluation of assistive technology for practitioners: A checklist arising from a participatory study with people with dementia, family and professionals. *Journal of Assistive Technologies, 6*(2), 123–135.

Goodrich, J., & stanley, E. (2014). Be seen and heard in the care discussion. *The Health Service Journal, 124*(6391), 26–27.

Goodwin, J., Cummins, J., Behan, L., & O'Brien, S.M. (2016). Development of a mental health smartphone app: Perspectives of mental health service users. *Journal of Mental Health, 25*(5), 434–440.

Gray, B., Robinson, C., Seddon, D., & Roberts, A. (2010). Patterns of exclusion for carers for people with mental health problems – The perspectives of professionals. *Journal of Social Work Practice, 24*(4, 6), 475–492.

Greenhalgh, T., Annandale, E., Ashcroft, R., et al. (2016). An open letter to The BMJ editors on qualitative research. *BMJ, 352*, i563.

Hendricks, N., Slegers, K., & Duysburgh, P. (2015). Codesign with people living with cognitive or sensory impairments: A case for method stories and uniqueness. *CoDesign, 11*(1), 70–82.

Hilgart, M.M., Ritterband, L.M., Thorndike, F.P., & Kinzie, M.B. (2012). Using instructional design process to improve design and development of internet interventions. *Journal of Medical Internet Research, 14*(3).

Holttum, S. (2014). Mental health recovery is social. *Mental Health and Social Inclusion, 18*(3), 110–115.

Iltanen-Tahkavuori, S., Wikberg, M., & Topo, P. (2011). Design and dementia: A case of garments designed to prevent undressing. *Dementia, 11*(1), 49–59.

Jones, M., Kimberlee, R., Deave, T., & Evans, S. (2013). The role of community centre-based arts, leisure and social activities in promoting adult well-being and healthy lifestyles. *International Journal of Environmental Research and Public Health, 10*(5), 1948–1962.

Kettley, S., Kettley, R., & Lucas, R. (2016). From human-centred to person-centred design. In I. Kuksa, & T. Fisher (Eds.), *Design and Personalization* (pp.170–191). London: Routledge.

Kim, R., & Cho, G. (2013). Effectiveness of the smart healthcare glove system for elderly persons with hypertension. *Human Factors and Ergonomics in Manufacturing, 23*(3), 198–212.

Larkin, M., Boden, Z.V.R., & Newton, E. (2015). On the brink of genuinely collaborative care: Experience-based co-design in mental health. *Qualitative Health Research, 25*(11), 1463.

Lin, R.J., Ramakrishnan, S., Chang, H., Spraragen, S., & Zhu, X. (2013). Designing a web-based behavior motivation tool for healthcare compliance. *Human Factors and Ergonomics in Manufacturing & Service Industries, 23*(1), 58–67.

Locock, L., Robert, G., Boaz, A., Vougioukalou, S., Shuldham, C., Fielden, J., Ziebland, S., Gager, M., Tollyfield, R., & Pearcey, J. (2014). *Testing* accelerated experience-based co-design: A qualitative study of using a national archive of patient experience narrative interviews to promote rapid patient-centred service improvement, *Health Services and Delivery Research, 2*(4), 1–150.

Malinverni, L., Mora-Guiard, J., Padillo, V., Valero, L., Hervás, A., & Pares, N. (2017, June). An inclusive design approach for developing video games for children with Autism Spectrum Disorder. *Computers in Human Behavior, 71*(C), 535–549.

Margrove, K., Heydinrych, K., & Secker, J. (2013). Waiting list-controlled evaluation of a participatory arts course for people experiencing mental health problems. *Perspectives in Public Health, 133*(1), 28–35.

Mckeown, E., Weir, H., Berridge, E., Ellis, L., & Kyratsis, Y. (2016). Art engagement and mental health: Experiences of service users of a community-based arts programme at Tate Modern, London. *Public Health, 130,* 29–35.

Mind (2017). *Mental Health Facts and Statistics.* Available at: https://www.mind.org.uk/information-support/types-of-mental-health-problems/statistics-and-facts-about-mental-health/how-common-are-mental-health-problems/#one. Retrieved 6 September 2019.

Morse, N., Thomson, L.J.M., Brown, Z., & Chatterjee, H.J. (2015). Effects of creative museum outreach sessions on measures of confidence, sociability and well-being for mental health and addiction recovery service-users. *Arts & Health: An International Journal of Research, Policy and Practice, 7*(3), 231–246.

Müllersdorf, M., & Ivarsson, A.B. (2012). Use of creative activities in occupational therapy practice in Sweden. *Occupational Therapy International, 19*(3), 127–134.

NHS England (2016). *Five Year Forward View for Mental Health.* Available from: https://www.england.nhs.uk/wp-content/uploads/2016/02/Mental-Health-Taskforce-FYFV-final.pdf. Retrieved 14 September 2018.

NHS Health Scotland (2016). *Good Mental Health for All.* Available from: http://www.healthscotland.scot/media/1805/good-mental-health-for-all-feb-2016.pdf. Retrieved 14 September 2018.

NHS Independent Taskforce (2016). *The Five Year Forward View for Mental Health.* Report. Available at: https://www.england.nhs.uk/wp-content/uploads/2016/02/Mental-Health-Taskforce-FYFV-final.pdf. Retrieved 6 September 2019.

Oh, H. (2014). Bridging vs. bonding: Achieving participatory parity in recovery communities. *Mental Health and Social Inclusion, 18*(2), 77–82.

Orlowski, S.K., Lawn, S., Venning, A., Winsall, M., Jones, G.M., Wyld, K., Damarell, R.A., Antezana, G., Schrader, G., Smith, D., Collin, P., & Bidargaddi, N. (2015). Participatory research as one piece of the puzzle: A systematic review of consumer involvement in design of technology-based youth mental health and well-being interventions. *JMIR Human Factors, 2*(2), e12.

Parsons, S., Millen, L., Garib-Penna, S., & Cobb, S. (2011). Participatory design in the development of innovative technologies for children and young people on the autism spectrum: The COSPATIAL project. *Journal of Assistive Technologies, 5*(1), 29–34.

Petersen, K., Hounsgaard, L., Borg, T., & Nielsen, C.V. (2012). User involvement in mental health rehabilitation: A struggle for self-determination and recognition. *Scandinavian Journal of Occupational Therapy, 19*(1), 59–67.

Pöllänen, S. (2015a). Elements of crafts that enhance well-being: Textile craft makers' descriptions of their leisure activity. *Journal of Leisure Research, 47*(1), 58–78.

Pöllänen, S. (2015b). Crafts as leisure-based coping: Craft makers' descriptions of their stress-reducing activity. *Occupational Therapy in Mental Health, 31*(2), 83–100.

Russ, L.R., Phillips, J., Brzozowicz, K., Chafetz, L.A., Plsek, P.E., Blackmore, C.C., & Kaplan, G.S. (2013). Experience-based design for integrating the patient care experience into healthcare improvement: Identifying a set of reliable emotion words. *Healthcare, 1*(3–4), 91–99.

Sanders, E.B., & Stappers, P.J. (2008). Co-creation and the new landscapes of design. *CoDesign: International Journal of CoCreation in Design and the Arts, 4*(1: Design Participation), 5–18.

Sangiorgi, D. (2011). Transformative services and transformation design. *International Journal of Design, 5*(2), 29–40.

Service Design Research Network UK (2018). http://imagination.lancs.ac.uk/activities/SDR_UK_Network. Retrieved 12 September 2018.

Stacey, G., & Stickley, T. (2010). The meaning of art to people who use mental health services. *Perspectives in Public Health, 130*(2), 70–77.

Stickley, T., & Eades, M. (2013). Arts on prescription: A qualitative outcomes study. *Public Health, 127*(8), 727–734.

Valenza, G., Lanatà, A., Paradiso, R., & Scilingo, E.P. (2014, May–June). Advanced technology meets mental health: How smartphones, textile electronics, and signal processing can serve mental health monitoring, diagnosis, and treatment. *IEEE Pulse, 5*(3), 56–59.

World Health Organisation (2013). *Mental Health Action Plan 2013–2020.* Available from: http://www. who.int/mental_health/publications/action_plan/en/. Retrieved 12 September 2018.

Wykes, T., & Brown, M. (2016). Over promised, over-sold and underperforming? – e-Health in mental health. *Journal of Mental Health, 25*(1), 1–4.

Yair, K. (2011). *Craft and Wellbeing Report.* Crafts Council. 31 March 2011. Available from: http://www. craftscouncil.org.uk/content/files/craft_and_wellbeing.pdf. Retrieved 12 September 2018.

14 Design for wellbeing

An applied approach to housing in later life

*An-Sofie Smetcoren, Liesbeth De Donder and
Dominique Verté*

Introduction

Demographic ageing within the European Union is likely to be of major significance in the coming decades. Increasing life expectancies and decreasing birth rates are reshaping the age pyramids of EU member states towards an older population structure (Eurostat, 2018). These demographic projections together with rapid changes in society (e.g., migration, globalisation, changing family structures) will have a significant impact on our housing sector, posing various challenges for future housing policies (Pittini & Laino, 2011). Both within recent housing policies as well as gerontological research, there has been a growing attention for the concept of 'ageing in place', which can be defined as 'the ability to live in one's own home and community safely, independently and comfortably, regardless of age, income or ability level' (Centers for Disease Control and Prevention, 2013). When reading this definition, it is clear that the design of the home environment plays a crucial role enabling older people to age in their preferred setting. Home could be considered as the primary context for growing old as this is the place where older people perform most of their daily activities. Furthermore, personal abilities, others around us and the 'context' we live in influence our subjective wellbeing (Nussbaum, 2001). In international research the 'context a person lives in' can be defined in various ways: as the community and its characteristics (e.g., Hooghe & Vanhoutte, 2011); the social structure of the neighbourhood one is living in (e.g., Gardner, 2011); and of course as the actual physical character of that environment, that is, the actual houses, buildings and interiors that surround us. One of the main critiques from environmental gerontologists is the decontextualisation of the process of ageing from the environment where it takes place (Peace et al., 2007). Therefore, this chapter will focus on the housing and neighbourhood design (the physical context) and its relation to the (objective and subjective) wellbeing of older people. Based on existing literature and results of the research project 'Entour-Age Noord', the authors will put forward important design principles for the future and formulate challenges relating to home environments and the wellbeing of older people.

Population ageing and diversity

Population ageing, which refers to the increasingly large proportion of older people within the total population, is according to United Nations (2013) one of the most significant and important challenges of our twenty-first century. Compared to 2017, it is expected that the number of people aged 60 and above globally will double by 2050 and the number of persons aged 80 and above is expected to triple by 2050 (United Nations, 2017a).

In 2017 19.4 per cent of the European population is aged 65 years or over, with the highest shares being in Italy (22.3 per cent), Greece (21.5 per cent) and Germany (21.2 per cent) (Eurostat, 2018). Like Europe, Belgium is challenged by a growing number of people in retirement age. In 2017, 24.6 per cent of the Belgian population was 60 years and older and the demographic projection expects that by 2050 this will shift to 32.4 per cent (United Nations, 2017b).

These demographic projections will have implications for various policy areas; from family policy, through labour market policy, to social protection systems such as pensions and health care (European Union, 2014, 2015; Rechel et al., 2013; United Nations, 2017b). Societies worldwide will need to take on responsibility to ensure the wellbeing of this ageing population on several domains of daily life, with specific attention for the most vulnerable groups among older people, such as older single households, older people with migrant backgrounds, older people with physical, mental and learning disabilities, and older people with chronic illnesses and multi-morbidities, etc.

This increasing number and proportion of older people, especially given its diversity, have a significant impact on our current health sector (Rechel et al., 2013) and also pose various challenges for current and future housing policies (Pittini & Laino, 2011). This chapter will elaborate on the importance of the housing and neighbourhood design (the context) and its relation to the objective and subjective wellbeing of older people. If societies want to support their citizens 'ageing *well* in place', they should provide housing and neighbourhoods adapted to meet the needs of their ageing populations.

Meaning of home environment in later life

Concept of ageing in place and age-friendly communities

In general, only a small percentage – less than 5 per cent – of people aged 60 and over live in an institutional setting (United Nations, 2017c). The majority of people reside in private households their entire life; however, the proportion of older persons in institutional arrangements is increasing with age. The report of the United Nations on *Living Arrangements of Older Persons* (2017c) indicates that in 2011 4.1 per cent of the Belgian population aged 60 years or over lived in an institutional setting. Disaggregated by age, the report shows that 1.5 per cent of those between 60 and 79 years reside in institutions and this percentage increases to 13.5 per cent among those aged 80 years and over. Among the community-dwelling older people (60 and older), data from the Belgian Ageing Studies pointed out that 95.2 per cent live independently (alone or with a partner) in a single-family house, an apartment or a studio. Only a minority live together with their children (2.5 per cent) or in alternative housing (2.3 per cent) (such as sheltered housing, kangaroo housing or collective housing) (De Witte et al., 2012).

In the last decade, in many European countries as well as in Belgium, there has been growing attention within research and policy for the concept of 'ageing in place'. Several scholars have demonstrated the wish of older people to remain in the familiar home environment for as long as possible (Löfqvist et al., 2013; Peace et al., 2011; Smetcoren, 2016; Wiles et al., 2012). In general, older people want to age in settings that are familiar in some way (Sixsmith & Sixsmith, 2008) and which reflect their own identity and the society in which they live (Peace et al., 2007). Furthermore, when reaching old age, there is a significant chance of being more attached to the dwelling, which possibly increases the desire to age in place in later life. Alongside this, both policy-makers and the public are largely in agreement and have responded to this desire (Cutchin, 2003; Golant, 2011), for example, by mediating ageing in place through the provision of formal care services, the promotion of home modifications and the development of adult daycare centres (Cutchin, 2003; Dury, 2018; Paraponaris, Davin, & Verger, 2012; Szanton et al., 2011). Additionally, there is the recent increasing tendency towards the organisation of community care for older people. This refers to the growing paradigm shift in which care for people in need becomes less institutionalised and, increasingly, becomes the responsibility of society. This paradigm shift in care for older people means that care takes place within the community, as opposed to institutionalisation, in addition, care is provided by the community, thereby underlining the role of informal caregivers (family, neighbours, volunteers, etc.) (De Donder et al., 2017). Older people are motivated to remain at home and will only make a move towards a residential care facility when the provision of informal and/or formal care within the home situation is no longer sufficient.

Taking in account all these tendencies – the ageing of the population, the wish to age in place and the move towards community care – both policy as well as public (e.g. community service organisations as well as citizens) are challenged by these tendencies – ageing populations, wish to age in place and move towards community care – to seriously rethink the design of both housing as well as communities which are accessible for all residents. A key player in raising awareness concerning this matter on a global level is the World Health Organisation (WHO). In 2007 the WHO launched the Age-Friendly Cities guide which aimed 'to engage cities to become more age-friendly so as to tap the potential that older people represent for humanity' (p. 1). An age-friendly community can be described as a community 'where older people are actively involved, valued, and supported with infrastructure and services that effectively accommodate their needs' (Alley et al., 2007, p. 4). Eight key domains were described that contribute to the development of age-friendly environments of which housing is considered one. Within the Age-Friendly Cities guide, it is stated that housing in which older people are supported to age comfortably and safely within the community to which they belong, is universally valued (WHO, 2007, p. 30). In order to create 'age-friendly housing' in the community, attention should go to affordability, essential services (water supply, electricity, sanitation, etc.), housing design, housing modifications, housing maintenance, access to services, community and family connections, different housing options and the close living environment (WHO, 2007). Adjoining this, the European Union is working on a European Reference Framework for Age-Friendly Housing (ERF-AFH) (Peine & Arentshorst, 2016). This reference framework is being co-created with national, relevant stakeholders from Europe and serves as a tool, resource and interaction platform. It offers guidance by using clear language and definitions to empower stakeholders to concerted and collaborative actions. At present, the concept of 'age-friendliness' is well known among policy and practice, however, it still requires greater recognition of the importance of housing in the lives of older people (Buffel et al., 2018). 'Home' should be considered as the primary context for growing old as this is the place where older people perform most of their daily activities.

Home as a social, emotional and psychological construct

Because of the growing number of older people who opt for ageing at home, conducting research on person–environment relationships with a focus on inclusive, flexible housing design remains a key focal point (Golant, 2015; Smetcoren, 2016; Wright et al., 2017). At first buildings, such as houses, are shaped as a result of an architect or housing developer's idea about what houses should look like, but, over time, as people live in their houses they give meaning to the physical structures and materials, which in return changes and eventually shapes them. On the one side, this refers to the house as a physical structure, a defined space providing shelter and protection for domestic activities, and, on the other hand, to the home as a social, cultural and emotional construct (Easthope, 2004; Oswald & Wahl, 2005). It is argued by Easthope (2004) that the 'home' should be considered as a significant type of place, whereby the concept of 'place' is located within time and space and whereby place provides the link between one's dwelling place and one's wellbeing and identity. Also Oswald & Wahl (2005, p. 22) point out that 'Addressing the meaning of home focuses attention on the relationship between the objective socio-physical setting and subjective evaluations, goals, values, emotions, and observable or potential behaviors that people pursue'. Across the life span, from childhood until late adulthood, people interact with their social and physical environment, 'which leads to meaningful representations of the self within the environment' (Oswald & Wahl, 2003, p. 568). When growing older, various researchers have emphasised the meaning of home in later life (Cristoforetti et al., 2011; Oswald & Wahl, 2005; Peace, Holland & Kellaher, 2011; Severinsen, Breheny & Stephens, 2015).

Oswald and Wahl (2005) describe three reasons why the immediate home environment becomes more important as people age. These contribute to our understanding of the role and variety of meanings assigned to the home. The first reason, 'sociostructural antecedents', refers to the typical household composition of community-dwelling older people. The majority of older people live independently in the community, either alone or with their partner. Only a small number of people live in a residential institution. Alongside this is the time a person spends living in the same home, which has also an influence on the meaning of home (Oswald & Wahl, 2005). Many older people have lived in their houses and neighbourhoods for a very long time, which can create strong attachments to place. The home covers memories and symbolises their entire life (Heylen et al., 2009, p. 232) and housing should be regarded *as an essential player in the unfolding of a life history* (Severinsen, Breheny & Stephens, 2016, p. 724). A second antecedent of the meaning of home in later life denotes the 'everyday life dynamics' (Oswald & Wahl, 2005). Older people tend to spend a higher amount of time within their immediate home environment because of a reduction in their action radius and because their home is the place where most of their daily activities occur. A German study by Brasche and Bischof (2005) about the daily time spent indoors indicated that on average people spend 15.7 hours at home. Older people in particular (aged 65 and older) were characterised by the longest period at home, namely 19.5 hours. Besides higher amounts of time spend inside the home, the immediate neighbourhood also provides opportunities for daily activities. The study of Föbker and Grotz (2006) demonstrated that more than half of the leisure activities of older people occurred in their immediate residential environment, for example 88 per cent of walks were performed within the neighbourhood. The home environment is significant for maintaining an active and healthy life (Sixsmith et al., 2014). Third, Oswald and Wahl (2005) point towards the 'health- and environment-related antecedents' of the meaning of home. 'The home acquires new meaning in old age because it serves to compensate for the reduced functional capacity of the aging individual, especially in very old age' (Oswald & Wahl, 2005, p. 25). Reaching old age can bring with it certain changes and losses on several levels: the social level (e.g., death of a spouse or of peers or friends) (Cristoferetti et al., 2011), the physical level (higher probability of health and mobility problems) (Balfour & Kaplan, 2002) and the psychological level (cognitive decline) (Jokela, Batty & Kivimäki, 2013).

When experiencing these life-changing events, the home environment acts as an important supportive resource for maintaining control over their lives and ensures the continuation of habits, daily structure and identity (Cristoforetti et al., 2011; Oswald & Wahl, 2005; Severinsen, Breheny & Stephens, 2016).

Home as control centre and a source of continuity

Taken as a whole, housing is one of the most important social determinants of a person's health during their lifetime (Shaw, 2004). A systematic review by Bambra et al. (2010) underlines that housing is one of the responsible domains for improving health for all age groups within the population. When growing older, needs and expectations within the home environment may alter, stressing the importance of ageing in an easily adaptable environment (Tinker et al., 2013). Dwellings adapted to the needs of their older residents play a crucial role in the possibility of continuing to live independently. Despite this knowledge, previous research has indicated that home environments can encompass certain risk factors influencing the health of older people. In terms of physical health, older people are at a higher risk of diseases and injuries inside the home (Mack & Liller, 2010; Shaw, 2004). A review by Mack and Liller (2010) concerning the epidemiology and burden of home injuries across different life stages in the US pointed out that the leading causes of home injury and deaths among older people are often housing-related: falls, burns, poisoning, natural or environmental exposure (exposure to excessive heat or cold) and suffocation. The dwellings of older people contain a high prevalence of hazards, with multiple hazards in rooms where they perform complex daily routines (e.g., the bathroom is the most hazardous room) (Carter et al., 1997). Furthermore, another study of Brookfield et al. (2015) revealed that stairs, very small spaces, the location and design of certain fixtures (e.g., height or design of cupboards, switches, sockets, etc.) create complicated everyday activities resulting in a less active, more sedentary lifestyle, which in turn contributes to health problems such as diabetes, cardiovascular complaints and premature mortality (Dempsey et al., 2014; Dunstan et al., 2012). However, even if housing is unsuitable in terms of functional decline, it remains of significant importance for maintaining continuity in older people's lives and is a key aspect in narrating their identity (Severinsen, Breheny & Stephens, 2016).

Few studies have examined the influence of interior design on older people's subjective wellbeing. For example, the early work of Lawton (1985) formulated the concept of 'control centres' that older people create in their home environment, which refer to favoured comfortable places at home where older people have the maximum feeling of autonomy and control. Lawton found some repeated characteristics such as: (1) the location of the control centre was often the living room (as age decreases and impairments increase, the living room becomes the main occupied space); (2) the focus of the 'control centre' was a favoured chair (often chosen by the participants with their present need in mind, e.g., offering good support); (3) a telephone and a television were placed within reach and sight of the chair ; (4) the chair was placed to have overview of the (front) door and a window (often so that the person could look outside); and (5) side tables were placed close to the chair and were covered with objects (e.g., remote control, medicine, magazines, pencil, photographs, etc.) and information (e.g., telephone numbers, magazines, etc.) of highest salience to the person (Lawton, 1985). Also meaningful objects around the house and photographs can symbolise a person's identity and life history (Sixsmith et al., 2014). These 'control centres' clearly indicate that older people also think about and arrange (or design) their interior in order to be in their comfort and control zones. Research of Wright and colleagues (2017) concerning design principles for people with complex and cognitive disability emphasises that architects ought to consider the physical, social, natural, symbolic and care environment in relation to the housing design and neighbourhood context for improved outcomes.

Given the results of these previous studies, it is clear that the physical structure and interior design of the physical environment people live in is of major concern for both physical as well as psychological wellbeing, and, thus, that they support or hinder ageing 'well' in place.

A need for alternative housing typologies: Insights from the Entour-Age Noord project

Background

The ageing population and the provision of age-friendly housing and neighbourhoods are a major challenge for all three regions in Belgium, but in particular for the Brussels-Capital Region. First of all, the group of older single households and older people with a migration background is rising (Knowledge Centre Housing & Care, 2016). Second, the Brussels region contains a (much) higher proportion of the general population that experience poverty compared to the two other regions in Belgium, 38.4 per cent of the Brussels population is at risk of poverty or social exclusion in comparison with 26.3 per cent in the Walloon region and 15.3 per cent in Flanders. The region also faces an increasing percentage of older people relying on a minimum income (Brussels-Capital Health and Social Observatory, 2015). As well as this, the housing stock also has its challenges: 30 per cent of the housing stock in the Brussels-Capital Region was built before 1919. Many dwellings in Brussels lack basic facilities and the most frequently mentioned problems are poor electricity, faulty heating systems, high risk of CO_2 intoxication and the presence of damp problems (Van Mieghem, 2011). Moreover, Winters & Heylen (2014) made a comparison using the European Union Statistics on Income and Living Conditions (EU-SILC) data for 2009 and Eurostat indicators. Their study concluded that poor housing outcomes (overcrowding, damp problems and housing cost overburden) turned out to be at their worst for the Brussels-Capital Region, with the best conditions being in the Flemish Region. There is also a gap between produced housing stock (3,800 units per year since 2003) and the expressed demand (5,000 units per year between 2001 and 2015) in the Brussels-Capital Region. This tension nourishes the rise in real estate prices and rent, which affects the most vulnerable income groups as there are a limited number of affordable dwellings available (Dessouroux et al., 2016).

This lasting crisis in the housing sector and the challenge of an increasing population ageing in place pointed to an innovative approach being needed to respond to the particular care needs of a diverse ageing population. The Brussels Institute for Research and Innovation (Innoviris) launched a collaboration with IWT[1] called 'Innovative Brussels Care'. One of the projects accepted for funding was 'Entour-Age Noord: Inspiring and innovative housing and work'. In close collaboration with different stakeholders, the objective of the Entour-Age Noord project was to develop various innovative and small-scale housing models for older people and to generate new work models within the field of housing and care for older people. The new housing as well as work models are designed to reinforce the quality of life of older people who are ageing in the neighbourhood while allowing them to choose the models best suited to their needs and wishes.

Co-creation of new housing models for later life

In order to answer to these aims, and given their complexity and multidimensionality, the project was divided into six different 'work packages' (WPs). Within these WPs the different stakeholders and end-users (older people, informal caregivers, neighbourhood residents, etc.) were involved during various activities (service design methodology, architectural workshops, inspiring visits, etc.) in order to co-create the answers and recommendations. In a first step, the persona technique was used to generate answers to the question 'for whom should we build?'. Personas can be described as conceptual models of targeted user group(s) and can be used to generate a shared understanding among the different stakeholders. 'The primary advantage of the multi-dimensional persona is to enable the development team to identify with target users, communicate effectively with them and to be a constant reminder to integrate user needs into the system' (Le Rouge et al., 2013, p. 255). Personas were created at the start of the design process and are based on field data, surveys, user interviews, observations and a combination of these (Nielsen & Hansen, 2014). Eight different personas were constructed, e.g., an independent persona, one who has a lot of energy, relies on him/herself and will do so as long as possible, willing to help others; or a persona in distress, a person who faces a cumulation of different problems (financial, housing, social, health, etc.). Personas were used to test the different developed conceptual models of housing.

During the project two future 'alternative' housing models were detailed on paper. Alternative housing can be understood by whatever form that does not fit within the traditional group (notably residential care facilities and single-family houses) (Lawton, 1981). These alternative housing schemes differ from traditional housing in several aspects and contain the following common characteristics (inspired by the early work of Powell Lawton in 1981): (1) they are more custom-built for people who cannot find a solution for their needs within the traditional housing types; (2) they are relatively small-scaled; (3) they include a certain degree of communal life; (4) these alternatives emphasise the ability of living independently (within a supportive and caring environment) and focus less on the availability of medical care. The first housing model focused on older people who wanted to 'share a house' as good neighbours, with private units and some common spaces, where residents could occasionally meet and talk, where good 'neighbourliness' is highly valued, and a 'social porter' is present to help residents with small questions. The second model is intended for older people who want to 'live together' in a familial atmosphere sharing a common house with private rooms, where residents meet every day in communal areas, where friendship, care and support are central, and where family members can play an active role.

In the discussions, several architectural and spatial design characteristics were raised by older people that are important for the development of future housing models for later life:

1) provide 'encounter-friendly' communal facilities (e.g., staircase, entrance, mailboxes, elevator, etc.) – these should be more than solely functional, also providing opportunities for casual social contact (e.g., noticeboard, a shared bookshelf, decorative

elements, a hallway that is wide enough, placement of plants/flowers which need maintenance and care);

2) provide a common space outside where residents can meet and interact (e.g., a garden or a terrace);
3) able to share basic functional areas (e.g., laundry facility/'salon-lavoir', common freezer, dumpster area, etc.)
4) have a polyvalent area for all sort of activities (but which can also act as a room for the neighbourhood);
5) have a spare room for guests (or as shelter for people in a crisis situation by working together with an organisation);
6) take into account guidelines on design for later life (e.g., wide doors, grab rails, etc.).

These characteristics are not limited to older adults but can be of interest to any age group. Each future housing development could take these suggestions into consideration. Most important is to involve the future residents in the decision-making process: which common rooms would they like to see realised? How do they want to manage these common rooms? For example, some people will prefer to have a shared laundry facility, but for others this will not be the case. And what about the presence of housing adaptations? For example, the study of Sixsmith et al. (2014) demonstrated that, for some older people, overcoming everyday challenges posed by one's frailties, such as stairs, resulted in feelings of achievement. And for some people in this study, adaptations were seen as symbolic of their frailty and thus they preferred an environment that was familiar and reflective of their identity rather than instrumentally supportive.

Conclusion

The main aim of this chapter was to give an overview and understanding of the meaning of the home environment in later life. The immediate home environment should be regarded as a significant place, whereby the concept of 'place' is located within time and space and whereby place provides the link between one's dwelling and one's wellbeing and identity (Easthope, 2004; Smetcoren, 2016; Stones & Gullifer, 2016). We would like to end this chapter with some thoughts to reflect upon and some recommendations that may be of interest for further research, with a focus on design research. First of all, previous research has clearly indicated the importance of the home environment for older people in general. However, several vulnerable groups, such as very old people, single older persons or seniors from low-income categories can benefit even more from living in accessible and age-friendly home environments, as they often lack the means (physical, psychological, financial, etc.) to initiate proper changes in their environmental situation. Those who have low competence are much more vulnerable to environmental demands than older adults with high competence (Iwarsson, 2005; Smetcoren, 2016). Providing accessible, pleasant environments could act as a buffer for less resilient groups.

Second, the Entour-Age Noord project and previous studies have stressed the involvement of older adults as a resource for residential developments (Means, 2007; Pirinen, 2016; Smetcoren, 2016). Also within the design practice, an end-user should be represented as a central figure, not as 'a passive resident' or 'an object that undergoes, tests and experiments', but as a 'leading subject' or 'an active agent' in decision-making processes. As Mallers, Claver and Lares (2014, p. 73) point out, 'Innovations in aging, such as cohousing and intentional neighbourhoods, have expanded aging-in-place to community-in-place, whereby residents have voice and environmental control over the design and sustainability of communities in which they live'.

Third, attention could be given to the interior design of home environments. Previous studies have focused largely on the physical layout and design of the home environment (such as the presence of staircases, thresholds (indoor/outdoor), distance to services, etc.) and how the home environment is congruent with older people's needs and goals (Golant, 2012; Rantakokko et al., 2014; Smetcoren, 2016). Petermans and Pohlmeyer (2014) state that, to date, numerous (interior) architects have focused to a large extent on how design can contribute to objective wellbeing of people, mainly by paying attention to aspects such as acoustics, isolation, heating and cooling facilities, accessibility, and sustainability of the built environment. However, these researchers stress the importance to take into account subjective wellbeing in future interior design research, in the course of which the interior space is reasoned to facilitate higher order needs (such as personal growth, self-acceptance, life satisfaction, positive emotions, engaging activities, etc.) (Petermans & Pohlmeyer, 2014). Research on the meaning and importance of interior design in later life is scarce and scientific knowledge on how home interior design affects subjective wellbeing is required. In order to fill this gap, it is recommended that researchers across different fields – including design, health and gerontology research – work in close collaboration with each other.

Note

1 IWT is the Flemish Government Agency for Innovation by Science and Technology.

References

Alley, D., Liebig, P., Pynoos, J., Banerjee, T., & Choi, I.H. (2007). Creating elder-friendly communities: Preparation for an aging society. *Journal of Gerontological Social Work*, *49*, 1–18.

Balfour, J.L., & Kaplan, G.A. (2002). Neighborhood environment and loss of physical function in older adults: Evidence from the Alameda County Study. *American Journal of Epidemiology*, *155*(6), 507–515.

Bambra, C., Gibson, M., Sowden, A., Wright, K., Whitehead, M., & Petticrew, M. (2010). Tackling the wider social determinants of health and health inequalities: Evidence from systematic reviews. *Journal of Epidemiology and Community Health*, *64*(4), 284–291.

Brasche, S., & Bischof, W. (2005). Daily time spent indoors in German homes – Baseline data for the assessment of indoor exposure of German occupants. *International Journal of Hygiene and Environmental Health*, *208*(4), 247–253.

Brookfield, K., Fitzsimons, C., Scott, I., Mead, G., Starr, J., Thin, N., Tinker, A., & Thompson, C.W. (2015). The home as enabler of more active lifestyles among older people. *Building Research & Information*, *43*(5), 616–630.

Brussels-Capital Health and Social Observatory (2015). *Brussels Poverty Report* [online]. Available from: http://www.observatbru.be/documents/publications/publications-pauvrete/rapportspauvrete.xml?lang=en (in Dutch)

Buffel, T., Handler, S., & Phillipson, C. (2018). Age-friendly cities and communities: A manifesto for change. In T. Buffel, S. Handler, & C. Phillipson (Eds.), *Age-Friendly Cities and Communities. A Global Perspective* (pp. 273–288). Bristol: Policy Press.

Carter, S.E., Campbell, E.M., Sanson-Fisher, R.W., Redman, S., & Gillespie, W.J. (1997). Environmental hazards in the homes of older people. *Age and Ageing*, *26*(3), 195–202.

Centers for Disease Control and Prevention (2013). *Healthy Places Terminology*. Available from: http://www.cdc.gov/healthyplaces/terminology.htm

Cristoforetti, A., Gennai, F., & Rodeschini, G. (2011). Home sweet home: The emotional construction of places. *Journal of Aging Studies*, *25*(3), 225–232.

Cutchin, M.P. (2003). The process of mediated aging-in-place: A theoretically and empirically based model. *Social Science & Medicine, 57*(6), 1077–1090.

De Donder, L., Smetcoren, A.-S., Dury, S., Van Regenmortel, S., Lambotte, D., … and Verté, D. (2017). *Zorginnovatie in Vlaamse proeftuinen. Onderzoek naar Actief Zorgzame Buurten in Brussel en Antwerpen* [Towards An Active Caring Community in Brussels and Antwerp] (in Dutch). Kenniscentrum WWZ. (Viewed April 2018). Available from: http://www.kenniscentrumwwz.be/sites/default/files/bijlagen/zorginnovatie.pdf

Dempsey, P.C., Owen, N., Biddle, S.J.H., & Dunstan, D.W. (2014). Managing sedentary behavior to reduce the risk of diabetes and cardiovascular disease. *Current Diabetes Reports, 14*(9), 1–11.

Dessouroux, C., Bensliman, R., Bernard, N., De Laet, S., Demonty, F., Marissal, P., & Surkyn, J. (2016). Housing in Brussels: Diagnosis and challenges. *Brussels Studies, 99.* (Viewed April 2018). Available from: http://journals.openedition.org/brussels/1353

De Witte, N., Smetcoren, A.-S., De Donder, L., Dury, S., Buffel, T., Kardol, T., & Verte., D. (2012). *Een huis? Een thuis! Over ouderen en wonen* [A House? A home! Housing in Later Life] (In Dutch). Brugge: Vanden Broele.

Dunstan, D.W., Howard, B., Healy, G.N., & Owen, N. (2012). Too much sitting – A health hazard. *Diabetes Research and Clinical Practice, 97*(3), 368–376.

Dury, S. (2018). Dynamics in motivations and reasons to quit in a Care Bank: A qualitative study in Belgium. *European Journal of Ageing.* (Viewed April 2018).

Easthope, H. (2004). A place called home. *Housing, Theory and Society, 21*(3), 128–138.

European Union (2014). *Population Ageing in Europe: Facts, Implications and Policies. Outcome of EU-funded Research.* (Viewed June 2018). Available from: https://ec.europa.eu/research/social-sciences/pdf/policy_reviews/kina26426enc.pdf

European Union (2015). *Social Protection Systems in the EU: Financing Arrangements and the Effectiveness and Efficiency of Resource Allocation.* Report jointly prepared by the Social Protection Committee and the European Commission Services. (Viewed June 2018). Available from: http://ec.europa.eu/social/main.jsp?catId=738&langId=en&pubId=7743&type=2&furtherPubs=yes

Eurostat (2018). *Population Structure and Ageing.* (Viewed June 2018). Available from: https://ec.europa.eu/eurostat/statistics-explained/pdfscache/1271.pdf

Föbker, S., & Grotz, R. (2006). Everyday mobility of elderly people in different urban settings: The example of the city of Bonn, Germany. *Urban Studies, 43*(1), 99–118.

Gardner, P. (2011). Natural neighbourhood networks – Important social networks in the lives of older adults aging in place. *Journal of Aging Studies, 25,* 263–271.

Golant, S.M. (2011). The quest for residential normalcy by older adults: Relocation but one pathway. *Journal of Aging Studies, 25*(3), 193–205.

Golant, S.M. (2012). Out of their residential comfort and mastery zones: Toward a more relevant environmental gerontology. *Journal of Housing for the Elderly, 26*(1–3), 26–43.

Golant, S.M. (2015). Residential normalcy and the enriched coping repertoires of successfully aging older adults. *The Gerontologist, 55*(1), 70–82.

Heylen, M., De Roeck, V., Kerkhof, I., Plessers, M., & Verheyen, E. (2009). *Atlas van de menselijke levensloop* [Atlas of the Human Life Course] (In Dutch). Leuven: Acco. (Viewed January 2018). Available from: https://www.plan.be/publications/publication.php?lang=nl&TM=46

Hooghe, M., & Vanhoutte, B. (2011). Subjective wellbeing and social capital in Belgian communities. The impact of community characteristics on subjective wellbeing indicators in Belgium. *Social Indicators Research, 100*(1), 17–36.

Iwarsson, S. (2005). A long-term perspective on person–environment fit and ADL dependence among older Swedish adults. *The Gerontologist, 45*(3), 327–336.

Jokela, M., Batty, G.D., & Kivim Ki, M. (2013). Ageing and the prevalence and treatment of mental health problems. *Psychological Medicine, 43*(10), 2037–2045.

Knowledge Centre Housing & Care Brussels (2016). *Masterplan Woonzorg Brussel 2014–2020* [Masterplan Care & Housing Brussels 2014–2020] (In Dutch). (Viewed January 2018). Available from: http://www.kenniscentrumwwz.be/sites/default/files/bijlagen/Fiche%20MP%20-%20Ouderen%20in%20cijfers_0.pdf

Lawton, M.P. (1981). Alternative housing. *Journal of Gerontological Social Work, 3*(3), 61–80.

Lawton, M.P. (1985). The elderly in context: Perspectives from environmental psychology and gerontology. *Environment and Behavior, 17*(4), 501–519.

Le Rouge, C., Ma, J., Sneha, S., & Tolle, K. (2013). User profiles and personas in the design and development of consumer health technologies. *International Journal of Medical Informatics, 82*, 251–268.

Löfqvist, C., Granbom, M., Himmelsbach, I., Iwarsson, S., Oswald, F., & Haak, M. (2013). Voices on relocation and aging in place in very old age – A complex and ambivalent matter. *The Gerontologist, 53*(6), 919–927.

Nielsen, L., & Hansen, K.S. (2014). Personas is applicable: A study on the use of personas in Denmark. *Proceedings of the SIGCHI Conference on Human Factors in Computing System (CHI'14)*, Ontario, Canada, pp. 1665–1674.

Nussbaum, M. (2001). *The Fragility of Goodness. Luck and Ethics in Greek Tragedy and Philosophy.* Cambridge: Cambridge University Press.

Mack, K.A., & Liller, K.D. (2010). Home injuries: Potential for prevention. *American Journal of Lifestyle Medicine, 4*(1), 75–81.

Mallers, M.H., Claver, M., & Lares, L.A. (2014). Perceived control in the lives of older adults: The influence of Langer and Rodin's work on gerontological theory, policy, and practice. *The Gerontologist, 54*(1), 67–74.

Means, R. (2007). Safe as houses? Ageing in place and vulnerable older people in the UK. *Social Policy & Administration, 41*(1), 65–85.

Oswald, F., & Wahl, H.-W. (2003). Place attachment across the life span. In J.R. Miller, R.M. Lerner, L.B. Schiamberg, & P.M. Anderson (Eds.), *The Encyclopedia of Human Ecology* (Vol. 2, pp. 568–572). Santa Barbara, CA: ABC-Clio.

Oswald, F., & Wahl, H.-W. (2005). Dimensions of the meaning of home in later life. In G.D. Rowles, & H. Chaudhury (Eds.), *Home and Identity in Late Life: International Perspectives* (pp. 21–46). New York, NY: Springer.

Paraponaris, A., Davin, B., & Verger, P. (2012). Formal and informal care for disabled elderly living in the community: An appraisal of French care composition and costs. *The European Journal of Health Economics, 13*(3), 327–336.

Peace, S., Holland, C., & Kellaher, L. (2011). 'Option recognition' in later life: Variations in ageing in place. *Ageing and Society, 31*(5), 734–757.

Peace, S., Wahl, A.-W., Mollenkopf, H., & Oswald, F. (2007). Environment and ageing. In J. Bond, S. Peace, F. Dittmann-Kohli, & G. Westerhof (Eds.), *Ageing in Society: European Perspectives on Gerontology* (Third Edition, pp. 209–234). London: Sage Publications Ltd.

Peine, A., & Arentshorst, M. (2016). *Towards a European Reference Framework for Age-Friendly Housing.* (Viewed March 2018). Available from: https://ec.europa.eu/digital-single-market/en/news/final-report-recommendations-european-reference-framework-age-friendly-housing

Petermans, A., & Pohlmeyer, A. (2014). Design for subjective wellbeing in interior architecture. *Proceedings 6th Annual Arch. Research Symposium: Designing and Planning the Built Environment for Human Wellbeing*, Oulu, Finland, pp. 206–218.

Pirinen, A. (2016). Housing concepts for and by the elderly: From subjects of design to a design resource. *Journal of Housing for the Elderly, 30*(4), 412–429.

Pittini, A., & Laino, E. (2011). *Housing Europe Review 2012. The Nuts and Bolts of European Social Housing Systems.* Published by CECODHAS Housing Europe's Observatory. (Viewed March 2018). Available from: http://www.housingeurope.eu/resource-105/the-housingeurope-review-2012

Rantakokko, M., Iwarsson, S., Vahaluoto, S., Portegijs, E., Viljanen, A., & Rantanen, T. (2014). Perceived environmental barriers to outdoor mobility and feelings of loneliness among community-dwelling older people. *The Journals of Gerontology Series A: Biological Sciences and Medical Sciences, 69*(12), 1562–1568.

Rechel, B., Grundy, E., Robine, J.-M., Cylus, J., Mackenbach, J.P., Knai, C., & Mckee, M. (2013). Health in Europe 6. Ageing in the European Union. *The Lancet, 381*(9874), 1312–1322.

Severinsen, C., Breheny, M., & Stephens, C. (2015). Ageing in unsuitable places. *Housing Studies, 31*(6), 714–728.

Severinsen, C., Breheny, M., & Stephens, C. (2016). Ageing in unsuitable places. *Housing Studies, 31*(6), 714–728. doi:10.1080/02673037.2015.1122175

Shaw, M. (2004). Housing and public health. *Annual Review of Public Health, 25*(1), 397–418.

Sixsmith, A., & Sixsmith, J. (2008). Ageing in place in the United Kingdom. *Ageing International, 32*(3), 219–235.

Sixsmith, J, Sixsmith, A, Malmgren Fänge, A, Naumann, D, Kucsera, C, Tomsone, S, Haak, M, Dahlin-Ivanoff, S., & Woolrych, R. (2014). Healthy ageing and home: The perspectives of very old people in five European countries. *Social Science and Medicine, 106*. (Viewed April 2018). Available from: https://www.sciencedirect.com/science/article/abs/pii/S0277953614000318

Smetcoren, A. (2016). *I'm Not Leaving!? Critical Perspectives on 'Ageing in Place'*. PhD thesis, Vrije Universiteit Brussel. Brussels: University Press.

Stones, D., & Gullifer, J. (2016). 'At home it's just so much easier to be yourself': Older adults' perceptions of ageing in place. *Ageing & Society, 36*(3), 449–481

Szanton, S.L., Thorpe, R.J., Boyd, C., Tanner, E.K., Leff, B., Agree, E., … and Gitlin, L.N. (2011). Community aging in place, advancing better living for elders: A bio-behavioral- environmental intervention to improve function and health-related quality of life in disabled older adults. *Journal of the American Geriatrics Society, 59*(12), 2314–2320.

Tinker, A., Kellaher, L., Ginn, J., & Ribe, E. (2013). *Assisted Living Platform – The Long Term Care Revolution*. (Viewed April 2018). Available from: https://www.ifa-fiv.org/wp-content/uploads/2013/11/HLIN-Report-LTC-Revolution.pdf

United Nations (2013). *World Population Ageing 2013*. Published by the Department of Economic and Social Affairs Population Division. (Viewed January 2018). Available from http://www.un.org/en/development/desa/population/publications/pdf/ageing/WorldPopulationAgeing2013.pdf

United Nations (2017a). *World Population Prospects: The 2017 Revision, Key Findings and Advance Tables*. Working Paper No. ESA/P/WP/248. Published by the Department of Economic and Social Affairs Population Division.

United Nations (2017b). *World Population Ageing 2017 – Highlights (ST/ESA/SER.A/397)*. Published by the Department of Economic and Social Affairs Population Division.

United Nations (2017c). *Living Arrangements of Older Persons: A Report on an Expanded International Dataset (ST/ESA/SER.A/407)*. Published by the Department of Economic and Social Affairs Population Division.

Van Mieghem, W. (2011). Zeven jaar ongezonde woningen in Brussel. Conclusies [Seven years of unhealthy housing in Brussels. Conclusions]. In Brusselse Bond van Recht op Wonen, ed. *7 jaar strijd tegen ongezonde woningen in Brussel: De balans* (In Dutch). Brussel: BBRoW.

Wiles, J.L., Leibing, A., Guberman, N., Reeve, J., & Allen, R.E.S. (2012). The meaning of 'ageing in place' to older people. *The Gerontologist, 52*(3), 357–366.

Winters, S., & Heylen, K. (2014). How housing outcomes vary between the Belgian regions. *Journal of Housing and the Built Environment, 29*(3), 541–56.

Wright, C.J., Zeeman, H., & Whitty, J.A. (2017). Design principles in housing for people with complex physical and cognitive disability: Towards an integrated framework for practice. *Journal of Housing for the Built Environment, 32*, 339–360.

World Health Organisation (2007). *Global Age-friendly Cities: A Guide*. (Viewed December 2017). Available from: http://www.who.int/ageing/publications/Global_age_friendly_cities_Guide_English.pdf

15 An international perspective on design for wellbeing

Leandro Miletto Tonetto

Studies on design for wellbeing (DfW) from all over the globe focus on products, technology, services, built environment and sustainability. Such studies are vital to the development of the research field but are not unique to any particular scientific community.[1] What seems to differentiate the scientific production within DfW from continent to continent are the underlying theoretical foundations and the social issues addressed by these studies.

The need for developing a view on wellbeing at an international level is related to three specificities and dissimilarities that characterise DfW. First, different theoretical and methodological perspectives (especially pragmatic and phenomenological) shape the way in which wellbeing is understood and investigated by different scientific communities. Second, wellbeing may be viewed as a final desired effect of design, but studies may also focus on stimuli or experiences that are proven to lead to wellbeing, such as the conciliation of internal conflicts and the improvement of social relationships. Third, some differentiation is seen in social issues that are addressed in distinct societies. These three aspects may confuse researchers and practitioners looking for theoretical and methodological parameters to ground their work. These parameters are explored in the following three sections. At the end of the chapter we offer five steps to guide future practice in the field of DfW.

Pragmatic vs phenomenological perspectives: Epistemological level

In design research throughout the globe, wellbeing is explored under distinct perspectives – pragmatism and phenomenology. These methodological roots provide different approaches to understand how wellbeing is addressed at an international level and help define how to conduct research on the subject.

Particular research communities do not adopt a single methodological perspective. Whereas Anglo-Saxon research more often applies pragmatic perspectives, phenomenologically oriented studies are more commonly seen in European and North American publications. Few or no phenomenological studies are observed in South America, Asia or Oceania.

Taken into account that pragmatism and phenomenology seem to be the most widely adopted approaches to DfW, in what follows, these approaches are discussed in more detail.

Pragmatism

Studies within DfW that report the development of industrial or large-scale distribution artefacts, such as products (e.g., Wu & Noy, 2010, UK) and mobile apps (e.g., Carey et al., 2016, Australia), are commonly associated with pragmatic theories and approaches throughout the international community. Design guidelines, tools and frameworks are recurrently aimed outcomes in this type of investigation (e.g., Ozenc, 2014, US).

Following the American tradition represented here by William James, pragmatism is concerned with practical, functional and applicable outcomes to design problems. Such an assumption brings the idea that design problems and artefacts designed to solve them are at different ends of a continuum. Therefore, there is a belief that designers should set a design brief – or receive one that is already clear and focused on a problem – to be able to produce valid and applicable solutions.

Design *for* wellbeing seems an appropriate expression to define the field, since researchers and practitioners deliberately try to manipulate design variables to influence wellbeing (Desmet & Pohlmeyer, 2013, Netherlands). DfW is clearly related to pragmatic research approaches that somehow try to 'predict' the likely effects of design on people's lives and use this information in applied projects. There is also a root and an inspiration in the positivist tradition that understands life from a cause-and-effect perspective.

Pragmatic approaches adopt both qualitative and quantitative methods to attain their objectives. Regardless of the nature of the data collected, there are clear concerns about neutrality, generalisation and replicability, which are typical of modern science. Two research papers serve as examples in this respect: Eaves, Gyi and Gibb (2016), from the UK, and Zuniga-Teran et al. (2017), from the US.

Eaves, Gyi and Gibb (2016) investigated the health and wellbeing of heavy manual construction workers, collecting qualitative data through interviews from a sample of 80 people. Although the authors did not offer a clear differentiation between health and wellbeing, the research focused on exploring ways to make the workers' tasks more comfortable, safer and easier to perform. Results pointed to over 250 design ideas aimed at increasing health and wellbeing, making the research strongly connected to pragmatism in its applicability.

In a similar pragmatic path to reach design ideas and guidelines, Zuniga-Teran et al. (2017) investigated how wellbeing is affected by the design of the neighbourhood in which respondents live. The author used a questionnaire to collect data from a sample of 486 individuals. Results point to city vegetation as an inducer of physical activity and wellbeing, and city maintenance as related to improved mental health and wellbeing.

Although research papers usually propose the individual or combined use of methods for pragmatically approaching DfW, some authors have attempted to create frameworks for that purpose. Examples are 'modes of transition' (Ozenc, 2014, US), which is briefly outlined next and 'positive design' (Desmet & Pohlmeyer, 2013, Netherlands), which is described in the next section.

Modes of transition is characterised by a three-stage design process – structuring human-centred design methods, scenario-based design and research through design. It provides designers with 'sensitising lenses' and guidelines to help structure human-centred design methods and processes. The design endorses the functional and experiential needs of users to promote their wellbeing. In the words of Ozenc (2014, p. 41), wellbeing helps users to 'thrive in their personal and social relationships; discover meaning in their daily and long-term interactions; balance their life modes (e.g., work, home and social time); and embrace their emotions and values'.

Pragmatism in DfW is related to the industrial tradition of design, which tends to split the design process into linear stages. It also points at the problem–solution binomial as different ends of a single continuum. As the examples reviewed in this section indicate, it is a practical approach not significantly connected to any particular geographic region, although slightly predominant in Anglo-Saxon research and practice.

Phenomenology

Focus on experience as a unique phenomenon to design personally shaped artefacts and spaces is usually associated to phenomenological approaches and theories. Clear phenomenological perspectives are less usual in general design studies on wellbeing, but they do consistently appear in architecture and interior design research (e.g., a European–Swedish study on health care experiences in a critical care setting by Olausson, Lindahl and Ekebergh, 2013), especially in research from Europe and North America.

Phenomenological approaches are grounded in the work of authors such as Edmund Husserl and Merleau-Ponty. Phenomenologist designers disregard the presumed neutrality of modern science, refraining from adopting its structured character. These approaches are not connected to generalisations and mass solutions, since every design process and user experience is seen as related to an individual's subjective consciousness (Mace, 2016, UK). Therefore, designers do not necessarily look for or believe in the clarity of design briefs, structured guidelines, stage-by-stage framework or pre-set tolls.[2] Consequently, the binomial 'problem–solution' is not representative of this approach. The experience of wellbeing is not seen as evocable by designed artefacts (e.g., built environment, products, services) as an individual response from the designer to the user. The user cannot be dissociated from the design process, and designed artefacts are not necessarily responses to clear design briefings.

General problems that relate to the design of replicable solutions are of no particular interest to phenomenologists, since experience itself is not commonly seen as replicable. In this chapter, a distinction is adopted to allow a clear differentiation between pragmatic and phenomenological approaches to DfW.

Design *and* wellbeing better characterise phenomenology-based approaches, indicating a relationship between the two concepts rather than an assumption that there is a devisable cause (design) *for* an intended effect (wellbeing). There is no belief in cause–effect perspectives, since they do not envision wellbeing as a manipulatable linear consequence of particular design stimuli. Therefore, phenomenology-based DfW naturally tends to favour qualitative methods.

The research in Poldma (2011), from Canada, provides a good example of phenomenology-based DfW. The author examines astronauts' experiences of living in zero gravity, analysing how interior design in space may address the relationships between humanity and technology. The author's approach was clearly phenomenological: 'We navigate spaces understanding and reacting to our perceptions, physiological, and psychological responses that are triggered by physical indicators to which all of our senses react' (p. 546). In this perspective, experience refers to living in a space here and now. Quoting Merleau-Ponty, the author states that the space is in constant movement, being the opposite of a static artefact to which we only respond to. Thus, rather than providing strict guidelines to lead the design process, the author indicates general approaches and design ideas, such as to design flexible small areas and devices that can change quickly in response to different activities astronauts will be involved in. Rejecting pragmatic and quantitative paths, Poldma (2011) indicates the use of qualitative design criteria alongside with current concrete approaches that dominate the design in zero gravity environments.

In a previous work, Poldma (2008) reinforces the ideas discussed above. Her perspective on DfW is grounded on the assumption that people's place in space at a particular time is in constant change; wellbeing is driven by their living experiences. Designing means not only to approach technical solutions for design problems, but also to work on crafting meaning in space and place for potential users.

In a conceptual study from the Netherlands, Megens et al. (2013) developed 'experiential design landscapes' (EDL), which is claimed to be an approach to design that places users in the centre of the design process. Users generate meaning for themselves, since self-generated meaning contributes to people's wellbeing. The theoretical basis to discuss the creation of meaning is phenomenology: 'Through the EDL method, by bringing open-ended design proposals based on open scripts and intentionality to society we can open up and explore societal transformation' (p. 4295).

In conclusion, phenomenology moves away from the industrial tradition of treating design problems and designed solutions as different ends of a continuum, rejecting cause–effect perspectives as a means to work towards a particular 'truth'. Every design project is seen as a unique phenomenon, which may involve users in an inimitable experience, being representative of reflective practices of the North American and European authors reported in this subsection.

Although inspiring many research articles, it is difficult to identify approaches for design and wellbeing that are solely influenced by phenomenology, as seen in Poldma (2008, 2011). Since design is an applied science, many researchers have also shown influences from pragmatism, as described in the following subsection. These influences are seen in the search for practical and useful applications of their designs that go beyond projects based on a specific person. They are aimed at influencing a broader group of people.

Coherence of integrated frameworks: Pragmatic phenomenology

As explored hereafter, some authors propose approaches that combine pragmatism and phenomenology. These approaches cannot be identified as geographically predominant. As seen in the studies reviewed previously, they vary along a continuum in which, at one extreme, pragmatism appears as a clear practice and, at the other, pure phenomenology is identified.

In philosophical terms, phenomenology and pragmatism have developed distinct methodological traditions. For many pragmatists, phenomenology has been often associated to subjectivism or even metaphysics; phenomenologists traditionally reject the philosophy behind pragmatism, commonly associating it to reductionism. Despite their opposing views, phenomenology and pragmatism have been jointly adopted in contemporary research (e.g., Bourgeois, 2002). In the DfW field the two approaches may be viewed as essentially contradictory, but they may also represent a coherent way of dealing with design as an applied science.

Design is an applied science and, as such, sometimes prioritises application purposes rather than epistemological coherence. To exemplify that, several times in which phenomenology is linked to wellbeing studies in the design field, a pragmatic phenomenological approach emerges, rather than a strict phenomenological approach per se.

Pragmatic phenomenology focuses on sensibility and experience, embracing experimental procedures and attention to particularity and plurality, prioritising uniqueness over generality (Craig, 2010). Such an integrated approach may be justified in design research by its usefulness.

A few authors seem to move towards pragmatic phenomenology approaches while attempting to draw generalisations from their results. An Australian example is found in Page and Richardson (2016) who investigate the design of interactive medical devices. The authors assume that every 'person centred design approach' (p. 9) that is inspired by phenomenology focuses on users' wellbeing. The authors have employed what they defined as a phenomenological attitude to research, though their aims were still connected to applicable results from experimentation (typical from pragmatism), which is the development of common ground to work in the intersections among design, human–computer interaction and medicine.

Ren and Strickfaden (2018) have integrated different research perspectives on wellbeing: existential, ecological and place-based. Although using a strong basis in Merleau-Ponty, the authors still synthesise their ideas in a reduction of the design process, which is a 'framework for the association of material environments and people with dementia' (p. 18).

In conclusion, pragmatic phenomenology is an alternative to integrate approaches that are seen as contradictory in other sciences. It adopts the phenomenological philosophy behind the concepts of perception, experience and wellbeing, but it is still grounded in practical applications and, somehow, in the usefulness of pragmatism.

Design for wellbeing or design to influence the predictors of wellbeing: Application level

There are two main ways in which we can design for wellbeing: addressing it directly or targeting its predictors.

In the first way of dealing with wellbeing through design – addressing it directly – researchers investigate and/or design explicitly to evoke higher levels of wellbeing; for example, inciting positive affect, inhibiting negative emotions, improving the general evaluation of people regarding their own lives, encouraging meaning in life and boosting the use of a person's virtues in everyday situations (Brey, 2015).

In experimental terms, DfW investigates or manipulates independent variables associated with the design, measuring their effects on wellbeing (dependent variables). Such an experimental approach commonly refers to constructs such as psychological or subjective wellbeing by North American and (especially) European authors (e.g., Easterbrook and Vignoles, 2015, UK).

Piper, Weibel and Hollan (2014, US), for instance, used audio-enhanced paper photos enabled by digital pen technology as a research technique to understand emotional wellbeing in late adulthood. The subjects were patients who had aphasia and advanced memory loss following a stroke. Results indicated that the artefacts produced by the technique had embedded emotional information and that they addressed various aspects of emotional wellbeing itself.

In another study, Easterbrook and Vignoles (2015) investigated the long-term impact of shared housing designed to foster positive relationships and wellbeing in its users. The authors have adopted direct measures of wellbeing and concluded that students who live in flats with features that encourage the use of communal areas (e.g., shared bathrooms) reported unintentionally meeting their flatmates more frequently. The number of encounters was a significant predictor of the strength of interpersonal bonds and degree of wellbeing.

Moving away from work focused on the effects of artefacts on wellbeing, but still dealing with the construct in a direct manner, some frameworks have been proposed for DfW.

Positive design (Desmet & Pohlmeyer, 2013), which is a movement initiated in the Netherlands, is a meaningful example. Based on a positive psychology background, professional designers aim to evoke higher levels of wellbeing. In this framework, designers target users' values, pleasure and personal significance to stimulate wellbeing.

In a second way to DfW, which is a research tradition spread throughout the globe, wellbeing itself is not always the primary target. This way consists in designing to stimulate the predictors of wellbeing. Most research work on design, independent of geographical origin, is identified with this pattern. The focus relies on human characteristics and experiences that are supposed to improve wellbeing, such as solving people's internal conflicts (Carey et al., 2016, Australia; Ozkaramanli & Desmet, 2012, Netherlands) and environmental interferences (Jackson, 2003, US; Taylor & Hochuli, 2015, Australia). These examples are explored next.

Carey et al. (2016) measured the effect of a mobile app called MindSurf on depression, anxiety and stress, which were considered predictors of wellbeing. The app allows people to explore their thinking to help solve internal conflicts. Decreased scores on the three measures were verified in university staff subjects after using the app.

Ozkaramanli and Desmet (2012) also focused on internal conflicts (conflicting concerns), investigating how design could stimulate sustainable eating habits through emotionally appealing concepts. The authors developed tools to support professionals in addressing users' conflicting concerns in the design process.

Jackson (2003, US) investigated human wellbeing in low-density urban living developments. There are public health arguments to support the improvement of greenery, natural light and visual and physical access to open spaces in urban areas. To increase health and social life, these improvements should be adopted in urban design. To facilitate the preservation of agricultural and natural areas for respite and recreation, urban spaces need to be close to civil and retail resources, and also offer cultural and business opportunities for the population.

In this perspective, there is a need to expand the focus of DfW from single artefacts, or sets of artefacts, to the design of an ecosystem. Theoretical work from Taylor and Hochuli (2015) indicates that fields such as urban design recognise that the delivery of walkable spaces, community spaces and green spaces tend to increase citizens' wellbeing. Nevertheless, these deliveries are insufficient to foster human wellbeing. The authors encourage the inclusion of environmental aspects, such as biodiversity and ecosystem functioning, in research on urban design. Therefore, both studies recognise wellbeing as achievable through the design of urban ecosystems.

As seen in the examples above, wellbeing is considered to be a long-lasting human experience that is not commonly considered to be directly targetable by design. There is no answer yet on how it can be evoked through design. Even though wellbeing does not have a unique definition, researchers deal with design variables that are perceived as its predictors. As a result, taking into account the lack of a longitudinal measure of wellbeing as outcome of design choices, many researchers – both pragmatic and phenomenologically driven – address its short-term predictors.

Social issues

This subchapter discusses how current research addresses social issues, indicating opportunities for local and intercultural projects. It does not aim to be an assessment of the relevance of the work from the authors hereafter mentioned.

Several papers address general issues that fit any society. Differently, a number of studies seem to reflect social concerns that underlie wellbeing in each culture. They were organised from macro-social issues to individual focuses[3], as follows:

a) Macro-social issues: some Australian studies revealed a focus on participatory democracy (Mcintyre-Mills & De Vries, 2010; Mcintyre-Mills, 2010), while European papers endorsed the importance of engaging citizens in the development of public buildings and spaces (Erikson & Wideström, 2014, Sweden), in questions regarding user-influencing design (manipulation of life through design), and in freedom and determination (Dorrestijn & Verbeek, 2013, Netherlands). Educating citizens for environmental issues was also a topic found in European studies (Schulze et al., 2015, Germany and Sweden).

b) Urban life and how the built environment can help shape it: this topic seems to be deeply explored in urban societies, including European research on the effect of green and sustainable spaces on human life (Douglas, Lennon & Scott, 2017, Ireland), and North American studies on urban nature (Knecht, 2004, US) and neighbourhood design (Zuniga-Teran et al., 2017, US). This type of issue was also identified in Australian research that focuses on design that supports midwifery practice in hospitals (Hammond, Homer & Foureur, 2017) and on how biodiversity and ecosystem functioning can enhance urban residents' wellbeing (Taylor & Hochuli, 2015).

c) Social relationships: they are explored in research carried out in developed countries. Examples include an investigation on cyberbullying in North America (Bowler, Knobel & Mattern, 2015, US) and social relationships in student housing in Europe (Easterbrook & Vignoles, 2015, UK).

d) Wellbeing and health (or wellbeing through health, or vice versa): relationships between the two topics were observed especially in Europe (King, Thomson & Darzi, 2014, UK), North America (Piper, Weibel & Hollan, 2014, US) and Australia (Pedell et al., 2015; Page & Richardson, 2016).

e) Worker´s wellbeing: it is a recurrent research focus in Europe (Edwards & Jensen, 2014, Denmark; Michel, O'Shea & Hoppe, 2015, Germany and Ireland; Eaves, Gyi & Gibb, 2016, UK) and Australia (Tyson, Lambert & Beattie, 2002).

f) Individual wellbeing: there is an emphasis on research to help solve internal (psychological) conflicts through design in Europe (Ozkaramanli & Desmet, 2012, Netherlands) and Australia (Carey et al., 2016), and in therapeutic activities and artefacts in Europe (De Couvreur et al., 2013, Belgium; Diedrichs et al., 2017, UK) and North America (Piper, Weibel & Hollan, 2014, US).

Research from Asia seems to focus on very technical aspects of design. Examples include Siu and Wai's (2011) study on how the design of public toilets may increase the wellbeing of visually impaired users in China, and Cho and Kim's (2015) research on cognitive aspects of smartphone usage among different generations. Technicality is not a rule and some exceptions are found, such as in Lee, Hung and Wu (2014, Taiwan), who investigated the relationships between the use of mobile applications for subjective wellbeing among middle-aged adults.

Developing countries, such as Chile, have a smaller body of publications in DfW. Since wellbeing is a very broad concept, research from these countries tends to focus on general topics that are not always connected with social development and wellbeing itself. An example is Vera-Vilarroel et al. (2016), who studied how colour could affect liking and the perception of safety in bike lanes in Chile.

Final considerations: Best practice guidance

International perspectives on DfW indicate that wellbeing can be targeted by design in different ways. They vary from distinct epistemological perspectives to particular application areas that reflect local issues and the scope of the design (e.g., stakeholders and the consequences of design for wellbeing). However, DfW still needs to learn how to deal with such complex issues not yet fully addressed by researchers (Brey, 2015).

Some aspects of design research on the topic may be viewed as examples of best practice. Five steps to best practice guidance in the field of DfW are presented hereafter.

First, define the theoretical perspective that underlies DfW in your study. It may be hard to simultaneously address theories and methods that assume that wellbeing can be objectively manipulated by researchers with others that reject such an assumption. These theoretical and methodological perspectives represent different approaches that were developed from very distinct epistemologies. If you try to mix methods, look for coherence in integrated research approaches. This is not a concern solely based on epistemic issues. DfW is grounded on theoretical contradictory or complementary perspectives on what wellbeing is. The scientific community would benefit from observing consistent theoretical–methodological research perspectives, well represented by works such as Poldma's (2011). Therefore, a challenge in future studies is the search for coherence between what is understood by the term wellbeing, methodological procedures associated with it and expected results.

Second, connect your research to the cultural particularities of your community. On one hand, of course general issues (e.g., the impact of using a specific device on wellbeing) tend to be of interest to any society. On the other hand, wellbeing is a multi-layered phenomenon that connects to local specificities that help in understanding its complexity. The experience of wellbeing is lived in a connected world, in which the effects of a project can only be evaluated by observing how contextualised users in a particular community are influenced by the design. There is no neutrality to allow us to observe how design affects the wellbeing of people in isolated contexts. Although wellbeing is important in a broad sense, societal issues, such as cyberbullying in North America (Bowler, Knobel & Mattern, 2015), must be addressed in DfW in order for it to reach its maximum potential.

Third, define the scope of your study. If possible, make a shift from an individual perspective (solely the assessment of isolated users) to social contexts, defining the stakeholders who will be involved in the investigation (e.g., policy-makers, urban planners, users). This shift may assist in understanding the complexity of wellbeing as a phenomenon deeply connected to an ecosystem. This shift is well represented by the Australian research on participatory democracy and systemic governance, which may be considered one of the best practices on the matter (Mcintyre-Mills & De Vries, 2010; Mcintyre-Mills, 2010).

Fourth, focus on the evaluation of the long-term effects of design on wellbeing even though its short-term impacts are also relevant. The shift in investigations from the short- to the long-term effects of design on human life is noticeable in research reported all over the globe. Some studies are representative of this shift, such as the European–Dutch framework proposed by Desmet and Pohlmeyer (2013). Although recognising the viability of measuring the isolated effect of a particular design on wellbeing, the need for considering its long-lasting effect is considered one of the foundations of this framework.

Fifth, avoid designing exclusively the material aspects of artefacts, and favour the design of systems. They offer a broader range of possibilities for human–design interaction in opposition to solo artefacts. The focus on designing systems is well represented by the studies of Jackson (2003, US) and Taylor and Hochuli (2015, Australia). These authors indicate the need for designing (eco)systems to foster wellbeing in urban living and exploring design elements, such as greenery, natural light and visual and physical household solutions.

As multifaceted as wellbeing is, so are the international research perspectives on DfW. By observing practices throughout the globe, it was possible to draw best practice guidance, consisting in the aforementioned five steps required in wellbeing studies. The bottom line of this chapter is the effort to understand what wellbeing and DfW are. There is not yet an agreement on what wellbeing is, how to address it in our research and what the most important variables and contexts for study are. Connecting our research communities is a way of looking for coherence in our work and defining how our design can benefit users and our societies.

Acknowledgements

The author would like to thank Dr Tiiu Poldma (School of Design, University of Montreal, Canada) for the very productive dialogues on phenomenology and pragmatism in the field of design for wellbeing. My thanks also to Taiane Malabarba for proofreading its final version.

Notes

1 This analysis has privileged journal papers, mainly from the past 15 years. There are two reasons for that. First, they tend to be peer-reviewed and therefore submitted to a screening process that is more rigorous than if compared to conference papers. Second, some conferences may attract audiences that are closer to their venues, potentially creating a bias in the analysis. Articles published in conference proceedings were included in the discussion whenever revealing differentials from a research community. Our search was limited to proceedings of large conferences (e.g., DRS and IASDR) from the past five years.
2 It is possible to adopt pragmatic approaches to phenomenological design. They are explored in the following subsection.
3 Examples are given to indicate similarities and diversity, and do not intend to represent continents by quoting individual countries or particular research communities.

References

Bourgeois, P. (2002). Phenomenology and pragmatism: A recent encounter. In A. Tymieniecka (Ed.), *Phenomenology World-wide: Foundations – Expanding Dynamics – Life-engagements: A Guide for Research and Study* (1st edition, pp. 568–570). Dordrecht: Springer.
Bowler, L., Knobel, C., & Mattern, E. (2015). From cyberbullying to well-being: A narrative-based participatory approach to values-oriented design for social media. *Journal of the Association for Information Science and Technology*, 66(6), 1274–1293.
Brey, P. (2015). Design for the value of human well-being. In J. Van Den Hoven, P. Vermaas, & I. Van Der Poel (Eds.), *Handbook of Ethics, Values, and Technological Design: Sources, Theory, Values and Application Domains* (pp. 365–382). Dordrecht: Springer.
Carey, T., Haviland, J., Tai, S., Vanags, T., & Mansell, W. (2016). MindSurf: A pilot study to assess the usability and acceptability of a smartphone app designed to promote contentment, wellbeing, and goal achievement. *BMC Psychiatry*, 16(442).
Cho, K., & Kim, C. (2015). The influence of generation in the usage of smart phone as a means of distributed cognition: An exploratory study on Baby boomer and Generation Y. In *Proceedings of*

IASDR2015: Interplay (pp. 418–430). Brisbane, November 2015. Brisbane: Queensland University of Technology.

Craig, M. (2010). *Levinas and James: Towards a Pragmatic Phenomenology*. Bloomington, IN: Indiana University Press.

De Couvreur, L., Dejonghe, W., Detand, J., & Goossens, R. (2013). The role of subjective well-being in co-designing open-design assistive devices. *International Journal of Design*, 7(3), 57–70.

Desmet, P. (2015). Design for mood: Twenty activity-based opportunities to design for mood regulation. *International Journal of Design*, 9(2), 1–19.

Desmet, P., & Pohlmeyer, A. (2013). Positive design: An introduction to design for subjective well-being. *International Journal of Design*, 7(3), 5–19.

Diedrichs, P., Atkinson, M., Garbett, K., Williamson, H., Halliwell, E., Rumsey, N., Leckie, G., Sibley, C., & Barlow, F. (2017). Evaluating a website designed to improve body image and psychosocial well-being among adolescent girls and their mothers: A cluster randomised controlled trial with mother-daughter dyads. *Journal of Adolescent Health*, 60(2), S6.

Dorrestijn, S., & Verbeek, P. (2013). Technology, wellbeing, and freedom: The legacy of utopian design. *International Journal of Design*, 7(3), 45–56.

Douglas, O., Lennon, M., & Scott, M. (2017). Green space benefits for health and well-being: A life-course approach for urban planning, design and management. *Cities*, 66, 53–62.

Easterbrook, M., & Vignoles, V. (2015). When friendship formation goes down the toilet: Design features of shared accommodation influence interpersonal bonds and well-being. *British Journal of Social Psychology*, 54(1), 125–139.

Eaves, S., Gyi, D., & Gibb, A. (2016). Building healthy construction workers: Their views on health, wellbeing and better workplace design. *Applied Ergonomics*, 54, 10–18.

Edwards, K., & Jensen, P. (2014). Design of systems for productivity and well being. *Applied Ergonomics*, 45(1), 26–32.

Erikson, E., & Wideström, J. (2014). Staging the interaction? Explorative interventions for engaging citizens in the development of public knowledge institutions. In *Proceedings of DRS 2014: Design's Big Debates* (pp. 1096–1108), Umeå, June 2014. London: Design Research Society.

Hammond, A., Homer, C., & Foureur, M. (2017). Friendliness, functionality and freedom: Design characteristics that support midwifery practice in the hospital setting. *Midwifery*, 50, 133–138.

Jackson, L. (2003). The relationship of urban design to human health and condition. *Landscape and Urban Planning*, 64(4), 191–200.

King, D., Thomson, P., & Darzi, A. (2014). Enhancing health and wellbeing through 'behavioural design'. *Journal of the Royal Society of Medicine*, 107(9), 336–337.

Knecht, C. (2004). Urban nature and well-being: Some empirical support and design implications. *Berkeley Planning Journal*, 17(1), 82–108.

Lee, S., Hung, Y., & Wu, F. (2014). Identifying mobile application design to enhance the subjective wellbeing among middle-aged adults. In *Universal Access in Human-Computer Interaction: Aging and Assistive Environments – 8th International Conference, UAHCI 2014, Held as Part of HCI International 2014* (pp. 289–299), Heraklion, June 2014. Cham: Springer.

Mace, V. (2016). The transfigured phenomena of domesticity in the urban interior. *Idea Journal*, 15, 16–37.

Mcintyre-Mills, J. (2010). Participatory design for democracy and wellbeing: Narrowing the gap between service outcomes and perceived needs. *Systemic Practice and Action Research*, 23(1), 21–45.

Mcintyre-Mills, J., & de Vries, D. (2010). Addressing complex needs: User-centric design to enhance wellbeing. *International Journal of Interdisciplinary Social Sciences*, 5(5), 11–31.

Megens, C., Peeters, M., Hummels, C., & Brombacher, A. (2013). Designing for behaviour change towards healthy living. In *Proceedings of the 5th International Congress of International Association of Societies of Design Research: Consilience and Innovation in Design* (pp. 4289–4296), Tokyo, August 2013. Tokyo: Shibaura Institute of Technology.

Michel, A., O'Shea, D., & Hoppe, A. (2015). Designing and evaluating resource-oriented interventions to enhance employee well-being and health. *Journal of Occupational and Organizational Psychology*, 88(3), 459–463.

Olausson, S., Lindahl, B., & Ekebergh, M. (2013). A phenomenological study of experiences of being cared for in a critical care setting: The meanings of the patient room as a place of care. *Intensive and Critical Care Nursing, 29*(4), 234–243.

Ozenc, F. (2014). Modes of transitions: Designing interactive products for harmony and well-being. *Design Issues, 30*(2), 30–41.

Ozkaramanli, D., & Desmet, P. (2012). I knew I shouldn't, yet I did it again! Emotion-driven design as a means to motivate subjective well-being. *International Journal of Design, 6*(1), 27–39.

Page, R., & Richardson, M. (2016). Co-creating narratives: An approach to the design of interactive medical devices, informed by phenomenology. In *Proceedings of DRS2016: Design + Research + Society – Future-focused Thinking* (pp. 1487–1498), Brighton, June 2016. London: Design Research Society.

Pedell, S., Constantin, K., D'Rosario, J., & Favilla, S. (2015). Humanoid robots and older people with dementia: Designing interactions for engagement in a group session. In *Proceedings of IASDR2015: Interplay* (pp. 1639–1655), Brisbane, November 2015. Brisbane: Queensland University of Technology.

Piper, A., Weibel, N., & Hollan, J. (2014). Designing audio-enhanced paper photos for older adult emotional wellbeing in communication therapy. *International Journal of Human-Computer Studies, 72*(8), 629–639.

Pohlmeyer, A. (2013). Positive design: New challenges, opportunities, and responsibilities for design. In *Design, User Experience, and Usability: User Experience in Novel Technological Environments, HCII 2013* (pp. 540–547), Las Vegas, July 2013. Berlin: Springer-Verlag.

Poldma, T. (2008). Dwelling futures and lived experiences: Transforming interior spaces. *Design Philosophy Papers, 6*(2), 141–155.

Poldma, T. (2011). The interior spatial environment: Dynamic 0g environments and human places. *Personal and Ubiquitous Computing, 15*, 539–550.

Ren, H., & Strickfaden, M. (2018). The active role of material things: An environment-based conceptual framework to understand the well-being of people with dementia. *Open Journal of Social Sciences, 6*, 11–23.

Schulze, J., Martin, R., Finger, A., Henzen, C., Lindner, M., Pietzsch, K., Werntze, A., Zander, U., & Seppelt, R. (2015). Design, implementation and test of a serious online game for exploring complex relationships of sustainable land management and human well-being. *Environmental Modelling & Software, 65*, 58–66.

Siu, M., & Wai, K. (2011). Designing public toilets to enhance the well-being of the visually impaired. *International Journal of Health, Wellness & Society, 1*(3), 137–145.

Taylor, L., & Hochuli, D. (2015). Creating better cities: How biodiversity and ecosystem functioning enhance urban residents' wellbeing. *Urban Ecosystems, 18*(3), 747–762.

Tyson, G., Lambert, G., & Beattie, L. (2002). The impact of ward design on the behaviour, occupational satisfaction and well-being of psychiatric nurses. *International Journal of Mental Health Nursing, 11*(2), 94–102.

Vera-Villarroel, P., Contreras, D., Lillo, S., Beyle, C., Segovia, A., Rojo, N., Moreno, S., & Oyarzo, F. (2016). Perception of safety and liking associated to the colour intervention of bike lanes: Contribution from the behavioural sciences to urban design and wellbeing. *PloS One, 11*(8), e0160399.

Wu, S., & Noy, P. (2010). A conceptual design of a wireless sensor actuator system for optimizing energy and well-being in buildings. *Intelligent Buildings International, 2*(1), 41–56.

Zuniga-Teran, A., Orr, B., Gimblett, R., Chalfoun, N., Guertin, D., & Marsh, S. (2017). Neighborhood design, physical activity, and wellbeing: Applying the walkability model. *International Journal of Environmental Research and Public Health, 14*(1), 76.

16 It's love, my friend! Some reflections on cultivating the positive design plot

Pieter M.A. Desmet

> One is not allowed in the modern culture to speak about love, except in the most romantic and trivial sense of the word. Anyone who calls upon the capacity of people to practice brotherly and sisterly love is more likely to be ridiculed than to be taken seriously. The deepest difference between optimists and pessimists is their position in the debate about whether human beings are able to operate collectively from a basis of love.
>
> (Donella Meadows, Dennis Meadows and Jørgen Randers, 1992, p. 233)

Introduction

What makes humans truly happy? A question of existential importance to each of us as individuals, as much as it is of professional importance to designers. A question that has gained urgency in an era in which the implicit assumptions of economic expansion driven by materialistic ideologies, which, for decennia, have pervaded our Western cultures, are increasingly questioned, and even rejected. In fact, the materialistic ideology seems to be denounced bankrupt, obsolete and overrun by its apparent and far-reaching social and environmental costs. We are in need for a new ideology; one that is more sustainable in the long run. An ideology that guides us in understanding the nature of the 'right striving' both at the level of societies and at the level of the individual person in the pursuit of happiness, providing us with guidance for our design practices. The authors of this book and many designers, teachers and researchers alike, have embraced a modern form of *humanism*, or humanistic psychology, as a constructive basis for this new ideology. Building on the philosophy of Socrates, advanced by Abraham Maslow, and reinvigorated by the positive psychology movement, the humanistic view adopts a holistic view on human existence, emphasising the positive human potential, all humans' inherent drive towards self-actualisation, and the process of realising and expressing one's own capabilities and creativity.

Traditionally, psychologists were reluctant to enter the arena of human happiness because they preferred to avoid 'value judgements' and were hesitant to make claims that their research had implications for how people ought to live. But in the last 20 years, impressive theoretical developments emerging within the field of wellbeing research suggest that it may now be possible to make such recommendations – not only on the basis of personal preferences, but on the basis of *data*. What do these data say about the 'right' kinds of goals to strive for? How, and under what circumstances, do such goals contribute to individual wellbeing? How do the goals that are 'right' for one individual impact the welfare of others? And, just as important, how can design support the achievement of these goals? These questions are at the heart of this book. By addressing a variety of topics, cases, tools and methods, the authors explored the possibilities of operationalising human happiness in design intentions, processes and outcomes. I was inspired by their optimism, compassion and willingness to be accountable for the impact of their work. I witness a similar excitement when talking to other designers and researchers who enter the arena of happiness-driven design: adopting a humanistic ideology (re)invigorates their passion for design, reconnecting their professional practices to their deeply held personal values.

In the same excitement I sometimes tell our design students that 'design is an act of love'. Design for subjective wellbeing – for happiness – as an act of love; it may be as simple as that. After all, love is an 'intense feeling of deep affection' or a 'great interest and pleasure in something', and design is *both*. Good design is both: It combines deep affection for the people who will use our designs with a profound pleasure in the act of designing. This book has examined design for happiness as an aspiring act of love, as activity, pursuit and outcome. A love that contributes perhaps as much to our own self-actualisation as it does to the happiness impact of our designs.

Seeking a new plot

In 2016, I visited an exhibition that had a lasting impact on me: The Neo-Prehistory 100 Verbs ('Neo-Preistoria 100 Verbi') exhibition of the XXI Triennale de Milano. Curated jointly by the eminent Andrea Branzi and Kenya Hara, it was as elegant as it was refined: exhibiting 100 human-made objects and 100 verbs. From Hold, Destroy and Kill, to Restore and Regenerate, each verb was connected to one object, strung together by Branzi and Hara to a journey across the history of humankind. Words which relate to actions which relate to objects. This simple relationship proved to be mesmerising. Each artefact was displayed as a unique and priceless piece, as if the exhibition was presenting human history to an alien from a remote planet. That afternoon, I got lost in the space, which was completely dark and multiplied by mirrors, creating an illusion of boundlessness infinity.

The verbs and related artefacts referred to the variety of human needs: utensils to get food and containers to store it, devices to kill and annihilate, and objects for communication, for writing and for travelling. Proceeding through the exhibition, the verbs related to increasingly sophisticated wishes and to artefacts that pushed forward the limits of the possible, like a winged suit to fly and a technological prosthesis to replace part of the human body. The exhibition expressed our never-ending evolving relationship with tools, from the Stone Age to this present day, destined by both human intelligence and stupidity, compassion and cruelty. A relationship we practise, but we will *never* oversee or control. The exhibition illustrates that design is in need of a realistic knowledge horizon. In the words of Branzi: 'One, far from utopian ideas and from the old optimism of a Modernity that has proved incapable of controlling what it induced.' One in which 'each individual is an exception and a potential but also a riddle that cannot be solved' (Branzi & Hara, 2016, p. 14).

Inspired by Branzi's words, I wonder about the knowledge horizon for happiness-driven design. What is our distinct or *unique* plot – our convincing discourse that cultivates our sprouting ideology? Developing this plot is one of the key challenges of the positive design movement. Design practices and processes are as diffuse as they are pervasive in the development of humankind. And yet, design is also as simple as a functional artefact, a tool. All 100 objects exhibited in the Neo-Prehistory exhibition are essentially tools, and, as a collection, their portrayal of design history was comprehensive. With design for wellbeing, we have reached a meta-level finale of tool delineation: design as a tool for happiness. It cannot be more definite than this, especially if we broaden the scope to the happiness of society and humanity at large. But what is the verb here? How does one *do* happiness? The best candidate seems to be to self-actualise or to *flourish* – 'To grow or develop in a healthy or vigorous way, especially as the result of a particularly congenial environment'.[1] What makes a particular design a tool for flourishing? As much as we can appreciate the infinite variations of the act of human flourishing, so it is difficult to imagine what *specific* tools can support it. Let's take the plant on my windowsill as an example. What does it need to flourish – to become its best possible self? Soil, water, sun and, perhaps, some occasional kind words. Would we consider the plant pot to be a 'wellbeing design', or the watering can a tool for flourishing, or the cloth I use to dust its leaves? Probably not. The plant flourishes, and design optimisation is circumstantial or a secondary affair – at most. The same applies to designs that intend to support human flourishing. If we frame wellbeing-driven design as contextual design, as circumstantial, all 100 objects in the Neo–Prehistory exhibition are essentially examples of wellbeing-driven design. All of them purport to enable human actions that may (directly or indirectly) contribute to their flourishing.

It seems that our current plot only tells half of the story, one of *intentions*. The concepts wellbeing, happiness and flourishing serve us well when describing design objectives. They fall short, however, as design criteria. *Any* design can be framed as design for wellbeing. All design facilitates some human action or experience, and all actions and experiences can potentially contribute to happiness: a pen is not a tool to write, but a means for meaning-ful self-expression and creativity. A shoe is not a tool to walk, but a means for discovery and self-development. At times, I have been amazed by the cunning creativity of design students who eloquently leverage concepts of positive psychology when explaining why and how their design project contributes to the wellbeing of the user. More than simply providing us with the language to frame the happiness intentions of our designs, our plot should also enable us to weigh the actual happiness impact, as compared to other concepts and existing designs, including the potential adverse or *ill*-being effects. In other words, we need a plot that does not only convince by inspiration but also by supporting the critical reflections and dialogue that are needed to make design decisions. Moreover, the plot should provide us with clear and useful criteria that operate as indicators of success. If we neglect to develop this analytical power, a formal knowledge that provides a sound basis for arguing for the rigour and legitimacy of design decisions, positive design may risk sliding into a meta-discourse serving as mere glitter dust to sprinkle our design practices, exploiting assumptions and filtering our observations and questionable extrapolations.

At the same time, we may not be able to develop this plot along the traditional path-ways towards scientific rigour. Providing proof of concept, for example, by demonstrating that principles from humanistic psychology have practical potential in design practices, may very well be impossible. Even showing the wellbeing impact of a particular and specific design may not be possible with traditional controlled intervention studies. We cannot develop our plot without also considering the challenge of developing a new form of validation, an alternative for the validity found in evidence-based cause–effect relation-ships. By focusing on that which we understand through empirical observation (omitting all that is unclear), the need for validation echoes the values of positivism, sharply con-trasting with the hermeneutic techniques that prevail in traditional design discourse. The empirical aspiration may be less evident than it seems, given the widely accepted critiques on positivism that precisely those things that are most meaningful to us may not allow for empirical observation. In other words, a design can have a wellbeing impact even if we are not able to prove it. A design may be partly responsible for an individual's wellbeing, and an individual's wellbeing may be partly dependent on that design, but this does not necessarily mean that we can expect to find causal relationships. One of our main challenges is to develop a new arsenal of methods to demonstrate and verify the rigour of positive design while respecting the phenomenological nature of design for wellbeing practice.

What hides in the noise

Twenty years ago, *Science* published an article about a mysterious, ground-breaking, powerful antidepressant (Enserink, 1999). The drug, dubbed MK-869, was invented by the pharmaceutical company Merck & Co. Based on encouraging clinical trials, it was set to become a new millennium drug for millions of people who take antidepressant medication every day. Analysts eagerly predicted that this drug would become a blockbuster, shaking up the $7 billion antidepressant market at the time (Langreth, 1999). However, shortly before launch, Merck suddenly decided to shelve it. What happened? MK-869 was struck by 'the curse of the placebo effect'. Merck explained in a press release that the company discovered that patients who had received a dummy pill in the clinical trial had done unexpectedly well. In fact, they did practically *as well as* those on MK-869, wiping out the rationale for the new drug (Enserink, 1999). In other words, a placebo, a look-alike pill made of milk sugar, was almost as effective as the real thing.

The fact that taking a faux drug can powerfully improve some people's (mental) health has long been considered an embarrassment to the serious practice of pharmacology. This placebo effect was traditionally considered to be nothing more than an inconvenient noise that must be controlled in order to discriminate a valid signal of specific treatment efficacy. Well, not any more. The placebo effect has recently emerged from the shadows of obscurity into the spotlight of stardom. By reframing it to 'contextual healing', health researchers have embraced the placebo effect as a profound opportunity for health treatments (see Miller & Kaptchuck, 2008). The contextual healing movement proposes that, instead of focusing exclusively on the therapeutic power of medical technology and thereby ignoring or dismissing context, we should see the context of the clinical encounter as a potential enhancer, and in some cases the primary vehicle, of therapeutic benefit. Factors that may play a role in contextual healing include the environment of the clinical setting, cognitive and affective communication of clinicians, and the ritual of administering treatment.

In the development of our positive design plot, there is something to be learned from this evolution in the 'health care research plot'. While biomedical science, motivated by the search for specific therapeutic efficacy, has long dominated health care research, contextual healing reaches back to a more humanistic premodern *art of medicine* that was more inclusive than diagnosing disease and administering effective treatments. Traditional biomedical science had pushed the holistic art of medicine into the corner of irrational charlatanism, and the promise of contextual healing research is to broaden the scope of knowledge development by re-embracing a holistic outlook. Parallel to the challenges of knowledge development in the domain of design for wellbeing, these researchers realise that the increasing scientific attention cannot rely on the methodologies that are used to prove medicine efficacy – the very same methodologies that render contextual healing as noise. Likewise, the effects of design for wellbeing interventions may very well be hidden in the noise. Design for wellbeing does not necessarily purport to relieve symptoms of ill-being but may just as well provide the contextual factors that contribute to human flourishing. Our arsenal of methods should support the idea that the context of an encounter can be the primary vehicle of wellbeing design, not only in design practices but also in the approaches that are used to verify the impact of design on human flourishing.

The prison inside me

Imagine your ideal holiday location. Your dreamed image may not include the experience of being locked up in a five-meter square cell, sleeping on the floor and using a toilet in the corner of the room. And yet, this idea is strangely appealing among many stressed-out South Koreans. To escape from high work pressure, they seek voluntary refuge in a 'prison hotel'. They act like real inmates, living in an empty cell without possessions or privileges. The prison was established in 2008 with workaholics as the target group. It has 28 cells and, although there are some daytime activities, the inmates spend most of their time alone, in their cells. The building looks like a real prison, inmates wear a uniform and meals are served through a slot in the doors. It is a huge success. Co-founder Noh Jihyang stated about her clients: 'Most of them were initially resistant because they were told it is jail. But after staying inside, they said it is not the small cell that is the prison, but rather the outside world' (as cited in Ghani, 2018).

Is this prison hotel a good example of wellbeing focused design? Well, it does provide the visitors with some happiness; a context for reflection, personal growth and bliss. So, yes. But at the same time there is a bitter taste to this happiness when we realise under what conditions a person needs to live to develop the need to lock themselves up in the first place. In South Korea the share of employees working very long hours is much higher than the average; it is the most overworked nation in Asia (OECD Better Life Index, 2019). This is a fundamental issue, a basic context for ill-being, from a social, physical and psychological point of view. The prison may alleviate some of the symptoms, but it doesn't solve the problem. How do we address tension between people's pursuit of happiness and the (sometimes harmful) societal environmental conditions of modern societies in our positive design plot? How do we maintain a solid realism that avoids the naivety of utopianism and the gloominess of nihilism? Our narration, as elegant and intelligent as it is, should avoid becoming only self-referential, ignoring the darkness, the violence and the contradictions that accompany human existence in this world, unable to find the means for sustainable peace and shared prosperity.

Parachute suit man

In 1912, 33-year-old Frantz Reichelt jumped to his death from the Paris Eiffel Tower. This was not a suicide, even though he jumped out of his own free will. Reichelt, who was a tailor and inventor, had designed a wearable parachute, a suit for aviators that would convert into a parachute, enabling them to survive a fall should they be forced to leave their aircraft. After some semi-successful tests with a dummy that he dropped from the top of his apartment building, he believed that a suitably high test platform would prove his invention's efficacy. After several petitions, he got permission to take his dummy to the Eiffel Tower. However, upon arrival, he made it clear that instead of using the dummy he intended to jump personally – to prove the worth of his invention. Despite the desperate attempts of his close friends to convince him to abandon the experiment, he jumped from the tower's first platform wearing his invention. The parachute failed to deploy and he made a 57-metre free fall.

This horrific stunt made a legend out of Reichelt, aka 'the parachute suit man'. I marvel at his conviction, his absolute and unreserved trust in his ideas, for which he was willing to pay with his life. And, of course, his stunt was one of infinite idiocy. Luckily, today's designers know better. Our current mantra is to iterate and prototype. Design follows an evolutionary development, with continuous improvement and working prototypes as the primary measure of progress. At the same time, design does not rely on mere evolution – it takes a stance, though not one as bold as Reichelt's conviction. Design cannot exist without taking a stance about its purpose, value and meaning. This applies to all design practice and most certainly to design for wellbeing as well. Since the 1960s attempts have been made to incorporate scientific knowledge into the design process. Design researchers started to work out the rational criteria of decision-making, with the ultimate aim optimising decisions. This research now includes the question of what constitutes wellbeing. Not all life goals and aspirations summed across individuals will allow sustainable living patterns and the life conditions of tomorrow that we shape today will certainly affect our wellbeing (Schmuck & Sheldon, 2001). As mentioned in the introduction, design research now has to start asking the question what are the 'right' goals to strive for, what are the goals designers should be developing tools for. We boldly have to re-enter the mosh pit of subjectivism, because wellbeing-driven design cannot exist without making claims about how people ought to live, implicitly or explicitly. History has proven many times that design and technology can cause harm and ill-being, in most cases unintentionally. In fact, some of the most destructive design visions have been fuelled by the ambition to contribute to human wellbeing. Indeed, this should not only make us cautious about making wellbeing claims, but it should also stimulate us to actively seek opportunities to develop pragmatic hybrid design methodologies that combine theory-based visionary power with open-minded iterative progression.

It's love, my friend

'It's the economy, stupid' – more than 25 years ago, this phrase became a famous key slogan of Bill Clinton's 1992 presidential campaign against the sitting president, George Bush. Leveraging the then-prevailing recession in the United States, this slogan helped him to successfully unseat Bush. While successful, this slogan represented, even then, an obsolete sentiment. One year before that, in 1991, Donella Meadows, Dennis Meadows and Jørgen Randers had published their influential book *Beyond the Limits*, which, by advocating an urgently needed sustainability revolution, provided a perspective that expressed much more care about people, the earth and the welfare of our future generations. In the concluding chapter (p. 232), they propose five tools to 'encourage the peaceful restructuring of a system that naturally resists in its own transformation' towards this revolution: Visioning, Networking, Truth-telling, Learning and *Loving*: 'In the quest of a sustainable world, it doesn't take long before even the most hard-boiled, rational, and practical persons, even those who have not been trained in the language of humanism, begin to speak, with whatever words they can muster, of virtue, morality, wisdom, and love.'

Design has undeniably played its role in the extensive and unmaintainable environmental exploitation that was propelled by the industrial revolution. But design also represents hope, pushing forward the limits of the possible towards a sustainable paradigm. In the positive design plot, designers generate value and meaning that transcends the mere economic value that is recognised by the bare instrumentalism of capitalism. Design for subjective wellbeing – for happiness – as an act of love; it may be as simple as that: love for the students we teach to become designers, love for the people who are affected by design practices and outcomes, and love for the pure bravery of transformation, for the refusal to be held back by the unknown, combined with the humble willingness to listen, observe and reconsider, to be accountable, to redesign and to start over if necessary. Our positive design plot – combining heroism with modesty, requires love.

At the start of this chapter, I mentioned the 100 objects in the Neo-Prehistory exhibition. Not surprisingly, one of the 100 verbs was to *love*. It was number 22, and it was accompanied by a simple but elegant prehistoric Japanese jade *magatame* (comma-shaped) bead, that traces back to the hunter-gatherer Jōmon period in Japanese prehistory. The shape represents the significant value in that which transcends oneself. I relish the idea that, to date, archaeologists and historians have been unable to determine the origins of the magatama form, which has resulted in a variety of alternative explanations (see Nishimura, 2018): magatama may have been modelled after the shape of an animal fang, a human foetus or the moon – and some even propose that it might symbolise the shape of the soul. Rather than determining which of these is the correct interpretation, we can enjoy a rich picture painted by the variety of meanings. This is where the love hides, between the lines, beyond both reason and the senses, complicated – and always inspiring.

Acknowledgements

I'd like to thank Willy Desmet, my father, for his thoughtful suggestions and for introducing me to the work of Donella Meadows, Dennis Meadows and Jørgen Randers, showing me the natural connection between the positive design initiative and the urgently required 'sustainability revolution'.

Note

1 https://en.oxforddictionaries.com/definition/flourish.

References

Branzi, A., & Hara, K. (2016). *Neo-Preistoria*; 100 Verbi. Milano: XX1T.

Enserink, M. (1999). Can the placebo be the cure? *Science*, *284*(5412), 238–240.

Ghani, F. (2018). Prison inside me: Providing Koreans peace and solitude in a sell (online article). Retrieved from https://www.aljazeera.com/indepth/features/prison-providing-koreans-peace-solitude-cell-180910135056915.html

Langreth, R. (1999). Merck hits a stumbling block in testing new antidepressant (online article). *The Wall Street Journal*. Retrieved from https://www.wsj.com/articles/SB917042966767618000

Meadows, D.H., Meadows, D.L., & Randers, J. (1992). *Beyond the Limits: Confronting Global Collapse, Envisioning a Sustainable Future*. Post Mills, VT: Chelsea Green Publishers.

Miller, F.G., & Kaptchuk, T.J. (2008). The power of context: reconceptualizing the placebo effect. *Journal of the Royal Society of Medicine*, *101*(5), 222–225.

Nishimura, Y. (2018). The evolution of curved beads (magatama) in Jōmon period japan and the development of individual ownership. *Asian Perspectives*, *57*(1), 105–158.

OECD (Organisation for Economic Co-operation and Development) (2019). *Better Life Index*. Retrieved from http://www.oecdbetterlifeindex.org/countries/korea/

Schmuck, P., & Sheldon, K.M. (2001). *Life Goals and Wellbeing. Towards a Positive Psychology of Human Striving*. Seattle, WA: Hogrefe & Huber Publishing.

Index

Note: Page numbers in bold represent the entries of Tables.